*Chinese Social Policy in a Time of Transition*

# International Policy Exchange Series

*Published in collaboration with the
Center for International Policy Exchanges
University of Maryland*

## Series Editors
Douglas J. Besharov
Neil Gilbert

*United in Diversity?
Comparing Social Models in Europe and America*
Edited by Jens Alber and Neil Gilbert

*The Korean State and Social Policy:
How South Korea Lifted Itself from Poverty and Dictatorship
to Affluence and Democracy*
Stein Ringen, Huck-ju Kwon, Ilcheong Yi, Taekyoon Kim, and Jooha Lee

*Child Protection Systems:
International Trends and Orientations*
Edited by Neil Gilbert, Nigel Parton, and Marit Skivenes

*The Age of Dualization:
The Changing Face of Inequality in Deindustrializing Societies*
Edited by Patrick Emmenegger, Silja Häusermann, Bruno Palier, and Martin Seeleib-Kaiser

*Counting the Poor:
New Thinking About European Poverty Measures and Lessons for the
United States*
Edited by Douglas J. Besharov and Kenneth A. Couch

*Social Policy and Citizenship:
The Changing Landscape*
Edited by Adalbert Evers and Anne-Marie Guillemard

*Chinese Policy in a Time of Transition*
Edited by Douglas J. Besharov and Karen Baehler

SCHOOL of
PUBLIC POLICY

# CHINESE SOCIAL POLICY IN A TIME OF TRANSITION

Edited by

DOUGLAS J. BESHAROV
KAREN BAEHLER

**OXFORD**
UNIVERSITY PRESS

Oxford University Press is a department of the University of Oxford.
It furthers the University's objective of excellence in research, scholarship,
and education by publishing worldwide.

Oxford   New York
Auckland   Cape Town   Dar es Salaam   Hong Kong   Karachi
Kuala Lumpur   Madrid   Melbourne   Mexico City   Nairobi
New Delhi   Shanghai   Taipei   Toronto

With offices in
Argentina   Austria   Brazil   Chile   Czech Republic   France   Greece
Guatemala   Hungary   Italy   Japan   Poland   Portugal   Singapore
South Korea   Switzerland   Thailand   Turkey   Ukraine   Vietnam

Oxford is a registered trademark of Oxford University Press in the UK and certain other
countries.

Published in the United States of America by
Oxford University Press
198 Madison Avenue, New York, NY 10016

© Oxford University Press 2013

All rights reserved. No part of this publication may be reproduced, stored in a
retrieval system, or transmitted, in any form or by any means, without the prior
permission in writing of Oxford University Press, or as expressly permitted by law,
by license, or under terms agreed with the appropriate reproduction rights organization.
Inquiries concerning reproduction outside the scope of the above should be sent to the
Rights Department, Oxford University Press, at the address above.

You must not circulate this work in any other form
and you must impose this same condition on any acquirer.

Library of Congress Cataloging-in-Publication Data
Chinese social policy in a time of transition / edited by Douglas J.
Besharov and Karen Baehler.
    pages cm.—(International policy exchange series)
Includes bibliographical references and index.
ISBN 978-0-19-999031-3 (alk. paper)
1. China—Social policy—20th century.  2. China—Economic
conditions—20th century.  I. Besharov, Douglas J.  II. Baehler, Karen J.
HN733.5.C44295 2013
320.60951—dc23
2012050201

978-0-19-999031-3

9 8 7 6 5 4 3 2 1
Printed in the United States of America
on acid-free paper

# CONTENTS

**Contributors** vii

1
**Introduction: Chinese Social Policy in a Time of Transition** 1
*Karen Baehler and Douglas J. Besharov*

2
**Welfare Regimes in the Wake of State Socialism: China and Vietnam** 18
*Jonathan D. London*

3
**Social Benefits and Income Inequality in Post-Socialist China and Vietnam** 48
*Qin Gao, Martin Evans and Irwin Garfinkel*

4
**Social Security Policy in the Context of Evolving Employment Policy** 68
*Barry L. Friedman*

5
**Urban Social Insurance Provision: Regional and Workplace Variations** 86
*Juan Chen and Mary E. Gallagher*

| | |
|---|---|
| **6** **Health and Rural Cooperative Medical Insurance**<br>*Song Gao and Xiangyi Meng* | 101 |
| **7** **The Quest for Welfare Spending Equalization: A Fiscal Federalism Perspective**<br>*Xin Zhang* | 121 |
| **8** **Financing Migrant Child Education**<br>*Jing Guo* | 142 |
| **9** **Labor Migration, Citizenship, and Social Welfare in China and India**<br>*Josephine Smart, Reeta Chowdari Tremblay and Mostaem Billah* | 160 |
| **10** **Ethnic Minorities and Trilingual Education Policies**<br>*Bob Adamson, Feng Anwei, Liu Quanguo and Li Qian* | 180 |
| **11** ***Danwei*, Family Ties, and Residential Mobility of Urban Elderly in Beijing**<br>*Zhilin Liu and Yanwei Chai* | 196 |
| **12** **Marriage, Parenthood, and Labor Outcomes for Women and Men**<br>*Yuping Zhang and Emily Hannum* | 223 |
| **13** **Implications of the College Expansion Policy for Social Stratification**<br>*Wei-Jun Jean Yeung* | 249 |
| **14** **The Evolving Response to HIV/AIDS**<br>*Zunyou Wu, Sheena G. Sullivan, Yu Wang, Mary Jane Rotheram and Roger Detels* | 270 |
| **Index** | 297 |

# CONTRIBUTORS

Bob Adamson
Department of International
   Education and Lifelong Learning
Hong Kong Institute of Education
Hong Kong, China

Feng Anwei
School of Education
University of Bangor, UK

Karen Baehler
Department of Public Administration
   and Policy
American University
Washington, DC, United States

Douglas J. Besharov
School of Public Policy
University of Maryland
College Park, Maryland, United States

Mostaem Billah
Department of Geography
Memorial University of Newfoundland
Newfoundland and Labrador, Canada

Yanwei Chai
Department of Urban and Economic
   Geography
Peking University
Beijing, P.R. China

Juan Chen
Department of Applied Social Sciences
Hong Kong Polytechnic University
Hong Kong, China

Roger Detels
School of Public Health
University of California Los Angeles
Los Angeles, California

MARTIN EVANS
Economic & Social Policy Specialist
UNICEF
New York, New York, United States

BARRY L. FRIEDMAN
The Heller School for Social Policy
    and Management
Brandeis University
Waltham, Massachusetts, United States

MARY E. GALLAGHER
Department of Political Sciences
University of Michigan
Ann Arbor, Michigan, United States

QIN GAO
Graduate School of Social Service
Fordham University
New York, New York, United States

SONG GAO
China Academy of Public Finance
    and Public Policy
Central University of Finance and
    Economics
Beijing, China

IRWIN GARFINKEL
School of Social Work
Columbia University
New York, New York, United States

JING GUO
Myron B. Thompson School of Social
    Work
University of Hawaii at Manoa
Honolulu, Hawaii, United States

EMILY HANNUM
Department of Sociology
University of Pennsylvania
Philadelphia, Pennsylvania,
    United States

ZHILIN LIU
School of Public Policy and
    Management
Tsinghua University
Beijing, P.R. China

JONATHAN D. LONDON
Department of Asian and
    International Studies
City University of Hong Kong
Hong Kong, China

XIANGYI MENG
China Academy of Public Finance
    and Public Policy
Central University of Finance and
    Economics
Beijing, China

LI QIAN
School of Foreign Languages
Northwest Normal University
Lanzhou, P.R. China

LIU QUANGUO
School of Foreign Languages
Northwest Normal University
Lanzhou, P.R. China

MARY JANE ROTHERAM
Center for HIV Identification,
    Prevention and Treatment Services
    (CHIPTS)
University of California Los Angeles
Los Angeles, California,
    United States

JOSEPHINE SMART
Department of Anthropology
University of Calgary
Calgary, Alberta, Canada

SHEENA G. SULLIVAN
National Centre for AIDS/STD
  Control and Prevention
Chinese Centre for Disease Control
  and Prevention
Beijing, China
School of Public Health
University of California Los Angeles
Los Angeles, California, United States

REETA CHOWDARI TREMBLAY
Department of Political Science
University of Victoria
Victoria, British Columbia, Canada

YU WANG
Chinese Centre for Disease Control
  and Prevention
Beijing, China

ZUNYOU WU
National Centre for AIDS/STD
  Control and Prevention
Chinese Centre for Disease Control
  and Prevention
Beijing, China

WEI-JUN JEAN YEUNG
Faculty of Arts and Social Sciences
National University of Singapore,
  Singapore
New York University
New York, New York, United States

XIN ZHANG
School of Public Administration and
  Policy
Renmin University of China
Beijing, China

YUPING ZHANG
Department of Sociology and
  Anthropology
Lehigh University
Bethlehem, Pennsylvania, United
  States

# *Chinese Social Policy in a Time of Transition*

# 1

# INTRODUCTION: CHINESE SOCIAL POLICY IN A TIME OF TRANSITION

## Karen Baehler and Douglas J. Besharov

The story of China's rapid economic transformation has been told many times, in many languages and from many different ideological perspectives, always accompanied by a now familiar, but still astonishing, litany of facts: the tenfold increase in gross domestic product (GDP) since 1978, the 7.1 percent annual decline in poverty during the same period, and the quadrupling of per capita income between the early 1980s and mid-1990s alone. Although China has ranked as a (perhaps *the*) major power for much of the past two thousand years, its recent return to global power status is viewed by many as "the big story of our age.... Like the rise and fall of Rome, the Ottoman Empire, the British Raj or the Soviet Union, it is the stuff from which grand narratives are wrought" (Leonard 2008, 5).

If China's rise is indeed the big story of our age and "one of the blessed miracles of modern economic history," as David Ignatius (2010) has written, then its social impacts deserve careful attention for reasons of sheer scale, if nothing else. With 12 percent of the world's GDP and 15 percent of the world's absolute poverty head count, China exerts considerable influence over global indicators of social and economic well-being. To take just one example, the Chinese economic miracle has thus far lifted 600 million people—more than the combined populations of North America and Russia—above the threshold for extreme poverty, defined by the World Bank as living on less than US$1.25 a day (Chen and Ravallion 2009). As a result, China accounted for over half of the world's progress in reducing severe deprivation during the past quarter century.

Beyond the significance of scale, China's experience deserves attention because of the new paradigms of social protection emerging from the Chinese government's efforts to blend socialist principles with the realities of market economics. Although the late 1970s marked a sharp break with the past and the beginning of an entirely new era dedicated to modernizing and opening up the Chinese economy, the design and implementation of specific economic and social reforms have proceeded gradually, by trial and error, with constant adaptation to changing internal and external circumstances. Rather than replacing the centrally planned economy with a market-based economy in one stroke, China's reformers chose to institute a "dual-track" system in which central planning and market arrangements would operate side by side in selected sectors of the economy for a time, while the country gradually learned how to succeed in the new track. Twenty-five years after the economist Zhang Weiying first put forward the idea of "dual-track pricing," the pricing component has been phased out, but other dimensions of a dual economy are being actively maintained. Alongside the blossoming of private enterprises, the state still employed roughly one-third of the urban labor force and accounted directly for 38 percent of China's GDP in the early 2000s (Pei 2006).

China's embrace of market mechanisms inevitably disrupted the social welfare arrangements of the pre-reform period, many of which depended heavily on guarantees of lifetime employment and access to social services provided by state-owned employers. The withering of employer-based social protection began in rural China in the 1980s, as policies designed to raise agricultural productivity by individualizing farming weakened social services that had been provided to farm families by the now defunct communes. In the cities, current and former employees of state-owned enterprises continued to receive health care coverage, pensions, and other supports from their workplaces for a time. But the burden of financing these programs was transferred gradually to a combination of employee, employer, and state contributions as policymakers moved more aggressively to reduce surplus labor. Health care and pension coverage for employees of private firms were left largely to the idiosyncratic policies of employers, with patchy development of government-run programs to fill the gaps. The push to streamline production in state-owned enterprises led to downsizing or closure of the less efficient, more heavily subsidized enterprises, while private firms were allowed to expand their activities. In the early days of the reforms, downsized enterprises were expected to provide their laid-off workers with basic living allowances, but this practice became financially unsustainable as the number of unemployed grew and grew.

Moreover, the steady shrinking of the "iron rice bowl" substantially increased income inequality in China, starting in rural areas as early as the 1980s and then moving to urban areas a decade later. Overall, inequality in China rose dramatically over the last two decades of the twentieth century but appears to have plateaued in the early twenty-first century (Herd 2010). It is too early to tell what

## Introduction: Chinese Social Policy in a Time of Transition 3

impact the global financial meltdown that began in 2007 will have on inequality and poverty in China over the next several decades. That crisis hit the country hard due to China's heavy reliance on exports, but growth figures climbed back into double digits in the last quarter of 2009, thanks in part to a massive stimulus intervention by the central government. Subsequently, as the U.S. recovery stalled and Europe's financial problems deepened, the Chinese economy showed signs of significant cooling. The GDP growth rate hit a three-year low in the second quarter of 2012, which brought renewed attention to long-standing concerns about structural problems in China's economy, including "unsteady development" fueled by "overheated investment" and trade surpluses; "uneven development" between urban and rural areas; and "uncoordinated development" between consumption and investment and across the primary, secondary, and tertiary sectors (Jiabao 2007).

Looking ahead, current and future Chinese governments have the potential to make unprecedented breakthroughs in social protection, but the next increments of progress will be harder to achieve than the earlier ones. According to World Bank analysts Ravallion and Chen (2007, 38), the policy changes of the early 1980s picked the "low-lying fruits of efficiency enhancing pro-poor reforms" by undoing many of the failed agricultural schemes of the Great Leap Forward and Cultural Revolution eras. The challenges to be addressed now are far more complex and span the full range of issues from financing retirement to improving the quality and availability of education for migrant children. This book aims to increase understanding of those challenges by closely examining social conditions and social policymaking aimed at addressing those conditions through the 1990s and into the first decade of the 2000s.

Earlier versions of most of the chapters of this volume were presented at a 2009 conference in Singapore sponsored by the Lee Kuan Yew School of Public Policy at the National University of Singapore, the University of Maryland's School of Public Policy, and the Association of Public Policy and Management. Entitled "Asian Social Protection in Comparative Perspective," the conference brought together established and emerging social policy researchers from nearly every continent to discuss social protection problems and policies throughout Asia in the areas of pensions and aging, health care, education, welfare, employment, housing, disabilities, and poverty. A large number of high-quality papers at the conference focused on Chinese social policy developments since the 1980s, including some comparisons of Chinese social policy with other countries, which led to the idea for this volume. Three additional papers have been added here to cover important topics not addressed by conference participants, and the conference papers have been updated. A second volume of papers from the Singapore conference is forthcoming, focused on issues of pensions and aging across Asia.

The Chinese economy has been in constant transition since the late 1970s, when the early market liberalization reforms began. With respect to social policy, the 1980s were marked by the first efforts to implement a cultural and ideological shift from collective to household responsibility and from employer-centered social insurance provision to a social protection system financed through general taxes and individual contributions as well as employer efforts. Initiatives during the 1980s included loosening the residential registration system to enable rural workers to migrate to cities where jobs were rapidly being created, decentralizing expenditure responsibility from the national government to provincial and local governments, instituting labor contracts, marketizing health care, reassigning responsibility for financing and delivering social insurance benefits, and establishing rudimentary unemployment insurance and pension pools. The 1980s were a period of growing awareness of market-reform-induced social problems that ranged from high out-of-pocket health care costs to the destabilizing effects of massive layoffs.

Policymakers responded to these challenges with an accumulation of incremental changes from the mid-1980s to the mid-1990s, including the creation of two major public assistance programs (an early version of unemployment insurance and the Minimum Livelihood Guarantee). In the late 1990s, the pace of social policymaking seemed to increase as the marketization of health care and housing rapidly expanded, the old socialist workplaces (*danwei*) were told to wind down their social services, and worker retrenchment reached a crescendo. From 1995–2006—the focal period for this book—the central government took a series of significant social policy decisions that included adopting a single, national pension plan for urban areas; standardizing unemployment insurance; (re)establishing nationwide rural health care coverage; including migrant children in urban education; introducing trilingual education policies in ethnic minority regions; expanding college enrollment; addressing the challenge of HIV/AIDS more comprehensively; and making social welfare spending more equal across provinces. This wave of reforms expanded access to many programs and went a long way toward consolidating the social policy framework that had gradually emerged in piecemeal fashion during the 1980s and early 1990s.

Unresolved is whether the resulting framework is adequate to address the problems generated by economic liberalization, demographic transition, and mass internal migration. Since 2007, an additional question has been added: Can the existing social protection framework cope with the global financial crisis and its impacts on China's workforce and social fabric? This volume does not aim to answer either of these questions directly. Instead, its purpose is to collect the evidence needed to understand the main streams of social policymaking, as well as their impacts on social conditions, that shaped the critical period of the late 1990s and early 2000s when the broad outlines of the current social protection system were being solidified. The policies inherited from that period are sure to change, and some will be replaced altogether in response to current and future pressures, but going forward, all new social policy decisions will need to work from the foundation laid during that vital period.

Introduction: Chinese Social Policy in a Time of Transition    5

*Chinese Social Policy in a Time of Transition* offers scholars, practitioners, students, policymakers, and anyone interested in the evolution of Chinese policymaking a composite snapshot of China's social policy foundation at its point of greatest maturation prior to the great global recession. Rather than comprehensively surveying the universe of Chinese social policy developments during this period (a task that would require multiple volumes), each chapter takes a slightly different element of the focal period's reforms in order to concentrate on particular phenomena of interest. Some chapters address selected policy questions within particular fields of social policy, such as health and education; other chapters survey whole swaths of programs in order to observe larger, cross-policy patterns of evolution and impact. Three chapters compare China's policymaking processes and outcomes with important benchmark countries—namely, Vietnam (another country making the transition from state socialism to greater market activity) and India (the world's second-largest country and one undergoing rapid development). Such comparisons are vital for understanding the Chinese situation in a larger context and drawing lessons from China's experience for other countries in transition.

The combination of detailed policy analyses, thematic analyses, and inter-country comparisons allows the reader to toggle between micro- and macro-level views, thereby gaining a fuller picture of China's social policy challenges, then and now, in a larger context. Students who encounter this book in a comparative social policy or public policy course will be introduced to a diversity of qualitative and quantitative analytical approaches to policy-oriented research as well as a range of topic areas. They will also find many unanswered questions, which should stimulate agendas for future research. With Chinese social policy in a seemingly continuous state of rapid change, there is a pressing need for the kinds of lessons that can be learned from both the finely focused studies and the broader, cross-policy analyses contained here.

## VARIETIES OF WELFARE REGIMES: WHAT COMES AFTER STATE SOCIALISM?

China has thus far defied the predictions of experts who argue that the economic transition from socialist central planning to capitalist markets must lead eventually to a political transition away from authoritarianism toward competitive democracy of one form or another. What has eventuated instead is a new hybrid phenomenon known as "market-Leninism" (Kristof 1993). In Chapter 2, "Welfare Regimes in the Wake of State Socialism: China and Vietnam," Jonathan London describes market-Leninism as the marriage of market-based economic institutions to Leninist forms of political organization, which include rule by elites in a one-party state.

London explores the implications of market-Leninism for social policy, using a comparison between China and Vietnam to highlight certain common narratives that distinguish this hybrid form of welfare regime from others found elsewhere in Asia and from other models of post-state-socialist welfare arrangements. Both China and Vietnam, for example, have experienced lags between the retreat of socialist welfare provision and the emergence of new forms of social protection. In the interim, as services such as health and education became commodified and individuals' out-of-pocket costs for those services rose dramatically, inequalities in access, take-up, and outcomes inevitably developed and grew. As the evidence of growing needs mounted, government came under increasing pressure in both countries to enlarge social security provision. Both countries responded with social program expansion, but these expansions took different forms, most of which can be explained by the differences in the two countries' political paths post-1980, a central theme expounded by London.

Alongside the shared qualities that characterize market-Leninism, China and Vietnam display important variations which developed as a result of their different exit paths from state socialism. For example, Vietnam's broader coalitions of ruling elites appear more responsive—on the whole—to the welfare needs of their population than their Chinese counterparts, as evidenced by Vietnam's more redistributive pattern of fiscal transfers. Although the ruling parties in both of these market-Leninist countries have tended to let economic development goals override aspirations for social well-being, subtle differences in underlying political culture and bureaucratic styles have led to relatively significant differences in social impact.

In Chapter 3, "Social Benefits and Income Inequality in Post-Socialist China and Vietnam," Qin Gao, Martin Evans, and Irwin Garfinkel further explore these differences in social impact, using national household survey data from China and Vietnam. Focusing on the early 2000s, they find that China spent significantly more on average for cash and in-kind benefits than did Vietnam. Within those larger expenditures, China displayed a wider rural-urban gap than Vietnam, with far more social spending flowing into urban areas compared to rural areas. Pensions dominated both countries' welfare packages (Vietnam especially), and Vietnam contributed a larger share of its total spending in the form of social welfare transfers compared with China. Health spending as a proportion of total social spending was roughly equal in the two countries, but education showed dramatic variation, with China's share of its own pie spent on education significantly larger than Vietnam's (although this result may be an artifact of measurement problems).

Despite the socialist rhetoric of equalization heard from these countries' leaders, social security arrangements in both China and Vietnam have an overall regressive effect, meaning that they channel more resources to higher income residents and families than to citizens at the bottom of the distribution. China's system appears to be more regressive than Vietnam's, according to Gao and colleagues' data. The implications for policy of these findings depend on what policymakers want to accomplish. If equalization is a genuine goal, then more effort is needed in both countries, but especially in China, to channel resources and programs toward the neediest households.

## MULTIPLE TRANSITIONS

Although the world's attention has focused predominantly on China's transition from a centrally planned socialist economy to an increasingly open, market-based economy, in Chapter 4, "Social Security Policy in the Context of Evolving Employment Policy," Barry Friedman identifies two additional types of transitions (aging and the shift out of agriculture) that will shape Chinese social policymaking going forward. He discusses all three transitions in the context of interactions and tensions between employment policy and pension policy.

With respect to employment policy, it is difficult to exaggerate the scale of the redundant worker problem in modern China. Even after the more aggressive policy changes of the 1990s and early 2000s halved the number of state-owned and state-controlled firms and put 45 million people out of work (i.e., 40 percent of the sector's labor force), China experts noted that there were still many firms sheltered under the protection of local and provincial governments whose officials did not want to be held responsible for cutting subsidies, putting firms out of business, and causing yet more joblessness (Bergsten et al. 2006). Chinese policymakers, like their counterparts everywhere, face an unhappy choice between economic performance and social protection. Whereas shedding excess labor is sure to improve an industry's productivity, retaining redundant workers is one way of securing household incomes and ensuring access to workplace-based social insurance benefits. Policies that focus on creating new jobs (typically in small- to medium-sized private firms) may ease the pain of restructuring by absorbing some of the country's excess workers, but these policies can only go so far.

Friedman describes how pension policies have been employed at various stages in the reform process to address the unemployment mega-problem—for example, by supporting early retirement, pooling contributions to spread the risk across enterprises, and setting up separate pension funds for contract workers. He presents evidence suggesting that some of these employment policy changes may have had adverse effects on retirees, particularly those at the lower end of the income distribution. Friedman also addresses conundrums associated with population aging and the soaring costs of pensions (the second major transition under way in China), as well as the problem of how to cover huge numbers of workers who have moved out of agricultural employment (the third transition). All three transitions appear throughout this book; they are central themes of China's post-reform experience.

## URBAN AND RURAL GAPS IN SOCIAL INSURANCE

As Friedman points out, support for the unemployed was largely a non-issue in pre-reform China because all workers were guaranteed lifetime employment in state-owned enterprises or agricultural collectives, and other forms of social protection, such as health care and pensions, were provided by one's employer. According to Chapter 5, "Urban Social Insurance Provision: Regional and Workplace Variations" by Juan Chen and Mary Gallagher, employees of state-owned enterprises still enjoyed advantages, compared with their counterparts working for domestically owned private firms, well into the 2000s. Chen and Gallagher's research also showed foreign-owned private enterprises to be more generous providers of workers' supports than Chinese-owned firms. Based on household surveys conducted in four Chinese cities, Chen and Gallagher found that access to social insurance covering old age, health care, and unemployment was highest for workers in majority state-owned and foreign-owned private enterprises and lowest for workers in domestically owned private collectives and the self-employed. As a result, regional disparities in economic development and ownership patterns tend to reproduce themselves in social insurance disparities, with workers in the fast-growing foreign investment hubs of the eastern provinces enjoying greatest access to social insurance.

In order to narrow continuing gaps in coverage, the authors recommend continued development of China's mixed model of public-private social insurance provision, but with enhancements that include making social insurance benefits portable across firms and regions, consolidating social insurance management centrally, and escalating enforcement of employers' obligations to provide coverage (with support through expansion of labor contracts). This policy agenda reflects Chen and Gallagher's research into the social attitudes of citizens, which revealed continued majority support for the idea of social insurance provided as a matter of right with contributions from employers, employees, and government. For various reasons, most Chinese workers (with the exception of migrants) do not seem inclined to put all their social insurance eggs in the state basket.

Chen and Gallagher's research illuminates the repercussions for social insurance of the first key transition noted above—the transition from state-owned to privately owned enterprises. Chapter 6 turns to the third transition, in which workers moved out of agricultural employment in large numbers, creating challenges not only for China's pension systems (as discussed by Friedman in Chapter 4), but also for health care and other social services following the collapse of the rural communes and the dismantling of related health care co-ops.

In "Health and Rural Cooperative Medical Insurance," Song Gao and Xiangyi Meng examine government efforts to address rural health disadvantages through the 2002 New Rural Cooperative Medical Scheme. Based on the fact that individuals and villages with lower incomes and poorer health were more likely to participate in the scheme than those with higher incomes and better health, the authors conclude that the scheme succeeded in closing some of the gaps in health services found in the Chinese countryside. This phenomenon of sicker people buying more insurance ("adverse selection") would have created potential financial problems for the new rural scheme, but those problems were solved by the achievement of nearly universal coverage as of 2011. Even prior to that point, according to Gao and Meng, the new program was accomplishing its goals of providing greater social protection to the most vulnerable citizens.

Gao and Meng also investigate the impacts of health insurance coverage on subjectively measured health outcomes. They find a strong positive relationship between insurance coverage and health status prior to introduction of the new scheme, but this relationship disappeared after 2002, probably because of the aforementioned tendency for disproportionately large numbers of sicker people (with poorer outcomes) to join the new scheme. The achievement of nearly universal coverage, including relatively healthy rural residents, allowed the scheme to build a larger, more diverse insurance risk pool to counteract the effects of adverse selection. Future research should investigate the quality of care being provided after 2002 and its impacts on health status.

## INTERREGIONAL TRANSFERS

In Chapter 7, "The Quest for Welfare Spending Equalization: A Fiscal Federalism Perspective," Xin Zhang goes beyond the specific issue of rural health care access to address the problem of place-based disparities in social outcomes more generally. Viewing the problem through the lens of fiscal federalism, Zhang finds some good news: Regional disparities in overall per capita spending appear to have shrunk between 1998 and 2006. Still, a region's level of economic development continues to be a determining factor in its per capita welfare spending. Central government transfers have not eliminated these kinds of inequities.

Zhang analyzes revenue and expenditure data to explore these and other issues of fiscal capacity and effort in the Chinese context, with a focus on the eternal question of how to balance centrally controlled redistribution with decentralized control over expenditures in order to achieve both equity (by smoothing access to resources across rich and poor regions) and efficiency (by allowing local people to decide which services they value most). Zhang concludes that centralized redistribution of revenues and decentralized expenditures are necessary and complementary arrangements that can be applied through the enhanced use of China's compound fiscal system.

The economic development orientation identified by Zhang requires large numbers of workers, many of whom must migrate from rural areas in the country's interior to urban areas on the coast in order to find jobs. This phenomenon of massive internal migration gives rise to a more specific question of fiscal policy: Who should pay to educate the children of migrating laborers? Jing Guo seeks to answer that question in Chapter 8, "Financing Migrant Child Education."

When parents move to the cities looking for work, some children are left behind in home districts to be cared for by grandparents or aunts and uncles, but many others accompany their parents. As a result, nearly 14 percent of China's migrant population consists of children under the age of 14 who are entitled (indeed, compelled) by Chinese law to receive nine years of state-funded education. In the 1980s and 1990s, migrant status was a major barrier to education because education financing was decentralized and local governments budgeted education funds based on household registration numbers. Migrant children fell between the cracks in this system: they were included in the budgets of their home districts, where they did not use services, and were excluded from the budgets of their actual areas of residence, where they needed services. Some urban areas addressed this problem by charging fees for migrant children, a practice that caused severe material hardship for many migrant families.

Guo tells the story of this highly controversial issue and explores how two local jurisdictions have implemented new national policies to address the problem. The national laws improved access to schooling for migrant children by tying responsibility for education delivery to the receiving jurisdictions and by forbidding the imposition of differential fees based on residency status.[1] The laws did not address local governments' financing concerns, however, and did not offer any fiscal relief for local and municipal jurisdictions faced with large numbers of migrant students. As a result, Guo finds substantial differences between Beijing and Zhejiang in their approaches to implementation, particularly the degree to which costs for migrant education are shared between provincial and municipal levels of government or borne entirely at the local level. This research sheds light on two general prerequisites to successful social policy reform in China: intergovernmental coordination and fiscal capacity equalization.

## WILL YOU STAY OR WILL YOU GO? THE SOCIAL POLICY CHALLENGES OF ROOTED AND UPROOTED COMMUNITIES

The dilemmas over financing education for migrant children arise from China's formal system of household registration known as *hukou,* which was embraced by the Communist Party as a mechanism for preventing the problems of economic and social instability that typically follow mass migrations from countryside to city. Many experts have called for a relaxation of *hukou,* on the grounds that it hinders both the optimal functioning of labor markets and the provision of social protection for migrants and their families (Herd, Koen, and Reutersvard 2010). In Chapter 9, "Labor Migration, Citizenship, and Social Welfare in China and India," Josephine Smart, Reeta Chowdari Tremblay, and Mostaem Billah explore the alternative view that China's household registration system has contributed positively to the modernization and economic viability of the Chinese countryside by ensuring that migrants maintain strong ties with their rural home districts and return eventually to those districts to apply the skills and knowledge that they learned in the cities.

The positive impacts of China's registration system pose a sharp contrast to the realities of internal migration in India, where migrants are free to go where they like and social benefits are not tied to place of birth or registration. According to Smart, Tremblay, and Billah, Indian migrants tend to move relatively short distances, often from one rural area to another, and usually between areas with similar income levels. Indians move around their country for a wide variety of reasons, including marriage (the reason for most female moves), whereas internal migration in China is almost entirely driven by job-seeking. Although the Indian data on migration are poor and difficult to interpret, the authors argue that there appears to be little if any net positive economic impact for the migrant-sending areas generally. In the specific category of rural-to-urban moves, Indian migration tends to be more permanent than Chinese migration, which means that India's rural areas miss out on the economic, cultural, and intellectual cross-pollination that return migration brings.

Although available evidence is not sufficient to determine whether the net impact of internal migration in each country is positive or negative, this chapter provides background for pursuing that important question in future research. As with the earlier chapters comparing China with Vietnam (see Chapters 2 and 3), Smart and colleagues' work on China and India underscores the value of intercountry comparisons for illuminating the complexities of major social policy challenges.

At the same time that Chinese policymakers need to address more effectively the opportunities and problems associated with internal labor migration on a massive scale, they also need to better understand the distinctive needs of those populations who maintain strong geographical and cultural ties to their places of origin. Not every rural dweller dreams of a factory job in Shanghai, and many of those who prefer to stay in the countryside belong to ethno-cultural minorities with deep traditions and strong group identities. Alongside the Han ethnic group, which constitutes over 90 percent of China's population, an additional 55 groups are officially recognized as discrete ethnic minorities, many of whose members live in enclaves around the country's periphery. In order to manage the phenomenon of regionally concentrated ethnic minorities and to promote "harmony" over secessionist unrest, more than 150 "autonomous areas" have been established since the founding of the People's Republic of China. These include a few large regions with international profiles, such as Tibet and Inner Mongolia, and many smaller prefectures, counties, and towns of various types.

In Chapter 10, "Ethnic Minorities and Trilingual Education Policies," Bob Adamson, Feng Anwei, Liu Quanguo, and Li Qian explore the tensions between social equity, economic development, national cohesion, and ethnic identity that arise in the course of making educational policies for areas of ethnic minority concentration. In particular, they trace the evolution of language education policy at the national level and identify four distinctive approaches to implementing trilingual language instruction policy that have emerged from various regions. They argue for a multilevel approach to trilingual education that allows for customization of local curricula to strike an effective balance within each region between standard Chinese, English, and the local mother tongue.

Just as present-day rural China is characterized by both anxious mobility and fragile permanence, so the same can be said about urban China, where the forces of change have not yet swept away the long-standing communities that grew up around postwar socialist workplaces. In Chapter 11, "*Danwei*, Family Ties, and Residential Mobility of Urban Elderly in Beijing," Zhilin Liu and Yanwei Chai describe how China's more than 60-year-old institution known as *danwei* has gradually evolved from a formal mechanism of socialist governance, economic production, and welfare allocation into a hub of social attachments and public services for elderly city dwellers. Although the term cannot be translated easily into English, *danwei* can be defined as "a generic term denoting the Chinese socialist workplace and the specific range of practices that it embodies," which in pre-reform times included housing, medical care, child care, kindergartens, sports teams, bathhouses, dining halls, and service companies (Bray 2005, 3). In the new Chinese economy, the employment and production niche once occupied by *danwei* has ostensibly been filled by market-based mechanisms, while the social functions of *danwei* have continued to evolve.

Based on in-depth interviews with elderly Beijing residents living in different types of residential communities, Liu and Chai find that *danwei* have become much more than work units or service delivery hubs for older cohorts of workers who spent the bulk of their adulthood working and living together in these compounds. As a result, many of the elderly residents in Liu and Chai's sample were reluctant to move away from the social interaction and support, as well as the access to public services, that they had come to depend upon within *danwei*. Many of these retirees preferred to stay in or near *danwei* housing because of the strong bonds of attachment and the "sense of belonging" that they had developed within these communities (Liu and Chai, this volume).

This chapter lays the groundwork for further research to explore how urban governance and public service delivery systems can adapt to the realities of "a relatively stable landscape of aging communities in the urban core" (Liu and Chai, this volume). To the extent that Chinese social policy can shape residential patterns going forward, it should aim for an optimal balance between labor mobility, community stability, family harmony, and availability of social services where people need them.

## EQUITY, FAMILY ARRANGEMENTS, AND EDUCATION

As *danwei* and other socialist institutions evolve, they influence not only residential patterns but also career and family formation pathways. Earlier socialist arrangements, such as workplace-based day care centers and canteens, made it somewhat easier to be a working mother in the pre-reform period. With these collective supports rapidly disappearing, it is perhaps predictable that young mothers would choose to work less and invest more in the private home

## Introduction: Chinese Social Policy in a Time of Transition 13

environment, thus expanding the gender gaps in employment and income. This and other gender dimensions of China's workforce transition are the subject of Chapter 12, "Marriage, Parenthood, and Labor Outcomes for Women and Men," by Yuping Zhang and Emily Hannum.

The multivariate data analysis presented in this chapter confirms and extends Zhang and Hannum's earlier research on the predictors of relative female earnings in China. Although significant progress has been made in equalizing access to college (see Chapter 12), women continue to be disadvantaged in education compared with men, a fact that becomes more significant as returns to education increase in the new economy. Years of formal education do not fully explain the gender gaps in employment and income, however; the missing variables, according to Zhang and Hannum, are marital status and child-bearing. Whereas women without children experience some gap in pay relative to men, that gap is significantly larger for married women and women with children, and it grows slightly with each additional child in the family.

Although this chapter does not offer policy recommendations, Chinese policymakers who want to narrow the gaps in workforce pay and participation for wives and mothers need to understand the changing nature of work-family conflict in the new economy. They need subtlety and creativity to design policies that preserve the gains in workforce gender equity that were achieved in the pre-reform era while recognizing the particular preferences of today's working-age population. Although *danwei's* direct role in Chinese life may be fading, the *danwei* experience offers many lessons for the future: accessible, affordable child care arrangements are central to this story.

The gender gap identified by Zhang and Hannum is just one of several equity "gaps" explored in Chapter 13, "Implications of the College Expansion Policy for Social Stratification," by Wei-Jun Jean Yeung. Yeung examines the impact of government's push to expand enrollment in tertiary institutions on access to higher education for selected population groups. Results of the multivariate analysis indicate a threefold increase in the overall odds of attending college after the policy was implemented and a possible spillover effect on high school completion: the improved chances of gaining college admission appear to have helped motivate higher graduation rates from secondary schools. In terms of equity impacts, the picture is mixed. In the 1990s and early 2000s, the odds of attending college increased dramatically for females, and modestly for rural dwellers, but decreased for ethnic minorities (non-Han). Family background characteristics, such as household income, parents' education, and parents' party membership, played a prominent role in determining college attendance both before and after the college expansion policy, with no significant change in the later period.

Although some groups experienced gains between the two periods, "staggering inequalities among subgroups" remained in the later period (Yeung, this volume). Rural/urban origin continues to be the best predictor of who will attend college, with rural youth attending at only 9 percent the rate of urban youth.

Efforts to further close the gap in college access will need to focus especially on youth disadvantaged by their rural *hukou* or ethnic minority origins and on youth from lower income households. The latter factor is likely to become more important due to steady increases in the share of college costs paid by households. Policymakers also need to pay attention to how overall quality of education may have changed following enrollment expansion and, with respect to equity, how socioeconomic and regional stratification of educational opportunities may be perpetuated by differences in admission rates to elite tertiary institutions. As debates continue about the inevitability of stark inequalities in a market-based economy, the issue of college access and affordability will play an important role in China's efforts to pursue economic growth and social harmony simultaneously.

## COLLABORATIVE POLICY LEARNING

The final chapter, "The Evolving Response to HIV/AIDS," by Zunyou Wu, Sheena G. Sullivan, Yu Wang, Mary Jane Rotheram, and Roger Detels, offers a glimpse of the types of policy development processes that will be needed to meet the many challenges posed by the multiple economic and demographic transitions described throughout this volume. Wu and colleagues tell the backstory to the 2006 *AIDS Prevention and Control Regulations* and the *Five-Year Action Plan to Control HIV/AIDS* (2006–2010). These two policies represent the culmination of 20 years of forward and backward moves by multiple units within the Chinese government. Following China's early responses to the HIV/AIDS threat, which took the form of containment via border security, understanding of the disease and its modes of transmission developed in fits and starts and eventually led to such highly promising programs as "needle social marketing" (i.e., needle exchange by a more acceptable name), condom distribution to commercial sex workers, counseling and peer education for high-risk groups, public education about prevention in schools, free HIV testing for the poor, and free anti-retroviral treatment for rural residents and the urban poor through public clinics. The road to these programs was built by trial and error in a series of pragmatic steps designed to meet various challenges as they emerged. Although the result is a relatively coherent policy framework, the process of getting there was neither strategic nor systematic; it closely resembled the processes seen in other areas of Chinese social policymaking in the reform period, as described throughout this volume, and especially by Friedman in Chapter 4.

The story of HIV/AIDS policy in China is a reminder of the often ad hoc nature of successful policy development. Key elements included patient accumulation and dissemination of scientific findings, the use of pilot projects to demonstrate feasibility and effectiveness of proposed interventions, leadership by influential figures willing to raise the public profile of the problem, and good, old-fashioned relationship-building among key individuals to marshal the resources and commitment needed to implement new programs. In 10 years' time, if social policymakers in China absorb the lessons put forth by Wu and colleagues based on the HIV/AIDS case, another volume of papers will need to be published recounting the more successful and more expeditious construction of coherent and effective policies to address education, underemployment and unemployment, health care, gender disparities, urban-rural disparities, financing anomalies, aging, migration, and the cultural and developmental needs of ethnic minorities, to name just a few of the social challenges that continue to accumulate in the new China.

## CONCLUSION

From the diversity of studies reported in this volume, a few overarching themes emerge, including the trend toward cost-sharing arrangements between employers, employees, and the state to finance social services; the gradual recognition of a need to expand risk pools for all types of social insurance beyond the enterprise and city levels; and the process of combining national mandates with local implementation, which leads to large variations in social protection coverage and compliance across municipalities, provinces, and autonomous regions. The "liberalization of people's mobility" (Smart et al., this volume) through the loosening of household registration rules has forced and is forcing changes in every area of social policy.

Chinese policymakers may have access to more resources in the coming decade as a result of large infusions of new funding for pensions, education, health care, and farm subsidies that began in 2010. The new spending appears to reflect the beginning of a possible rebalancing of the government's economic growth strategy away from a historically heavy emphasis on capital-intensive investments toward human capital-oriented investments designed not only to improve worker productivity but also to boost domestic consumption and thereby create jobs. Many commentators have been urging such a shift in policy, and the government's rhetoric has been promising it for some time, but it is difficult to predict how far the government will progress down that policy road in a highly uncertain global economic environment.

Looking ahead, many questions still need to be addressed by scholars and policy practitioners who want to help China move forward while also drawing lessons from China's experience for other parts of the developed and developing worlds. Some of these questions are the same in every country: how to insure against unemployment without reducing work incentives, how to nurture community attachments without hindering labor mobility, how to pay for ever increasing pension obligations without impoverishing current and future working-age generations, and how to support social norms of family care while ensuring adequate social protection at the population level. These are universal tensions within all socioeconomic systems, whether capitalist, socialist, or hybrid.

Other questions arise from China's distinctive history and reform agenda: how to shed large numbers of excess workers and make firms self-sufficient without causing massive hardship, how to sustain the positive social bonds that formed within pre-reform collectives and state-owned enterprises but adapt them to an economy where there is little room for the older types of enterprises, and how to fuel rural development without coercing people to stay in or return to the countryside, among many others. Since China's transition to market socialism began in the late 1970s, many countries have embarked on the exit path from state socialism toward different versions of a mixed economy, and their varied experiences provide a rich source of insights for answering these questions. Alongside continued research on China, substantially more comparative policy research is needed to identify the types of policies that seem to work best in a dynamic context of formidable economic, demographic, cultural, and industrial transitions.

This book has assembled a series of thoughtful analyses about a critical phase in China's social policy evolution, which, we hope, will help readers to draw lessons for other countries as well as for Chinese policymakers. It is offered in the spirit of mutual learning with high expectations for continued international dialogue.

## NOTE

1 This paralleled obligations for urban employers to make pension benefits available to migrant workers, as noted by Friedman (this volume, Chapter 4).

## REFERENCES

Bergsten, C. Fred, Bates Gill, Nicholas R. Lardy, and Derek Mitchell. 2006. *China: The balance sheet*. Washington, DC: Peterson Institute for International Economics.

Bray, David. 2005. *Social space and governance in urban China: The danwei system from origins to reform*. Palo Alto, CA: Stanford University Press.

Chen, Shaohua, and Martin Ravallion. 2009. *The developing world is poorer than we thought, but no less successful in the fight against poverty*. Policy Research Working Paper No. 7403 (revised version), Development Research Group, World Bank.

Herd, Richard. 2010. *A Pause in the growth of inequality in China?* Economics Department Working Papers No. 748. Paris: OECD.

Herd, Richard, Vincent Koen, and Anders Reutersward. 2010. *China's labour market in transition: Job creation, migration and regulation.* Economics Department Working Papers No. 749. Paris: OECD.

Ignatius, David. 2010. The trouble with China's economic bubble. *Washington Post.* March 11, p. A21.

Jiabao, Wen. 2007. Premier Wen Jiabao's press conference. March 17. http://www.fmprc.gov.cn/eng/zxxx/t304313.htm (accessed February 2010).

Kristof, Nicholas D. 1993. China sees "Market-Leninism" as way to future. *New York Times.* September 6.

Leonard, Mark. 2008. *What does China think?* London: Fourth Estate.

Pei, Minxin. 2006. The dark side of China's rise. *Foreign Policy* (online). http://www.foreignpolicy.com/articles/2006/02/17/the_dark_side_of_chinas_rise (accessed March 2010).

Ravallion, Martin, and Shaohua Chen. 2007. China's (uneven) progress against poverty. *Journal of Development Economics* 82(1): 142.

# 2

# WELFARE REGIMES IN THE WAKE OF STATE SOCIALISM: CHINA AND VIETNAM

Jonathan D. London

## INTRODUCTION

This chapter examines the evolution of welfare regimes in contemporary China and Vietnam.[1] Specifically, it examines how the degeneration of state-socialist regimes and the evolution of new political economies in their wake have shaped institutional arrangements governing the provision of and payment for education and health services and their stratification effects. A foundational assumption of welfare regimes analysis is that welfare institutions evolve interdependently with prevailing political and economic institutions. That is, historically emergent combinations of political and economic institutions that define a given political economy—and express the precise relation between state and economy—profoundly affect welfare and stratification. Analyzing welfare regimes in China and Vietnam raises interesting questions about the nature and dynamics of their political economies and more general questions about how welfare regimes evolve in the transition from one form of political economy to another. The common assumption that welfare regimes reflect the structured interests of dominant political and economic actors and thus serve to reproduce that regime is reasonable but tends to invite an excessively static perspective. This chapter argues that welfare regimes and stratification in contemporary China and Vietnam may not be understood without appreciating their properties under state-socialism and how specific paths of extrication affected their degeneration and subsequent development under a new form of political economy.

The first section discusses the extent to which earlier and more recent literature on welfare regimes can inform the study of welfare regimes in both the transition from and wake of state-socialism, before examining the degeneration of state-socialist welfare regimes in China and Vietnam, respectively. The second section explicates core features of the political economies that have emerged in China and Vietnam in the wake of state-socialism, arguing that they are best characterized as market-Leninist regimes. In market-Leninist regimes, market economic institutions develop in subordination to Leninist principles of political organization. This specific combination of institutional attributes and its attendant effects on welfare, stratification, and political consciousness distinguishes market-Leninist regimes from other forms of political economy. The final section examines the development of welfare regimes in China and Vietnam in the wake of state-socialism. It is argued that areas of divergence in the two countries' welfare regimes reflect not only differences in wealth but also qualitative differences in the politics of redistribution in both countries.

The terminal crisis of state-socialism involves the erosion of one welfare regime and its replacement with another. Among formerly state-socialist countries, Vietnam and China are frequently lumped together as instances of "gradual" market transitions. But perhaps the crucial shared feature of market transition is the ability of Leninist states to survive the erosion of state-socialist economic institutions and to employ markets to promote state goals, such as the political supremacy of the Communist Party. The way that this occurred in Vietnam and China differed, however, which in turn affected the subsequent development of their respective welfare regimes.

## WELFARE REGIMES IN THE PATH FROM STATE-SOCIALISM

Globally, the degeneration of state-socialist regimes took place differently in different settings, but in all cases the impetus for change arose from systemic failures in state-socialist economic institutions and the tremendous political pressures this brought to bear on Leninist states. Most fundamentally, administrative allocation of capital and labor generated perverse incentives that promoted soft-budget constraints and resulted in conditions of general scarcity (Kornai 1980). Promoting and sustaining capital accumulation under such conditions proved untenable. In this section, I consider the extent to which existing literature on welfare regimes can aid in analyzing what happened to welfare in the transition from state-socialism. The features of market transitions in China and Vietnam are examined, and the degenerative effects of transition on these countries' welfare regimes explained.

### Welfare Regimes and Institutional Change

In recent years, welfare regimes analysis has gained currency among analysts of social policy and welfare institutions worldwide. However, welfare regimes analysis is not without controversy. Some analysts have questioned the value of the term altogether. The term "welfare regime" refers to distinctive sets of institutional arrangements that govern the creation and allocation of welfare. It first emerged in studies of welfare states under advanced capitalism in Western Europe and North America (Esping-Andersen 1987, 1990). Welfare regimes analysis aims to explicate the historical determinants and stratification effects of welfare regimes across time and space.

A second generation of analysis has sought to protract the ambit to other economic and regional settings (Gough 2000; Gough and Wood and Gough 2006), such as middle-income and poor countries, including East Asia (Cook and Kwon 2007; Goodman et al. 1998; Gough 2001; Holliday 2000; Kwon 1998; Park 2008), South Asia (Davis 2004), Latin America (Barrientos 2004), and Africa (Bevan 2004). The extension of welfare regimes analysis to developing countries is now well-established. As Gough and Wood have emphasized, the point was never to simply apply the original framework, but rather, to extend its fundamental ideas to new contexts, thereby clarifying differences between welfare institutions in wealthier and poorer parts of the world economy. Perhaps inevitably, this second generation has often resulted in highly descriptive and sociologically thin taxonomical studies that fail to attend to the original aims of welfare regimes analysis, that is, to explain historical variation and convergence in welfare regimes in relation to the developmental attributes of political economies. Additionally, there are relatively few—if any—attempts to theorize the diversity of welfare regimes in formerly state-socialist settings within this growing body of "second generation" literature. (For an exception, see Deacon 2000; Sotiropolous et al. 2003.) Surely, the diversity of these settings poses obstacles, as there are at least 33 formerly state-socialist countries. Otherwise, another disincentive lies in the sheer historical scope of such an undertaking.

Yet, a standard assumption of welfare regimes analysis is that a country's welfare institutions exist and develop in interdependent relation with other social, political, economic, and cultural institutions. It is by extension reasonable to expect that the evolution and involution of state-socialism significantly affects the development of subsequent welfare regimes. Studying welfare regimes under both state-socialism and in the transition from state-socialism to a new form of political economy is a huge task indeed, and welfare regimes analysis offers a useful interpretive frame. In this chapter, attention is directed first to the general nature of the market transition, and then to the specific ways in which this unfolded in Vietnam and China.

## Paths from State-Socialism

As the command economy was the economic foundation for one-party rule, citizens' dependence on officials for the satisfaction of needs was the basis of official power (Oi 1985, 1989; Walder 1983, 1986, cited in Walder 1995). Hence, departures from and systemic problems in the planned economy were always a potential source of political decline (Walder 1995). State-socialist regimes responded differently to these pressures. In some instances, states sought to arrest any significant deviations from the formal institutions of central planning. Peasants who went to market were arrested or shot. In others instances, states tolerated deviations and even sought to co-opt them eventually through various liberalizing reforms. In Hungary, for example, the development of markets was accelerated by state assistance, which provided an increasingly systematic legal infrastructure to institutionalize the market (Kornai 2000). Either way, by the carrot or the stick, efforts to reform state-socialist economies could not address the systemic inefficiencies of actually existing planned economies. Nor could they counteract the weak and perverse incentives that ultimately spelled their doom.

Since the late 1980s, scholars have been concerned to understand the historical antecedents, political logic, and various outcomes of market transition. Academic literature has progressed from an at-times simplistic and normative debate about the putative advantages or disadvantages of "rapid" versus more "gradual" approaches to market reforms to more fine-grained analyses of the transition, the latter distinguished by a greater attention to institutions. As the standard caricature goes, Russia and Eastern European countries took a rapid approach, while China took a gradual one.[1] Vietnam, more populous than any of the Eastern European state-socialist countries save for Russia, is seldom mentioned.

## Vietnam's Market Transition

Vietnam's transition to a market economy was a 10-year process of institutional decay. As core institutions of state-socialism gradually lost their force, the coherence of the economy diminished to a point at which it threatened even the maintenance of basic state functions. In the aftermath of war, the circumstances that confronted the Communist Party of Vietnam (CPV) were hardly favorable. War damage and international isolation, economic scarcity, and limited state capacities undermined the viability of state-socialist developmentalism. The 1978 military engagement in Cambodia removed a lethal threat but proved costly, given that it resulted in a border war with China, evolved into a protracted occupation, and resulted in a U.S.-Sino embargo lasting until the mid-1990s. These factors, which inflicted enormous pressure on a weak economy, meant that Vietnam ranked among the poorest countries in Asia throughout the 1980s. Nonetheless, the principal mechanisms underlying the slow death of state-socialism lay at the micro-foundations of the Vietnamese economy.

By the late 1970s, Vietnam was failing to achieve the aim of state-socialism, in which all economic actors in a planned economy—from agricultural producers to state-owned industrial enterprises—create and accumulate value to achieve social reproduction and advance the political and economic causes of the state. War, inadequate infrastructure, and insufficient energy and food did not help matters. Across all sectors, aggravated scarcity prevailed and incentives remained poor. In this context, the survival strategies of both enterprises and individuals deviated increasingly from the diktat of central planning (Beresford 1997; Fforde and de Vylder 1996). Economic producers in Vietnam (including state-owned enterprises) adopted increasingly brazen "fence breaking" strategies that contravened state norms by the 1980s.

As the most noted foreign analysts of Vietnam's market transition have pointed out, "reform"—with its implication of a top-down ex ante plan of action—fails to describe accurately what was occurring in the country (Fforde and de Vylder 1996). Cognizant of the breakdown of planning, central government agencies sought to contain "spontaneous" reforms by introducing successive rounds of top-down measures that aimed to control, limit, and steer the processes of change that were already occurring, primarily by legalizing practices and setting formal limits. This strategy legitimized change but did not slow it, nor did it address the fundamental problem of incentives.

It is significant that the first marketizing measures introduced in Vietnam first occurred in the enterprise sector, where a coalition of enterprise managers and provincial leaders pushed the reluctant center to reform. Output-contracts in agriculture were introduced only in the 1980s. In both cases, these post hoc measures improved economic incentives and boosted outputs by allowing economic producers to engage in market exchange. Yet market reform is a double-edged sword. This limited liberalization also accelerated and expanded the diversion of economic resources from the central budget, which in turn undercut the financial bases of state functions, including its limited welfare functions (as addressed below). Politically, the powers of the central state vis-à-vis the localities weakened, compromising its fiscal integrity and resulting in an acute crisis that ended with the abandonment of core state-socialist institutions.

Crucially, Vietnam's transition culminated in 1989 when an acute fiscal crisis caused the state to dramatically accelerate marketization, principally through the removal of dual prices and subsidies. As it would turn out, however, this would not be a protracted political and fiscal decline of the central state vis-à-vis the localities. While localities enriched by marketization would gain autonomy (e.g., the so-called VNĐ10 Billion Club, a name that referred to their budgetary contributions), this was merely relative. Fiscal transfers to, and then away from, the center remained significant and grew in scale. By the 1990s, when the state began undertaking significant administrative decentralization, it had already regained its financial footing, securing[2] and strengthening its redistributive functions, even if its allocative capacity remained weak. Thus, while scholars of Vietnam (and the present author included) have commonly emphasized the decentralization of political power, some perspective is needed. Although it is certainly the case that social life in contemporary Vietnam is much more decentralized than formal institutions would suggest, the central state has maintained an important redistributive and steering role. The question then becomes one of how beholden central power brokers became to national, local, and sector-based constituencies.

## China's Market Transition

China's economic reforms are better known. A heavy industry priority model applied in the capital-scarce but politically charged environment of the 1950s and 1960s was designed to spur industrialization by transferring value from rural areas to urban ones. Instead, it resulted in chaos. The "Great Leap Forward" produced the greatest famine in human history. More generally, violent collectivization and poor incentives to peasants and workers diminished productivity. Even more so than in Vietnam, Chinese state-socialism produced sharp chasms between urban and rural areas, where the terms of trade exploited the same peasants that had enabled revolution. Still, one notable feature of state-socialism in China is that the enterprise sector—in particular, industrial enterprise—grew and developed rather substantially. Nonetheless, systemic inefficiencies in China resembled those in other state-socialist economies, where poor incentives begat low productivity and general economic malaise.

In contrast, the market reforms that began in the late 1970s created a stream of new economic resources and improved economic incentives in agriculture. Enterprise reforms designed to improve incentives for workers also granted partial autonomy to state economic units and later incorporated retention of profits and foreign exchange. Profit remittances to the central budget were replaced with a profit tax in 1983, while the government permitted enterprises to sell output in excess of centrally determined quotas on the market a year later. As the quote by Lin and colleagues (1994, 14) aptly illustrates, "once a small crack was opened, it was pried apart even wider" and led eventually to the dismantling of the state-socialist model. Developments in the agriculture sector were even more important. Similar to that which occurred in Vietnam later, agricultural "reform" in China began secretly in the form of the output contract system—by authorities secretly leasing land and dividing procurement obligations—and was later approved by local and higher authorities. By 1981, 45 percent of China's localities had instituted such a system, and this figure increased to 98 percent in two years (Lin et al. 1994, 14). Lin and colleagues estimate that almost half the 42 percent growth in output between 1978 and 1994 is attributable to productivity gains permitted by the reforms, a finding reinforced by many other studies.

The rapid growth of township and village enterprises (TVEs) was another key development in China's path from state-socialism. Enterprise reforms liberalized access to credit, raw materials, and markets, while the new stream of rural savings from agricultural reforms created a resource base for both investment in and demand for TVE output. In the decade between 1981 and 1991, the number of TVEs grew by 26 percent, the sector's share of employment by 11 percent, and its output value by nearly 30 percent. In 1992, TVE output represented some 32 percent of the nation's total, while the total share of industrial output from non-state enterprises increased from 22 percent in 1978 to 52 percent (Lin et al. 1994).

Overall, China's economy was highly decentralized whether pre- or post-transition, reinforced by market reforms that conferred upon sub-national and local units of government increasing financial discretion. The dependence of localities on local economic units for revenue—and the corresponding need for local units to compete in regional and national markets—created powerful incentives for local officials to adopt a developmentalist outlook (Shirk 1993). This was often detrimental to essential social services. As Andrew Walder (2003) and numerous others have noted, cadres in China were quick to realize that their incomes and living standards, as well as those of their families, were closely related to the prosperity of "their" localities. Furthermore, they realized that they were likely to benefit from liberalization more than most, even if they no longer possessed a strict monopoly over the allocation of labor and capital. Although this has also been the case in Vietnam, differences in the political logic of economic reforms in both countries meant different implications for their welfare regimes.

## The Demise of State-Socialist Welfare Regimes

The economic institutions of state-socialism were designed to ensure security through the administrative and redistributive allocation of capital, full employment, and welfare-producing goods such as housing, education, and health services. Outside the household sphere, welfare allocation was—in principle—to occur through the planned economy. According to plan, economic security hinged on employment, which was guaranteed to all. Essential social services such as education, health care, and various forms of social insurance were to be financed and allocated through various state units, ranging from provincial and local administrative units to productive enterprises.

In practice, the actual allocation of welfare reflected the limitations of particular economies, while stratification outcomes reflected the distributive biases inherent in bureaucratic allocation. Just as market coordination in capitalist societies exhibited patterns of inequality owing to unequal relations to capital and to the means of production, state-socialist administrative coordination gave rise to inequalities reflective of unequal relations to institutions of bureaucratic allocation (Szelényi and Manchin 1987).

These unequal relations hinge not only on one's affiliation with the Communist Party and state, but also to one's functional position within the planned economy. Bureaucratic allocation under state-socialism is subordinated to a specific developmental logic—one that seeks to finance the development of heavy industry and cities through savings from agriculture. This drove the dualism in state-socialist economies, where the quality and scope of welfare services offered in rural areas were more limited than in cities. However, in both town and country, welfare allocation depended on resources that were either transferred from above or mobilized at the local level.[3] This formal dependence became evident in the course of transition from state-socialism. As the flow of resources dwindled, malaise in welfare institutions gathered pace, necessitating a new financial basis.

Scholars of market transition have noted the devastating impact of market transition on welfare institutions, yet crucial here is identifying what the transition entailed. Drawing on and extending Polanyi's (1957) distinction between reciprocal, formal, and redistributive forms of market coordination, Szelényi (1978) noted that under state-socialism (a modern instance of the redistributive state), households frequently resorted to illicit reciprocal and market exchange relations in order to make ends meet. Nonetheless, the flow of economic resources and opportunities for mobility remained dependent on bureaucratic allocative institutions, even as the latter were typically subject to various kinds of rent-seeking.

Market transition promised to flatten the state-socialist opportunity structure by providing greater economic freedom to those previously subject to administrative exclusion. Hence Nee (1989, 663), among others, hypothesized in his "market transition theory" that the transition[4] would "shift sources of power and privilege to favor direct producers relative to redistributors." Undoubtedly, market transition has flattened opportunity structures in some respects. As a general matter, however, it appears that Nee underestimated the extent to which the politically connected would be able to convert their political capital into economic opportunity following state-socialism's demise. In terms of welfare allocation and stratification, the development of and eventual preponderance of markets over other means of economic coordination created new market-based inequalities. These were in turn ameliorated only by administrative and redistributive means, or by individual households engaging in various forms of reciprocal exchange and self-exploitation.

The problems for countries undergoing market transition were (1) the significant time gap—essentially a generation—between the collapse of the state-socialist welfare regime and economic recovery; and (2) the adoption of new formal institutions governing welfare that were strangely more liberal than even the most capitalist of welfare states. This minimalist approach to social welfare has been observed across the formerly state-socialist countries, suggesting a degree of institutional convergence. The subsequent development of welfare regimes in these societies is examined in the final section.

## THE DEGENERATION OF STATE-SOCIALIST WELFARE

### Regimes in Vietnam and China

Such broad assumptions remain inadequate in explaining particular instances of change, and the specific conditions under which economic and welfare institutions developed and then collapsed in the transition from state-socialism profoundly affected their subsequent development in Vietnam and China. There also exist categorical differences in the interests, capacities, and incentive structures of policy elites in both countries during and after the transition period, which can be explicated in concise terms.

In Vietnam, the fiscal crisis of the central state, combined with the disintegration of collectivist arrangements, rapidly eroded institutional arrangements for financing education and health.[5] This would prove especially damaging to schooling in rural areas. As the 1980s wore on, the gradual dissolution of agricultural collectives gathered pace. In economic terms and with respect to living standards, the shift to household production in agriculture and the expansion of markets provided some immediate relief. This was not the case for the welfare regime, where the already paltry amount of local resources available for education and health declined even further.

The withering of state-socialist economic institutions necessitated a reworking of the financial and fiscal bases of formal schooling. In 1989, the CPV took its first step away from the universalist principles that had guided education policies since the 1950s, when the (rubber-stamp) National Assembly met in a special session to pass a constitutional amendment permitting the state to charge school fees. The results were devastating. Whether sharp declines in enrollment at the time were predated or exacerbated by the introduction of fees is the subject of some debate. What is clear however, is that enrollment rates fell sharply and dropout rates soared. Between 1989 and 1991, dropouts increased by up to 80 percent in secondary schools in some areas, while new enrollments declined by upward of 30 percent nationally and would not recover to 1985 levels until the mid-1990s. Even though the country gained 10 million school-age children between 1980 and 1990, Vietnam registered only a minor increase in its gross enrollment.

With hyperinflation and evaporating state budgets in the late 1980s, national and local investments in education and health fell sharply in real terms. Workers in these sectors faced declining wages from an already low base. In many areas, especially rural ones, teachers and medical staff were not compensated for months. Responding to new opportunities, they expanded their economic activities outside the state sector, or left their professions altogether in search of a living wage. The quality of education and health services deteriorated, and the state-socialist welfare regime lay in ruins.

In China, the gap between urban and rural areas characteristic of the pre-reform period became sharper, as the fiscal capacities of Rural People's Communes declined precipitously with the advent of the household responsibility system (White 1998). Urban systems eroded more slowly, particularly in the "prestigious" heavy industrial sector, where workers' benefits were protected. In the late 1970s, major economic reforms reshaped the health care system in China. The results were manifold—government financing was decentralized; enterprise reforms required health facilities to be self-supporting; greater economic openness allowed imports of modern medical technology and drugs; greater mobility of the population aided both patients and health workers in moving around the country; and salary reforms increased incentives for health worker performance.

The beginning of the 1980s saw the central government introduce fiscal decentralization, which weakened the influence of central health policy on health service activities. Provincial and municipal health departments, county and city health bureaus, and township and town health centers came to enjoy a considerable degree of autonomy. They also came more directly under the authority of local governments. The "financial responsibility system" served to further weaken the influence of national health policy. Hospitals and other health institutions were required to maximize non-budgetary sources of revenue and did so by charging fees for their services. The reforms resulted in a shift of resources from lower to higher levels, from rural to urban areas, from preventive to curative services, and from planning and management to market forces (Huong et al. 2006, 33–37).

To summarize, the following features of the decline of welfare regimes are as follows:

- The breakdown of state-socialist economic institutions involves a change of welfare regime, though the way in which this plays out varies from country to country;
- Vietnam's transition was a gradual process, culminating in a fiscal crisis and the collapse of institutional arrangements governing the finance of education and health; whereas China's transition, though initiated by bottom-up deviations from the planned economy, nonetheless resembled a top-down reform effort;
- In Vietnam, the fiscal crisis of the state at the end of the 1980s resulted in retrenchment and greater decentralization, but within a unified polity; whereas in China, the transition undercut the power of the central state vis-à-vis the provinces, while fiscal policies encouraged a "eating in separate kitchens" system;
- In China, decentralization took the form of fiscal federalism in which local units of government resembled actual governments in their own right; whereas in Vietnam, a practically unitary fiscal system remained intact, and the political economy was characterized by significant inter-governmental redistribution;
- Both Vietnam and China experienced the commodification of education and health, though the way that this unfolded, its effects, and responses to it have varied.

Having established the basic contours of the degeneration of state-socialist welfare regimes, the focus is now thrust at the development of welfare regimes in the wake of state-socialism. An essential step here is appreciating the institutional attributes of the political economy that succeeded the state-socialist regime.

## THE POLITICAL ECONOMY OF MARKET-LENINISM

The transformation of formerly state-socialist societies is among the most important developments of our times. Much of the existing literature on these societies is focused on changes in economic and political institutions, or on changes in social policies. But this chapter is concerned with a somewhat broader question: How do welfare regimes develop in the wake of state-socialism? It has been noted above that in any political economy, institutional arrangements governing the creation and allocation of both welfare and stratification are broadly determined by the nexus of politics and economy. This basic insight directs our attention to that nexus in China and Vietnam, and to how it structures welfare and stratification.

A distinctive type of political economy has developed in China and Vietnam following state-socialism, and along with it, a particular kind of welfare regime. Market economic institutions and market-based strategies of accumulation in both countries have developed in subordination to Leninist political institutions. This particular combination of political and economic institutions forms the essence of market-Leninism (London 2009, 2011). In what follows, I identify characteristic attributes of market-Leninism and explain why we might expect them to exhibit distinctive welfare regimes. At the same time, I argue that there are important qualitative differences in the features of market-Leninism observed in Vietnam and China. These differences, as I contend, owe not only to different historical and material circumstances, but also to the different paths these countries took to and from state-socialism, coupled with their particular historical and contemporary features of class and bureaucratic politics.

## Political Institutions of Market-Leninism

In Vietnam and China, communist parties have survived the erosion of state-socialist economic institutions by using markets to promote political imperatives, including eternal social order under one-party rule, economic accumulation, social welfare, and legitimacy and consent among the ruled. It is clear that the political continuities and changes in both countries differ from other state-socialist states that experienced political revolution. With respect to continuity, the communist parties of Vietnam and China maintain a deep sense of corporate identity, and their activities continue to penetrate the grassroots. Yet, the notion that Vietnam and China have skirted political change is problematic.

Market transitions in both countries entailed considerable changes in the nature and internal politics of the state, as well as a fundamental reconstitution of state-society relations. While it must be conceded that relations between state and society are always complex, they are necessarily reciprocally determinant. The state is a product of society and affects social life through its policies, but it is simultaneously shaped and constrained by actors and structures outside it. Obviously, the nature of Vietnam's and China's external relations has changed considerably, including their political engagement with the international order. The divergent features of political change within both countries are, as I will argue, responsible for some important differences in their welfare regimes today.

## Economic Institutions and Trajectories of Economic Change

Vietnam and China are market economies ruled by Leninist parties. To suggest they are market-socialist understates the importance of the party in organizing the economy and exaggerates the importance of socialist aims. Calling them "capitalist" suggests the supremacy of liberal economic institutions, such as private property, and the presence of a dominant capitalist class. The label "capitalism with Vietnamese or Chinese characteristics" is too vague to be meaningful. In fact, market reforms in both countries grew from the cracks in state-socialist economic institutions, and their character has and continues to be heavily shaped by the political logics of the Communist Party—hence, the befitting term "market-Leninism."

We can clarify trajectories of economic change in Vietnam and China by differentiating them from what occurred in other state-socialist settings. Szelényi and King (2005) have distinguished three ideal-typical paths of transition from state-socialism. Where the transition occurred through a "revolution from above," state elites orchestrated change according to a "blueprint" architected by neoliberal economists, resulting in the *nomenklatura* (and its clients) being transformed into a "grand bourgeoisie." Such was the Russian path. The case of other Eastern European societies such as Hungary resembled a "revolution from without." An alliance of technocrats and elites adopted neoliberal blueprints but blocked attempts at appropriation by the *nomenklatura*, in addition to forging economic alliances with foreign investors and multinational capital (Szelényi 2010, 3).

Although all the formerly state-socialist regimes in Eastern Europe passed through a period of state retrenchment, differences in path-dependent effects of the transition between Russia and Central and Eastern Europe have been unmistakable (Szelényi 2008b, 170). Russia's economy, having recovered from the lost decade of the 1990s, when gross domestic product (GDP) fell by 50 percent, has had its market institutions developed and become more entrenched. The commanding heights of its political economy are contested by a neo-patrimonial elite and business "oligarchs"—remnants of the *nomenklatura*. Contrastingly, Eastern European countries such as Poland and Hungary have continued to adopt formal market institutions that are in many respects more liberal than those in the United States and the United Kingdom. The engine behind economic growth has moved from massive foreign investment initially to one propelled by a developing domestic bourgeoisie that comprises in part a large contingent of former state managers.

Yet even if subsequent political configurations vary considerably, Communist Party rule ended in both ideal-typical Eastern European experiences, a phenomenon that Szelényi and King (2005) contrast with a third approach, termed the "Chinese" or "East Asian" path. Here, the transition involved a process of "transformation from below," to be combined later with developmental statism. The declining coherence of the centrally planned economy in Vietnam spurred a coalition of Southern reformers and enterprise leaders to champion market reforms during the 1980s. Over the course of the 1990s and into the present, Vietnam's economic policies have appealed to various constituencies within the state, rather than conforming to a coherent developmentalist plan. State policies are aimed at securing control over the commanding heights of the economy while simultaneously preventing the development of an independent bourgeoisie. What has emerged instead is a state business class whose favorable position within or on the borders of state power has enabled it to exploit market opportunities for personal gain.

Contrastingly, agricultural reforms, first introduced in the late 1970s and then extended across the country, led to the generation and accumulation of rural savings in China. These were in turn channeled into hybrid and private firms, as well as the reforming state enterprise sector (Oi 1999). Moreover, economic growth was further catalyzed by a combination of rising domestic demand (based on aforementioned savings), surging foreign investment, and access to the giant U.S. and European markets. The political logic of economic reform that evolved in the 1980s and 1990s reflected China's decentralized enterprise structure. Piecemeal economic reforms transformed enterprise managers into enterprise owners, while the "eat in separate kitchens" fiscal model meant that provinces maintained a degree of financial autonomy from the center. Provinces have thus been able to pursue developmentalist economic policies in a way largely unseen in Vietnam.

China today, as Szelényi (2008b, 171) notes, resembles "capitalism" from above more than during the early stages of its transition. Particularly, SOEs have been appropriated by well-placed officials and their clients, all of whom have benefited disproportionately from multinational capital. SOE privatization further suggests movement toward capitalism, alongside Walder's (2003) observation of the rise of an economic elite separate from the state. In both countries, however, communist parties have overseen a process of migration from the peripheries of world capitalism to central points in the international division of labor.

## DIVERGENCE IN EAST ASIA'S MARKET-LENINIST WELFARE REGIMES

Analysts of formerly Eastern European state-socialist countries have sought to explain the evolution of institutional arrangements governing welfare in the wake of state-socialism (e.g., Deacon 2002; Haney 2002; Kornai 1997; Sotiropolous et al. 2003). Broadly, these studies are consistent with the idea that cross-national variation in the character of welfare institutions reflects divergent class configurations and class politics in the path toward a market-based political economy (Eyal et al. 1998; King 2001a, 2001b, 2002). These class dynamics are the product of unique social histories and institutional attributes, including levels of development, timing of industrialization, and struggles for power among competing social groups in dynamic domestic and international contexts (King 2001b;

Szelényi et al. 2005, 2008a). But few—if any—studies have explicitly sought to understand convergences and divergences in the welfare institutions of China and Vietnam. And while a thorough analysis cannot be achieved within the scope of a short chapter, a concise exploration of these questions yields intriguing insights that potentially contribute to existing literature on welfare institutions in both countries and to the broader theoretical literature on welfare regimes.

The welfare regimes that Vietnam and China display today share core similarities. Within the eroded shell of state-socialist institutions, both countries have experienced the commodification of most essential services under the rule of communist parties that profess a commitment to achieving "socialist-oriented" market economies. Economic development policies and corresponding patterns of production and distribution have intensified regional and class inequalities, while state policies have shifted institutional responsibility for the provision of and (especially) payment for essential social services from the state to households. This, in turn, has fostered the intensification of market-based social inequalities. In both countries, emerging social inequalities and raw contradictions between received rhetoric and practices have generated pressure on the state to respond to the destructive impacts of commodification with ameliorative policies and programs of varying significance. In both countries, communist parties continue to profess a long-term commitment to universalist principles and programs, even as the manner in which institutions are actually evolving casts doubt. The stratification outcomes in both Vietnam and China exhibit a dual and overlapping character. The resilience of Leninist political organization continues to generate inequalities of access to power and, by extension, mediates allocation of economic resources and opportunities. In the meantime, these relations of political domination are—at every social scale—suffused with and reinforced by market-based inequalities. The similarities of both countries' welfare institutions are striking, as are simmiliarities and differences in the indicators of wellbeing observed in both countries, and depicted in Tables 2.1–2.3.

The significance of the data presented in the tables is addressed at greater length below. What bears emphasis here, is that there are important differences in these countries' welfare regimes that are not easily explained simply by disparities in size or wealth per se. Intriguingly, for example, Vietnam rivals or "outperforms" China across a number of indicators of well-being, including life expectancy and access to basic education and health services, despite being poorer. As depicted in Table 2.3, the Vietnamese state spends a larger proportion of its GDP on health and education than China. More strikingly still, recorded rates of inequality are significantly greater in China than in Vietnam, as measured by Gini and other indicators. This possibly owes to the comparatively more redistributive character of Vietnam's state, which Malesky et al. (2011) contend is more pluralistic than that of China. Data from 2001 to 2006 also indicate that Vietnam's fiscal system and welfare regime are more redistributive than those of China, suggesting that Vietnam is less unequal.

Table 2.1. General Indicators, Vietnam and China, 1990–2010

|  | Vietnam |  |  | China |  |  |
|---|---|---|---|---|---|---|
|  | 1990 | Latest | (Year) | 1990 | Latest | (Year) |
| GDP (US$ million) | 6,472 | 103,571 | (2010) | 354,644.36 | 5,878,629 | (2010) |
| GDP per capita (US$) | 98.04 | 1,172 | (2010) | 310.19 | 4,392 | (2010) |
| Foreign Direct Investment, net flow (US$ million) | 180 | 7,600 | (2009) | 3,478 | 78,192 | (2009) |
| GDP Growth (annual %) | 5 | 6.8 | (2010) | 4 | 10.3 | (2010) |
| Percent of Agriculture in GDP | 38.7 | 20.9 | (2009) | 26.9 | 10.3 | (2009) |
| Percent of Industry in GDP | 22.7 | 40.2 | (2009) | 41.3 | 46.3 | (2009) |
| Percent of Service in GDP | 38.6 | 38.8 | (2009) | 31.8 | 43.4 | (2009) |
| Human Development Index | 0.61 | 0.572 | (2010) | 0.627 | 0.663 | (2010) |
| Mid-Year Population (million) | 66.02 | 89.028 | (2010) | 1,143.33 | 1,354.14 | (2010) |

*Source:* UNDP and World Bank data and statistics.

Malesky and colleagues attribute divergent patterns of inequality in Vietnam and China to differences in the structure of elite coalitions at the national level. They contend that Vietnam's comparatively broader elite coalition, in which local constituencies can effectively impose constraints on the politburo and by extension national policies, promotes greater distribution across provinces and greater public services provision than in China. As evidence, they submit that between 2001 and 2006, equalizing fiscal transfers in Vietnam were 5.73 percent, relative to just 1.71 percent in China. Further, for the same period,[6] Vietnam outpaced China by spending an average of 9 percent of GDP on infrastructure, poverty alleviation, and national targeted programs, compared to China's 2 percent. Indeed, while Vietnam has embraced administrative decentralization, it has not embraced the kind of fiscal federalism that one observes in China. In Vietnam there is comparatively greater emphasis on funding norms that guarantee the provision of essential social services at local levels of governance. But the conclusions drawn from this rather brilliant analysis need to be treated with caution, as they tell us little about the character of welfare regimes at their micro-foundations. One may also reasonably inquire as to whether China's gigantic stimulus spending in 2009 and 2010 has altered the situation and accords with the authors' findings. These concerns become clearer through a concise explication of the features of welfare regimes in each country.

## Vietnam

Vietnam has experienced extraordinary changes over the last two decades, rising from among the world's "least-developed" countries in the early 1990s to being on the cusp of "middle-income country" status today. Its rapid economic growth

**Table 2.2.** Health Indicators, 1990–2010

|  | Vietnam | | | China | | |
|---|---|---|---|---|---|---|
|  | 1990 | Latest | (Year) | 1990 | Latest | (Year) |
| Life Expectancy at Birth (years), Female | 67 | 76.6 | (2009) | 70 | 75.1 | (2009) |
| Life Expectancy at Birth (years), Male | 63 | 72.7 | (2009) | 67 | 71.6 | (2009) |
| Crude Birth Rate (per 1,000 people) | 31 | 16.9 | (2009) | 21 | 12 | (2009) |
| Crude Death Rate (per 1,000 people) | 7 | 5.4 | (2009) | 7 | 7.3 | (2009) |
| Infant Mortality Rate (per 1,000 live births) | 38 | 19.5 | (2009) | 38 | 16.6 | (2009) |
| Total Fertility Rate (births per woman) | 3.7 | 2 | (2009) | 2.2 | 1.8 | (2009) |
| Maternal Mortality Ratio (per 100,000 live births) | 160 | 56 | (2008) | 95 | 38 | (2008) |
| Proportion of Births Attended by Skilled Health Personnel (%) | 95 | 87.7 | (2006) | 50[a] | 97.8 | (2006) |
| Prevalence of Underweight (% of children under age 5) | 41[b] | 20.2 | (2008) | 19 | 4.5 | (2005) |
| Under-Five Mortality Rate (per 1,000 live births) | 53 | 23.6 | (2009) | 49 | 19.1 | (2009) |
| Proportion of 1-Year-Old Children Immunized Against Measles (%) | 88 | 97 | (2009) | 98 | 94 | (2009) |
| Daily per Capita Protein Supply (Grams) | 50 | 65 | (2003) | 65 | 82 | (2003) |
| Daily per Capita Calorie Supply (Calories) | 2,148.8 | 2,616.70 | (2003) | 2,709.0 | 2,940.20 | (2003) |
| Population with Access to Improved Water Sources (%), Rural | 59 | 92 | (2008) | 59 | 82 | (2008) |
| Population with Access to Improved Water Sources (%), Urban | 90 | 99 | (2008) | 99 | 98 | (2008) |
| Population with Access to Improved Sanitation (%), Rural | 30 | 67 | (2008) | 7 | 52 | (2008) |
| Population with Access to Improved Sanitation (%), Urban | 58 | 94 | (2008) | 64 | 58 | (2008) |
| Government Expenditure for Health (% of GDP) | .8 | 1.5 | (2009) | 2 | 1.92 | (2009) |
| Health Expenditure, Public (% of total health expenditure) |  | 38.7 | (2009) |  | 50.1 | (2009) |

*Notes:* ADB Key Indicators and World Bank data and statistics.
*Source:* a refers to 1988; b refers to 1993.

## 34 CHINESE SOCIAL POLICY IN A TIME OF TRANSITION

Table 2.3. Education Indicators, 1990–2010

|  | Vietnam ||| China |||
| --- | --- | --- | --- | --- | --- | --- |
|  | 1990 | Latest | (Year) | 1990 | Latest | (Year) |
| Gross Primary School Enrollment Ratio (%), Female | 103 | 103 | (2009)[a] | 120 | 115 | (2009) |
| Gross Primary School Enrollment Ratio (%), Male | 111 | 109 | (2009)[a] | 130 | 111 | (2009) |
| Gross Secondary School Enrollment Ratio (%), Female | 31 | 89 | (2009)[a] | 42 | 81 | (2009) |
| Gross Secondary School Enrollment Ratio (%), Male | 33 | 85 | (2009)[a] | 55 | 76 | (2009) |
| Gross Tertiary Enrollment Ratio (%), Female | 1 | 13 | (2005) | 2 | 25 | (2009) |
| Gross Tertiary Enrollment Ratio (%), Male | 2 | 19 | (2005) | 4 | 24 | (2009) |
| Net Enrollment Ratio in Primary Education (%) | 90 | 88 | (2005) | 97 | 99 | (2003) |
| Ratio of Girls to Boys in Education of Primary Level | 0.93 | 0.89 | (2009)[b] | 0.93 | 103.9 | (2009) |
| Ratio of Girls to Boys in Education of Secondary Level | 0.91 | 0.99 | (2009)[b] | 0.75 | 106.6 | (2009) |
| Ratio of Girls to Boys in Education of Tertiary Level | .. | 0.76 | (2002) | 0.52 | 106.8 | (2009) |
| Literacy Rate, 15 Years and Over (%), Female | 87 | 90.5 | (2009) | 69 | 90.9 | (2009) |
| Literacy Rate, 15 Years and Over (%), Male | 94 | 95.2 | (2009) | 87 | 96.9 | (2009) |
| Proportion of Pupils Starting Grade 1 Who Reach Grade 5 (%) | 80 | 99.4 | (2010)[c] | 86 | 99 | (2002) |
| Government Expenditure for Education (% of GDP) | 1. | 5.3 | (2008) | 4 | 3.5 | (2006) |

Notes:
a. Calculated based on the MOET statistics and population census 2009
b. Ministry of Education (Vietnam) statistics
c. Multiple Indicator Cluster Survey, Socialist Republic of Vietnam, ICS, 2011
Source: ADB Key Indicators and World Bank data and statistics.

and declining poverty indicators have attracted worldwide attention, having experienced momentous changes across the entire range of its social institutions, including its welfare regime. Using an internationally defined poverty line, Vietnam's poverty head count declined from nearly 60 percent in the early 1990s to 16 percent in 2006 (World Bank 2008).

These changes began when the Vietnamese government adopted a series of welfare institutions that shifted responsibility onto households in the early 1990s, in a move from the principles of socialist "universalism" to a hybrid system in which the state provides a floor of basic services and a system of safety nets for certain population segments. Today, the government seeks to combine public, household, and other sources of finance in a way that ensures all Vietnamese access to essential social services. Viewed politically, the CPV appears intent on promoting the development of a welfare regime that combines market and redistributive elements.

Rapid economic growth over the last two decades has enabled increases in both state and household expenditures on essential social services, but institutional responsibility for the payment of these services has been shifted onto households, placing a greater proportional burden on poorer households. This shift started in the early 1990s when the country faced massive state retrenchment, as evidenced by education and health policies. By the mid-1990s, up to 80 percent of total (i.e., public and private) health expenditures and half of education expenditures were out-of-pocket—a remarkable inversion of the principles that had governed the provision and payment for health services under state-socialism (London 2009, 2010). Still, the economic growth that followed has enabled steady expenditure increases amidst the shifting shares. Education spending increased continuously, whereas health spending has remained low. Still, access to education and health has improved, as measured by enrollments and utilization of public services, respectively. However, there are large gaps in the quality of services between regions, and accessing services with quality above basic levels has become highly contingent on out-of-pocket payments. Moreover, in the context of rapid and (in respects) hasty decentralization, transfers of funds to localities often result in largess and waste, or go into projects that effectively commercialize nominally public services, or both.

The Vietnamese government is presently expanding a range of safety nets and insurance schemes, and the fate of these programs will indeed be of great importance. Currently reaching millions of Vietnamese, they merely soften rather than absorb the blow of large medical and educational costs. Their absolute size is not large. Total expenditure for national target programs increased by six- to sevenfold between 2002 and 2006, but only roughly 2 percent of recurrent spending was allocated to national target programs in the 2008 state budget (MOF 2009). While the idea of highly commodified education and health systems may not conform to CPV rhetoric, it is nonetheless a real institutionalized feature of social life in contemporary Vietnam (London 2006, 2003).

In the wake of state-socialism, the most important developments in the education sector were (1) the large increases in the volume of economic resources committed to education; (2) the shifts in the core principles and institutions governing the provision and payment for education toward the aforementioned hybrid system, which has increasingly subordinated education to market principles; and (3) the increasing scale of education, as indicated by significant increases in enrollment and by numbers of schools and other educational outlets. These trends, albeit being discernible across all levels of formal education and regions of the country, have nonetheless manifested differently across these levels and regions. Vietnam has steeply increased the volume of economic resources for private and public educational purposes from 1 percent since the early 1990s to 3.5 percent of an increasingly large GDP in 2005 (MOF 2006; GSO 2010). These increases have been fueled by rapid economic growth, which has been sustained at around 7 to 8 percent per annum.[7]

Here, a closer examination of increases in public and private expenditures helps us to appreciate the significance of growth. Following slow growth in the early 1990s, public spending on education has grown significantly in both absolute terms and as a proportion of Vietnam's GDP. Today, education represents nearly 20 percent of the state budget expenditure, compared to 10.9 percent in 2005, and is expected to remain at or above this level for the foreseeable future (Ministry of Planning and Investment 2006). A large proportion of public spending goes to teachers' wages, but the government has also sought to expand the geographical coverage of the educational system. The explosion of "private" (i.e., household) education spending also ranks among one of the most notable developments in Vietnam's education system. Up until the late 1980s, all education in Vietnam was (in principle) state-financed, whereas household expenditure accounts for at least half of total education spending today by most estimates. This increase is made possible partly by economic growth and increasing household incomes, where per capita GDP has increased from less than US$200 in the early 1990s to US$1,064 by 2009 (GSO 2010).

This increased spending by households is also the product of specific education policies. Since 1989, the education system has moved from one wholly financed by the state budget to a hybrid system combining state and household responsibility. By law, primary education is available at no direct charge to all children. In reality, virtually all aspects of education have become increasingly subject to market principles. Even though the state continues to play a major role in education finance, its policies signaling intent to expand rather than reduce its role in some fields notwithstanding, it has actively sought to shift financial responsibility onto households. This policy thrust was viewed as a sheer necessity in the early 1990s, given the acute fiscal crisis then. The state began promoting household spending under the guise of "socialization," defined by Party members as a process whereby "all of society assumes responsibility" for education. The analysis of education finance in Vietnam defies the conventional categorizations of "public" and "private," where the boundaries are rendered murky. Often, private payment for education takes place within nominally public educational institutions, while "public" schoolteachers frequently derive large proportions of their income from providing education privately outside school hours, and with tacit approval from state authorities. Table 2.4 indicates household education expenditure from 2002 to 2010.

In contrast, public spending on health has remained low (in international terms) but the government has maintained a commitment to providing preventive

Table 2.4. Average Expenses on Education per Capita in the Past 12 months (Unit: VND 1,000)

|  | 2002 | 2004 | 2006 | 2008 | 2010 |
| --- | --- | --- | --- | --- | --- |
| Poorest | 236.2 | 305.6 | 275.9 | 696 | 1019 |
| Near Poor | 345.2 | 502.7 | 563.1 | 1194 | 1735 |
| Middle | 467.0 | 652.0 | 1051 | 1586 | 2383 |
| Near Rich | 740.9 | 1024.9 | 1585 | 2176 | 3521 |
| Rich | 1418.5 | 1752.5 | 2443 | 3787 | 6722 |

Source: GSO (2010).

health service. This bears contrast with China, which, despite higher spending on health since 1990, lacks comparable investments in preventive medicine. The collapse of Vietnamese state-socialist institutions in the late 1980s placed the financial viability of the state-run health sector in question. However, the government—first with foreign donor support and later on its own—has effectively preserved and strengthened the state-run health network. State health providers remain the most important providers of health services.

Improvements in the country's health status since 1989 may be linked not only to general improvements in living standards and infrastructure, as well as a corresponding decline in the burden of infectious diseases, but also to the state's maintenance of a basic floor of health services, primarily through the continued public and donor-supported finance of commune health stations (CHS) and public hospitals. The CHSs were always a core element in Vietnam's national health system. However, they faced acute shortages, owing principally to an absence of local sources of financial support during the early 1990s. In 1994, Vietnam's prime minister issued Decision 58, permitting use of the central budget to pay or supplement salaries for three to five CHS staff in each commune through province budgets. Although most of this supplemental funding came from foreign donors, Decision 58 is credited with improving the income and morale of CHS workers and perhaps even rescuing the primary health system of the country. No such policy support was given to primary care providers in China (Huong et al. 2006).[8]

Besides stabilizing salaries, the state has had some degree of success in increasing the numbers and coverage of the CHS. In 1993, 800 communes in Vietnam lacked a CHS, while 88 lacked both a CHS and a health worker. By 2002, 93 percent of communes had a trained midwife, and 90 percent of hamlets (under the commune level) had at least one active health worker. Two years on, 98 percent (or all but 149) of communes had a CHS and at least one health worker, while 67.8 percent of communes had a doctor (Ministry of Health 2005). The central government further reasserted its role by specifying funding norms. In 2002, Circular 2002 required all CHSs to maintain a basic operational budget of at least 10 million VND per year, not including wages or funds for health for the poor.

It also established a range of compulsory funding norms for the CHS, holding the local People's Committee accountable for shortfalls (Huong et. al. 2006). By 2006, Vietnam counted some 10,672 state-run clinics at commune and precinct levels. This figure increased to 11,699 four years later, suggesting that it was a growth sector (GSO 2007, 559).

Still, these achievements in education and health should not be exaggerated. In fact, Vietnam already displays a tiered system of social services, particularly in health services. As corroborated by recent data, the expenditure of the wealthiest 20 percent of households on electricity and water are 11.7 times higher than that of the poorest households, while spending 3.1, 5.9, and 12.3 times more on health care, education, and leisure, respectively, than poorer households (General Statistics Office [GSO] 2007, 2010). In 2006, over a third of Vietnam's children remained malnourished; 2009 data indicate that nearly 20 percent of children are underweight, while 32 percent experience stunting (National Institute of Nutrition 2009). The current trend toward decentralization of "public" services will generate powerful incentives toward further commodification of services. It is unclear whether presumptive declines in the dependence of rich localities on the central budget will translate to increased expenditures in poorer ones. The increasing private provision of education, health, and other social services lacks adequate regulatory mechanisms, as is the case with public service provision.

## China

It is fair to state that the provision and payment for basic education and (especially) health care in the wake of state-socialism do not rank among China's greatest "success stories." However, equally notable is that public spending on both sectors has risen very rapidly in recent years and may undermine the assertions raised by Malesky and colleagues above. The account developed for this chapter draws on previous analyses by the Asian Development Bank (ADB; 2007), Min Xin Pei (2006), and recent World Bank data. These and other studies indicate that China was ranked 114th in public education spending globally in 1990, spending below 2 percent of GDP into the late 1990s, as compared to the average of 3.4 percent for low-income countries (ADB, various years) such as India, Mexico, Brazil, and the Philippines.

Chronic underinvestment in both policies and programs to get children to school were compounded by the tendency of local and central government units to shirk centrally mandated responsibilities, to invest in physical infrastructure and higher education, and to contribute to the commercialization of health services provision. In 1998, following two decades of economic reform, only 85 percent of the school-aged population had access to primary and middle school, the figure being a mere 40 percent in the poor western regions. The late 1990s saw a middle-school dropout rate of 42 percent, ranging from 30 to 50 percent in some parts of the south. Furthermore, the issue of school fees has been a glaring problem, and efforts to rein fees have been ongoing for at least a decade. Even though the central government has mandated schools to charge a single all-inclusive fee, it is too early to gauge the effectiveness of this intervention (Yang 2005).

The distribution of education expenditure, where localities are largely responsible for spending on compulsory education, could imply that local units of government finance education adequately. Specifically, townships account for 78 percent, counties for 9 percent, and provinces for 11 percent (Su 2002, cited in Pei 2006, 171); whereas 94 percent of all central government education spending went to higher education, and only 0.5 percent on primary and secondary education (Wang 2002). Yet, a closer examination of poorer and remote areas at the outset of the last decade revealed that government units there typically allocated less than what was mandated by the central government (Rong and Shi 2001). Even though the State Council committed itself to "further strengthening" education in rural areas in 2003, problems in poorer regions have lingered. Continued deficiencies of food and clothing, coupled with parents' desires to keep children at home for farm work, and informal payments have hampered the success of getting these children to school (Shen and Kang 2003). Alternatively, campaigns by local authorities to universalize compulsory education landed some localities in severe debt. At a national level, spending on education has increased, and the government continues to strive for 4 percent of its GDP as a target. Nonetheless, the commoditization of education that took place during the 1980s and 1990s will be difficult to reverse in the near term.

Perhaps, too, the defining feature of the development of the Chinese health system is its failure to deliver health services to the poor, especially in rural areas, and is possibly attributed to the fact that spending is heavily tilted toward urban areas. At 3.5 percent of GDP, overall public spending on health is inadequate, even if this figure is considerably higher than Vietnam's. Between 1978 and 1991, state spending on rural health services declined from 21.5 to 10.5 percent. There was also a concomitant increase in the cost of health care from 2 to 3 percent of total income in 1990 to about 11 percent in 1998, and this has continued to rise (Liu et al. 2000, cited in Saich 2004). Arguably, covering all curative (ambulatory/hospital) services lies beyond the state's ability, but failures in the areas of preventive health are costly. Health expenses have emerged as a major cause of poverty. The ratio of cost per inpatient admission to monthly income per capita was 23 and 42 percent for the second-lowest and lowest income quintile of the population, respectively, in 2003 in rural areas. It is suggestive that a survey of rural areas found that use of outpatient services among those reporting illness declined from 67 to 55 percent (Huong et al. 2006) in the 10-year period following 1993. Noteworthy here is Tony Saich's (2004) argument that the dramatic rise in health care disparity between urban and rural areas is among the new inequalities that have arisen from financial decentralization, among other reforms. This is reinforced by a 1998 World Bank study, which found that 22 percent of people in localities in high-income areas were covered by a cooperative medical facility, compared to just 1 to 3 percent in poorer areas (Zhu et al. 2001).

However, China's health system is presently undergoing important changes. In recent years the public share of total expenditure on health has risen sharply, from 40.7 percent in 2006 to 50.1 percent by 2009 (World Bank 2011). In his outstanding analysis of recent developments in China's health system, Wang (2010) identifies a marked turn in health policy, with the state contributing greater resources and corresponding increases in the number and accessibility of public health facilities, after more than a decade of malign neglect. Wang states that in February 2008, the state took aggressive steps to expand, making full coverage of officially registered urban dwellers within reach. No doubt, China's health system remains beset with inadequacies, including but not limited to paltry or even absent arrangements for migrant workers. The quality and accessibility of services in poor and remote rural areas remain abysmally poor in comparison with that in cities. Nonetheless, with 3 trillion dollars in foreign exchange, China has the financial means and perhaps now even the political will to deliver a comprehensive health system in a way that could not be envisaged in the Vietnamese case. Sharp increases in total central transfers are indicative of this reality (Table 2.5). No doubt, China's increasingly inverted demographic pyramid, coupled with political tensions arising from the government's past neglect and commercialization of the health system, has given health policy an acute urgency. Also widely noted is the increasing demand for quality education.

Table 2.5. Central Transfers in China

|      | Central Transfers* | GDP*       | Transfer/GDP |
|------|--------------------|------------|--------------|
| 1996 | 2,178.02           | 71,176.59  | 3.06         |
| 1997 | 2,856.67           | 78,973.03  | 3.62         |
| 1998 | 3,321.54           | 84,402.28  | 3.94         |
| 1999 | 4,086.61           | 89,677.05  | 4.56         |
| 2000 | 4,665.31           | 99,214.55  | 4.70         |
| 2001 | 6,001.95           | 109,655.17 | 5.47         |
| 2002 | 7,351.77           | 120,332.69 | 6.11         |
| 2003 | 8,261.41           | 135,822.76 | 6.08         |
| 2004 | 10,407.96          | 159,878.34 | 6.51         |
| 2005 | 11,484.02          | 184,937.37 | 6.21         |
| 2006 | 13,501.45          | 216,314.43 | 6.24         |
| 2007 | 18,137.89          | 265,810.31 | 6.82         |
| 2008 | 22,990.76          | 314,045.43 | 7.32         |
| 2009 | 32,602.59          | 340,506.87 | 9.57         |

Notes: * In 100 millions of yuan
Source: China fiscal yearbook (zhongguo caizheng nianjian) 1997–2010.

## CONCLUSIONS

Vietnam and China are not merely poorer cousins of the so-called "productivist" regimes of East Asia. The principles, institutions, and bureaucratic politics governing the creation and allocation of welfare in Vietnam and China are, in my view, distinctive from those of other countries. This owes in part to the existence of a political culture in which universalist values, however disregarded, remain a fixture of the political discourse, bringing real pressures on those in power.

Both Vietnamese and Chinese social policies and welfare may be subordinate to developmentalist economic policies in a manner similar to the East Asian productivist regimes (Holiday 2000), yet both draw on repertoires of political discourse fundamentally different from the other countries. The ruling parties in Vietnam and China profess a commitment to universalism and, more important, have polities steeped in market-Leninism. The coincidence of commodified essential services and polarizing class structures is generating social tensions and political pressures that challenge the legitimacy and capacities of ruling elites. Yet, however corrupted socialism in China and Vietnam may be, ruling elites retain a belief (if self-serving at times) that universalism is an ethic unto itself, and this cannot be said for other regimes in East Asia or, for that matter, North America and Europe. As the wealth of Vietnam and China increases, so too will the capacity of their governments to devote resources to the promotion of education and health, and so too will the capacity of organized citizens to bargain in their own interests. Vietnam and China are more Leninist than socialist, but neither are these countries ruled by a capitalist class or a state oriented mainly toward capitalist interests per se.

Alongside shared market-Leninist attributes, Vietnam and China also display distinctive differences that lie beyond their social histories and the circumstances of extrication from state-socialism, but rather in the trajectories of social change since. Differences in the countries' bureaucratic politics, class configurations, and social policies have generated different welfare regimes and patterns of stratification. It is arguable that although China is much wealthier, Vietnam's Communist Party has displayed greater determination in maintaining redistributive allocations of capital and in advancing universalist principles of social citizenship. Despite spending less on health and education, Vietnam has been more committed to ensuring access to preventive health services and basic education. China's greater wealth notwithstanding, its faster growth and continental size means that one must pay heed to caution when making comparisons, even if the shared features of both political economies warrant it. Further, that Vietnam has outperformed China on many significant health and education indicators—at least until recently—reinforces the fact that we are dealing with similar but distinctive countries.

Nor should the progressiveness of Vietnamese or Chinese market-Leninism be overstated. States in both countries combine Leninist tactics of political organization with market-based strategies of accumulation and social policies that exhibit both redistributive and neoliberal elements. Unequal forms of citizenship imposed under state-socialism are reproduced and transformed in a manner that preserves the political supremacy of the Communist Party, while creating new market-based opportunities and inequalities. Terms such as "market socialism" or "capitalism with Chinese/Vietnamese characteristics" are inadequate as descriptors of the welfare regimes in these countries. In contrast, the term "market-Leninism" rejects the widely held but false notion that planned or market economies have any inherent political character. The market-Leninist welfare regimes in Vietnam and China demonstrate that as a class-based determinant of distributive outcomes, Leninist political organization is ultimately much more important than socialism per se, at least for now.

## NOTES

1 From the beginning, theoretical literature on the so-called "transitional countries" tended to reflect the biases, normative commitments, and ignorance of its authors, who were typically scholars or technocrats with little direct experience with state-socialism. For example, the IMF and its academic sympathizers dispensed advice that the best path forward for economic reforms was a shock therapy approach. This approach, which proved disastrous in many respects, was based on rigid neoclassical assumptions as well as political calculations. The operative assumption, that a gradual approach to reform would galvanize opposition and prevent reforms of any depth, was reasonable in some respects. But the treatment—radical retrenchment of the state—produced a vacuum of economic governance. Over the course of the 1990s, the size of Russia's economy declined by half, while gangster-capitalism under the aegis of the old *nomenklatura* ruled the day.
2 Through revenue from trade.
3 Hence the absurdity of the common and mistaken claim that social welfare services under state-socialism were "free."
4 At least in China, and perhaps beyond.
5 The continuing poor performance of Vietnam's economy was compounded by the country's political and economic isolation under the U.S.-Sino embargo.
6 Equalizing transfers augment budget transfers to poorer provinces at the expense of richer ones.
7 Official poverty rates have declined, from 58 percent in 1993 to less than 11 percent (under a higher poverty ceiling) in 2006. Poverty declines in Vietnam are even steeper than in China (Ministry of Planning and Investment 2006).
8 Formerly, localities were responsible for paying local health workers' wages at the commune level. Decision 58/QĐ-TTg of 3/2/1994.

## REFERENCES

Asian Development Bank (ADB), *Key Indicators* 38. (Manila, Philippines: Asian Development Bank, 2007), 4–15.

Barrientos, Armando. 2004. Latin America: Towards a liberal and informal welfare regime. In *Insecurity and welfare regimes in Asia, Africa and Latin America: Social policy in development contexts*, eds. I. Gough et al., 121–168. Cambridge: Cambridge University Press.

Beresford, Melanie. 1990. Vietnam: Socialist agriculture in transition. *Journal of Contemporary Asia* 20(4): 466–486.

Beresford, Melanie. 1997. Vietnam: The transition from plan to market. In *Introduction to the political economy of Southeast Asia*, eds. R. Robison and G. Rodan, 179–204. Melbourne: Oxford University Press.

Bevan, Phlippa. 2004. The dynamics of African insecurity regimes. In *Insecurity and welfare regimes in Asia, Africa and Latin America: Social policy in development contexts*, eds. I. Gough et al., 202–253. Cambridge: Cambridge University Press.

Bian, Yangjie. 1994. *Work and inequality in urban China*. Albany: State University of New York Press.

Bryant, John. 1998. Communism, poverty, and demographic change in North Vietnam. *Population and Development Review* 24(2): 235–269.

Cheng, Xiaonong. 1995. Weichi Wending Yu Shenhua Giage: Zhongguo Mienling de Jueze (Transition vs. stability: China's dilemma). *Dangdai Zhongguo Yanjiu* (Modern China Studies) *1–2*: 84–106 (in Chinese).

Cook, Sarah, and Kwon Huck-Ju. 2007. Social protection in East Asia. *Global Social Policy* 7(2): 223–229.

Davis, Peter. 2004. Rethinking the welfare regime approach in the context of Bangladesh. In *Insecurity and welfare regimes in Asia, Africa and Latin America: Social policy in development contexts*, eds. I. Gough et al., 255–286. Cambridge: Cambridge University Press.

Deacon, Bob. 2000. Eastern European welfare states: The impact of the politics of globalization. *Journal of European Social Policy* 10(2): 146–161.

Deacon, Bob. 2001. *The social dimension of regionalism: A constructive alternative to neo-liberal globalization*. GASPP Occasional Paper No. 8.

Deacon, Bob. 2002. Globalization and the challenge for social security. In *Social security in the global village*, eds. R. Sigg and C. Behrendt. International Social Security Series No. 8. 17–30. New Brunswick, NJ: Transaction Publishers.

Dixon, John E. 1981. *The Chinese welfare system, 1949–1979*. New York: Praeger Publishers.

Esping-Andersen, Gøsta. 1987. The comparison of policy regimes: An introduction. In *Stagnation and renewal in social policy: The rise and fall of policy regimes*, eds. Martin Rein, Gøsta Esping-Andersen, and Lee Rianwater, 3–12. Armonk, NY: M. E. Sharpe.

Esping-Andersen, Gøsta. 1990. *Three worlds of welfare capitalism*. Princeton, NJ: Princeton University Press.

Esping-Andersen, Gøsta. 1999. *Social foundations of postindustrial economies*. Oxford: Oxford University Press.

Evans, Peter B., Dietrich Rueschemeyer, and Theda Skocpol. 1985. *Bringing the state back in*. Cambridge: Cambridge University Press.

Eyal, Gil, Ivan Szelenyi, and Eleanor Townsley. 1998. *Making capitalism without capitalists: Class formation and elite struggles in post-communist central Europe*. London: Verso.

Fforde, Adam, and Doug Porter. 1995. Public goods, the state, civil society and development assistance in Vietnam: Opportunities and prospects. Paper prepared for the Vietnam Update conference, Canberra, Australian National University.

Fforde, Adam, and Stefan de Vylder. 1996. *From plan to market: The economic transition in Vietnam*. Boulder, CO: Westview.

General Statistics Office (GSO). 2007. *Ket Qua Tom Tat Khao Sat Muc Song Ho Gia Dinh 2006* (Summary of the 2006 Household Living Standards Survey, GSO, Socialist Republic of Vietnam).

General Statistics Office (GSO). 2010. Household Living Standards Survey, Socialist Republic of Vietnam.

Goodman, R., G. White, and H.-J. Kwon. 1998. *The East Asia welfare model: Welfare Orientalism and the state*. London: Routledge.

Gough, Ian. 2001. Globalization and regional welfare regimes: The East Asian case. *Global Social Policy* 1(2): 163–189.

Gough, Ian. 2004. Welfare regimes in development contexts: A global and regional analysis. In *Insecurity and welfare regimes in Asia, Africa and Latin America: Social policy in development contexts*, eds. I. Gough et al., 15–48. Cambridge: Cambridge University Press.

Gough, Ian, and Geoff Wood. 2004. Introduction. In *Insecurity and welfare regimes in Asia, Africa and Latin America: Social policy in development contexts*, eds. I. Gough et al., 1–11. Cambridge: Cambridge University Press.

Haney, Lynne Allison. 2002. *Inventing the needy: Gender and the politics of welfare in Hungary*. Berkeley and Los Angeles: University of California Press.

Hinton, William. 1990. *The great reversal: The privatization of China, 1978–1989*. New York: Monthly Review Press.

Holliday, Ian. 2000. Productivist welfare capitalism. *Political Studies* 48: 706–723.

Howard, Pat. 1991. Rice bowls and job security: Urban contract labour system. *The Australian Journal of Chinese Affairs* 25: 93–137.

Huong, Dang Boi, Sarah Bales, et al. 2006. *Ensuring health care for the rural poor in Vietnam and China: A state or market approach?* Hanoi: Medical Publishing House.

Hussain, Athar. 1994. Social security in present-day China and its reform. *The American Economic Review* 84(2): 276–280.

Kasza, Gregory J. 2006. *One world of welfare: Japan in comparative perspective.* Ithaca, NY: Cornell University Press.

Kaufman, Joan, and Gita Sen. 1993. Population, health and gender in Vietnam: Social policies under the economic reforms. In *The challenge of reform in Indochina*, ed. Bjorge Lunggren, 259–292. Cambridge, MA: Harvard University Press.

Kerkvliet, Benedict J. T. 1995. Rural society and state relations. In *Vietnam's rural transformation*, eds. Benedict J. T. Kerkvliet and Douglas Porter. 65–96. Boulder, CO: Westview.

Kerkvliet, Benedict J. T. 2000. *Political shortcomings in North Vietnam's agricultural collectives, 1960s–1980s.* Canberra: Research School of Pacific and Asian Studies, Australian National University.

Kerkvliet, Benedict J. T. 2003. Authorities and the people: An analysis of state-society relations in Vietnam. In *Postwar Vietnam: Dynamics of a transforming society*, ed. Hy Van Luong. 27–54. Singapore: Rowman and Littlefield.

King, Lawrence P. 2001a. Making markets: A comparative study of postcommunist managerial strategies in Central Europe. *Theory and Society* 30(4): 494–538.

King, Lawrence P. 2001b. *The basic features of post-communist capitalism: Firms in Hungary, the Czech Republic and Slovakia.* Westport, CT: Praeger Press.

King, Lawrence. 2002. Postcommunist divergence: The transition to capitalism in Poland and Russia. Paper presented at the American Sociological Association Annual Meeting, August, Chicago.

Kornai, Janos. 1980. Hard and "soft" budget constraint. *Acta Oeconomica* 2(3–4): 231–245.

Kornai, Janos. 1997. Editorial: Reforming the welfare state in postsocialist societies. *World Development* 25(8): 1183–1186.

Kornai, Janos. 2000. What the change of system from socialism to capitalism does and does not mean. *Journal of Economic Perspectives* 14(1): 27–42.

Kwan, Yui-Huen Alex. 2012. Personal communication. February 2012.

Kwon, Huck-Ju. 1998. Democracy and the politics of social welfare: A comparative analysis of welfare system in East Asia. In *The East Asian welfare model: Welfare Orientalism and the state*, eds. Roger Goodman, G. White, and H.-J. Kwon, 27–74. London: Routledge.

Lin, Justin Yifu, Fang Cai, and Zhou Li. 1994. *China's economic reforms: Pointers for other economies in transition?* Policy Research Working Paper Series 1310, World Bank.

London, Jonathan D. 2003. Vietnam's mass education and health systems: A regimes perspective. *American Asian Review* 21(2): 125–170.

London, Jonathan D. 2006. Vietnam: Education in a "socialist periphery." *Asia Pacific Journal of Education* 26(1): 1–20.

London, Jonathan D. 2009. Vietnam and the making of market-Leninism. *Pacific Review* 22(3): 373–397.

London, Jonathan D. 2011. Market-Leninism. Working paper, Southeast Asia Research Centre, City University of Hong Kong. <http://www6.cityu.edu.hk/searc/Data/FileUpload/330/WP124_12_JLondon.pdf>.

London, Jonathan D. (Forthcoming). Welfare regimes in China and Vietnam. *Journal of Contemporary Asia.* Scheduled for publication in late 2013.

Malesky, Edmund, Regina Abrami, and Yu Zheng. 2011. Institutions and inequality in single-party regimes: A comparative analysis of Vietnam and China. *Comparative Politics* 43(4): 409–427.

Ministry of Education and Training (MOET). 2000. Bao Cao: Chueyn De Giao Duc. Unpublished report, Ha Noi.

Ministry of Health. 2005. Cac giai phap tai chinh y te cho nguoi ngheo [Health financing measures for the poor]. Unpublished research report, Ha Noi.

Ministry of Planning and Investment. 2006. The five year socio-economic development plan. Ha Noi. March.

National Institute of Nutrition. 2009. *Nutrition in Vietnam.* Ha Noi: National Institute of Nutrition.

Nee, Victor. 1989. A theory of market transition: From redistribution to markets in state socialism. *American Sociological Review* 54: 663–681.

Oi, Jean C. 1985. Communism and clientelism: Rural politics in China. *World Politics* 37(2): 238–266.

Oi, Jean C. 1999. *Rural China takes off: Institutional foundations of economic reform.* Berkeley and Los Angeles: University of California Press.

Park, Yong Soo. 2008. Revisiting the welfare state system in the Republic of Korea. *International Social Security Review* 61(2): 3–19.

Pei, Min Xin. 2006. *China's trapped transition: The limits of developmental autocracy.* Cambridge, MA: Harvard University Press.

Polanyi, Karl. 1957. *The great transformation: The political and economic origins of our times.* Boston: Beacon Press.

Rong, Xue Lan, and Tianjian Shi. 2001. Inequality in Chinese education. *Journal of Contemporary China* 10(26): 107–124.

Shirk, Susan. 1993. *The political logic of economic reform in China.* Berkeley and Los Angeles: University of California Press.

Siach, Anthony. 2004. *Governance and politics of China,* 2nd ed. New York: Palgrave Macmillan.

Sotiropoulos, Dimitri A., Ileana Neamtu, and Maya Stoyanova. 2003. The trajectory of post-communist welfare state development: The cases of Bulgaria and Romania. *Social Policy & Administration* 37(6): 656–673.

Szeléenyi, Ivan. 1978. Social inequalities in state-socialist redistributive economies: Dilemmas for social policy in contemporary socialist societies of Eastern Europe. International *Journal of Comparative Sociology* 19 (1–2): 63–87.

Szelényi, Ivan. 2008a. A theory of transitions. *Modern China* 34(1): 165–175.

Szelényi, Ivan. 2008b. Varieties of post-communist capitalisms: Convergences and divergences. In *Perceptions and images of China,* eds. Heinz-Dieter Assmann,

Thomas M. H. Chan, and Karin Moser v. Filseck, 13–35. Baden-Baden: Nomos Verlag.

Szelényi, Ivan. 2010. Capitalism in China? Comparative perspectives. In *Chinese capitalisms: Historical emergence and political implications*, ed. Yin-wah Chu, 199–223. London: Palgrave Macmillan.

Szelényi, Ivan, and Robert Manchin. 1987. Social policy under state socialism. In *Stagnation and renewal in social policy: The rise and fall of policy regimes*, eds. Martin Rein, Gøsta Esping-Andersen and Lee Rianwater, 102–142. Armonk, NY: M. E. Sharpe.

Szelényi, Ivan, and Lawrence P. King. 2005. Postcommunist economic systems. In *Handbook of economic sociology*, 2nd ed., eds. Neil Smelser and Richard Swedberg, 206–232. Princeton, NJ: Princeton University Press.

Walder, Andrew G. 1986. *Communist neo-traditionalism: Work and authority in Chinese industry*. Berkeley and Los Angeles: University of California Press.

Walder, Andrew G. 1995. The quiet revolution from within: Economic reform as a source of political decline. In *The waning of the communist state: Economic origins of political decline in China and Hungary*, ed. Andrew G. Walder, 1–24. Berkeley and Los Angeles: University of California Press.

Walder, Andrew G., ed. 2003. Elite opportunity in transitional economies. *American Sociological Review* 68(6): 899–916.

Wang Shaoguang. 2010. China's double movement in health care. *Socialist Register 2010*, vol. 46: 249–270.

White, Christine P. 1986. Everyday resistance: Socialist revolution and rural development, The Vietnamese case. *Journal of Peasant Studies* 13(3): 49–63.

White, Gordon. 1998. Social security reforms in China: Towards an East Asian model? In *The East Asian welfare model*, eds. Roger Goodman, Gordon White, and Kwon Huck-Ju. 175–197. New York: Routledge.

Wood, Geoff, and Ian Gough. 2006. A comparative welfare regime approach to global social policy. *World Development* 34(10): 1696–1712.

World Bank. 2008. *Social Protection*. Vietnam Development Repoert 2008. Hanoi: ADB, DFID, EC, the German Development Cooperation, and World Bank.

Zhu, W., Q. Tian, et al. 2001. Research on equity of health service in rural areas of Henan Province. *Journal of Health Economic Research* 1: 27–29.

# 3

# SOCIAL BENEFITS AND INCOME INEQUALITY IN POST-SOCIALIST CHINA AND VIETNAM

Qin Gao, Martin Evans, and Irwin Garfinkel

## INTRODUCTION

China and Vietnam share a border and much socialist ideology. During the past quarter century, they have both adopted pro-market economic reforms, resulting in a combination of rapid economic growth and significant poverty reduction. With an average annual gross domestic product (GDP) growth rate of 9.7 percent since 1980, China "has had the largest and fastest poverty reduction in history" (World Bank 2008, 22). The World Bank estimates that the poverty rate in China fell from 64 percent in 1981 to 7 percent in 2007, using a "cost of basic needs" poverty line (World Bank 2008). Vietnam has also made remarkable progress since its economic reform was launched in 1986. Its annual GDP growth rate averaged 7.4 percent since 1988 and remained above 8 percent since 2005. The poverty rate in Vietnam fell from 53 percent in 1993 to 16 percent in 2006, using consistent "cost of basic needs" measures derived by the World Bank. As two of the world's most successful transition economies, China and Vietnam continue to emphasize economic growth over other developmental goals.

Despite many similarities, China and Vietnam have very different levels of economic and social development. People in China enjoy a much higher level of real standard of living than those in Vietnam. Using the 2005 Purchasing Power Parity (PPP) developed by the World Bank (World Bank 2008), per capita GDP in China was US$6,100 in 2008, compared to US$2,900 in Vietnam (U.S. Central Intelligence Agency [CIA] 2009). At the same time, income inequality is more prominent in China than in Vietnam. In 2004, the lowest income decile households in China accounted for only 1.6 percent of total income, while the top decile commanded 34.9 percent of total income. In contrast, these figures were 2.9 percent and 28.9 percent, respectively, in Vietnam (CIA 2009).

Another important difference between the two countries has been their commitment to and development of social benefits. While China's rapid economic growth has been accompanied by cutbacks in its urban social benefit system (Gao 2006, 2008, 2010), rising income inequality and emerging social problems call for broader and stronger social protection (Gao and Riskin 2009). Vietnam took core decisions on economic reform later than China and thus can learn from the social and political problems that China's rapid growth generated. Indeed, policymakers in Vietnam have explicitly aimed to link growth with equalizing policies to avoid some of the severe urban-rural disparities and other forms of inequality that have developed during China's economic expansion (Evans and Harkness 2008). In a conceptual analysis of the welfare regimes of China and Vietnam, London (2013, chapter 2 of this volume) concludes that social policies and welfare in both countries are subordinate to economic development policies, despite commitments from the governments of both countries to universalism.

To provide empirical evidence on social welfare developments in the two countries and to draw implications for ongoing policy changes, this chapter compares the size and structure of social benefits in China and Vietnam in the early 2000s using national household survey data. It also examines the impact of social benefits on income inequality during the study period and contrasts the urban and rural systems within and between the two countries. The analysis reported here provides a valuable snapshot of social welfare outcomes in the two countries following the critical 1990s period of policy reform (in Vietnam) and policy consolidation and maturation (in China) and before the onslaught of global economic and financial crisis in 2007.

The social benefit system refers to social welfare provisions to support or improve the well-being of individuals and families. In this chapter, we examine the social benefit package that families receive, including cash transfers and in-kind benefits. Cash transfers include pensions, work-related social insurance, unemployment insurance, and public assistance. In-kind benefits include health and education benefits. Housing and food, two other forms of important in-kind benefits, are not included in our empirical analyses due to the lack of comparable data between the two countries. The inclusion of the various benefits examined here enables us to provide a comprehensive examination and comparison of the social benefit systems in the two countries.

The analysis reported here finds that the size of China's social benefit system—as measured by the share of social benefit income in total household income—was more than twice that of Vietnam; in both countries, benefits were distributed in a regressive manner; and the Vietnamese system was less regressive than the Chinese system. Pensions and social welfare transfers were more prominent in Vietnam, while education benefits were more generous in China.

The urban-rural gap in social benefit provision was much wider in China than in Vietnam: Chinese urban residents enjoyed significantly more benefits than their rural peers, while Vietnamese urban residents had only a modest advantage over their rural peers. Based on these comparative analyses, implications for social policy developments in both countries are discussed.

## SOCIAL BENEFIT SYSTEMS IN CHINA AND VIETNAM: AN OVERVIEW

### The Chinese Social Benefit System

Because social benefit provision mechanisms are embedded in the fundamental structural distinctions between urban and rural China, they differ substantially across the two areas. The urban social benefit system has undergone significant cutbacks from the comprehensive coverage and generous provision that characterized it before the economic reforms, while the rural social benefit system has remained minimal (Gao 2006, 2008, 2010; Gao and Riskin 2009).

The urban social benefit system was an inherent part of the "full employment" policy in urban China before the economic reforms were launched in the late 1970s. Under the pre-reform regime, almost all working-age urban residents were employed in state-owned or collective enterprises and received various social benefits through their work units (Davis 1989; Guan 2000; Saunders and Shang 2001; Wong 1998). These social benefits have been much curtailed since the economic reforms, mainly to facilitate market restructuring and stimulate economic growth (Croll 1999; Gao 2006; Leung 2003).

The reforms of the urban social benefit system have focused on shifting the financing of social benefits from state-owned and collective enterprises to general taxes and individuals so that the enterprises can concentrate on increased production and efficiency. Housing, which was widely provided at low or no cost before the reforms, has been privatized. Food assistance, a major benefit to urban residents during the pre-reform period, has vanished. Pensions, health benefits, and other work-related social insurance (such as maternity, sickness, and industrial injury) have begun to require individual contributions and have shifted to a wider risk pooling scheme across enterprises. Meanwhile, however, the government has taken a larger and more direct role in providing a safety net for the very poor. Unemployment insurance and Minimum Livelihood Guarantee (MLG, or *dibao*), the major public assistance program, have been established and enforced since the early to mid-1990s to meet the basic needs of many who have been left behind by both the economic and welfare reforms (Gao 2006, 2010; Li and Piachaud 2004; Solinger 2002; Tang, Sha, and Ren 2003).

Rural social benefits have always been marginal in coverage and minimal in provision, before and since the economic reforms (Gao 2008, 2010; Gao and Riskin 2009; Guan 2000; Saunders and Shang 2001). Only about 1.5 percent of rural residents have had access to pensions due to their prior employment in state-owned or collective enterprises. Traditionally, there have been three safety-net programs in rural China. The "Five Guarantees" program has existed to provide for the rural elderly, disabled, and minors who had no family support or income sources to meet five basic needs: food, clothing, medical care, housing, and burial expenses. This system, however, has not served the target population in most rural areas sufficiently (Cook 2001; Davis 1989). Two other public assistance programs—the natural disaster relief system and the collective welfare fund—have also been in place, aiming to protect the vulnerable from natural disasters and human misfortunes (Guan 2000; Saunders and Shang 2001; Zhu 2002).

Building on expansions of the urban MLG and in an effort to address the inadequacy of the existing public assistance programs, the rural MLG was established nationwide in 2007 after a series of provincial experiments. The rural MLG aims to provide cash subsidies to poor families so that they can meet basic local living standards. The majority of the recipients have low incomes because of chronic illness, disability, old age, and/or an adverse natural living environment. The total number of rural MLG recipients more than doubled from 16.1 million in January 2007 to 38.8 million in October 2008 (Ministry of Civil Affairs [MCA] 2008).

Before the economic reforms, the Rural Cooperative Medical System (RCMS) provided basic health services and wide coverage to rural residents. It was financed by three sources: (1) premiums deducted from rural families' annual incomes, usually set at a small proportion of income, ranging from 0.5 to 5 percent; (2) a portion of the collective welfare fund contributed by collective agricultural production or rural enterprises; and sometimes (3) subsidies from higher level governments, which were mainly used to compensate health care workers and purchase medical equipment. However, this system collapsed after the economic reforms were launched, leaving many rural residents unable to afford the dramatically increasing health care expenses (Bloom and Fang 2003; Liu 2004; Rösner 2004). To address this gap, the government has gradually restored the RCMS since the mid-1990s, renaming it NRCMS (New Rural Cooperative Medical Scheme) and implementing it nationwide in 2008. The NRCMS is a heavily subsidized voluntary health insurance program for rural residents. The government—central and local—is responsible for about 80 percent of NRCMS expenditures. The central government provides subsidies to the less developed provinces in the western and central areas. In 2008, the government contributed 80 yuan for each participant, whereas individuals contributed 20 yuan. Although the coverage is 100 percent in principle, it is important to note that actual beneficiaries were only about 30 percent of all rural residents in 2007. The low take-up rate was due to the insufficiency of funds to cover all those in need, on the one hand, and the low efficiency in expense reimbursement, on the other (Gao 2010; Mao 2008).

## The Vietnamese Social Benefit System

Although a stated goal of the current Vietnamese government has been to achieve universality, the term "universal" bears a very different meaning from that used in current European discussions, in which the term denotes forms of benefits that are provided based on certain circumstances with no test of income. Universalism in Vietnam refers to a wide and sometimes confusing range of provisions. The role of contributory social security is central, but the coverage from such provisions is only about one-third of all working people, even with a rapidly expanding, urban-based, formally employed workforce. The liabilities carried over from the socialist era are huge. The cadres who were employed in government and state-owned enterprises have fully protected pension rights under the current contributory system based on their previous employment—for which there are no contributory records. This results in a large expenditure on pensions directly from the state budget. The cohorts of formally employed workers have contributory protection for maternity, sickness, industrial injury, and health insurance under a separate scheme. Access to contributory pensions through voluntary social insurance has expanded greatly since 2004 and represents one element of the "universal" approach (World Bank 2007).

The health insurance system to assist in access to health care has developed alongside the process of health finance reform that saw the introduction of user-charges, purchaser-provider finance models, and some privatization of hospital services, all of which was termed "socialization." The universal approach for health care first provides automatic free access to health care services for all children aged five and younger, those who qualify for war disablement and survivors benefits, and the very few who receive the basic social assistance safety net (World Bank 2007; Evans et al. 2007). Voluntary health insurance was introduced initially for all schoolchildren (although the mixture of commune-level charges and obligations makes it difficult to describe this system as "voluntary" in practice) and then was extended to the remainder of the population. Uptake of voluntary health insurance has been high but has suffered from adverse selection, with the elderly and those with high medical needs often most likely to join the program, with their contributions paid by younger and fitter family members. The combination of eroding socialist universal provision of primary health care and the selective uptake of health care by those with insurance coverage has led to a crisis in health insurance funds and health care finance.

Non-contributory transfers exist for two main groups. First, war veterans, the disabled, and survivors of those killed in the long wars of independence receive a mix of cash transfers and benefits in kind (such as housing support and health care). Members of this group are largely older persons and form a cohort who will die off over the next decade or more. However, there is also a younger cohort, the members of which have suffered from congenital handicaps as a result of dioxin (Agent Orange) exposure associated with U.S. munitions and stores from the 1970s. The second group receives a small range of categorical, means-tested social assistance benefits. Eligibility criteria for this group include being disabled, orphaned, or suffering from HIV/AIDS and having income below the official poverty line.

Additionally, Vietnam provides cash transfers to offset the impact of user charges for health care and education for some low income groups, such as poor elderly people, and those living in geographically remote areas with poor infrastructure and high numbers of disadvantaged ethnic minority groups. These transfers, particularly transfers that help with health care costs, are very important in areas of the country where coverage by social insurance pensions are low. Indeed, in areas such as the Mekong Delta and other regions of South Vietnam, such transfers make up the largest element of the social protection package (Evans et al. 2007).

## DATA AND METHODS

### Data

We use two national household survey data sets to conduct the analyses: the China Household Income Project 2002 survey (CHIP) and the Vietnam Household Living Standards 2004 Survey (VHLSS). CHIP is a national, cross-sectional study designed by a team of Chinese and Western scholars and conducted by the Institute of Economics at the Chinese Academy of Social Sciences. Thus far, three waves of data have been collected, in 1988, 1995, and 2002. Samples of the CHIP study were drawn from larger National Bureau of Statistics samples using a multistage, stratified probability sampling method. With sample provinces from eastern, central, and western regions of China, the CHIP study is nationally representative and arguably the best publicly available data source on Chinese household income and expenditures (Gustafsson, Li, and Sicular 2008; Khan and Riskin 2005; Riskin, Zhao, and Li 2001). The 2002 CHIP urban surveys contain 6,835 households or 20,632 individuals, while the rural surveys include 9,200 households or 37,968 individuals.

VHLSS is carried out by the Vietnam General Statistical Office and collects data on living conditions in households across Vietnam. The 2004 survey is the second of a planned biannual survey project spanning 2002 to 2010. The VHLSS sample households were randomly selected from a commune register, including representative samples of communes from all provinces and regions. The effective sample size for VHLSS 2004 survey is 9,140 households containing 40,359 individuals (Evans et al. 2007).

### Measures and Methods

We adopt a comprehensive measure of total household per capita income, which includes market income, cash and in-kind social benefits, and private transfers. Market income includes the sum of individual earnings from waged employment and all other income sources from the market, such as income from private enterprises, property income, and income from family farming and non-farm activities. Tax payments and any social security contributions are deducted.

Social benefits are composed of cash transfers and in-kind benefits. Cash transfers include social insurance and social welfare income, while in-kind benefits include education and health. Education benefits were not directly asked about in the CHIP surveys. We impute households' education benefits in China by assigning the average government per capita spending on education for students enrolled in schools when surveyed. Such imputations are done by education level (i.e., elementary, junior high, and senior high schools, respectively) and by urban and rural areas. The imputations are only our first approximations and fall short in two dimensions. In the aggregate they equal only about half the officially reported totals. Furthermore, because we assume that benefits are distributed on a mean per capita government spending basis, we likely underestimate inequality of the distribution of education benefits in China. Education benefits surveyed in VHLSS included government supports on tuition fees, school materials, and scholarships. Public schooling benefits in Vietnam are not imputed due to lack of reliable administrative data. Thus the value of education benefits is severely understated in Vietnam. But because education benefits are more equally distributed in both countries than other social welfare benefits, and (more importantly) far more underreported in Vietnam than China, we are relatively confident that their full inclusion in both countries would only strengthen our central conclusion that benefits are less regressively distributed in Vietnam than in China. Health benefits were asked about directly in CHIP, measured as the health care expenses covered by the government and employers plus self-estimated market value of health care services. Health benefits in VHLSS were measured by the government transfers to offset user charges for health services. Two other types of important in-kind benefits—housing and food—were surveyed in CHIP but not in VHLSS. Based on calculation using CHIP data, in 2002, housing benefit made up 1.6 percent and food assistance made up 0.3 percent of total household income for Chinese families on average. We do not have reliable Vietnamese administrative data to simulate these benefits; therefore they are excluded from this study.

Expenditures on cash transfers, health, and education, and total social welfare expenditures as a percentage of GDP in 1998 as reported by the International Monetary Fund (IMF) and World Bank are presented in the top panel of Table 3.1 for both China and Vietnam. Not surprisingly, in view of China's per capita GDP being twice that of Vietnam, China devoted nearly one and a half times as much of its GDP to social welfare expenditures as Vietnam—9.87 percent as compared to 6.78 percent. As shown in the bottom panel of Table 3.1, in both countries, education accounted for 40 percent of total social welfare spending in 1998. In China, cash transfers also accounted for 40 percent of total spending, while for Vietnam the figure was only 30

**Table 3.1.** Social Welfare Expenditures as a Percentage of GDP and Proportions of Social Security, Health, and Education in Total Social Welfare Expenditure (%)

|  | Social Security | Health | Education | Total |
|---|---|---|---|---|
| Social Welfare Expenditures as a Percentage of GDP using IMF and World Bank 1998 data* | | | | |
| China | 4.00 | 1.87 | 4.00 | 9.87 |
| Vietnam | 2.00 | 2.00 | 2.78 | 6.78 |
| Proportions of Social Security, Health, and Education in Total Social Welfare Expenditure | | | | |
| China | | | | |
| IMF and World Bank 1998 data | 40 | 20 | 40 | 100 |
| CHIP 2002 survey data | 53 | 23 | 24 | 100 |
| Vietnam | | | | |
| IMF and World Bank 1998 data | 30 | 30 | 40 | 100 |
| VHLSS 2004 survey data | 73 | 23 | 5 | 100 |

\* *Source:* Authors' calculations based on social welfare expenditure data taken from IMF Government Finance Statistics Yearbook (1998) and GDP data taken from the World Bank World Development Indicators.

percent. Vietnam spent 30 percent of the total on health as compared to only 20 percent for China.

The bottom panel of the table also compares the composition of social welfare expenditures for both countries as reported in official aggregate data (i.e., IMF and World Bank 1998 data) with the composition reported in our two micro data sets. Though there are many reasons for the official aggregate data to differ from the survey data—the years are not the same, cash benefits are typically underreported in surveys, the value of public education benefits is neither reported nor simulated in Vietnam—the comparisons are still useful. In China, the proportion of education benefits as reported in the micro data is too low compared to the official data. This is because our estimates of education only include education expenditures from elementary school to high school, while the official data also include expenditures on early childhood education, higher education, and other education expenditures such as technical schools and continuing education. The discrepancy between official and survey data in education in Vietnam is even larger. Only 5 percent of total benefits analyzed in the Vietnam survey data are education benefits, despite the fact that 40 percent of total welfare benefits in the country are devoted to education. Again, this is because public schooling education benefits are not reported in the Vietnam survey data.

The major task of this study is to compare the impacts of the social benefit systems on income inequality within China and Vietnam. As an explicit redistributive mechanism, the social benefit system reallocates resources to improve the economic well-being of certain subgroups, as well as for the purpose of overall social justice. We compare the allocation of social benefits—both total and specific—across income quintiles of China and Vietnam. The higher the proportion of social benefits received by lower income quintiles, the more progressive the social benefit system. We further examine whether and to what extent the income redistribution through social benefit transfers raised or reduced overall income inequality. This is achieved by comparing pre- and post-transfer income inequality levels. Four different inequality measures are used to capture the impacts of social benefits on income inequality. First, we use the Gini coefficient, which reflects overall income distribution and is the most widely used measure of inequality. Second, we use the ratio of incomes of those at the 90th and 10th percentiles (hereafter P90/P10 ratio) to show the relative income distance between the top and bottom of the income distribution. Third, to reveal whether social benefits affect the top and bottom of the income distribution differently, we adopt two additional inequality measures: the ratio of incomes of the 90th to 50th percentile (hereafter P90/P50 ratio), which measures the top of the distribution, and the ratio of incomes of the 50th to 10th percentile (hereafter P50/P10 ratio), which measures the bottom of the distribution (Garfinkel, Rainwater, and Smeeding 2006).

## SIZE OF SOCIAL BENEFITS AND URBAN-RURAL CONTRAST

Measured by the share of social benefits in total household income, the size of China's social benefit system was much larger than that of Vietnam. As shown in Table 3.2, in 2002, social benefits made up 19 percent of total household income in China. Note that this figure is much higher than the proportion of total welfare transfers as a percentage of GDP presented in Table 3.1 (9.87 percent). The major reason for this difference, we believe, is that in China a large proportion of taxes are on production and do not therefore get reported as personal income. It is also possible that incomes are underreported. By way of contrast, in 2004, social benefits on average were only 4 percent of Vietnamese families' household income. If we are missing most of education, which is close to 3 percent, as shown in the official data in Table 3.1, the total social benefits add up to about 7 percent, which is consistent with the IMF and World Bank figures. Market income and private

**Table 3.2.** Composition of Household Income in China and Vietnam (%)

|  | China 2002 |  |  | Vietnam 2004 |  |  |
| --- | --- | --- | --- | --- | --- | --- |
|  | National | Urban | Rural | National | Urban | Rural |
| Market Income | 79.0 | 72.8 | 91.8 | 86.0 | 84.3 | 87.1 |
| Social Benefits | 19.2 | 25.6 | 6.0 | 4.3 | 4.8 | 4.0 |
| Private Transfers | 1.8 | 1.6 | 2.3 | 10.0 | 10.9 | 8.9 |
| Total Household Income | 100.0 | 100.0 | 100.0 | 100.0 | 100.0 | 100.0 |

Social Benefits and Income Inequality in Post-Socialist China 57

transfers played different roles in China and Vietnam. Market income comprised a larger proportion of total household income in Vietnam (86 percent) than in China (79 percent). Private transfers were a much more significant component in Vietnam (10 percent of total household income) than in China (2 percent).

The urban-rural gap in social benefit provision was much wider in China than in Vietnam: Chinese urban residents enjoyed significantly more benefits than their rural peers, while Vietnamese urban residents had only modest advantage over their rural peers. In urban China, social benefits on average made up slightly more than a quarter of total household income. In contrast, the proportion of social benefits in total household income in rural China was only 6 percent. To further illustrate this huge urban-rural gap, Figure 3.1 contrasts the population shares and the proportions of total social benefits received by urban and rural households. In 2002, the rural population made up 61 percent of the national population, but enjoyed only 10 percent of total national social benefits. In Vietnam, the proportion of social benefits in total household income was similar in the two areas (i.e., 4.8 percent in urban areas and 4.0 percent in rural areas).

The roles of market income and private transfers were also different by urban and rural residency in both countries. As shown in Table 3.2, the share of market income in total household income was larger in rural areas than in urban areas in both countries. However, this difference is more prominent in China (91.8 percent in rural areas, relative to 72.8 percent in urban areas) than in Vietnam (87.1 percent in rural areas, relative to 84.3 percent in urban areas). The regional

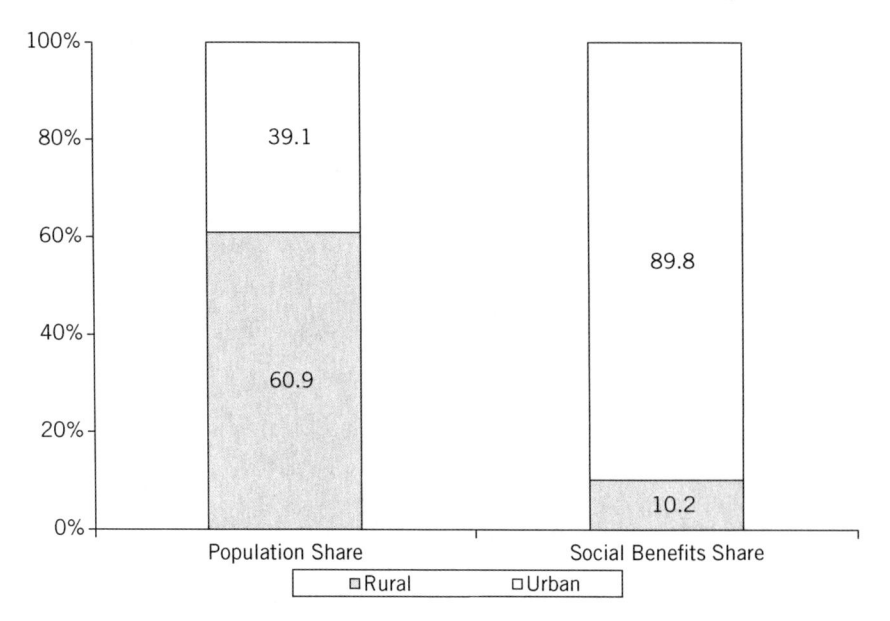

**Figure 3.1.** Contrast Between Population Share and Social Benefit Share in Urban versus Rural China

## 58   CHINESE SOCIAL POLICY IN A TIME OF TRANSITION

pattern for private transfers also differs across the two countries: in China, private transfers contributed more to total household income in rural areas (2.3 percent) than in urban areas (1.6 percent), while in Vietnam, private transfers played a larger role in urban areas (10.9 percent of total household income) than in rural areas (8.9 percent).

## URBAN-RURAL DIFFERENCES IN SOCIAL BENEFIT STRUCTURE

The urban-rural difference in social benefit structure was also much sharper in China than in Vietnam, as is evident in Table 3.3. Nearly 60 percent of social benefits in urban China were from cash transfers, while the rural residents only had 6.7 percent of total social benefits in the form of cash transfers. More specifically, pensions were very generous in urban China, making up 53.9 percent of total social benefits, but they constituted only 6.2 percent of rural social benefits. Rural residents did not benefit from any work-related social insurance income, while urban residents had 3 percent of their social benefits from this source. Social welfare was also more generous in providing a safety net for the urban poor than for their rural peers, making up 1.7 percent of total urban social benefits and only 1 percent of total rural social benefits. Health benefits also favored the urban residents, providing slightly more than a quarter of total social benefits, while rural residents had only 0.5 percent of their social benefits from health care. Education was the predominant rural social benefit, accounting for more than 90 percent of total rural social benefits, relative to 15.7 percent in urban areas. However, it is important to remember that the size of the rural social benefit system was

Table 3.3. Composition of Social Benefits in China and Vietnam by Urban-Rural Residence (%)

|  | China 2002 ||| Vietnam 2004 |||
| --- | --- | --- | --- | --- | --- | --- |
|  | National | Urban | Rural | National | Urban | Rural |
| Cash Transfers | 53.4 | 58.7 | 6.7 | 72.6 | 79.4 | 72.5 |
| Social Insurance: Pensions | 49.1 | 53.9 | 6.2 | 61.8 | 73.0 | 57.3 |
| Social Insurance: Work-related | 2.7 | 3.0 | 0.0 | 1.6 | 2.0 | 1.4 |
| Social Welfare | 1.6 | 1.7 | 1.0 | 9.2 | 4.4 | 13.8 |
| In-kind Benefits | 46.6 | 41.3 | 93.3 | 27.4 | 20.6 | 27.5 |
| Education | 23.5 | 15.7 | 92.8 | 4.8 | 3.2 | 4.9 |
| Health | 23.0 | 25.6 | 0.5 | 22.6 | 18.4 | 22.4 |
| Total Social Benefits | 100.0 | 100.0 | 100.0 | 100.0 | 100.0 | 100.0 |

Social Benefits and Income Inequality in Post-Socialist China    59

much smaller than the urban one, as presented above, and thus the seemingly large 90 percent figure actually corresponds to only 5.6 percent of total rural household income.

The urban-rural disparity in social benefit structure was much smaller in Vietnam than in China. The majority of social benefits took the form of cash transfers in both urban and rural Vietnam, making up 79 percent and 73 percent of total social benefits, respectively. Among cash transfers, pensions dominated in both urban and rural areas, representing 73 percent and 57 percent of total social benefits, respectively. Notably, social welfare played a much larger role in rural Vietnam, making up 14 percent of total social benefits, relative to only 4 percent in urban areas. Health benefits were the major in-kind transfers, making up 18 percent and 25 percent of total social benefits in respective urban and rural areas. Education benefits were marginal in both areas, accounting for 3 percent of total urban social benefits and 5 percent of total rural social benefits.

## DISTRIBUTION OF SOCIAL BENEFITS: PROGRESSIVE OR REGRESSIVE?

Overall, the social benefit systems in China and Vietnam were both regressive, as measured by the shares of total social benefits received by income quintiles. However, the regressivity in China was much more severe than in Vietnam, as illustrated in Figure 3.2. In both countries, social benefits did not favor the poor and increasingly rewarded the higher income groups. In Vietnam, the poorest

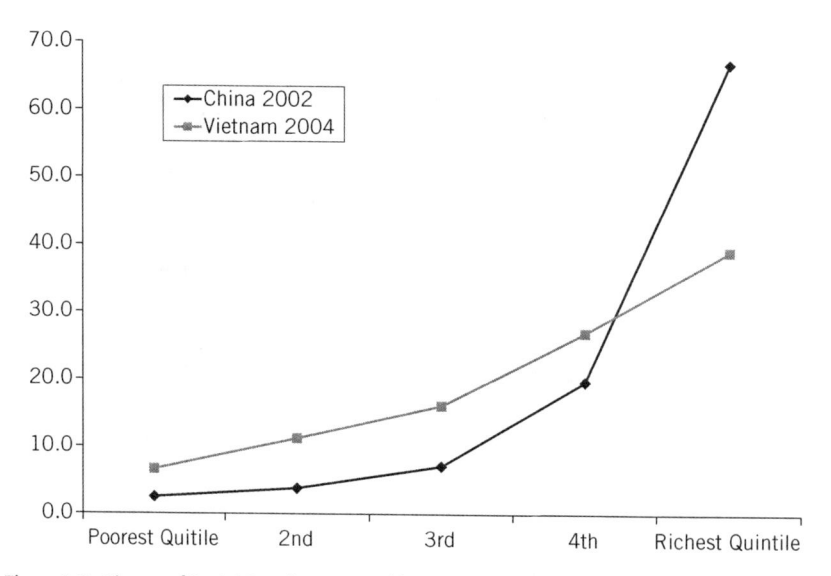

**Figure 3.2.** Shares of Social Benefits Received by Income Quintiles in China and Vietnam (%)

income quintile received 6.6 percent of all social benefits, while the top quintile received almost 40 percent. This gap between the rich and the poor was larger in China, where the lowest income quintile enjoyed 2.5 percent of all social benefits, while roughly two-thirds of all social benefits went to the richest income quintile.

The high regressivity of the Chinese social benefit system is driven by drastically uneven provisions in urban and rural benefits as well as the much more regressive distribution of urban social benefits compared to the rural system. Because the vast majority of social benefits (nearly 90 percent as shown in Figure 3.1) in China were received by urban residents and the overall income level of urban residents was more than three times that of rural residents, the higher income quintiles in China were predominately from urban areas and thus enjoyed much more social benefit than the lower income groups. Further, urban social benefits were distributed much more regressively than rural benefits based on results from the income quintile measures. The top income quintile in urban China received more than half of all urban social benefits, while the top income quintile in rural China enjoyed only 27.5 percent of all rural social benefits. In contrast, the urban-rural differences in social benefit provision and their distribution across income quintiles in Vietnam were much smaller, contributing to less severe regressivity in the Vietnamese social benefit system relative to the Chinese system.

Among social benefits, health assistance, work-related social insurance, and pensions were the most regressive, while social welfare was the least regressive in both countries. In China, as illustrated in Figure 3.3, the richest income quintile enjoyed 93 percent of all health benefits, 76 percent of all work-related social

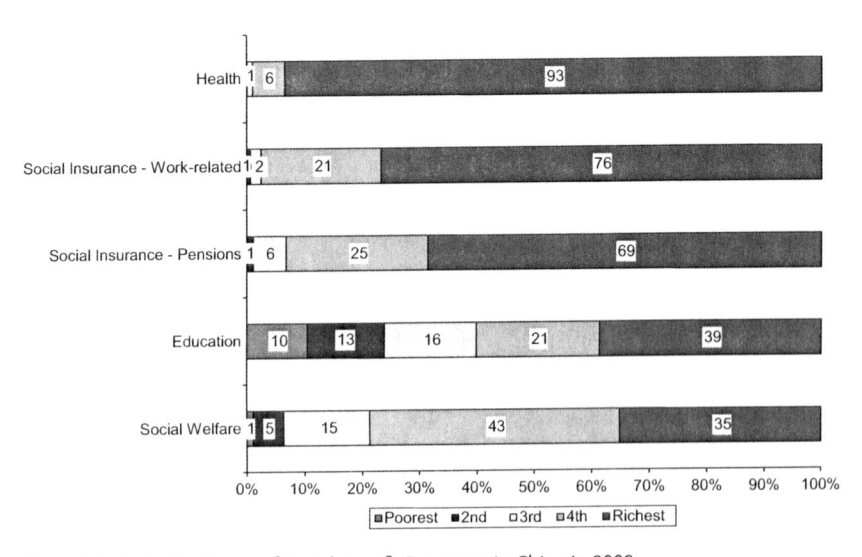

Figure 3.3. Quintile Shares of Social Benefit Programs in China in 2002

Social Benefits and Income Inequality in Post-Socialist China    61

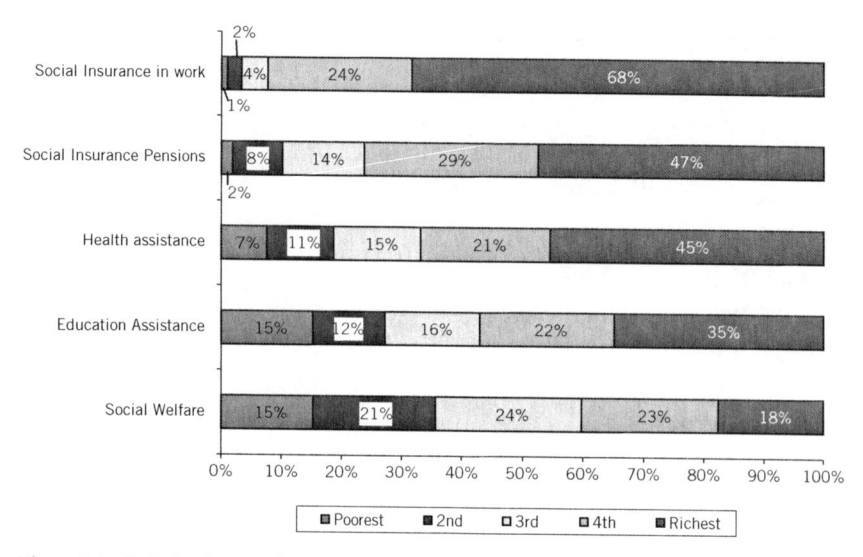

**Figure 3.4.** Quintile Shares of Social Benefit Programs in Vietnam in 2004

| Program | Poorest | 2nd | 3rd | 4th | Richest |
|---|---|---|---|---|---|
| Social Insurance in work | 2% | 4% | 24% | | 68% |
| Social Insurance Pensions | 1% | 8% | 14% | 29% | 47% |
| Health assistance | 2% | 7% | 11% | 15% | 21% | 45% |
| Education Assistance | 15% | 12% | 16% | 22% | 35% |
| Social Welfare | 15% | 21% | 24% | 23% | 18% |

insurance, and 69 percent of all pensions. In Vietnam, as shown in Figure 3.4, the top income quintile received 68 percent of all work-related social insurance, 47 percent of total pensions, and 45 percent of all health benefits. Social welfare favored the lower income groups in both countries and particularly so in Vietnam, serving its safety net function. In China, education benefits were more progressive than social welfare, but still disproportionately favored the top two income quintiles. This is because the per capita education expenditures that we use to impute education benefits for China have huge gaps between the rural and urban areas, and urban children on average receive more years of education. As we discussed above, the higher income quintiles concentrate in the urban areas, and the lower income quintiles concentrate in rural areas.

How does the exclusion of education expenditures in Vietnam influence these results? In view of the fact that education benefits are one of the least regressively distributed benefits in China and that inequality in both market incomes and social benefits and between urban and rural residents is less in Vietnam than in China, we conclude that if we were to simulate public education benefits in Vietnam, they would further reduce the regressivity of benefits in Vietnam.

## IMPACT OF SOCIAL BENEFITS ON INCOME INEQUALITY

Social benefits shaped overall income inequality differently in the two countries. In Vietnam, social benefits reduced overall income inequality, but the Chinese social benefit system increased overall income inequality. Not only is the distribution of social benefits more regressive than in Vietnam, but the distribution of

Table 3.4. Impact of Social Benefits on Income Inequality in China and Vietnam

|  | (a) Market Income | (b) + Private Transfers | (c) + Social Benefits | (d) − Taxes | (c)−(b) (b) |
|---|---|---|---|---|---|
| **China 2002** | | | | | |
| *Overall Inequality* | | | | | |
| Gini Coefficient | 0.452 | 0.450 | 0.465 | 0.463 | +3.1% |
| P90/P10 Ratio | 8.265 | 8.271 | 8.489 | 8.448 | +2.6% |
| *Top of Distribution* | | | | | |
| P90/P50 Ratio | 3.176 | 3.156 | 3.252 | 3.199 | +3.0% |
| *Bottom of Distribution* | | | | | |
| P50/P10 Ratio | 2.604 | 2.618 | 2.611 | 2.639 | −0.3% |
| **Vietnam 2004** | | | | | |
| *Overall Inequality* | | | | | |
| Gini Coefficient | 0.409 | 0.408 | 0.401 | 0.401 | −1.7% |
| P90/P10 Ratio | 6.345 | 6.288 | 6.172 | 6.102 | −1.8% |
| *Top of Distribution* | | | | | |
| P90/P50 Ratio | 2.657 | 2.697 | 2.687 | 2.665 | −0.4% |
| *Bottom of Distribution* | | | | | |
| P50/P10 Ratio | 2.387 | 2.331 | 2.299 | 2.288 | −1.4% |

Chinese benefits is also more unequal than the market income distribution. Not only is the Vietnamese distribution of social benefits less regressive than that of China, but it also has an equalizing effect on incomes overall. This is because social benefits in Vietnam, though regressive, are less unequally distributed than market incomes. Table 3.4 presents the impact of social benefits on income inequality using the four inequality measures described earlier. Compared to the inequality level based on the income definition of market income plus private transfers, the inclusion of social benefits in China lifted the overall income inequality level to a Gini Coefficient of 0.465 (from 0.450), an increase of 3.1 percent, and a P90/P10 ratio of 8.489 (from 8.271), an increase of 2.6 percent. In contrast, the Vietnamese income inequality level was reduced to a Gini Coefficient of 0.401 (from 0.408), a decrease of 1.7 percent, and a P90/P10 ratio of 6.172 (from 6.288), a decrease of 1.8 percent, by social benefit transfers.

Did social benefits affect the top and the bottom of the income distributions differently? Social benefits in China enlarged the income inequality gap at the top of the income distribution (by 3 percent) but reduced income inequality at the bottom (by 0.3 percent). Therefore, the disequalizing impact of social benefits in China was largely driven by the favorable transfers to the richer income groups. The Vietnamese social benefit system, however, reduced income inequality at

Social Benefits and Income Inequality in Post-Socialist China 63

both the top (by 0.4 percent) and the bottom (by 1.4 percent) of the income distribution.

## SOCIAL BENEFITS FOR RURAL-TO-URBAN MIGRANTS

It is important to note that the above analyses exclude the migrants in both countries. Since the mid-1990s, rapid economic growth in both China and Vietnam has led to significant levels of migration, mainly from rural to urban areas. In China, the number of migrants jumped from 18 million in 1989 to 70 million in 1993 and to 150 million by 2004 (Liang 2001; Gao, Yang, and Li, 2012). Migrants now make up 11 percent of the national population and more than 20 percent of urban residents. However, migrants receive very limited social benefits. They usually do not qualify for rural benefits because they are of working age with earning capabilities. Meanwhile, they are not entitled to any urban social benefits due to the lack of registered local city resident status. CHIP contained a sub-survey of 2,000 migrant households (5,318 individuals). Results from the CHIP migrant data show that, in 2002, less than 5 percent of migrants received any pensions, unemployment insurance, or health benefits (Gao 2006). In fact, the taxes and fees that they paid exceeded the subsidies they received (Khan and Riskin 2005).

Vietnam has also had large and mostly unmeasured migration into urban areas. Current evidence from a range of surveys show inflows and outflows from selected urban and rural areas, respectively (GSO and UNFPA 2004; Le and Nguyen 1999), but the true extent of migration and reliable estimates of populations will only be apparent with the publication of the 2009 Census. The VHLSS sample was constructed using administrative commune-based records of registered households. Therefore, the "unregistered" households are missing from VHLSS. The growing migrant population in Vietnam are mostly "unofficial" and do not have official registration status in the destination communes. While registration is supposed to limit migration without official sanction, the actual effect is to establish significant populations that are extra-legally resident. A migration survey conducted in 2004 estimated that more than 50 percent of migrants living in rental houses are unregistered (GSO and UNFPA 2004). Furthermore, many migrants do not live in private households but rather in dormitories or other group residential accommodations, which are excluded from the survey. Similar to migrants in China, the lack of official registration status also prevents the Vietnamese migrants from access to government transfers and services.

Due to the lack of accurate estimation of the level of social benefits received by the Chinese and Vietnamese migrants, we can only speculate about what the national pictures would look like if migrants were to be included. Because most migrants are either ineligible for or not actual beneficiaries of social benefits, excluding migrants would most likely overestimate the generosity of total social benefits. Because the average incomes of migrants remain much lower than those of urban residents, the regressivity of social benefits would most likely be underestimated when migrants are omitted from the data.

## CONCLUSION AND DISCUSSION

Using national household survey data, this chapter has compared the size, structure, and progressivity of the social benefit systems in China and Vietnam and has examined their impacts on income inequality. It also has contrasted the urban and rural systems within and between the two countries. China's per capita GDP is twice that of Vietnam, and the proportion devoted to social welfare transfers is nearly one and a half times larger. Both countries devote about 40 percent of social spending to education. In both countries, social welfare benefits are distributed regressively, but the Vietnamese system was much less regressive than the Chinese system. The urban-rural gap in social benefit provision was much wider in China than in Vietnam: Chinese urban residents enjoyed significantly more benefits than their rural peers, while Vietnamese urban residents had only modest advantage over their rural peers.

Some common challenges emerge for both China and Vietnam to address in future social policy reforms. First and most important, the two systems are both quite regressive, favoring high income groups and ignoring low income groups through social benefit transfers. This pattern of regressivity diverges from these countries' socialist ideologies while also posing a possible obstacle to continued economic development. Recent policy trends in both countries suggest that the two governments indeed are moving their social policies toward a fairer and more just direction. Second, as mentioned earlier, both countries have increasing numbers of migrants who are much neglected by the current social benefit systems. This policy gap communicates a serious lack of respect for migrants' basic rights and may also become a source of social unrest. It is also promising that the Chinese government has made efforts to address this situation in recent years (Gao, Yang, and Li, 2012).

Based on the comparative results reported in this chapter, the two countries can learn from each other to enhance their future social policy developments. China can draw policy implications from the Vietnam case in two respects. First, the progressivity of the Chinese social benefit system can be improved, as the Vietnamese system demonstrates. As the Chinese government strives for a "Harmonious Society," a more equalizing distribution of resources is essential to provide some basic security to those left behind by both market developments and social policy changes. Greater equalization is also important for ensuring social stability and avoiding social unrest as China continues to prioritize economic growth among other developmental goals.

Second, China's huge urban-rural disparity needs to be addressed. Several recent government initiatives have begun to fill this gap. These include eliminating agricultural taxes, continuing the expansion of the NRCMS, providing free compulsory education to rural and migrant children, and expanding MLG and other public assistance programs to support the rural poor. The outcomes of these initiatives, especially their redistributive effects, require close observation and await evaluations.

The Vietnamese social benefit system can also draw lessons from the Chinese case in two regards. First, the overall size of Vietnam's social benefit system can be enlarged, especially as the government strives for "universal coverage." The current level of social benefit provision (i.e., only 4.3 percent in total household income) is much lower than the levels in most advanced industrialized countries (i.e., 20 percent or more). Second, education benefits appear to be very limited based on estimates in this study. This could be a reflection of actual provision, but could also be due to the estimation method used. Further research needs to achieve a clear and accurate estimation of this important benefit. If actual education benefits are at such a low level, the Vietnamese government needs to broaden its coverage and improve its benefit level, as education is the key to a nation's sustained prosperity.

## REFERENCES

Asian Development Bank. 2004. *Poverty profile of the People's Republic of China*. Manila: Asian Development Bank. http://www.adb.org/publications/poverty-profile-peoples-republic-china.

Bloom, G., and J. Fang. 2003. *China's rural health system in a changing institutional context*. Institute of Development Studies Working Paper No. 194. Brighton, UK: Institute of Development Studies.

Carrin, G., A. Ron, H. Yang, et al. 1999. The reform of the rural cooperative medical system in the People's Republic of China: Interim experience in 14 pilot counties. *Social Science & Medicine* 48(7): 961–972.

Cook, S. 2001. *After the iron rice bowl: Extending the safety net in China*. Institute of Development Studies at the University of Sussex, Discussion Paper 377.

Croll, E. J. 1999. Social welfare reform: Trends and tensions. *China Quarterly* 159: 684–699.

Davis, D. 1989. Chinese social welfare: Policies and outcomes. *China Quarterly* 119: 577–597.

Evans, Martin, Ian Gough, Susan Harkness, Andrew McKay, Huyen Dao Thanh, and Ngoc Do Le Thu. 2007. *How progressive is social security in Vietnam?* UNDP Policy Dialogue Paper. http://www.undp.org.vn/digitalAssets/21/21874_7589_SS_Progressive__E_.pdf.

Evans, Martin, and Susan Harkness. 2008. Social protection in Vietnam and obstacles to progressivity. *Asian Social Work and Policy Review* 2(1): 30–52.

Gao, Q. 2006. The social benefit system in urban China: Reforms and trends from 1988 to 2002. *Journal of East Asian Studies* 6(1): 31–67.

Gao, Qin. 2008. The Chinese social benefit system in transition: Reforms and impacts on income inequality. *Annals of the New York Academy of Sciences* 1136: 342–347.

Gao, Qin. 2010. Redistributive nature of the Chinese social benefit system: Progressive or regressive? *The China Quarterly* 201(1): 1–19.

Gao, Qin, and Carl Riskin. 2009. Explaining China's changing inequality: Market vs. social benefits. In *Creating wealth and poverty in contemporary China*, eds. D. Davis and F. Wang, pp. 20–36. Palo Alto, CA: Stanford University Press.

Gao, Qin, Sui Yang, and Shi Li. (2012). Labor contracts and social insurance participation among migrant workers in China. *China Economic Review* 23(4): 1195–1205.

Garfinkel, Irwin, Lee Rainwater, and Timothy Smeeding. 2006. A re-examination of welfare states and inequality in rich nations: How in-kind transfers and indirect taxes change the story. *Journal of Policy Analysis and Management* 25(4): 897–918.

GSO and UNFPA (General Statistics Office and United Nations Population Fund). 2004. *The 2004 Viet Nam Migration Survey: Major findings*. Vietnam: Statistical Publishing House.

Guan, X. 2000. China's social policy: Reform and development in the context of marketization and globalization. *Social Policy & Administration* 34(1): 115–130.

Gustafsson, B, S. Li, and T. Sicular. 2008. *Inequality and public policy in China*. Cambridge: Cambridge University Press.

Khan, Azizur Rahman, and Carl Riskin. 2005. China's household income and its distribution, 1995 and 2002. *The China Quarterly* 182: 356–384.

Le, M. T., and D. V. Nguyen. 1999. Remittances and the distribution of income. In *Health and wealth in Vietnam: An analysis of household living standard*, eds. Haughton, Dominique, et al., 167–182. Singapore: Institute of Southeast Asian Studies.

Leung, J. C. 2003. Social security reforms in China: Issues and prospects. *International Journal of Social Welfare* 12: 73–85.

Li, B., and D. Piachaud. 2004. *Poverty and inequality and social policy in China*. London: Centre for Analysis of Social Exclusion, London School of Economics. http://sticerd.lse.ac.uk/dps/case/cp/CASEpaper87.pdf.

Liang, Zai. 2001. The age of migration in China. *Population and Development Review* 27(3): 499–524.

London, Jonathan. 2013. Welfare Regimes in the Wake of State Socialism: China and Vietnam. Chapter 2 of this volume.

Liu, Y. 2004. Development of the rural health insurance system in China. *Health Policy and Planning* 19(3): 159–165.

Ministry of Civil Affairs (MCA). 2008. Monthly administrative data on MLG. MCA Department of Planning and Finance. http://cws.mca.gov.cn/article/tjsj/dbsj/ (accessed December 8, 2008).

Riskin, Carl, Renwei Zhao, and Shi Li. 2001. *China's retreat from equality: Income distribution and economic transition.* Armonk, NY: M. E. Sharpe.

Rösner, H. J. 2004. China's health insurance system in transformation: Preliminary assessment, and policy suggestions. *International Social Security Review* 57(3): 65–90.

Saunders, P., and X. Shang. 2001. Social security reform in China's transition to a market economy. *Social Policy & Administration* 35(3): 274–289.

Solinger, D. J. 2002. Labour market reform and the plight of the laid-off proletariat. *China Quarterly* 170: 304–326.

Tang, J., L. Sha, and Z. Ren. 2003. *Zhongguo Chengshi Pinkun yu Fanpinkun Baogao [Report on poverty and anti-poverty in urban China].* Beijing, China: Huaxia Press.

Wong, L. 1998. *Marginalization and social welfare in China.* London and New York: Routledge/London School of Economics.

World Bank. 2007. *Social protection: Vietnam development report 2008.* Hanoi: World Bank.

World Bank. 2008. *China Quarterly Update* (February). http://siteresources.worldbank.org/INTCHINA/Resources/318862-1121421293578/cqu_jan_08_en.pdf (accessed August 19, 2008).

Zhu, Y. 2002. Recent developments in China's social security reforms. *International Social Security Review* 55(4): 39–54.

# 4
# SOCIAL SECURITY POLICY IN THE CONTEXT OF EVOLVING EMPLOYMENT POLICY

Barry L. Friedman

## INTRODUCTION

Before China began its reforms in 1978, it provided maximum job security for its urban workers in state-owned enterprises (SOEs). Many countries have policies to protect jobs in various ways, but in China, jobs for SOE workers were guaranteed for life. As the reforms began, there was growing recognition that this system might need to change, alongside concerns about the difficulty in doing so. Although worker redundancy was seen as an impediment to enterprise efficiency, dismissing masses of redundant workers in the midst of a large influx of new entrants to the labor force was seen as a possible recipe for social instability. The evolution of post-reform employment policy in China has been driven by this unresolved tension between reducing redundancy and preserving stability. For about 20 years, employment policy attempted to avoid hard choices on the way to a painless transition, but the pain finally arrived in the 1990s in the form of large-scale layoffs.

Alongside lifetime job security, other core features of the pre-reform social protection system for urban SOE workers were also distinctive, especially the provision of benefits by each enterprise to its own workers. In many countries, portions of social protection are provided by enterprises, often voluntarily, but in pre-reform China, virtually all standard social insurance benefits, including pensions, were provided by individual enterprises under government mandates that tied the social protection system directly to the job security system. If workers were to lose their jobs, they would also lose their benefits, which made it difficult for economic reformers to attack redundancy without also finding a way to make benefits portable across enterprises. The link between social security and job security also extended to the pension system, which was called on from time to time to retire workers earlier in the hope of opening more jobs to younger workers. Using pension policy as a tool of employment policy blurs the boundary between these policy domains, and when this occurred, employment goals generally functioned as the driving force.

While job security and employer mandates were major targets of reform in the transition from socialism, they were not the only concerns of policy. In addition to considerations of the transition from socialism, there was a growing awareness of a demographic transition characterized by population aging that would create significant, long-run problems for the pension system and other social protection benefits. As concerns about population aging began to affect policy deliberations, pension considerations increased in priority, but solutions to the problem were still constrained by employment goals.

One other major feature of China's social protection system is its dual nature. Urban residents have access to a well-developed set of benefits, but benefits for the large mass of rural residents have emerged only slowly and on a separate (and sometimes unequal) track from urban social insurance, thus mirroring the urban-rural differences in economic opportunities. In yet one more transition, employment policy has changed to accommodate the movement of rural workers out of agriculture, although rural workers have only recently gained initial access to the urban pension system. The increased involvement of rural workers in the urban economy will eventually challenge the current dual urban and rural pension systems.

It has been observed that Chinese reforms do not tend to proceed according to a coherent strategic plan. Instead, problems are perceived and then solutions are sought, one step at a time, in an almost experimental way. That same unsystematic process can be seen in the evolution of social protection reforms, which began with multiple goals (often in conflict with each other), rather than a unitary vision, and proceeded through a learning process in which policymakers often tried to avoid painful choices, but eventually were compelled to make trade-offs. Despite the messy, trial-and-error process of policy design, the end result sometimes appears coherent, even effective, albeit with continued unresolved challenges (Naughton 1996, 1).

This chapter uses the juxtaposition of pension and employment policy to highlight the inherent dilemmas and trade-offs faced by Chinese policymakers in light of the three transitions—the economic shift toward markets, the aging of the population, and the movement of rural workers out of agriculture—with emphasis on the transition away from socialism. In addition to tracing the evolution of pension benefit structures outside enterprises and the links between this process and the demise of guaranteed jobs, the chapter uses data from the Chinese Household Income Projects (CHIP) for 1995[1] and 2002[2] to explore possible adverse effects of the late 1990s labor retrenchment policies on pension benefits and work patterns among older workers, with particular attention to the mixing of pensions and work.

## THE TRANSITION FROM SOCIALISM

The old Maoist planning and social protection system was distinctive even among East Bloc countries. Two features of the old urban system were particularly important for social protection and for comparison to other countries. First, while many countries protect job security by regulating the ability of companies to dismiss workers, the old Chinese system occupied the extreme end of that policy continuum by prohibiting dismissal by SOEs completely: jobs were guaranteed for life. Reformers came to call this system the "iron rice bowl." Second, whereas some countries provide certain social benefits through employers (such as health insurance in the U.S.)—either voluntarily or through mandates—most social benefits in pre-reform China were provided to workers by their enterprises, and SOEs were mandated to provide these benefits, including pensions. SOEs had to meet not only their social protection obligations, but also their requirements under the economic plan.

Chinese reformers came to view both of these features as problematic and designed reforms to move away from the extreme versions of the lifetime job guarantee and employer provision of social benefits. At first there was a long period of gradual reform, aiming at a gentle transition away from guaranteed jobs. Many innovations were tried, but the underlying problems remained. Despite increasingly focused efforts to reduce redundancy among enterprise workers, the reforms could not be completed without some pain, and policymakers learned just how difficult it is to shift away from job security and benefit mandate programs when that becomes the policy goal.

### The Employment-Driven Evolution of Transition Policy

SOEs had substantial social obligations alongside their production requirements under the economic plan. In addition to providing social benefits for their workers, the policy of guaranteed jobs meant that enterprises were required to support workers even if they were made redundant. Enterprises had always met these obligations because the state subsidized them when necessary, but reformers worried about the financial burden on government as the scale of redundancies grew. In response to these problems, one of the early goals of the reforms was for enterprises to stand on their own without subsidy. The Twelfth Central Committee of the Communist Party in October 1984 specified the "task of invigorating enterprises as the key to reforming the national economy" (World Bank 1990, 2). But eliminating subsidies would require changes in the social protection obligations of enterprises. At the same time, reformers faced a serious urban unemployment problem that had been concealed during the Cultural Revolution of the Mao era, when 17 million young people were sent to the countryside to work in agriculture. When the reforms began in 1978, these people began returning to their cities at the same time that a large demographic cohort of new workers was reaching working age and seeking jobs. These factors combined to produce an official urban unemployment rate of 5.4 percent in 1979, with higher rates in the largest cities (Naughton 1996, chapter 2). Some officials in the former Ministry of Labor and Personnel who looked at the subsidy and redundancy problems urged that the iron rice bowl be smashed, but other officials feared that a campaign against the job guarantee would only add to unemployment.[3] The initial reforms focused on creating jobs rather than smashing the iron rice bowl. The tension between reducing redundancy and increasing unemployment has been an ongoing feature of Chinese employment policy.

Pension policy was used almost immediately to deal with unemployment. Pensions for workers in SOEs had been established as part of labor insurance regulations in 1951 and had been managed by the All-China Federation of Trade Unions. However, the Federation was dissolved in 1966 during the Cultural Revolution, and the full responsibility for pensions passed to enterprises, particularly SOEs, as enterprise mandates (Dixon 1981, chapter 4). Thus, mandated enterprise provision of benefits was an accidental outcome of the earlier conflict, but nevertheless a significant problem for the reformers to deal with. During the Cultural Revolution, retirement was discouraged in spite of official retirement ages of 60 for men and 55 for women. Faced with the unemployment problem in 1978, the reformers switched direction and encouraged not only retirement, but also early retirement. The *ding ti* system between 1978 and 1983 allowed workers to pass their jobs to their children if they would retire (World Bank 1990, 3). It was an early case of using pensions as part of employment policy.

In the mid-1980s, a series of reforms in both employment and pension policy seemed to prepare a legal basis for attacking redundancy, and the transition was almost seamless in terms of actual outcomes. A labor contract system began in 1986. Existing workers continued as permanent employees, but new workers were hired under contracts of limited duration, from one year up to five or ten years (White 1987, 367). Contract workers did not have lifetime jobs, but they could not be fired until the end of their contracts, and at least initially most contracts were renewed when they expired. The legal basis for dismissal was established, but initially it was estimated that 90 percent of workers were reemployed at the end of their contracts (World Bank 1990, 60). Also in 1986, an unemployment insurance (UI) program was established to protect those who did lose jobs. However, benefits were limited to workers dismissed for specific reasons: their enterprise went bankrupt or was undergoing streamlining; they were not reappointed at the end of their contract; or they were fired for disciplinary reasons (World Bank 1990, 65). Initially, UI was not widely used. After a new law permitted bankruptcy, there was one bankruptcy in Shenyang in 1986, but for several years, the law was hardly used (World Bank 1990, 61).

Alongside the employment reforms, pension reforms were adopted, with implications for an eventual attack on redundancy. The problem of an aging population was perceived first at the enterprise level. Since each enterprise paid for the pensions of its own workers on a current basis, older enterprises with older workforces had much higher pension costs. A survey of enterprises conducted by the World Bank found newer enterprises with 60 or even 90 workers per retiree, but some older enterprises had barely two (World Bank 1990, Table 2.5, 33). This impaired the profitability of older enterprises, the more and less productive ones alike, putting all such enterprises at a competitive disadvantage for no other reason than that they were established earlier and thus had to pay pensions to more retirees. To deal with this problem, State Council Document 77 called for the establishment of pension pools, most of which operated at the city level beginning in 1986 (World Bank 1990, 10–11). Within a pool, there was a common contribution rate (discussed during multiple visits to the Ministry of Labor in 1986–1989). Enterprises with pension costs below the rate would contribute to the pool. Those with costs above the rate would receive funds from the pool. At first, when enterprises were still the agents that paid the pensions, the pools functioned as clearinghouses that allowed uniform pension expenditures across enterprises in order to eliminate competitive disadvantages. The pools also facilitated further employment reforms, such as setting contribution rates appropriately so that pensions could be paid to workers whose enterprise went bankrupt. Pension pooling was thus a necessary step toward allowing bankruptcies. Pooling could also facilitate worker mobility, at least within a city. If a worker changed jobs, she could turn to the pool for her pension, rather than going back to her old enterprise for a part of it.

Actual pooling practices were shaped by developments in employment policy. Following the introduction of labor contracts, separate pension pools with different contribution rates were established for contract and permanent workers. The reasoning behind this segmentation was that contract workers would expect to contribute to the pools, but permanent workers were not used to contributing since they were hired under the earlier expectation that enterprises would cover all pension costs; officials clearly did not want to antagonize the permanent workers. Separate pools were also established for workers in collective enterprises, again with different contribution rates. These practices illustrate how new developments in employment policy influenced pension policy in ways that made pooling less efficient. The State Council Resolution on the Reform of the Pension System for Enterprise Workers of 1991 called for the uniform treatment of all kinds of enterprise workers, with equalized contribution rates and provincial-level pooling. However, differences remain across cities and provinces in implementing these reforms (Salditt, Whiteford, and Adema 2007, 17). Although the learning process has led officials gradually to improve regulations and practices, reforms are still not complete.

## Social Security Policy in the Context of Evolving Employment Policy

The reforms of the 1980s set up a framework for addressing redundancy, but the approach was gentle, and policy held back the pace of dismissals. In spite of numerous attempts to improve enterprise efficiency and increase jobs through active employment policy, the redundancy problem continued into the 1990s and contributed significantly to the perpetuation of numerous loss-making enterprises. The state's willingness to extend subsidies or loans to keep weak enterprises afloat steadily eroded, and support grew for measures such as closure, transformation, and consolidation (Liu and Wu 2006, 124). The strongest action came in September 1997 with the Fifteenth Party Congress's approval of the *xiagang,* or layoff, policy (Solinger 2002, 304). This was intended to be a temporary policy giving enterprises the right to lay off large numbers of redundant workers. A laid-off worker would receive a monthly benefit somewhat above the official minimum living standard of the city and would be assigned to a Re-employment Service Center, all funded jointly by her enterprise and the city. If new employment was not found within two or three years (depending on the city), the laid-off worker would be reclassified as unemployed and would begin receiving UI benefits (discussions at Ministry of Labor and Social Security, July 2000). "Laid off" thus became an official category, distinct from "unemployed," and statistical sources began reporting data on it separately. According to official data, the number of workers in laid off status reached 6.1 million in 1998, the first full year of the policy, rising to 6.57 million in 2000, and then gradually declining to 2.6 million in 2003. The data also show substantial rates of reemployment (Institute of Labor Studies 2004, 9). In terms of employment alone, it appears that the layoff policy had a substantial, perhaps temporary effect, but a fuller analysis is needed.

Existing literature documents various adverse effects of reforms, for example, on inequality, including increases in inequality in China associated with retrenchment that predated the 1997 *xiagang* policy. Using household survey data, Appleton and colleagues estimated the statistical probability of layoff to be over 11 percent in 1999, although it differed substantially across individuals; the average unemployment spell appeared to last 24 months, but possibly longer because many of the spells included in the study were not yet completed at the time of analysis (Appleton, Knight, Song, and Xia 2002). Additional studies have found increases in urban poverty following retrenchment (Solinger 2002; Liu and Wu 2006; Saunders and Lujun 2006). Looking not only at income, but also at all kinds of capital, Davis and colleagues have demonstrated increasing inequality favoring those with political connections and public sector jobs (Davis, Bian, and Wang 2005). Among other things, these articles raise the question of whether the social protection system in China is adequate to deal with the employment upheavals that the transition from socialism entails.

Although previous studies illustrate adverse effects, they generally do not identify the specific reform policies responsible for the adverse effects. In view of the importance of the layoff policy, it would be desirable to have an identified test of its effects. Appleton, Knight, Song, and Xia (2002) provide the most detailed study of employment effects, but do not test for a separate effect of the layoff policy, perhaps because available data are not adequate.

## Evidence on the Impact of the *Xiagang* Policy on Pensions

Pension reforms were intended, among other things, to protect retirees in case of layoffs and might be expected to increase both pension participation and benefits. On the other hand, if the layoffs were disruptive enough and interfered with the implementation of the pension policies, pensions could have been adversely affected. Consider first positive effects. The development of pooling could assure pensions to workers from bankrupt enterprises or to those who had been laid off. Drawing on the pools could protect the pensions of workers whose enterprises no longer existed or were unable to pay. Moreover, revisions in the pension formula could protect pension amounts for laid-off workers. Other positive factors for pensions (not related to the *xiagang* policy) are that more recent cohorts of retirees may have had higher wages and thus would receive higher pensions, and that the government occasionally increased particular pension components. Negative effects would be possible if the pension reforms were not implemented before the layoffs began. Implementation schedules differed by city. It is possible, for example, that a worker lived in a city where the pool was not yet operating smoothly.

Depending on the balance between positive and negative factors, it is possible that the net outcome for pensions could go either way, or perhaps in different directions for different people. If considering only the mean outcome, it would be surprising if the net outcome were negative, for this would indicate a very disruptive effect of layoffs on pensions, along with slow implementation of pension reforms. Making a negative outcome even more unlikely is the possibility that many laid-off workers were still too young to retire and that the main impact of the layoff policy may have fallen on a younger cohort. Thus, a negative finding would make a fairly strong case that layoffs were having adverse effects on pensions, while a positive effect would not rule out the possibility of adverse pension effects for some segments of older people. Some workers might get no pension or a low pension, while many others might get the pension normally expected. A comparison of mean outcomes before and after the *xiagang* policy would thus be only a weak test of its effects. It would be desirable to keep track of the overall pension distribution to see if an increase in low pensions occurs.

The CHIP surveys were conducted in 1995, before the large retrenchment that began in 1998, and again in 2002, after the layoffs were well underway, with a high rate of layoffs still continuing. We first present before and after comparisons of pension receipt and pension amounts. For the reasons given above, these are weak tests.[4] We then look at the distribution of pension amounts to see whether pensions went down at the lower end of the distribution.

# Social Security Policy in the Context of Evolving Employment Policy

*Was there a reduction in the receipt of pensions?* The proportion of people receiving a pension is calculated relative to the population of those eligible. Men were eligible for a pension at age 60, although those who worked in more difficult circumstances were eligible at 55. Women in managerial positions were eligible at 55, and other women at 50. The calculations here take all men over 55 and all women over 50 as the relevant population. A small number received pensions before these ages, but they are omitted. It turns out that in 1995, 63 percent of the older population received pensions; in 2002, that group increased to 69 percent. Since the proportion might differ systematically across people, a logistic regression was run to get an adjusted estimate of the difference between years. The year effect was estimated as the coefficient of a time dummy variable (2002 cases being the ones) while controlling for a set of demographic variables.[5] The logit estimate predicted an even larger increase in the probability of receiving a pension. The marginal effect for the difference in probability between 1995 and 2002 was 14 percent and strongly significant. It appears that the composition of the elder subsample in 2002 was quite different from that of 1995. It was more female; there was less work experience; and fewer workers were from SOEs—all factors likely to be associated with less pension receipt. Apparently, the controls help adjust for these differences in sample, which otherwise result in an underestimate of the difference based on raw means alone. But both approaches are consistent in showing an increase in pension receipt after the start of the retrenchment policy. Thus, there is no direct evidence that the layoff policy was hindering pension receipt. This does not rule out the possibility of adverse effects on just a portion of the elderly. As indicated above, there are ample reasons to expect pension receipt to rise. The lack of a negative effect here indicates only that any negative effects were not large enough to offset the positive effects.[6]

*Was there an adverse effect on pension amounts and their distribution?* Two kinds of comparisons can provide information on pension amounts. First, the 1995 sample can be compared to the 2002 sample. Second, within the 2002 sample, those who retired before 1998 can be compared to those who retired from 1998 on (1998 was the first year of extensive layoffs). The comparison of the 1995 and 2002 samples yields an interesting insight, but no evidence on the effects of layoffs. The comparison within the 2002 sample is the most promising indication that there was an adverse effect on pensions.

Consider first the comparison between 1995 and 2002. Adjusting for inflation in the urban consumer price index, the average real pension went up by 66 percent, or at an annual rate of 7.5 percent. Looking across the distribution, there are similar real increases in every decile. This is not a story of adverse effects between the two years. Pensions went up faster than prices, so real pensions grew. However, if pensions are deflated by the rate of wage inflation rather than price inflation, the story is reversed. The average wage-deflated pension goes down for the whole sample by around 20 percent, or about 3 percent a year, and by similar amounts in each decile. The wage-deflated pension gives information on how pensions are doing relative to wages. The price-deflated pension shows that the purchasing power of pensioners rose in real terms, but since wages grew substantially faster than prices, retirees were falling behind relative to workers. This result reflects partly that the pension indexing formula deliberately used a rate lower than the rate of wage inflation in an effort to control the growth in pension costs. It is probably not the effect of layoffs. To check the result while controlling for other factors, the log of pension income was regressed on the same covariates as in the previous logit estimation. For the log of the price-deflated pension, the coefficient of year was .582 and strongly significant. This suggests an approximately 58 percent increase in the real pension between the two years, controlling for the other variables, a result consistent with the growth in the simple mean. However, for the log of the wage-deflated pension, the coefficient of year was -.156, again highly significant, indicating a decline of approximately 15 percent, and again consistent with the result for the simple mean.

Turning now to the comparison within the 2002 sample, the pension data are all from the same year, so the inflation adjustment makes no difference. The mean pension of those who retired in 1998 or later was lower by about 8 percent, compared to those who retired before 1998. Controlling for other variables in a regression of the log of the pension, the dummy for retiring in 1998 or later had a coefficient of -.057, significant at the 5 percent level, indicating that pensions were on average lower by about 5.7 percent. However, the distribution of effects may be more important than the mean effect. There is more than one way to explore differences across the pension distribution. The pension at each decile can be found, and then the difference at each decile can be calculated. This gives a comparison across the distribution by decile, but without controlling for other variables. Alternatively, a quantile regression allows the calculation of coefficients separately at each decile of the distribution. In particular, the coefficient of the dummy for retiring in 1998 or later can be calculated, controlling for other factors. The dependent variable is still the log of the pension, but now it is calculated separately at each decile along the log pension distribution. Results for both the simple mean comparisons by decile and the quantile regression coefficients of the dummy for retiring in 1998 or later are presented in Table 4.1.

The mean differences show pensions consistently lower across the whole distribution, although the bottom two deciles and the top one stand out with larger differences. The quantile regressions tell a more interesting story. The difference in pension is largest at the lowest deciles and then gets steadily smaller. The 10 percent decile has the largest difference, and it is significant at the 10 percent level, with a p value of .054. From the 50 percent decile and up, the differences are too small to be significant. These results give the strongest indication yet that something adverse was happening to those who retired in 1998 or later and who were in the bottom half of the pension distribution. Of course, it is not

**Table 4.1.** Differences in Pensions Between Those Who Retired in 1998 or Later and Those Who Retired Before 1998: Mean Comparisons and Quantile Regression Coefficients by Decile

| Deciles (percents) | 10 | 20 | 30 | 40 | 50 | 60 | 70 | 80 | 90 |
|---|---|---|---|---|---|---|---|---|---|
| **Mean pensions (yuan)** | | | | | | | | | |
| Retired before 1998 | 3,807 | 4,583 | 5,199 | 5,881 | 6,637 | 7,627 | 8,905 | 10,869 | 14,331 |
| Retired 1998 and later | 3,056 | 4,114 | 4,911 | 5,594 | 6,361 | 7,278 | 8,465 | 10,131 | 12,914 |
| Percent difference | −19.7 | −10.2 | −5.5 | −4.9 | −4.2 | −4.6 | −4.9 | −6.8 | −9.9 |
| **Quantile regression** | | | | | | | | | |
| Coefficient of retired 1998 and later | −.116 | −.073* | −.050* | −.054* | −.039 | −.037 | −.005 | .036 | .029 |
| S.E. | .060 | .028 | .021 | .021 | .027 | .024 | .029 | .032 | .040 |

Dependent variable of the quantile regressions is log pension.
Control variables are dummies for gender, SOE employee, age in 5-year categories (50 to 54, 55 to 59, and 65 and over, with 60 to 64 the omitted category), and province. Years of education and years of work are also included.
Standard errors calculated by bootstrapping with 100 repetitions.
N = 3,039 for quantile regression. For the means, N = 1,086 for those who retired in 98 or later, N = 1,959 for those who retired before 1998.
*significance at 5 percent level or less.

definitive that layoffs were the cause, but this is possible evidence of a pension problem concentrated at the lower end of the distribution during the period of retrenchment.

## THE DEMOGRAPHIC TRANSITION

According to the World Bank, it took 140 years for France to double the proportion of its old people from 9 to 18 percent of its population, but China is expected to do the same in just 34 years, reaching 18 percent by 2026 (World Bank 1994, 34). The discovery of the aging problem in China has led to a new focus on the specific problems of the pension system. In keeping with the patterns described earlier in this chapter, employment policy constrained one aspect of pension policy—the retirement age—but otherwise pension issues became an area of concern on their own. Chinese policy first addressed aging issues at the enterprise level by instituting pooling. As officials became more aware of the scope of the aging problem internally and in other countries, they began to address problems in the whole system. The urban Chinese pension system was in a situation similar to those in many industrial countries that were also experiencing rapid population aging. Chinese officials began to study social security programs around the world in order to get ideas on how to address the problems in their own country.

As in many other countries, Chinese pensions were paid out of the contributions of current workers on a pay-as-you-go (PAYGO) basis, but there was growing recognition that this can be problematic in a system with rapid population aging. By the mid-1980s, officials were learning about the possibilities for pre-funding, or setting aside funds in advance, to cover at least part of future pension obligations. By the late 1980s, there was intense interest in Singapore's fully funded system of individual accounts under its Central Provident Fund,[7] although not everyone agreed about that system's virtues. Many officials were uneasy about the prospect of individual accounts, and as more information was collected, officials became more aware of the problems associated with switching systems. In particular, there was the potential for two massive types of costs, one to fund the individual accounts, and the other to meet the legacy costs—promises made to existing retirees but not funded—for those already at or near retirement.

In the early 1990s, the idea of notional accounts gained attention, particularly in Shanghai, based on policies being considered in Sweden and finally adopted there in 1994 (Konberg, Palmer, and Sunden 2006, 449). Notional accounts, which elsewhere came to be called non-financial defined contribution (NDC) plans, are individual accounts in which contributions are credited, interest is credited on the accumulation, and the total bookkeeping accumulation at retirement is used to determine a pension. The term "notional" refers to the fact that actual funds from worker contributions may not be deposited in the account. Thus, an NDC plan is an unfunded version of an individual account, operated on a PAYGO basis. The Swedish NDC system includes elements to maintain the financial balance of the system, unlike the typical PAYGO system (Palmer 2006). Chinese advocates saw in notional accounts a way to start individual accounts without having to fund them initially. However, the early plans lacked the Swedish features that could contribute to financial discipline for the system.

By 1995 there was not yet agreement on a single Chinese pension plan. The Circular on Deepening of Reform of Pension Insurance System (State Council Document 6 of 1995) called for the eventual development of a single national plan, but then allowed cities to choose between two alternatives. One, which had emerged from the original Shanghai proposals, called for individual accounts with some notional features. The other called for a common benefit plus an earnings-related benefit, with provision for a voluntary individual account as a supplement. Finally, faced with the awkwardness of two coexisting systems, agreement was reached on a single plan. State Council Document 26 of 1997 called for a base benefit of 20 percent of the average city wage plus an individual account. It appeared that in many cities, the individual accounts set up under the

Social Security Policy in the Context of Evolving Employment Policy 79

new rules would be notional and not funded. In 2000 an experiment in Liaoning Province was started to investigate further the feasibility of funding the individual accounts (Drouin and Thompson 2006, 20–21). Chinese and foreign analysts have had continuing concerns about the financial condition of the system and what to do about it. Early estimates of the implicit pension debt suggested a moderate problem, with estimates of 94 percent of 1998 gross domestic product (GDP) (Dorfman and Sin 2000), 71 percent of 2000 GDP (Wang, Xu, Wang, and Zhai 2001), and 141 percent of 2001 GDP (Sin 2005).

The full range of policy issues related to pension financing is beyond the scope of this chapter. However, one aspect relevant to the theme of this chapter is the retirement age. Increasing the retirement age from its current low levels (60 for men, 55 for women in management positions, lower for both groups among blue-collar workers) would be one way to reduce the unfunded pension liabilities, and foreign experts often recommend this (for example, World Bank 1996, 20). People who worked longer would contribute more and withdraw less from the system. However, I have frequently heard concern from officials who do not want an increase in the number of older workers in the workforce, given their worries about finding enough jobs for others. It would help to know more about the labor market for older workers in China to judge whether these concerns are realistic. Do older workers want or need to work? Are they substitutes for younger workers? While these questions are difficult to answer, we can get some information on work and retirement patterns of older workers from the CHIP data.

The surveys did ask about work and retirement, but these were given as mutually exclusive choices. In other countries, many people seek bridges to retirement in which they withdraw from work gradually. (For an early study in the U.S., see Doeringer 1990.) Table 4.2 shows the percentages of people with wages, pensions, or both for several age categories. Based on eligibility for pensions, the table includes women over 50 and men over 55. The first row of the table is thus women only.

The percent receiving a wage (columns 1 plus 2) diminishes from 55 percent to 11 percent going down the table to older age categories. In spite of the official

Table 4.2. Percent of Pension-Eligible People Who Receive Wages, Pensions, or Both

| Age | N | 1<br>Wage, no pension | 2<br>Wage and pension | 3<br>Pension, no wage | 4<br>Other |
| --- | --- | --- | --- | --- | --- |
| 50–54 | 1041 | 31.8 | 22.9 | 35.4 | 9.9 |
| 55–59 | 1000 | 32.7 | 19.7 | 39.2 | 8.4 |
| 60–64 | 886 | 8.4 | 18.6 | 63.0 | 10.0 |
| >64 | 1494 | 1.2 | 10.0 | 70.2 | 18.5 |
| All | 4421 | 17.0 | 17.0 | 53.6 | 12.5 |

barriers from retirement-age policy, there is a strong interest in work among these age groups, even extending to those above the retirement age, but especially in the younger age categories. The percent receiving a pension (columns 2 plus 3) increases from 58 percent to 80 percent as age increases. It is worth noting that 17 percent of the total sample receives both a wage and a pension, but this number declines in the older age categories from 23 percent to 10 percent. Whether from necessity or choice, we do not know, but close to a fifth of older workers appear to have a mixed road to retirement that involves receiving a pension while still continuing to work. The work patterns shown here result when people can get pensions at relatively younger ages.

For many years, employment concerns have constrained aspects of pension policy, and the local administration of pension policy has been a barrier to labor mobility. Recent reforms promise to reduce these constraints. A new national Social Insurance Law became effective on July 1, 2011, which calls for a unified social security system to facilitate labor mobility. Individuals will be able to transfer accrued rights to a social security pension when moving from one province or city to another. When calculating a pension, total years of service will be accounted for, no matter where the person worked and was covered (U.S. Social Security Administration 2011, 4). However, new laws can be implemented slowly, and the timetable for this law is not yet clear.

Concerning the retirement age, Shanghai is allowing workers to delay retirement voluntarily to age 65 beginning on October 9, 2010 (AsiaNews. IT 2010). This is initially a trial limited to private-sector employees with certain technical skills, but it is expected that it will be extended to other groups. Shanghai has the largest share of the aged population among Chinese cities, and its pension deficit is rising (U.S. Social Security Administration 2010, 2). This illustrates that strong pension pressures can affect employment rules. Also, Shanghai is often a leader in policy reform, and there is a chance that other cities might eventually follow its lead.

## THE TRANSITION FROM AGRICULTURE

While the urban pension system is fairly well developed and extensive, rural pensions emerged later on a separate track. Different ministries administered the dual urban and rural pension policies, and even after administrative reorganizations, the rural system remained separate from the urban system. Following years of experiments with rural pensions, a new experimental initiative was introduced in 2009 to strengthen the rural system. Benefits were based on individual contributions, but in addition, the government for the first time subsidized a part of the benefit (Chen 2009). Originally expected to be implemented gradually up to 2020, the timing was accelerated in 2011, increasing the proportion to be covered by 2011 from 40 percent to 60 percent and completing coverage by

2013 (U.S. Social Security Administration 2011, 4). The Social Insurance Law of 2011 is described as a unified system that covers everyone, rural and urban, and the accelerated expansion of coverage is moving it to comprehensive coverage. However, benefits still differ by rural-urban location, so it remains in some ways a dual system, facing many of the same challenges as before.

One such challenge is the migration of large numbers of rural people to work in cities. Formerly, rural migrants with rural household registration would have to go back home if they needed any social benefits, as they were not covered under urban programs. But laws have changed. Not only is it easier now for those with rural registration to get work in cities, but also they are entitled by law to pension benefits from urban employers. Thus, there are two systems for rural people, the urban system for those who are being absorbed into the urban economy and the rural system for the majority who remain in the countryside. Although the systems are distinct, the people are not, and they can move back and forth between different locations and legal statuses in search of work.

For now, it would be difficult to link the existing systems. Bringing rural people who work in the countryside into the urban system has disadvantages, because urban contribution rates are high due to high legacy costs from unfunded obligations. Not only would rural residents have to pay high contribution rates without receiving any of the benefits from those legacy costs, but also, rural residents have lower wages, so a higher contribution rate would be relatively more burdensome to them. For these reasons, it seems likely that urban and rural systems will remain separate for the foreseeable future. But looking ahead, if labor mobility increases, the boundary between systems may blur, and people may find ways to game the dual systems. Eventually, when rural incomes rise and more rural people are able to participate in urban pensions, it may be feasible to open the question of integrating the systems.

## FOLLOW-UP ON EMPLOYMENT POLICY

The double concerns of promoting labor market flexibility and efficiency while protecting the rights of workers continue to this day, and tensions between the two goals also persist. A new China Employment Law was adopted in January 2008 to govern the terms of labor contracts. According to the new law, a labor contract specifying the terms of employment should be written within one month of the start of employment. Starting contracts usually specify a fixed duration, but after 10 years, the worker may receive an open-ended contract. There is also the option of a temporary contract until a project is finished. Contracts regulate termination, requiring advance notice in many cases and severance pay of one month for every year of work. There is also a provision that the state will gradually make individual pension accounts portable across the country, a provision formalized in the Social Insurance Law of 2011.

After the introduction of the new labor law, the global economic crisis began in China as elsewhere. Mass layoffs of workers occurred, with rural migrant workers particularly affected. Companies sought ways to avoid the new law. They delayed writing contracts, or if contracts already existed, some companies closed down in order to avoid paying workers what they were owed. There were cases of owners simply disappearing after workers filed claims for back pay and severance (Canaves 2009, A6). The government introduced temporary measures to ease the burden on employers, including a provision that employers having economic difficulties could apply for a moratorium or reduction in social security contributions (Fair Labor Association Blog 2009). As in the past, this policy dealt with short-term employment problems at the expense of the long-run problems of social security. But China did recover more quickly than many other countries. The temporary measures ended, and its new labor law is intact.

## CONCLUSION

China's reformers have been determined to move away from the old system of complete employment security while avoiding mass unemployment. Implementing that vision required new structures to pay pensions and other benefits so that employers could be freed to focus on productivity and global competitiveness. For 15 years, reforms were gradual in an effort to preserve jobs. UI was established, bankruptcy allowed, and pension pools set up to serve workers displaced from their enterprises, but these forms were not much used at the start. With little progress being made to reduce redundancy, it was finally decided to have a major retrenchment in employment at SOEs beginning after 1997. Other investigators have found considerable pain in terms of increased poverty and inequality resulting from the overall reform process, but have not attributed the adverse effects to specific actions such as the layoff policy. We found limited indications of a possible adverse effect on pension recipients, but the evidence is still indirect, and the full effects of the layoff policy remain to be evaluated. In the end, China could not avoid pain in its transition from socialism, but the extent of that pain has still not been fully documented.

The demographic transition affected primarily the pension system. Aging brought problems similar to those in industrial countries. China has studied pension developments in other countries closely and has debated pension policy intensely. It has made reforms, which will probably need further revision. Worries about employment have constrained any increase in the retirement age that might improve the financial balance of the pension system. While it is difficult to confirm the empirical validity of this finding, data were presented showing sizable amounts of work among older people and even close to 20 percent of the older cohorts both working and drawing pensions. Beginning in 2010, there was an easing of retirement age rules in Shanghai, perhaps an early sign of more changes to come.

The transition from agriculture is a major long-run challenge for pension policy. A new policy in 2009 sought to expand rural pensions with subsidies from government. At the same time, employment policy has made it easier for rural people to seek work in urban enterprises. Legal changes now make rural migrants eligible for urban pension programs. China will eventually have to make decisions on whether to integrate rural and urban pension systems. It appears that such integration is still far away, although employment developments like increased migration or rapidly rising rural wages might hasten it.

Although Chinese social protection seems unique, it shares features with other countries, including efforts to reduce employment rigidities, concerns about population aging, challenges associated with a segmented urban-rural pension system that resembles dual approaches in the developing world, and complex interactions among social and economic policies that make comprehensive, long-term policy planning difficult and place a premium value on intelligent incrementalism. In particular, this chapter has highlighted patterns of both synergy and obstruction between employment and pension policies, with employment concerns usually dominating social welfare concerns. Will these patterns continue, and perhaps intensify, in the wake of the global financial crisis? Future research should explore that question.

## NOTES

1 Riskin, Carl, Zhao, Renwei, and Li Shi. Chinese Household Income Project, 1995 [Computer file]. ICPSR version. Amherst, MA: Political Economy Research Institute [producer], 2000. Ann Arbor, MI: Inter-university Consortium for Political and Social Research [distributor], 2000.
2 Li Shi. Chinese Household Income Project, 2002 [Computer file]. ICPSR version. Ann Arbor, MI: Inter-university Consortium for Political and Social Research [distributor], 2008.
3 Based on interviews by the author in 1984.
4 Before and after comparisons are always limited by the fact that other things happening at the same time might be affecting the results. It might be easier to identify the effects of the *xiagang* policy if we could identify which pensioners had been laid off before retirement. There is a question on the questionnaire about *current* employment status, but retirement and laid-off status are mutually exclusive alternatives in this question. There is no information about past layoff status for a pensioner.
5 Control variables used were dummies for gender, SOE employee, age in 5-year categories (50 to 54, 55 to 59, and 65 and over, with 60 to 64 the omitted category), and province. Years of education and years of work were also included. The sample size was 6,418.

6 Other complications include the possibility that some other factor was increasing pension participation. Perhaps also those laid off were more eager to begin a pension, lacking other alternatives. Finally, there is the possibility of error. In 2002, almost all who did not have positive pensions had a zero entry. But in 1995, most who did not receive pensions had a missing code. The data instructions warn that missing does not necessarily mean zero. Thus, perhaps 1995 participation was underestimated.
7 There were meetings in several cities around the country in 1989 and 1990 to introduce local officials to ideas about individual accounts and their potential uses, and I was invited to some of these, along with officials from Singapore.

## REFERENCES

Appleton, S., J. Knight, L. Song, and Q. Xia. 2002. Labour retrenchment in China: determinants and consequences. *China Economic Review 13*(2–3): 252–275.

AsiaNews. IT. 2010. Pension reform begins in Shanghai. http://www.asianews.it/news-en/Pension-reform-begins-in-Shanghai-19628.html (October 4).

Canaves, S. 2009. Factory closures strain China's labor law. *Wall Street Journal*, January 17.

Chen, L. 2009. New pension plan to benefit China's 900 million farmers. *Global Times*. http://www.globaltimes.cn/content/454406.shtml (August 5).

China State Council. 1995. Circular of the state council on deepening of the pension insurance system. Document 6 of 1995. Beijing.

China State Council. 1997. Decisions on the establishment of the Unified Basic Pension System for Enterprise Workers. Document 26 of 1997. Beijing.

Davis, D., Y. Bian, and S. Wang. 2005. Material rewards to multiple capitals under market-socialism. In *social transformations in Chinese societies*, eds. Y. Bian, K. Chan, and T. Cheung, *1*: 31–58. Leiden, The Netherlands: Brill.

Dixon, J. 1981. *The Chinese welfare system, 1949–1979.* New York: Praeger.

Doeringer, P. B. 1990. *Bridges to retirement.* Ithaca, NY: Cornell University Press.

Dorfman, M., and Y. Sin. 2000. *China: Social security reform, technical analysis of strategic options.* Human Development Network. Washington, DC: The World Bank.

Drouin, A., and L. H. Thompson. 2006. *Perspectives on the social security system of China.* International Labor Organization. ESS Paper Number 25. Geneva, Switzerland.

Fair Labor Association Blog. 2009. China answers global crisis with new labor market policies. http://www.fairlabor.org/blog/entry/china-answers-global-crisis-new-labor-market-policies (May 20).

Institute for Labor Studies, Ministry of Labor and Social Security of China and International Labor Organization. 2004. *Study on labor market flexibility and Employment Security for China.* Beijing, China.

Khan, A. R., and C. Riskin. 2001. *Inequality and poverty in China in the age of globalization.* New York: Oxford University Press.

Konberg, B., E. Palmer, and A. Sunden. 2006. The NDC reform in Sweden: The 1994 legislation to the present. In *Pension reform: Issues and prospects for non-financial defined contribution (NDC) schemes,* eds. R. Holzmann and E. Palmer, 449–466. Washington, DC: The World Bank.

Liu, Y., and F. Wu. 2006. The state, institutional transition and the creation of new urban poverty in China. *Social Policy and Administration* 40(2): 121–137.

Naughton, B. 1996. *Growth out of the plan.* Cambridge: Cambridge University Press.

Palmer, E. 2006. What is NDC? In *Pension reform: Issues and prospects for non-financial defined contribution (NDC) schemes,* eds. R. Holzmann and E. Palmer, 17–33. Washington, DC: The World Bank.

Riskin, C., R. Zhao, and S. Li. 2001. *China's retreat from equality.* Armonk, NY: M. E. Sharpe.

Salditt, F., Whiteford, P., and Adema, W. 2007. *Pension reform in China: Progress and prospects.* Paris: OECD Social, Employment and Migration Working Papers No. 53.

Saunders, P., and S. Lujun. 2006. Poverty and hardship among the aged in urban China. *Social Policy and Administration* 40(2): 138–157.

Sin, Y. 2005. *China: Pension liabilities and reform options for old age insurance.* Washington, DC: The World Bank.

Solinger, D. J. 2002. Labour market reform and the plight of the laid-off proletariat. *The China Quarterly* 170: 304–326.

U.S. Social Security Administration. 2010. *International update, November 2010.* http://www.ssa.gov/policy/docs/progdesc/intl_update/2010-11/index.html.

U.S. Social Security Administration 2011. *International update, August 2011.* http://www.ssa.gov/policy/docs/progdesc/intl_update/2011-08/index.html.

Wang, Y., D. Xu, Z. Wang, and F. Zhai. 2001. *Implicit pension debt, transitional cost, options and impact of China's pension reform.* World Bank Working Paper 2555.

White, G. 1987. The politics of economic reform in Chinese industry: The introduction of the labor contract system. *The China Quarterly* 111: 365–389.

Wikipedia. 2009. China Employment Law (translation). http://en.wikipedia.org/wiki/China_Employment_Law.

World Bank. 1990. *China: Reforming social security in a socialist economy.* Report No. 8074-CHA: Washington, DC.

World Bank. 1994. *Averting the old age crisis.* Washington, DC: Oxford University Press.

World Bank. 1996. *China pension system reform.* Report No. 15121-CHA: Washington, DC.

# 5

# URBAN SOCIAL INSURANCE PROVISION: REGIONAL AND WORKPLACE VARIATIONS

Juan Chen and Mary E. Gallagher

## INTRODUCTION

Since the mid-1980s, the Chinese government has introduced a series of reforms to replace the old urban social security system established under the planned economy with a new social insurance system corresponding to the market economy. The main feature of the reforms was the introduction of cost-sharing: in order to finance the social insurance system, funds are contributed jointly by enterprises, individuals, and the state (Frazier 2006; Maitra et al. 2007; Nyland et al. 2006). Although the reforms have led to the expansion of social insurance coverage from state-owned enterprises to all urban enterprises, regardless of ownership type and employees' *hukou* (household registration) status, there are still great disparities in accessing social insurance benefits arising from differences in workers' *hukou* status and types of workplace ownership (Nielsen et al. 2005). The social insurance reforms were initiated at the national level, but the implementation of these regulations was delegated to localities, which led to the "segmentation" of social insurance provision across regions (Zheng and Sun 2008).

Various studies have documented the reform process and the changes in China's social insurance provisions from the perspective of government policy design and implementation (Lin and Kangas 2006; Zhu and Nyland 2005), but few researchers have examined the extent of Chinese workers' participation in these programs, the expectations and attitudes of Chinese workers toward their contributions, and the variations across regions and types of workplace ownership. Using data from the China Labor Survey (2005), which was conducted in four cities representing different geographic locations and levels of economic development, we examine social insurance provision in urban China from the workers' perspective. We focus particularly on the variations in workers' access to social insurance according to region and workplace ownership. Based on our analysis, we suggest possible approaches to reduce the disparities in social insurance provision during the reform process—approaches that take into account Chinese workers' expectations and attitudes.

## REFORMS AND EXPANSION

Before market-oriented economic reforms were introduced in China in the 1980s, its urban residents were well organized in their workplaces (*danwei*), which provided lifetime employment, medical benefits, and retirement pensions. Employees of state-owned enterprises, in particular, were in an "iron rice bowl" system and enjoyed guaranteed employment and cost-free pensions and medical benefits (Lü and Perry 1997; Walder 1986). From the perspective of state-owned enterprises adapting to market-oriented economic reforms, the old social welfare and insurance system was considered a burden that blunted their competitive edge. Government responded to these concerns by releasing state-owned enterprises from the obligation to provide social welfare, such as housing and child care, and social insurance, such as medical benefits and retirement pensions (Leung 1994).

In the 1990s, the Chinese government enacted a series of medical and pension reforms that introduced cost-sharing in the financing of social insurance. Where the state had once been the sole provider of virtually cost-free medical and pension benefits, the new enterprise-based welfare and insurance system shifted the obligation to individuals, who were required to contribute to their own medical benefits and future retirement funds. Costs are now distributed among workers, employers, and the state (Frazier 2006; Maitra et al. 2007; Nyland et al. 2006).

The social insurance reforms relieved state-owned enterprises from shouldering the entire responsibility for welfare provision. The reforms also led to the expansion of social insurance coverage from state-owned enterprises to all urban enterprises, regardless of their ownership. The same social insurance system now is applied to foreign enterprises, domestic private enterprises, and individual businesses. China's newly developed system includes old-age insurance, medical insurance, and unemployment insurance. The premiums and coverage for each insurance scheme are defined in the regulations issued by the Chinese central government and are summarized below.

## Old-Age Insurance

The new old-age insurance system for Chinese employees in urban areas was initiated in 1997 and combines pooled funds and personal accounts. Insurance premiums are jointly paid by employers and employees. The premiums paid by enterprises cannot exceed 20 percent of their total salary disbursement. Each province, autonomous region, and municipality determines its own proportion of the enterprise premium payment. Employees pay 8 percent of their wages as premiums. Self-employed individuals and those with flexible employment pay an amount equivalent to approximately 18 percent of the average wage in their locality. Initially, old-age insurance was reserved for employees of state-owned enterprises and collectively owned enterprises in urban areas. In 1999, this coverage was expanded to include foreign enterprises, domestic private enterprises, and all other types of businesses in urban areas. Provinces, autonomous regions, and municipalities decided whether to include self-employed persons in accordance with the specific conditions in their localities. In 2002, the basic old-age insurance coverage was expanded to all those with flexible employment.

## Medical Insurance

China's basic medical insurance system also combines pooled funds and personal accounts. The funds are contributed by both employers and employees. Employers pay 6 percent of the business's total salary disbursement. Employees contribute 2 percent of their wages. The program now covers all employers and employees in urban areas. People with flexible employment, including individual business owners, migrant workers, and temporary workers, can also participate in the basic medical insurance program.

## Unemployment Insurance

The unemployment insurance system for urban workers was standardized in 1999. The premiums are paid jointly by employers and employees. Employers pay 2 percent of their total salary disbursement, and individuals pay 1 percent of their wages. All enterprises and institutions in urban areas must participate in the unemployment insurance program. In the case of migrant workers, employers must pay the unemployment insurance premiums, but the workers are not required to contribute. Unemployment benefits come in a lump sum rather than in monthly payments for eligible migrant workers.

After years of trial and error, the Chinese social insurance system has assumed a concrete shape, and the number of participants continues to increase. The enrollments in the old-age insurance, medical insurance, and unemployment insurance schemes were 155.06 million, 109.02 million, and 79.75 million, respectively, in 2003 (Information Office of the State Council 2004). By the end of 2006, enrollment numbers had reached 187.66 million, 157.32 million, and 111.87 million, respectively. The annual increase was about 7 percent during the first five years of the 2000s (Zheng and Sun 2008). The rising enrollment trend continued after 2006, especially in the medical insurance scheme, which reached 237 million urban residents in 2010 (National Bureau of Statistics 2011).

## SEGMENTATION AND DISPARITY

Through various reforms, the former enterprise-based social welfare system in urban China has been transformed into a jointly funded, state-managed social insurance system (Lin and Kangas 2006). Although the design of the system was the result of long deliberation, two key issues of policy implementation remain problematic: the regional differences in social insurance management and disparities in employer compliance.

The social insurance reforms were initiated at the national level; however, the implementation of these regulations was delegated to localities, which has led to great variations in compliance, premiums, and benefits across provinces, autonomous regions, and municipalities. The phenomenon was given the name "segmentation" by Zheng and Sun (2008). Wang (2008) argues that regional disparities in economic development are the underlying cause of disparities in social insurance development. According to Wang (2008), the rankings of the old-age insurance development index (OIDI) are consistent with the level of economic development across localities: Guangdong, Shanghai, and Zhejiang are the top three, whereas Hainan, Tibet, and Chongqing are the bottom three. In general, the east coast has the highest levels of social insurance, followed by the middle inland region. The western inland area has the lowest level.

Employer non-compliance has also been a significant barrier to the implementation of equitable social insurance reforms in China. Private-sector firms are more likely to fail to pay social insurance premiums for their employees than state-owned enterprises (Gao 2001). Western and Japanese enterprises tend to adopt the good practices of their native countries (Chan 2001). Zhu and Nyland (2005) argue that the lack of an effective enforcement mechanism is the major reason for such discrepancies. In Shanghai, for example, the annual audit of businesses' insurance premiums only covers a small percentage of the firms registered. The probability of being found guilty of non-compliance is low, and, even if a business is charged, the penalties are mild. Analysis of data collected in Shanghai shows that the rate of non-compliance with social insurance obligations on the part of businesses is between 70 and 80 percent (Maitra et al. 2007; Nyland et al. 2006).

In addition, access to social insurance is still affected by workers' *hukou* status (i.e., whether they live and work in the same area where they are registered; if not, they qualify as internal migrants). Although government policy has expanded social insurance coverage to include workers with flexible employment, social insurance accounts are not portable across provinces. Nielsen and colleagues (2005, 353) note that, "there is little likelihood the majority of migrant workers who have moved to China's towns and cities will be able to access the social insurance benefits traditionally available to those with urban registration." Migrant works are, therefore, reluctant to participate in the various insurance schemes.

Although the reforms have turned China's social insurance system into a cost-sharing enterprise, Chinese workers are still inclined to believe that the government should assume full responsibility for social security. As Zhu and Nyland (2005, 67) observe, "This is particularly significant in a society that, because of its Communist history, accepts social protection is a right." Meanwhile, because of rapid economic development in the past 30 years, people also believe that the state now has the financial resources to cover social security.

Although existing studies provide useful analyses of policy development and implementation, little research has been devoted to the workers' perspective. The extent of Chinese workers' participation in social insurance programs is still unclear, and workers' attitudes toward their expected contributions have not been studied. In this chapter, we attempt to shed light on these issues by asking the following questions:

1. What kinds of social insurance coverage do workers have access to? Do they receive employer-provided old-age insurance, medical insurance, and unemployment insurance?
2. How does workers' social insurance coverage vary by region and workplace ownership? Which groups of workers still do not have access to social insurance coverage?
3. What are the workers' attitudes regarding sharing the responsibility of contributing to social insurance funds? Do they think that the employers are contributing the right amount, too much, or too little? More specifically, how do workers feel about financing old-age insurance? Do they think that the state should assume most of the responsibility? Or do they accept or prefer commercial pension insurance plans?

## DATA AND METHODS

Data for this study came from a household survey that we conducted in four cities in China in 2005. While the survey's particular focus was knowledge of, and attitudes toward, labor law and labor law disputes involving Chinese workers, it also included questions concerning workers' social insurance coverage and their feelings about social protection and sharing its costs. We confined our survey to four cities—Foshan, Chongqing, Wuxi, and Shenyang—that represent a wide range of characteristics. They vary in terms of geography, industrial sectors (and types of ownership), economic development, and integration with the global economy through trade and investment.

*Foshan*, in southern coastal China, was one of the first areas to be opened up to foreign investment and trade. It has a high level of economic development and is closely integrated with the global economy. The industrial sector is dominated by foreign and private businesses.

*Chongqing*, in southwest inland China, is the only municipality directly under the central government in western China. It is less integrated with the global economy and has a lower level of foreign direct investment than the coastal areas. Chongqing has a large state-owned enterprise sector and high levels of layoffs and unemployment.

*Wuxi*, in central coastal China, has a moderately high level of economic development, varied ownership, and increasing integration with the global economy. In Wuxi, there are few layoffs and low rates of unemployment.

*Shenyang*, in northeast inland China, is the capital of Liaoning Province. It is less integrated with the global economy and has a lower level of foreign direct investment than the southern and central coastal areas. Shenyang has a large state-owned enterprise sector, and the rates of layoffs and unemployment are high.

The survey's target population was people between 18 and 65 who had work experience and resided in dwellings within the city limits. The survey employed global positioning system and geographic information system (GPS/GIS) spatial probability sampling techniques (Landry and Shen 2005). Respondents (both permanent residents and migrant workers) were chosen by means of a four-stage population-proportional-to-size sampling. The number of respondents in the completed sample was 4,112 (over 1,000 in each city), and the overall response rate was 73 percent. In this study, we focus on workers who were employed at the time of interview and exclude those who were unemployed or did not participate in the labor market. The final sample for our analysis included a total of 2,531 workers in the four cities.

Our analysis is composed of two parts. The first part focuses on workers' access to social insurance provision. We present descriptive statistics on workers' access to social insurance coverage in each city. We then report the findings of bivariate and multiple regression analyses that we conducted to discover the associations between workers' access to social insurance provision and workplace ownership, controlling for individual characteristics, such as age, gender, education, and residence. We estimated separate models for the four cities in our study. In the second part of our analysis, we examine workers' attitudes toward sharing payment for social insurance and responsibility for social security provision, particularly for old-age insurance. The results presented are primarily descriptive in this section. Survey design effects (stratum, cluster, and individual weight) were taken into account throughout the analysis to make the weighted sample represent the target population.

## RESULTS

Table 5.1 presents the descriptive statistics of workers in each city and the variations in workers' access to old-age insurance, medical insurance, and

Table 5.1. Descriptive Statistics of Workers in Four Cities: China Labor Survey, 2005

|  | Foshan | Chongqing | Wuxi | Shenyang |
|---|---|---|---|---|
| Demographic Characteristics | | | | |
| Age (years) | 32.3 | 34.8 | 35.0 | 34.7 |
| Gender (female) | 42.4% | 40.0% | 42.1% | 43.9% |
| Education | | | | |
|    Middle school or less | 28.2% | 37.0% | 26.1% | 29.2% |
|    High school graduate | 36.5% | 30.4% | 39.4% | 28.8% |
|    College and above | 35.3% | 32.6% | 34.6% | 42.0% |
| Residency (*hukou* in the city) | 76.9% | 74.7% | 79.2% | 82.7% |
| Labor Contract | | | | |
| Signed Some Form of Contract | 60.1% | 47.2% | 62.5% | 48.0% |
| Workplace Ownership | | | | |
| Majority State-owned Enterprise | 12.3% | 23.8% | 28.8% | 22.8% |
| Domestic Private Collective Enterprise | 29.7% | 28.9% | 21.1% | 18.8% |
| Foreign Enterprise or Joint Venture | 9.3% | 3.2% | 8.9% | 6.3% |
| Self-employed[a] | 29.7% | 27.6% | 21.0% | 25.7% |
| Government and Shiye Danwei | 18.9% | 16.4% | 20.1% | 26.4% |
| Receive Social Insurance from Workplace | | | | |
| Old-Age Insurance | 61.5% | 45.5% | 73.4% | 55.4% |
| Medical Insurance | 68.5% | 44.4% | 77.1% | 57.8% |
| Unemployment Insurance | 40.1% | 24.0% | 52.7% | 37.8% |
| Sample N | 689 | 631 | 623 | 588 |

*Note:* Survey design effects (stratum, cluster, and individual weight) were taken into account in the estimations.
[a] Including individual business owners, migrant workers, temporary workers, etc.

unemployment insurance. The average age of workers in the sample is 34. About 42 percent are female. Chongqing has the highest percentage of workers with middle school education or less (37 percent), and Shenyang has the highest percentage of workers with some college education or more (42 percent). The majority of the workers have *hukou* in the city of residence (about 78 percent), and the percentage of migrant workers ranges from 20 percent in Wuxi and Shenyang to 25 percent in Foshan and Chongqing.

In terms of variations in workplace ownership across cities, Foshan has the lowest percentage of state-owned enterprises (12 percent) and the highest percentage of domestic private enterprises (30 percent) and foreign enterprises (9 percent). The enterprise ownership composition in Wuxi is diverse, with a high percentage of both state-owned enterprises (29 percent) and foreign enterprises (9 percent). Both Chongqing and Shenyang have a higher percentage of state-owned enterprises (about 23 percent) and a lower percentage of foreign enterprises (3 percent and 6 percent, respectively).

Access to social insurance coverage varies greatly across the four cities. Workers in Wuxi have the highest rates of access to all three schemes: about three-quarters have old age and health insurance, and more than half have unemployment insurance. Foshan ranks second among the four cities, followed by Shenyang. Workers in Chongqing have the worst social insurance coverage: only about 44 percent of workers in Chongqing have old-age insurance and medical insurance, and less then one-quarter are covered by unemployment insurance.

How does workers' access to social insurance vary according to workplace ownership in each city? Table 5.2 presents the results of a bivariate analysis of workers' access to social insurance and types of workplace ownership. In general, the majority of those employed by state-owned enterprises and foreign enterprises have access to social insurance coverage. In all four cities, workers in domestic private enterprises and those who are self-employed have less access

**Table 5.2.** Bivariate Analysis of Social Insurance Provision and Workplace Ownership in Four Cities: China Labor Survey, 2005

|  | Foshan | Chongqing | Wuxi | Shenyang |
|---|---|---|---|---|
| Receive Old-Age Insurance from Workplace | | | | |
| Majority State-owned Enterprise | 86.0% | 85.9% | 89.6% | 89.1% |
| Domestic Private Collective Enterprise | 60.0% | 35.5% | 65.1% | 41.3% |
| Foreign Enterprise or Joint Venture | 82.0% | 66.6% | 98.5% | 77.2% |
| Self-employed[a] | 40.4% | 11.9% | 32.1% | 17.3% |
| Government and Shiye Danwei | 70.6% | 57.1% | 91.0% | 68.4% |
| Receive Medical Insurance from Workplace | | | | |
| Majority State-owned Enterprise | 93.5% | 74.7% | 91.6% | 80.4% |
| Domestic Private Collective Enterprise | 68.0% | 32.2% | 73.8% | 41.2% |
| Foreign Enterprise or Joint Venture | 97.9% | 62.8% | 98.5% | 75.4% |
| Self-employed[a] | 47.5% | 15.0% | 35.0% | 13.8% |
| Government and Shiye Danwei | 71.5% | 67.8% | 94.4% | 88.6% |
| Receive Unemployment Insurance from Workplace | | | | |
| Majority State-owned Enterprise | 61.8% | 50.6% | 69.9% | 58.9% |
| Domestic Private Collective Enterprise | 37.6% | 16.7% | 51.0% | 26.9% |
| Foreign Enterprise or Joint Venture | 56.2% | 59.2% | 78.9% | 66.4% |
| Self-employed[a] | 27.9% | 4.5% | 16.5% | 4.5% |
| Government and Shiye Danwei | 41.3% | 24.3% | 56.1% | 53.0% |
| Sample N | 689 | 631 | 623 | 588 |

Note: Survey design effects (stratum, cluster, and individual weight) were taken into account in the estimations.
[a] Including individual business owners, migrant workers, temporary workers, etc.

to all three social insurance schemes. The workers in Chongqing and Shenyang who work in domestic private enterprises or who are self-employed have even less access than workers in Foshan and Wuxi in similar situations.

We further employ logistic regression techniques to model the associations between workers' access to social insurance provision and workplace ownership, controlling for individual characteristics, such as age, gender, education, and *hukou* status. We also include a variable in the model that indicates whether the respondent signed some form of labor contract with the enterprise. This variable enables us to determine whether labor contracts decrease the incidence of non-compliance on the part of the employers and increase workers' insurance coverage. We estimate separate models for the four cities. The regression results are reported in Table 5.3.

The results from the regression estimations are consistent with those in the bivariate analysis. After controlling for workers' demographic characteristics, workers who are in domestic private enterprises and who are self-employed are still less likely to have access to social insurance than those working in state-owned enterprises and foreign enterprises. The patterns are generally consistent across the four cities, with only one exception: in Wuxi the difference between domestic private enterprises and state-owned enterprises is only marginally significant.

The regression results also indicate that workers who are less educated are less likely to have social insurance coverage. Moreover, there are still significant differences in accessing social insurance according to *hukou* status: migrant workers are at a disadvantage.

Workers who signed some form of contract are more likely to have social insurance coverage in all three schemes and across the four cities. The coefficients are significant and indicate that labor contracts may function as an effective form of legal support and encourage employer compliance in the provision of social insurance benefits.

How do Chinese workers view the social insurance reforms? In Table 5.4, we present descriptive data on workers' attitudes toward sharing payment for social insurance and responsibility for social insurance, particularly regarding old-age insurance.

Among workers who receive social insurance from their workplace, about 60 percent think that the employers' portion of contribution to the insurance funds is appropriate. Between one-quarter and one-third of workers think that the workplace does not contribute enough. Few workers think the workplace contributes too much. In general, workers still expect that the workplace should assume the main responsibility for payments to various social insurance funds.

The above results are consistent with the responses we received to several further questions concerning old-age insurance. The majority of workers surveyed think that the employer and the worker should contribute to the old-age insurance fund, and that they should not rely on the government or a private insurance policy. This attitude is less likely to be held by workers in Foshan. Consistently,

Table 5.3. Multiple Regressions of Social Insurance Provision among Workers in Four Cities: China Labor Survey, 2005

|  | Old-Age Insurance ||||| Medical Insurance ||||| Unemployment Insurance ||||
|---|---|---|---|---|---|---|---|---|---|---|---|---|
|  | Foshan | Chongqing | Wuxi | Shenyang | Foshan | Chongqing | Wuxi | Shenyang | Foshan | Chongqing | Wuxi | Shenyang |
| Demographic Characteristics |||||||||||||
| Age (years) | 0.062** (0.021) | 0.066** (0.012) | 0.041** (0.014) | 0.081** (0.017) | 0.054+ (0.027) | 0.063** (0.013) | 0.034* (0.015) | 0.084** (0.028) | 0.037* (0.017) | 0.058** (0.018) | 0.047** (0.012) | 0.059** (0.015) |
| Gender (female) | −0.308 (0.336) | 0.358* (0.173) | 0.144 (0.418) | −0.652** (0.233) | −0.155 (0.230) | −0.275 (0.255) | 0.309 (0.445) | 0.031 (0.229) | 0.142 (0.285) | 0.066 (0.262) | −0.189 (0.228) | 0.156 (0.182) |
| Education |||||||||||||
| Middle school or less (reference) |||||||||||||
| High school graduate | −0.064 (0.388) | 1.178** (0.309) | 0.161 (0.391) | 0.116 (0.233) | 0.212 (0.358) | 0.617* (0.252) | 0.085 (0.453) | 0.032 (0.294) | −0.227 (0.376) | 1.473** (0.382) | 0.445 (0.386) | −0.158 (0.311) |
| College and above | 0.775* (0.364) | 1.872** (0.294) | 1.109** (0.473) | 1.491** (0.447) | 1.312** (0.415) | 1.547** (0.234) | 1.678** (0.519) | 1.675** (0.541) | 0.905** (0.381) | 1.669** (0.349) | 1.022 (0.608) | 1.006** (0.339) |
| Residency (*hukou* in the city) | 0.605+ (0.344) | 0.414 (0.318) | 0.926* (0.362) | 0.913+ (0.533) | 0.446 (0.318) | 0.584* (0.241) | 0.575 (0.498) | 1.049* (0.507) | 0.981* (0.411) | 0.748 (0.509) | 0.934** (0.311) | 0.678+ (0.349) |
| Labor Contract |||||||||||||
| Signed Some Form of Contract | 1.178** (0.247) | 1.021** (0.245) | 1.865** (0.331) | 1.754** (0.348) | 1.087** (0.352) | 0.896** (0.196) | 1.872** (0.368) | 1.191** (0.318) | 0.702** (0.215) | 0.917** (0.226) | 1.018** (0.168) | 1.666** (0.308) |

(*Continued*)

Table 5.3. (Continued)

| | Old-Age Insurance | | | | Medical Insurance | | | | Unemployment Insurance | | | |
|---|---|---|---|---|---|---|---|---|---|---|---|---|
| | Foshan | Chongqing | Wuxi | Shenyang | Foshan | Chongqing | Wuxi | Shenyang | Foshan | Chongqing | Wuxi | Shenyang |
| **Workplace Ownership** | | | | | | | | | | | | |
| *Majority State-owned Enterprise (reference)* | | | | | | | | | | | | |
| Domestic Private Collective Enterprise | -1.073** (0.383) | -1.704** (0.367) | -0.806+ (0.438) | -1.922* (0.706) | -1.742** (0.571) | -1.152** (0.289) | -0.626 (0.398) | -1.183* (0.436) | -0.747* (0.335) | -0.907+ (0.492) | -0.249 (0.343) | -0.747* (0.286) |
| Foreign Enterprise or Joint Venture | -0.124 (0.748) | -0.464 (0.543) | 2.327+ (1.230) | 0.240 (0.691) | 1.219 (1.050) | 0.216 (0.466) | 1.747 (1.179) | 0.897 (0.552) | -0.341 (0.605) | 1.121* (0.437) | 1.031** (0.363) | 1.278* (0.519) |
| Self-employed | -1.588** (0.567) | -2.849** (0.545) | -1.717** (0.453) | -2.558** (0.467) | -2.265** (0.498) | -1.922** (0.383) | -1.966** (0.388) | -2.414** (0.426) | -0.830** (0.250) | -1.951** (0.420) | -1.530** (0.410) | -2.263** (0.445) |
| Government and Shiye Danwei | -0.554 (0.466) | -1.637** (0.401) | 0.384 (0.435) | -1.616* (0.623) | -1.617* (0.695) | -0.273 (0.258) | 0.522 (0.498) | 0.482 (0.401) | -0.703* (0.296) | -1.144* (0.438) | -0.656* (0.313) | -0.220 (0.317) |
| Constant | -1.728+ (0.954) | -2.941** (0.700) | -1.943* (0.818) | -3.071** (0.861) | -0.579 (0.873) | -3.080** (0.486) | -1.208 (0.913) | -3.989** (1.471) | -2.544** (0.837) | -4.820** (1.115) | -3.012** (0.831) | -4.160** (0.686) |
| Wald F Statistics | 20.11 (10,25) | 31.93 (10,22) | 23.68 (10,26) | 20.33 (10,25) | 20.90 (10,25) | 41.25 (10,22) | 22.79 (10,26) | 18.73 (10,25) | 22.08 (10,25) | 108.91 (10,22) | 24.57 (10,26) | 6.98 (10,25) |

*Note:* Survey design effects (stratum, cluster, and individual weight) were taken into account in the estimations. Standard errors in parentheses; ** p<0.01, * p<0.05, + p<0.1.

Urban Social Insurance Provision 97

**Table 5.4.** Attitudes Toward Social Insurance Provision among Workers in Four Cities: China Labor Survey, 2005

|  | Foshan | Chongqing | Wuxi | Shenyang |
|---|---|---|---|---|
| *Attitudes of Workers Who Receive Social Insurance from Their Workplace:* | | | | |
| Payment for Old-Age Insurance | | | | |
|   Workplace portion too high | 3.2% | 2.0% | 2.4% | 3.2% |
|   Workplace portion appropriate | 62.8% | 63.9% | 65.9% | 56.1% |
|   Workplace portion too low | 26.0% | 26.9% | 23.9% | 33.2% |
|   Don't know or no answer | 8.1% | 7.2% | 7.8% | 7.5% |
| Payment for Medical Insurance | | | | |
|   Workplace portion too high | 2.4% | 2.4% | 1.2% | 1.2% |
|   Workplace portion appropriate | 53.7% | 56.5% | 61.3% | 57.5% |
|   Workplace portion too low | 34.6% | 30.5% | 28.8% | 34.6% |
|   Don't know or no answer | 9.3% | 10.7% | 8.7% | 6.7% |
| Payment for Unemployment Insurance | | | | |
|   Workplace portion too high | 3.6% | 2.3% | 2.2% | 1.1% |
|   Workplace portion appropriate | 57.0% | 62.7% | 58.6% | 62.2% |
|   Workplace portion too low | 27.5% | 28.4% | 28.2% | 26.0% |
|   Don't know or no answer | 11.9% | 6.7% | 11.1% | 10.6% |
| *Attitudes toward Old-Age Insurance Provision among All Workers:* | | | | |
| Who do you think should pay for the old-age insurance? | | | | |
|   Government | 32.2% | 20.8% | 25.4% | 35.4% |
|   Workplace and worker | 46.7% | 64.4% | 64.6% | 59.3% |
|   Private insurance purchase | 9.1% | 5.7% | 4.8% | 1.9% |
|   Don't know or no preference | 11.9% | 9.1% | 5.2% | 3.4% |
| People should not rely on *danwei* in providing old-age insurance, because *danwei* is only a workplace. | | | | |
|   Strongly agree | 5.9% | 6.3% | 5.9% | 3.1% |
|   Moderately agree | 25.1% | 24.7% | 28.9% | 18.3% |
|   Moderately disagree | 52.1% | 43.4% | 45.3% | 51.3% |
|   Strongly disagree | 11.5% | 18.6% | 16.9% | 24.9% |
|   Don't know or no answer | 5.4% | 7.0% | 3.0% | 2.4% |
| Having old-age insurance is each citizen's basic right. | | | | |
|   Strongly agree | 53.9% | 67.2% | 66.2% | 72.1% |
|   Moderately agree | 33.5% | 23.2% | 26.7% | 23.9% |
|   Moderately disagree | 4.2% | 3.5% | 3.2% | 2.6% |
|   Strongly disagree | 1.2% | 0.0% | 0.3% | 0.0% |
|   Don't know or no answer | 7.1% | 6.1% | 3.6% | 1.4% |

*(Continued)*

Table 5.4. (Continued)

|  | Foshan | Chongqing | Wuxi | Shenyang |
|---|---|---|---|---|
| China is not yet rich enough to provide universal old-age insurance. | | | | |
| Strongly agree | 17.5% | 23.8% | 14.6% | 24.6% |
| Moderately agree | 54.4% | 46.3% | 56.2% | 51.3% |
| Moderately disagree | 19.8% | 18.6% | 22.5% | 16.0% |
| Strongly disagree | 2.6% | 2.7% | 3.5% | 4.0% |
| Don't know or no answer | 5.7% | 8.7% | 3.1% | 4.1% |

*Note:* Survey design effects (stratum, cluster, and individual weight) were taken into account in the estimations.

workers in Foshan are also the least likely to agree that people should still rely on their workplace to provide old-age insurance.

From the perspective of citizens' rights, the majority of the workers (nearly 90 percent) believe that old-age insurance is a basic right. However, when asked whether China is rich enough to provide universal old-age insurance for all citizens, about 70 percent are realistic about the current level of development in China and agree that China is not yet rich enough to provide universal old-age insurance.

In addition to the descriptive statistics presented above, we have employed multiple regression techniques to model the associations between workers' attitudes toward social insurance provision and workplace ownership for each city, controlling for individual characteristics (results not shown). The regression results do not indicate any common or significant associations between workers' attitudes toward social insurance provision and workplace ownership across the four cities. The only exception is in Wuxi, where the self-employed are more likely to support the view that people should not rely on *danwei* in providing old-age insurance, because *danwei* is only a workplace.[1]

## DISCUSSION: SOCIAL INSURANCE REFORMS IN THE CHINESE CONTEXT

China's gradual introduction of market-oriented economic reforms during the last 30 years has radically transformed its social insurance system; rather than an "iron rice bowl" provided by the workplace, there is a new social insurance system in which costs and responsibilities are shared among workers, employers, and the state. This study's explicit focus on the workers' views on access to, and shared responsibility for, social insurance coverage addresses a key question affecting the viability of social insurance reforms in China: How have the people responded to the government-initiated policy design and implementation?

The results of this study provide a clear picture of Chinese workers' views on the social insurance reforms and of the disparities in social insurance coverage according to region and by workplace ownership. Workers in cities of high economic development (Foshan and Wuxi) have better social insurance provisions than those in cities of low economic development (Chongqing and Shenyang). Although the government's current policy requires social insurance coverage to be extended to all workers, regardless of workplace ownership, coverage for workers in domestic private enterprises and the self-employed still lags behind that provided for workers in state-owned and foreign enterprises.

To address the segmentation and disparity in social insurance provision across regions and types of workplace ownership, social insurance regulation and fund management must be centralized. In order to achieve this, the central government should consolidate social insurance management, ensure employer compliance, and make the benefits transferable across regions and workplaces. Labor contracts may provide employers with a legal initiative to comply with social insurance provisions during this process.

While workers still expect the workplace to provide social insurance benefits and believe that old-age insurance is each citizen's basic right, they are also aware of the state of China's economy and do not expect the government to establish an old-age insurance system for all citizens. Although the majority of workers are realistic about the current situation in China, the findings of different expectations and attitudes toward social insurance provision among workers in Foshan and the self-employed in Wuxi also indicate that the design and implementation of current government policies are likely to be met with various responses across regions, and that the viability of social insurance reforms in China may continue to vary across different forms of workplace ownership for the foreseeable future.

## NOTE

1  See Chapter 11 for an extended discussion of *danwei*.

## REFERENCES

Chan, A. 2001. *China's workers under assault: The exploitation of labor in a globalizing economy*. Armonk, NY: M. E. Sharpe.

Frazier, M. W. 2006. Pensions, public opinion, and the graying of China. *Asia Policy* 1: 43–68.

Gao, S. 2001. Issues and future perspective on the transition of China's pension system towards pooling funds system (in Chinese). In *Restructuring China's social security system: Funding, operation and governance*, ed. M. K. Wang, 131–135. Beijing: China Development Publishing House.

Information Office of the State Council. 2004. *China's social security and its policy*. Beijing.

Landry, P., and M. Shen. 2005. Reaching migrants in survey research: The use of global positioning system to reduce coverage bias in China. *Political Analysis 13*: 1–22.

Leung, J. C. B. 1994. Dismantling the iron rice bowl: Welfare reforms in the PRC. *Journal of Social Policy 23*(3): 341–361.

Lin, K., and O. Kangas. 2006. Social policymaking and its institutional basis: Transition of the Chinese social security system. *International Social Security Review 59*(2): 61–76.

Lü, X., and E. J. Perry. 1997. *Danwei: The changing Chinese workplace in historical and comparative perspective*. Armonk, NY: M. E. Sharpe.

Maitra, P., R. Smyth, I. Nielsen, C. Nyland, and C. Zhu. 2007. Firm compliance with social insurance obligations where there is a weak surveillance and enforcement mechanism: Empirical evidence from Shanghai. *Pacific Economic Review 12*(5): 577–596.

National Bureau of Statistics. 2011. *China statistical yearbook 2011*. Beijing: China Statistics Press.

Nielsen, I., C. Nyland, R. Smyth, M. Zhang, and C. J. Zhu. 2005. Which rural migrants receive social insurance in Chinese cities? Evidence from Jiangsu survey data. *Global Social Policy 5*(3): 353–381.

Nyland, C., R. Smyth, and C. J. Zhu. 2006. What determines the extent to which employers will comply with their social security obligations? Evidence from Chinese firm-level data. *Social Policy & Administration 40*(2): 196–214.

Walder, A. G. 1986. *Communist neo-traditionalism: Work and authority in Chinese industry*. Berkeley: University of California Press.

Wang, H. 2008. China's regional disparities in economic development and level of old-age insurance (in Chinese). Beijing: *China Network of Social Security*.

Zheng, B., and S. Sun. 2008. China's 30 years of social security reform (in Chinese). In *Blue book of development and reform (no. 1): China's 30 years of reform and opening-up (1978–2008)*, ed. D. Zou, Chapter 22. Beijing: Social Science Academic Press.

Zhu, C. J., and C. Nyland. 2005. Marketization, globalization, and social protection reform in China: Implications for the global social protection debate and for foreign investors. *Thunderbird International Business Review 47*(1): 49–73.

# 6
# HEALTH AND RURAL COOPERATIVE MEDICAL INSURANCE

Song Gao and Xiangyi Meng

## INTRODUCTION

The report of the Commission on Macroeconomics and Health of the World Health Organization (WHO) states:

> Improving the health and longevity of the poor is an *end* in itself, a fundamental goal of economic development. But it is also a *means* to achieving the other development goals relating to poverty reduction. The linkages of health to poverty reduction and to long-term economic growth are powerful, much stronger than is generally understood. (World Health Organization 2001)

Thus, health, an important type of human capital, appears to be one important determinant of economic growth (for examples, see Weil 2007; Bloom, Canning, and Sevilla 2004). Poor people in developing countries are, on average, much less healthy than their counterparts in the developed world. One public policy option for improving *poor* people's health is to provide (subsidized) health insurance, which can be justified by the positive externality of health and the lack of affordability of health care for poor people. The empirical literature on the impact of health insurance on health status finds a significantly positive effect (for a survey of previous research, see Levy and Meltzer 2001).

China developed a nationwide rural health insurance system in the 1950s, and about 90 percent of rural villages were covered by the Rural Cooperative

Medical System (RCMS) by the mid-1970s (Liu 2004). However, research on the impact of health insurance on health outcomes is rare in China, possibly due to both the difficulty and cost involved in the measurement of health status, and the lack of panel data tracing the same individuals over a long enough period of time. Most studies on China have been focused on health care financing, utilization, or participation decisions (see Liu, Rao, and Hsiao 2003; Wang et al. 2006; Wang and Rosenman 2007; Zhang et al. 2004; and Wagstaff et al. 2009). Since improving health outcomes is the ultimate goal of public policy in providing insurance to poor people, this chapter endeavors to fill this void by assessing the impact of rural cooperative insurance on subjective health measures in China. Our results show that, prior to the new insurance scheme of 2003, individual participation in rural cooperative insurance had a significantly positive impact on self-reported health, while there is no evidence of any significant impact for the new scheme after 2003. This differential impact is probably due to the existence of individual adverse selection under the new scheme, biasing the coefficient downward to zero. We find no evidence of similar bias prior to the new scheme.

The chapter is organized as follows: the next section contains a brief history of the development of China's rural cooperative medical schemes from 1955 to present; the subsequent sections present a discussion of methodology, a description of the data we use, a discussion of our main results, and our conclusions.

## BRIEF HISTORY OF COOPERATIVE MEDICAL SCHEMES

### Rural Cooperative Medical System (RCMS), Pre-2003

China's RCMS started in the 1950s at the village level, then spread from a few counties to most of the rural areas and peaked during the "Cultural Revolution" (1970s), at which time around 90 percent of Chinese rural residents were covered (Liu and Cao 1992). RCMS was an integrated part of the overall collective system for agricultural production and social services (Zhang 1992) and was managed by the RCMS Committee, consisting of the village administrative representatives and village clinics. The management committee collected the participants' premiums and managed the program; meanwhile, the participating villages provided matching funds as premium subsidies out of their welfare fund.[1] Each village operated a clinic and provided free service for patients' visits. For drugs at the clinic, some villages charged nothing, while others required some co-payments. The patients with severe diseases could be referred to a commune or county hospital or even higher level hospitals, and their outpatient and inpatient expenses (50–60 percent) would be reimbursed through the RCMS plan (Liu and Cao 1992). In summary, the RCMS plan could be considered a medical care scheme consisting of both insurance coverage and welfare subsidies. The World Bank praised it as a significant contribution to both the improvement of China's health situation and the increase in people's life expectancy, and the plan was acclaimed a successful "healthcare revolution" (World Bank 1992).

The cooperative system, with easy access to village/county clinics and health services, contributed to China's success in providing basic health care to the poor rural population when China was still a very underdeveloped country. However, severe problems arose following the overhaul of the once highly acclaimed, universal health care system in the 1980s, which accompanied market reforms in rural areas and the shift from a collective to a household responsibility system—a combination of changes that directly eroded the financial base of the Rural Cooperative Medical System. In effect, the collective welfare fund that supported RCMS premiums collapsed. Medical costs escalated during the privatization of rural healthcare, with one direct result being low health insurance coverage for rural populations. By 1984, the number of villages covered had dropped to 4.8 percent from 90 percent in the pre-reform era. This situation prompted the central government to launch a nationwide "rural primary health care" program in 1989, which resulted in a 10 percent increase in the coverage of RCMS villages by 1994 (Carrin et al. 1999). However, in spite of this effort, overall coverage was still relatively low, with only 9.5 percent of rural residents insured in 1998 (Liu 2004). With such low coverage, rural Chinese were exposed to health and financial risks, which may have had long-term negative effects on economic development when the uninsured could not obtain medical care and poor, sick people were driven further into poverty traps. Liu, Rao, and Hsiao (2003) estimated the impact of medical expenditures on the poverty head count rate and concluded that the number of rural households living in poverty was increased by 44.3 percent due to heavy medical spending.

Wagstaff et al. (2009) provide an excellent review of the old scheme: trends in health outcomes, inequalities in health and health care utilization, out-of-pocket spending and financial protection, the impacts of insurance, and so on. As their summary of the literature indicates, however, very few studies have looked at the impact of health insurance on individuals' health. Our research seeks to fill that gap and to provide a new perspective on both old and new rural cooperative medical systems.

## New Rural Cooperative Medical System (NCMS)

In October 2002, the Chinese government announced a new initiative to gradually establish the New Rural Cooperative Medical System (NCMS) focusing on inpatient care. This new initiative was launched in 2003 and was planned to cover the entire rural population by 2010 (State Council 2002). NCMS is a matching fund composed of central government subsidy, county government contributions, and individual contributions (poor rural residents' contributions are waived), with an individual premium at 10 yuan per person per year. The subsidies from central and local governments are large—originally 20 yuan, and 40 yuan since 2006.

One distinct feature of this new scheme is that it is operating at the county level instead of the village level. There is considerable heterogeneity in the specific benefits packages across counties in terms of services covered (especially outpatient versus inpatient), deductibles, expenditure caps, and co-payment rates. The NCMS program is voluntary, and the enrollment unit is required to be the household rather than the individual. By requiring all of the members of a household (whether sick or well) to participate in the program together, or opt out together, policy designers hoped to reduce the adverse selection problem, but in practice there were many partially enrolled households—a fact that suggests the persistence of adverse selection (Wang et al. 2006). Adverse selection is a classic problem in insurance markets. In the case of health insurance, it refers to the fact that people with worse health are more likely to buy health insurance plans, thus driving premiums beyond the limits of affordability and defeating the purpose of insurance to spread the financial risks and costs of illness across a broad population of more and less healthy people. Without a large enough budget to provide health insurance to everyone under a universal coverage scheme, measures are needed to ensure that the costs of any insurance program are covered either through differential pricing (charging sicker people higher premiums) or by limiting coverage of expenditures. Otherwise the insurance program will not be financially sustainable. Requiring all household members to take up the program brings a greater mix of more and less healthy people into the insurance pool and reduces adverse selection. Under this arrangement, the degree to which adverse selection persists is a function of health status differences across households.

It is not necessarily the case that providing a new subsidized insurance scheme will attract all rural residents to the program. Wang and Rosenman (2007) studied the differences between rural residents' perceived need and actual demand for health insurance and found that "only less than half of the rural residents realize the need of health insurance and only one fifth of them actually purchase it." In another study Zhang et al. (2004) collected data before the start of the new insurance system and focused on the farmers' willingness to join NCMS; they found the probability of an individual farmer's willingness to join to be only 50 percent, and both community-level and individual-level social capital were positively associated with this probability. Wagstaff et al. (2009) used the difference-in-differences method to evaluate the new rural cooperative insurance scheme in 15 counties (10 were program pilots). They found lower enrollment among poor households and higher enrollment among households with chronically sick members. Wang et al. (2006) also found that individuals with worse health status were more likely to enroll in NCMS than individuals with better health status, thus demonstrating the existence of adverse selection despite efforts by the new scheme's designers to use households rather than individuals as the enrollment unit. This problem clearly stems from incomplete compliance and the local practice of allowing partial household enrollment.

The NCMS program focuses on catastrophic diseases. Moreover, due to limited funding sources, many services are either not provided or only partially provided. These limitations raise an important policy question about the likely impact of participation on insured residents' utilization of both preventive and medical care. Wagstaff (2009) found that the new insurance scheme increased outpatient and inpatient utilization by 20 to 30 percent on average, but the impact was unevenly distributed. No impact on out-of-pocket spending or utilization was found among the poor, which means that the percentage increase in utilization among the non-poor was higher than 20 to 30 percent.

Notwithstanding the above uncertainties about the impacts of NCMS, on January 21, 2009, the Chinese government announced that an additional 850 billion RMB[2] (roughly US$125 billion) would be spent collectively by the central and local governments over the next three years on five specific areas:

1. Expanding insurance coverage to over 90 percent of the population, and substantially increasing the amount of subsidies for residents to enroll in NCMS in 2010.[3] That goal was achieved by the end of 2009, at which point NCMS had spread to 2,716 counties and covered 833 million rural residents, accounting for over 90 percent of the total rural population. Correspondingly, the average amount of subsidy spent on inpatient care increased from 690 RMB in 2003 to 1,180 RMB in 2009.

2. Establishing a national basic medicine system and mandating NCMS to include these basic medicines as reimbursable;

3. Increasing government spending on public health services, thereby reducing the inequality of basic public health services across regions;

4. Establishing a comprehensive system of primary care facilities, focusing on county hospitals, township health centers, village clinics in remote areas, and community health centers in poor urban areas; and

5. Reforming the public hospital system.[4]

Although it is still too early to draw conclusions about the progress of this call for further reforms, several researchers have applauded the policy move as a step in the right direction. However, many are still worried that the hoped-for improvements might not occur until some other systematic reforms are in place. For example, Wagstaff et al. (2009) emphasize two other reforms. First, they argue that it is imperative to make "a shift from reimbursement insurance to a contractual model where insurers pay providers and copayments become set on a per case basis rather than a fee-per-item-of-service basis." Second, they argue that it is crucial to reform the role of government in setting prices for drugs and procedures that are not covered under the insurance, "eliminating providers' incentive to shift demand from covered to uncovered services." Yip and Hsiao (2009) make similar observations.

As described above, most studies of the impact of NCMS have used data either from the pilot period or from the first two years or so of the new program. Therefore, nothing has been learned about the relative longer term impact of NCMS. Our data covers both the pre-program period, prior to 2003, and the phasing-in period of the new scheme, which allows us to have a wide enough window to evaluate the impact of health insurance on health status, if there is any. Thus, even if we could not find any impact of NCMS due to data limitations (3 years after the introduction of NCMS), any positive impact found under the old schemes will suggest possible positive gains for the health of rural households under NCMS.

## EMPIRICAL METHODOLOGY

The key dependent variable in the empirical analysis is individual health outcome. There exists a large body of literature on using survey-based health measures as indicators of various components of health or overall health. These health measurements are usually divided into two categories: objective and subjective. Objective measures often include specific physical limitations such as Activities of Daily Living (ADL) and disease indicators. For subjective health measures, individuals often answer a global question on self-assessment of health. That question is asked in the following way in our study: "Right now, how would you describe your health compared to that of other people at your age: excellent, good, fair, or poor?" It has been shown that subjective, self-rated health is a robust indicator of general physical health status in terms of morbidity, disability, and mortality. The China Health and Nutrition Survey (CHNS) provides only limited information about interviewees' disease history, while all adults were asked to rate their health in the above four-scale question. Therefore we consider the self-reported health status as the best available overall health measure in this study. We code the self-report of health as a four-scale variable with values of 1 to 4 (1 representing poor health, 4 representing excellent health).

The main independent variable is the individual's rural cooperative insurance status in the previous survey year, which is also self-reported (details are available in the following section). As noted above, most studies use concurrent insurance status with data spanning, at most, a couple of years; these studies do not take into account the time needed for health insurance to have any effect on health. With the longer period covered by our sample, we use the individual's health insurance status in the previous period as our insurance variable.

### Identification

To identify the causal effects of health insurance on health improvement, the ideal is to randomly assign health insurance to individuals. Although we do not have random assignment in this study, other features of the available data help ensure the validity of the results:

1. *Exogenous variation in individual probability of taking up the insurance.* The cooperative feature of this rural insurance scheme means that either it is a collective action of all individuals in a certain village, or it is enacted by command from the district government, whose executive level is above villages in rural China's administrative ladder. This implies two possibilities: one is that the individual probability of taking up the insurance will be zero if the village has no such arrangements, regardless of whether the collective action to set it up failed or the district government neither had interest in nor could afford its setup; the other possibility is that, even in a village with this insurance setup, there is still a large degree of variation in individual participation rate across each village, due to either adverse selection or lack of trust in local governments. Therefore we argue that the fact that a village has such an insurance scheme[5] increases individuals' participation rate *exogenously*. Our main identification strategy is to use the existence of village cooperative insurance as an instrument for individuals' insurance status. Besides its indirect effect on health through individual health insurance, the existence of village health insurance has no direct effect on health.

2. *Self-reported health as perceptions of health.* "While important, perceptions are likely related to values, background, beliefs, and information, all of which are systematically related to socioeconomic characteristics, including wages and income" (Strauss and Thomas 1995). One possibility is that people with little access to health care (due to lack of insurance) might feel that they are in better health, while people who use health care report worsened health, even if their objective health measure actually improved (Strauss and Thomas 1995). But this should be a concern only if we found a significantly negative impact of health insurance on self-reported health. A significantly positive impact will serve as a lower bound of the *true* effect.

3. *Adverse selection.* One big concern is that adverse selection—the phenomenon in which people with worse health are more likely to take up insurance—would bias our estimate of health impacts downward to zero in statistical terms due to unobserved differences in health status between the treatment and comparison groups. However, as discussed above, a significantly positive impact of health insurance participation on self-reported health will serve at least as a lower bound of the *true* effect.

## Econometric Model

For ease of calculation, exposition, and interpretation, we further collapse the four-scale self-reported health measure to a 0–1 variable, with 1 being good health (including good and excellent health) and 0 being bad health (including so-so and bad health). We first estimate an ordered Probit model using the four-scale dependent variable without controlling for the endogeneity of individual insurance participation to get preliminary measurement of the relationship between health insurance and health outcome. Then we perform an instrumental Probit model analysis based on the pooled data of six waves (1991–2006) with individual cooperative insurance being instrumentalized; cluster estimation is performed to adjust standard errors for possible serial correlation for any given individual. The standard setup in the literature starts with a latent index model as the following,

$$HS^*_{i,t+1} = \beta_1 COOPins_{i,t} + \beta_2 HS_{i,t} + \beta_3 X_{i,t+1} + \varepsilon_{i,t+1} \qquad (1)$$

where $HS^*$ is the individual's latent[6] health status, $COOPins$ is an indicator variable taking on 1 if the individual has cooperative health insurance, $HS_{i,t}$ is the lagged self-reported health, and $X$ is the vector of all other demographic and economic factors, including age, age squared, sex, education levels, occupation (agricultural vs. non-agricultural), marital status, household size, and household per capita income, to control for individual and household heterogeneity. We also include village dummies and year dummies to tease out the administrative differences and aggregate shocks to all these villages.

Then

$$\Pr ob(HS_{i,t+1} = 1) = \Phi(HS^*_{i,t+1} > 0) \qquad (2)$$

where $\Phi$ is the normal CDF.

To purge the possible endogeneity of individual health insurance, we use the existence of a village insurance scheme as the instrumental variable to individual enrollment status.[7] We will present both the first step and the second step results.

## DATA

This chapter uses longitudinal data from the China Health and Nutrition Survey (CHNS). The first round of the survey was conducted in 1989, and six follow-up surveys were collected in 1991, 1993, 1997, 2000, 2004, and 2006. This longitudinal survey is designed to catch the ongoing changes in China in the last 20 years in health and nutrition, family planning, demographic, and economic factors. It was conducted in nine provinces (Guangxi, Guizhou, Heilongjiang, Henan, Hubei, Hunan, Jiangsu, Liaoning, and Shandong), which differ in geography, economic development, public resources, and health indicators. Both urban and rural areas are randomly selected using a multistage cluster process. About 4,400 households and 19,000 individuals were interviewed. This survey covers a period of reform in China, and it is expected to demonstrate how the society and Chinese people are responding to these changes. Individual surveys, household surveys, and community surveys are conducted separately, with detailed questions about health-related issues, as well as demographic and economic information, including health status, health insurance coverage, health behaviors, and health care utilization at the individual level, the medical provider level, and the community level (health facilities level).

Health and Rural Cooperative Medical Insurance   109

This chapter examines the influence of rural cooperative health insurance on the health outcomes of insurance participants. Therefore we focus the analysis on rural residents only. As previously mentioned, participation in the rural cooperative health insurance system experienced a dramatic decrease due to health care system reform since the 1980s, and it remained at a constant low level for many years. In 2003, the Chinese government began to experiment with the new rural cooperative health insurance program in selected areas and expanded it to the national level afterward. This coincided with a big jump in participation after 2003. Because the promotion of the rural cooperative health insurance system usually focuses on the county level, questions about participation are asked at both the individual and community levels. In order to capture such effects and other village heterogeneity, we use community (village) level data as controls, such as the time-varying village average income (reported by the village leader) and village fixed effects, in addition to individual-level reporting.

We use self-reported health as the overall health outcome measurement, and therefore must drop the 1989 data because that year's survey did not ask the question about self-reported health. Second, we drop children and adolescents younger than 16 because the survey did not ask about their subjective health status, which results in a sample of 7,223 respondents in 1991, 7,133 in 1993, 7,599 in 1997, 6,577 in 2000, 7,037 in 2004, and 6,861 in 2006. Finally, in order to utilize as much information as possible, we pool all six waves of data together.

Table 6.1 shows the rural cooperative insurance take-up rates by individual and village over the years 1991–2006.[8] Even though 2003 was the starting year of the new rural cooperative insurance, we still observed changes between 1991 and 2000 given the existence of the old RCMS. With the exception of 1997, when

**Table 6.1.** Cooperative Insurance Take-up Rate (%)

| Year | 1991 | 1993 | 1997 | 2000 | 2004 | 2006 |
|---|---|---|---|---|---|---|
| **Individual insurance** | | | | | | |
| % of insured villagers | 5.45 | 0.17 | 10.8 | 6.37 | 10.4 | 37.5 |
| Number of villagers | 7,223 | 7,133 | 7,599 | 6,577 | 7,037 | 6,861 |
| **Village insurance** | | | | | | |
| % of villages with co-op insurance | 11 | 3.94 | 33.9 | 17.5 | 22.9 | 60.8 |
| Number of villages | 127 | 127 | 124 | 120 | 144 | 143 |

*Notes:* Whether a village provided cooperative insurance in either 1991 or 1993 was NOT asked. However, we partially infer the information from individual insurance status: if the number of villagers having cooperative insurance in a certain village is at least 2 (using 2 as a cutoff point to avoid reporting error), we label this village as one of the villages that provide cooperative insurance; otherwise, this village is labeled as having no cooperative insurance. So a potential measurement error is that some villages that provided cooperative insurance even though no one in the village participated are mislabeled as having no cooperative insurance. Although there is a big attrition in 1997 (with Liaoning province being dropped due to non-participation in the survey and Heilongjiang province being added to the sample), dropping these two provinces from our sample does not change the above trend.

the participation rates of both individuals and villages were higher,[9] all other years were lower than 10 percent. A surprising finding is that the lowest rates occurred in 1993, which is inconsistent with previous findings by Carrin et al. (1999). This is probably due to methods of data collection in 1993, as well as reporting bias. The take-up rates were higher after 2003 due to the launch of the new insurance plan, which is consistent with the statistics disaggregated by provinces (Table 6.2). Moreover, the provincial data demonstrate dramatic variation across provinces, with Jiangsu and Shandong having cooperative insurance over all years and much higher participation rates than those of other provinces. One possible explanation could be that the two provinces had a relatively better economic situation during the study period. Table 6.3 shows the average village per capita income (adjusted for inflation to 2006) by insurance status over years. It consistently reveals that those villages under cooperative insurance coverage were richer than their uninsured counterparts. For example, the per capita income of participating villages was about 67 percent, 97 percent, 52 percent, 85 percent, 32 percent, and 21 percent higher than that of non-participating villages in 1991, 1993, 1997, 2000, 2004, and 2006. The income gap between insured villages and uninsured villages dramatically drops after 2003, which implies that more poor villages participated in the new cooperative health scheme.

Table 6.4 indicates the average of the four-scale self-reported health status by insurance status. A higher score implies better health. We find that insured people had better average health than uninsured people before 2006 (except 1993), but the situation changed in 2006, with uninsured people faring better than insured people, although the difference is not significant. This might be due to the strong self-selection into the new insurance coverage after 2003, as poorer people with worse health gained access to the health insurance scheme without much cost. Thus, people with poorer health were more likely to participate in the new insurance scheme than healthier people. Alternatively, as discussed above, perhaps the poor residents who were previously uninsured began to feel less healthy once they acquired insurance and sought medical advice. Going to the doctor may have reduced their self-reported health. This makes the health outcome and health insurance status simultaneously affect each other, resulting in a possible endogeneity in our estimation for the post-2003 waves of data. To reduce such effects, we use cooperative insurance in the previous period as our main policy variable to explore whether it has any influence on Chinese rural residents' health. Insurance status in the previous period is a better indicator than current insurance status, because it takes into account the time lag between starting insurance coverage, seeking treatment, and achieving better health.

Basic demographic and economic information is shown in Table 6.5. We define people as elderly if they are older than 55. Over the course of the study, the sampled individuals are getting older. It is not surprising that very few people in rural China received high school education or beyond, while the percentage of people who graduated from high school increases over years. Over the period

**Table 6.2.** Cooperative Health Insurance Take-up Rate by Province (%)

| | Liaoning | Heilongjiang | Jiangsu | Shandong | Henan | Hubei | Hunan | Guangxi | Guizhou |
|---|---|---|---|---|---|---|---|---|---|
| 1991 | 0.13 | — | 38.3 | 0.36 | 0.20 | 7.08 | 0.12 | 0 | 0 |
| 1993 | 0.27 | — | 0.46 | 0.24 | 0.11 | 0.12 | 0 | 0.1 | 0.09 |
| 1997 | — | 0 | 27.9 | 30.5 | 18.1 | 4.97 | 1.05 | 3.77 | 0 |
| 2000 | 0 | 0 | 30.1 | 15.8 | 1.48 | 0.73 | 0 | 3.50 | 2.87 |
| 2004 | 0 | 7.8 | 50.2 | 14.1 | 0 | 5.63 | 11.4 | 0.44 | 5.09 |
| 2006 | 50.4 | 42.6 | 59.4 | 41.2 | 24.9 | 46.5 | 13.9 | 25.7 | 35.6 |

**Table 6.3.** Average Per Capita Income by Cooperative Insurance Status (Yuan)

| Year | 1991 | 1993 | 1997 | 2000 | 2004 | 2006 |
|---|---|---|---|---|---|---|
| Villages with cooperative insurance | 3,606 | 5,088 | 4,429 | 6,572 | 6,946 | 6,973 |
| Villages without cooperative insurance | 2,158 | 2,586 | 2,910 | 3,555 | 5,241 | 5,769 |

covered by the study, more rural residents quit their agricultural jobs, migrating to urban areas or taking up non-agricultural jobs. The per capita income of each household has been adjusted for local inflation and reflects the real income level, using 2006 as the base year. The per capita income of rural residents increased by 1.9 times over the course of the study, from 1991 to 2006.

## RESULTS

Table 6.6 presents the preliminary regression results of an ordered Probit analysis without controlling for the endogeneity of individual insurance participation. Even though the coefficients of such models cannot be interpreted directly, they can reflect the direction and magnitude of variables of interest. The impact of the lagged measure of individual cooperative insurance is significant and positive on individual's health status. In other words, health insurance coverage appears to improve people's health. The baseline health score also affects current health significantly, which is consistent with Grossman's health production theory. The *Break* dummy is the time dummy to indicate whether the data are from 2004 and 2006, that is, after the launch of the new rural cooperative insurance. Although the *Break* dummy is not significant, its interactive terms with individual insurance and village insurance have significantly negative impacts on health. The summary statistics suggest that after the 2003 launch of the new cooperative insurance plan, more people with worse health participated. The negative interactive coefficients imply that villages with an overall poorer health situation are more likely to participate in the new insurance, and individuals with poorer health are more likely to take up the insurance. It is widely known that economic condition is one determinant in health insurance take-up. Table 6.3 (above) shows a decreasing gap in incomes

**Table 6.4.** Self-Reported Health Status by Cooperative Insurance

| Year | 1991 | 1993 | 1997 | 2000 | 2004 | 2006 |
|---|---|---|---|---|---|---|
| Insured | 2.84 | 2.41 | 2.95 | 2.85 | 2.71 | 2.60 |
| Uninsured | 2.84 | 2.84 | 2.84 | 2.75 | 2.67 | 2.66 |

**Table 6.5.** Summary Statistics on Demographics

| Variables | 1991 | 1993 | 1997 | 2000 | 2004 | 2006 |
|---|---|---|---|---|---|---|
| Male | 0.5 | 0.5 | 0.51 | 0.48 | 0.49 | 0.48 |
| Age | 37.49 | 38.17 | 39.73 | 42.77 | 45.70 | 47.44 |
| Elder | 0.16 | 0.17 | 0.19 | 0.22 | 0.29 | 0.33 |
| Married | 0.7 | 0.7 | 0.71 | 0.78 | 0.84 | 0.85 |
| Education (>=High School) | 0.1 | 0.11 | 0.12 | 0.14 | 0.16 | 0.18 |
| Han Ethnicity | 0.84 | 0.84 | 0.86 | 0.84 | 0.86 | 0.86 |
| Household Size | 4.65 | 4.61 | 4.33 | 4.07 | 3.87 | 3.97 |
| Real Per Capita Income (2006 Yuan) | 2,312 | 2,679 | 3,453 | 4,293 | 5,627 | 6,618 |
| Agriculture | 0.74 | 0.7 | 0.7 | 0.67 | 0.62 | 0.6 |

between insured villages and uninsured villages over time. From another perspective, it reflects that more villages with lower income and poorer health have participated in the program.

In addition, we find that rural male residents were more likely to have better health than females and that marital status was not a significant predictor of health status after we controlled for economic situation and baseline health status. The natural aging process significantly deteriorated people's health. More individual income provided more access to health care and generated better health outcomes. From the macro level, we found that, apart from Heilongjiang and Shandong, all of the other six provinces demonstrated overall worse health status compared to Jiangsu province. This might be attributed to both economic status and environmental conditions.

Table 6.7 presents the results of the marginal effects of individual cooperative health insurance on different health outcomes. Cooperative insurance significantly influenced all four health outcomes. It reduced the probability of having poor health by 2 percentage points and the probability of having fair health by 9 points. In contrast, it increased the probability of having good health by 4 percentage points and the probability of having excellent health by 7 points.

Surprisingly, we find that the launch of the new rural cooperative insurance scheme had negative effects on health outcomes. To explore this non-intuitive result further, we estimated the effects of health insurance on health status separately in both pre- and post-2003 periods, using an instrumental variable approach. The IV Probit results are presented in Table 6.8. For the first stage results, the existence of cooperative insurance schemes at the village level had a significantly positive impact on individual insurance participation both pre-2003 and post-2003, with a larger magnitude during the latter period (post-2003). The t statistics, although not reported here, are in the 60–90 range, and the explained variation in the first stage is 30–40 percent. These statistics imply that the existence of some cooperative

## 114 CHINESE SOCIAL POLICY IN A TIME OF TRANSITION

Table 6.6. Effects of Rural Cooperative Health Insurance on Health Outcomes

| Variables | Coefficients |     |
|---|---|---|
| Individual Insurance (t-1) | 0.307 | *** |
| Village Insurance (t-1) | 0.015 |  |
| Health (t-1) | 0.294 | *** |
| Individual Insurance * Break | −0.269 | *** |
| Village Insurance * Break | −0.147 | ** |
| Break | 0.006 |  |
| Have other Insurance | 0.058 |  |
| Male | 0.208 | *** |
| Age | −0.026 | *** |
| Age squared | 0.000 |  |
| Elder (55 plus) | −0.083 | * |
| Married (1/0) | −0.037 |  |
| Higher Education (1/0) | −0.020 |  |
| Han Ethnicity (1/0) | −0.038 |  |
| Household Size | 0.008 |  |
| Adjusted Per Capita Income (Yuan) | 0.000 | *** |
| Agricultural Job (1/0) | −0.065 | ** |
| Liaoning | −0.106 | * |
| Heilongjiang | 0.247 | *** |
| Shandong | 0.207 | *** |
| Henan | −0.178 | *** |
| Hubei | −0.205 | *** |
| Hunan | −0.052 |  |
| Guangxi | −0.367 | *** |
| Guizhou | −0.270 | *** |

Significance levels: ***1%; **5%; *10%.

insurance scheme is a potentially strong instrumental variable determining individual (household) participation decisions, because an individual cannot participate if he or she lives in a village without such a scheme. The better the baseline health was, the higher the probability of participating in cooperative insurance

Table 6.7. Marginal Effects of Individual Cooperative Insurance on Health

| Self-reported Health | Poor Health | Fair Health | Good Health | Excellent Health |
|---|---|---|---|---|
| Marginal Effects | −0.019*** | −0.087*** | 0.040*** | 0.067*** |

Significance levels: ***1%; **5%; *10%.

**Table 6.8.** Effects of Rural Cooperative Health Insurance on Health Outcomes by Time

| Variable | pre–2003 | | post–2003 | |
|---|---|---|---|---|
| First Stage | | | | |
| Village Insurance (t–1) | 0.356 | *** | 0.908 | *** |
| Health (t-1) | 0.006 | * | −0.004 | |
| Adjusted Per Capita Income | 0.000 | | 0.000 | * |
| Male | −0.003 | | −0.002 | |
| Age | 0.000 | | 0.003 | *** |
| Age squared | 0.000 | | 0.000 | *** |
| Married | 0.005 | | 0.007 | |
| Higher Education | −0.009 | * | −0.021 | *** |
| Han Ethnicity | 0.001 | | −0.001 | |
| Household Size | 0.001 | | −0.004 | ** |
| Village Per Capita Income | 0.000 | | 0.000 | |
| Second Stage | | | | |
| Individual Insurance (t-1) | 0.592 | *** | −0.214 | |
| Health (t-1) | 0.226 | *** | 0.418 | *** |
| Adjusted Per Capita Income | 0.002 | *** | 0.001 | *** |
| Male | 0.159 | *** | 0.219 | *** |
| Age | −0.023 | *** | −0.031 | *** |
| Age squared | 0.000 | | 0.000 | |
| Married | −0.008 | | −0.004 | |
| Higher Education | 0.153 | *** | 0.095 | |
| Han Ethnicity | −0.068 | | 0.050 | |
| Household Size | 0.031 | *** | 0.004 | |
| Village Per Capita Income | −0.002 | | −0.001 | |

Significance levels: ***1%; **5%; *10%.

was before 2003. However, this effect disappeared after 2003. After purging the endogenous individual insurance effects in the second stage, we find that having cooperative insurance in the previous period improved current health status in a significant way before 2003, while this effect is totally gone after 2003.

As mentioned above, this is probably caused by the adverse selection of individual villagers when they have the choice of participating in the cooperative insurance scheme. To examine this, we did a simple test for the existence of adverse selection. Table 6.9 shows the marginal effects of health and village-level insurance on individual insurance take-up before and after 2003. People with bad health are more likely to join in the pre-2003 period. However, after we control for village-level insurance, individual health status becomes insignificant, which shows that using village-level insurance as the instrument could purge individual

Table 6.9. Relationship Between Individual Insurance, Health, and Village Insurance

| pre-2003 | | | post-2003 | | |
|---|---|---|---|---|---|
| **Without Village Insurance** | | | **Without Village Insurance** | | |
| Good Health | −0.014 | ** | Good Health | −0.041 | *** |
| **With Village Insurance** | | | **With Village Insurance** | | |
| Good Health | 0 | | Good Health | −0.038 | *** |
| Village Insurance | 0.5 | *** | Village Insurance | 0.59 | *** |

Significance levels: ***1%; **5%; *10%.

adverse selection. For the post-2003 estimation, with or without controlling for village-level insurance, health status persistently has significantly negative effects on individual insurance take-up, implying that poor health increases the individual probability of taking up the insurance. This difference between the two periods supports our previous claim that adverse selection might bias the health effects coefficient down to zero, even if there is actually a significantly positive effect of insurance status on health status as found in the literature.

## CONCLUSION

The determinants of individuals' health include initial health endowments and health investment. In rural China, people invest in health mainly by spending out of pocket on health care, which most rural peasants, especially the poor, find unaffordable. To reverse the post-1980 trend of declining insurance coverage, the Chinese government launched the new cooperative health insurance scheme in 2003 and expanded it to 90 percent of the rural population by 2010. This study contributes to the literature by evaluating whether cooperative health insurance—both the old and new—improves health or not, and how large the effects are.

Using a unique longitudinal data set (CHNS), which provides a long enough time span and an arguably good instrument for measuring health insurance take-up, we find both statistically and economically significant effects of cooperative health insurance on Chinese rural residents' health after controlling for initial health status, other health investment, the launch time of the new health insurance plan, and other related factors. The old rural cooperative health insurance scheme had a robust positive effect on subjective health, while the new one has not yet shown any impact. The latter result might be attributed to two factors: first, the period between taking up the new insurance scheme and improving health is not long enough for us to see any effect; second, adverse selection characterizes the new insurance scheme.

The problem of adverse selection is now on the verge of disappearing due to near-universal participation in the NCMS, and so may be future opportunities to measure the effects of participation on health status using comparison-group methods. By 2008, the NCMS basically covered all rural areas. By 2011, the NCMS covered 0.832 billion people, and the individual participation rate was over 96 percent. With the goal of universal health insurance coverage in rural areas largely secured and the comparison group of rural people without insurance nearly eliminated, the counterfactual for policy research no longer exists. Service coverage has expanded alongside increased participation: By 2011, hospitalization expenses within the policy scope were reimbursed up to 70 percent, and more than 85 percent of the covered areas enforced the outpatient services. In 2012, the Chinese government raised the standard NCMS subsidy per person and expanded medical coverage to include additional diseases such as uremia and lung cancer (Chinese Government Work Report 2012).

Future research should continue to track the impacts of the new scheme, even after it achieves 100 percent universal coverage, by evaluating the effects of differential insurance terms on health. Our research on the effects of the old cooperative insurance supports the policy recommendation that providing poor people with access to health care improves their health, which is beneficial for economic growth, and this conclusion reinforces the consensus among most scholars. As NCMS coverage expands and the adverse selection problem fades away, policymakers no longer need to worry about attracting healthier people into the scheme and can focus instead on the growing challenge of providing health services to mobile rural residents.

## NOTES

1 The welfare fund is a collective fund accumulated over time by retaining a fixed portion of village earnings every year.
2 This is the total amount to be spent for both rural and urban residents. As our focus is on rural cooperative medical systems, we will list only those spending areas that are directly relevant to rural residents.
3 The total amount of subsidy from central and local governments increased further to 120 RMB in 2010, a sixfold increase since the inception of NCMS. http://www.mof.gov.cn/zhengwuxinxi/caijingshidian/zgxww/201001/t20100106_256631.html, 2010.
4. The standing conference of the State Council of China adopted "Guidelines for Furthering the Reform of Health-care System in Principle" (Ministry of Health of China).
5 Even though, during the health care reform that began in the 1980s, the majority of rural villages had lost their cooperative health insurance coverage, there are still some villages that kept the old RCMS coverage for different reasons. Most such villages were located in eastern coastal areas with better economic development conditions. By November 1997, the coverage rate in Guangzhou and Dongguan was about 30%, and it exceeded 70% in

Shenzhen and Foshan. However, in central and western China, especially in the poor areas, the RCMS coverage was below 3.24% (Song 2007). The old RCMS mainly focused on providing basic health care and drugs, while the NCMS focuses on catastrophic diseases to relieve the poverty burden caused by diseases. The NCMS has gradually taken the place of the old RCMS, with diversified coverage in terms of benefits, services, and reimbursement according to the local economic development of each county. This variable can measure the overall health care access situation of a specific district.

6 Latent variables are variables that are not directly observed but can be inferred from other variables that are observed and measured.

7 The instrumental variables (IV) approach is designed to estimate causal relationships when controlled experiments are not feasible. Statistically, the benefit of using the IV method is that it allows consistent estimation of the causal variable when some of the explanatory variables are correlated with the error terms, which occurs when there is reverse causation, unobserved omitted variables, or measurement error. To put it differently, the IV method allows consistent estimation when there are unobserved confounding factors in establishing the causal relationship.

8 The community survey only asked about village cooperative insurance since 1997. Therefore, based on individual health insurance status for each village, we construct the existence-of-village-health-insurance variable for 1991 and 1993, using the following criteria: if no one has any cooperative insurance within a certain village, this village is considered to have no cooperative health scheme. If there are at least two villagers who report having cooperative health insurance, we regard the corresponding village as having a cooperative insurance scheme. If only one individual in a village reported having this insurance, we label the village as having no health insurance, to avoid the case that it is due to typing error in the survey. This is just a minor change, which should not have any substantial effect. Dropping 1991 and 1993 data altogether does not change our main results.

9 In January 1997, the Chinese central government made "The Decision about Health Care Reform and Development" and tried to reestablish the cooperative medical scheme in rural China through experiments in some chosen areas. Hence, we observe a higher RCMS coverage rate in 1997. However, this was not a successful experiment, in that it covered only 17 percent of rural villages and only 9.6 percent of rural residents participated in it.

## REFERENCES

Baker, M., M. Stabile, and C. Deri. 2004. What do self-reported, objective, measures of health measure? *Journal of Human Resources* 39(4): 1067–1093.

Bloom, D. E., D. Canning, and J. Sevilla. 2004. The effect of health on economic growth: A production function approach. *World Development XXXII*: 1–13.

Carrin, G., A. Ron, H. Yang, H. Wang, T. H. Zhang, L. C. Zhang, S. Zhang, Y.D. Ye, J. Y. Chen, Q. C. Jiang, Z. Y. Zhang, J. Yu, and X. S. Li. 1999. The reform of the rural cooperative medical system in the People's Republic of China: Interim experience in 14 pilot counties. *Social Science and Medicine* 48: 961–972.

Chinese Government Work Report. 2012. Delivered at the Fifth Session of the Eleventh National People's Congress on March 5, 2012. Beijing. Wen Jiabao, Premier of the State Council. China.

Currie, J., and B. C. Madrian. 1999. Health, health insurance and the labor market. In *Handbook of labor economics,* vol. 3C, eds. Orley Ashenfelter and David Card, 3309–3416. New York: Elsevier Science.

Levy, H., and D. Meltzer. 2001. *What do we really know about whether health insurance affects health?* Economic Research Initiative on the Uninsured Working Paper Series, December. University of Chicago.

Liu, X., and H. Cao. 1992. China's cooperative medical system: Its historical transformations and the trend of development. *Journal of Public Health Policy* 13(4): 501–511.

Liu, Y. L. 2004. Development of the rural health insurance system in China. *Health Policy and Planning* 19(3): 159–165.

Liu, Y. L., K. Q. Rao, and W. C. Hsiao. 2003. Medical expenditure and rural impoverishment in China. *Journal of Health, Population and Nutrition* 21(3): 216–222.

Mackenbach, J. P., C. W. Looman, and J. B. van der Meer. 1996. Differences in the misreporting of chronic conditions, by level of education: The effect of inequalities in prevalence rates. *American Journal of Public Health* 86(5): 706–711.

Song, S. Y. 2007. The historical inspection on rural cooperative medical scheme system in China from 1955–2000. *Journal of Qingdao University of Science and Technology (Social Sciences)* 23(3): 60–75.

State Council. 2002. *Decisions of the state council on strengthening rural healthcare.* State Council, Beijing: China (in Chinese).

Strauss, J., and D. Thomas. 1995. Health, nutrition, and economic development. *Journal of Economic Literature* 36(2): 766–817.

Wagstaff, A., M. Lindelow, J. Gao, L. Xu, and J. C. Qian. 2009. Extending health insurance to the rural population: An impact evaluation of China's new cooperative medical scheme. *Journal of Health Economics* 28:1–19.

Wagstaff, A., W. Yip, M. Lindelow, and W. Hsiao. 2009. China's health system and its reform: A review of recent studies. *Health Economics* 18: S7–S23.

Wang, H. H., and R. Rosenman. 2007. Perceived need and actual demand for health insurance among rural Chinese residents. *China Economic Review* 18: 373–388.

Wang, H., L. C. Zhang, W. Yip, and W. Hsiao. 2006. Adverse selection in a voluntary rural mutual health care health insurance scheme in China. *Social Science and Medicine 63*: 1236–1245.

Weil, D. N. 2007. Accounting for the effect of health on economic growth. *The Quarterly Journal of Economics 122*(3): 1265–1306.

World Bank. 1992. *China: Long-term issues and options in the health transition.* Washington, DC: World Bank.

World Health Organization. 2001. *Macroeconomics and health: Investing in health for economic development.* Report of the Commission on Macroeconomics and Health. Geneva: World Health Organization.

Yip, W., and W. Hsiao. 2009. China's health care reform: A tentative assessment. *China Economic Review 20*: 613–619.

Zhang, L. C., H. Wang, L. S. Wang, and W. Hsiao. 2004. Social capital and farmers' willingness-to-join a newly established community-based health insurance in rural China. *Health Policy 76*: 233–242.

Zhang, Z. 1992. Review of the early period of the Cooperative Medical System. *Chinese Health Economics 6*: 54–62 (in Chinese).

# 7

# THE QUEST FOR WELFARE SPENDING EQUALIZATION: A FISCAL FEDERALISM PERSPECTIVE

Xin Zhang

## INTRODUCTION

Market-oriented reforms in China have resulted in rich regions having more per capita welfare spending than poor regions. Thus, welfare-spending equalization across regions is required in order to build a more equitable society. Viewed from a fiscal federalism perspective, the two goals of continued economic growth and greater equalization of social welfare spending can be pursued simultaneously through a compound fiscal system of centralized revenue collection and decentralized spending, supported by transfers from the central government.

This chapter uses descriptive statistics, regression analysis, and factor analysis to explore the proposition that fiscal federalism embedded in a market economy can deliver both economic welfare and social welfare via this compound model. Two distinctive approaches to fiscal equalization are formulated empirically—one based on the power of economic development to boost fiscal capacity (i.e., a jurisdiction's ability to raise revenue) and the other based on public spending priorities. The underlying patterns in these two models support both sides of the fiscal federalism coin and, in particular, confirm the central role of public expenditures in equalizing social welfare outcomes across regions.

## CHINA'S COMPOUND FISCAL SYSTEM

China has been transitioning from a centrally planned economy toward a market-oriented economy since the late 1970s. The transition started in rural areas with the family-based contractual scheme. In the mid-1980s, it extended to urban areas with a strategy of reforming the state sector to achieve efficiency gains while letting the non-state sector boom. Thanks to the logic of market efficiency, enterprise corporations in both the state and non-state sectors have served as the engines of China's economic growth.

Between 1978 and 2010, China's gross domestic product (GDP) expanded from 364.52 billion to 40,120.20 billion RMB yuan, while per capita GDP rose from 381 to 29,992 RMB yuan. During that period, the average growth rate of GDP was 15.80 percent and the average growth rate of per capita GDP was 14.62 percent, without adjusting for inflation. Rapid growth was accompanied, however, by increasing inequality. The Gini coefficient measuring inequality of income distribution increased from 0.30 in the early 1980s to 0.47 in 2010, reflecting growth in income polarization across regions, sectors, and population groups.

To address concerns about rising inequality and to balance market efficiency with social equity,[1] the Hu-Wen administration of contemporary China has stated its intention to establish a "harmonious society," in the sense of the "Great Society" of the United States in the 1960s, by means of equalizing access to social services such as education, health care, social security (including social welfare and relief), and affordable housing. This is China's vision for sustainable development into the twenty-first century, which can be seen clearly in spending trends over the past several decades. For example, from 1978 to 2010, the share of social services expenditure (including transfer payments, education, social security, and health care) in total expenditures increased from 13 to 35 percent. According to welfare economics, this shift makes sense, because the welfare state can take care of social equity while the free market handles economic efficiency (Barry 1999). Thus, in the process of turning large swaths of the Chinese economy over to market forces, the focus of governmental functions has shifted from directly producing economic goods and services to managing the economy through less direct means and replacing the pre-reform system of enterprise-based social protection with government programs for social welfare.

At the same time that public spending has been shifting from economic production to social protection, China's unitary fiscal system also has been passing through several remarkable stages toward a compound fiscal system of expenditure decentralization and revenue centralization (see Figures 7.1 and 7.2). In the early 1980s, while a fiscal policy of the substitution of tax payments for profit remittances was enacted to separate government from state-owned enterprises, a revenue-sharing scheme was introduced to delineate fiscal responsibilities between central and provincial governments (Wong 1991).

Following the decline of central revenue from 1984 to 1993 that resulted from fiscal decentralization (Ma 1995), fiscal revenue re-centralization has resulted

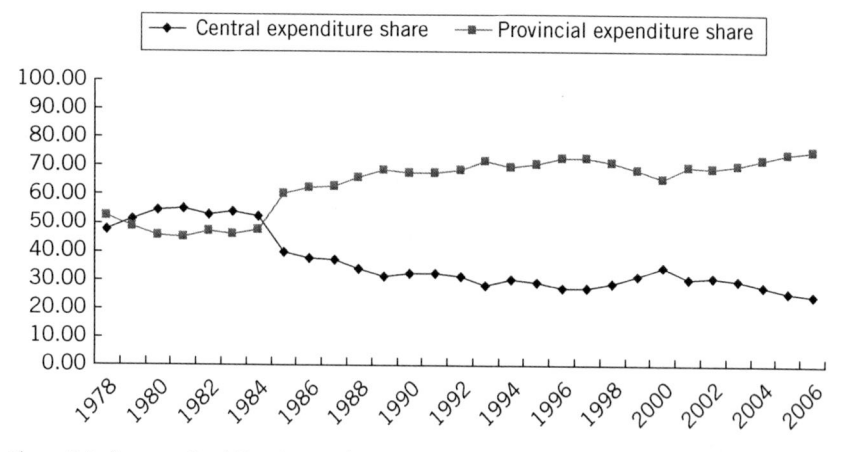

The Quest for Welfare Spending Equalization 123

**Figure 7.1.** Decentralized Fiscal Expenditure System in China, 1978–2006. *Source:* China State Statistical Yearbook (2003 and 2007)

from the 1994 fiscal reforms and the goal of building a common market nationwide (see Figure 7.2). The 1994 fiscal reforms focused on (1) rebalancing the functional expenditure assignment between central and provincial governments; (2) rebalancing the tax revenue assignment between central and provincial governments; and (3) instituting tax rebates and transfer payments from central government to provincial governments. In practice, the central government has spent about 30 percent of its revenue to reimburse provincial governments using matching formulas, but the reimbursement formula has been biased toward the contributions rather than the needs of provincial governments, except for minority nationality regions (Martinez-Vazquez et al. 2008).

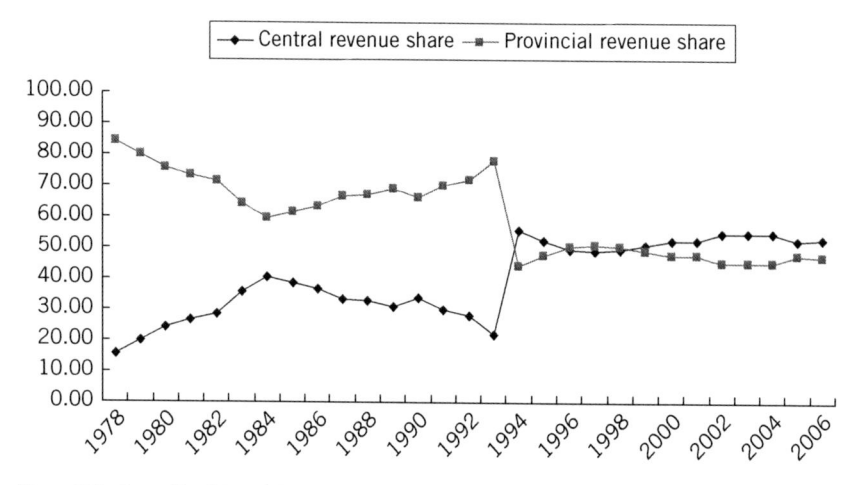

**Figure 7.2.** Centralized Fiscal Revenue System in China, 1978–2006. *Source:* China State Statistical Yearbook (2003 and 2007)

The administration of Hu Jintao and Wen Jiabao, which began in 2002, ratified the goal of equalizing essential social services for all the people as part of a national development priority, and greater fiscal equalization across regions was argued to be the necessary next step for its implementation. In order to realize a development strategy of balanced, sustainable, and "people-oriented" economic growth, while also enabling disadvantaged groups and less developed regions to share in the fruits of sustained economic growth (the harmonious society), some leveling of fiscal capacity was needed across rich and poor regions.

Conventional wisdom supports the mixed economy of market and government, in which the market takes care of economic growth while the government looks after social protection. Although globalization poses threats to the well-balanced mixed economy by pushing countries to focus almost exclusively on commercial competitiveness at the expense of other priorities, it has been argued that the welfare state can survive the internationalization of markets, at least in developing countries (Rieger and Leibfried 1998; Pierson 2001; Rudra 2002). The survival of the welfare state ultimately depends on its ability to sustain the fiscal capacity (i.e., capacity to raise sufficient revenues) that is needed to meet public demand for social services, including social security and welfare. Some scholars address the problem of welfare-state capacity by calling for alternative approaches to delivering social services through privatization or promoting a larger role for nongovernmental organizations (Savas 1977; Salamon 1995). Others insist on protecting a central role for the state and ensuring government provision of core goods and services (Stiglitz 1988; Bailey 1991).

The fiscal federalism literature offers a different set of solutions to the problem of welfare-state capacity in the form of a compound fiscal system that can generate better performance in the delivery of social services and meet multiple goals of economy, efficiency, effectiveness, equity, and responsiveness (Oates 1972, 1999; Ostrom 1991). According to the fiscal federalism literature, this can be accomplished by combining decentralized spending with a centralized system of transfer payments that serves to equalize fiscal disparities at the sub-central levels (Mikesell 1995; Adamovich and Hosp 2003). In a system of this type, fiscal revenue and fiscal expenditure, like two sides of a coin, need to be balanced at the local level to achieve fiscal equivalence, which often makes central transfer payments from the national level necessary in order to equalize fiscal capacities across rich and poor jurisdictions at the sub-national level (Olson 1969; Musgrave et al. 1987). Such a compound fiscal system of expenditure decentralization (see provincial expenditure share in Figure 7.1) and revenue centralization (see central revenue share in Figure 7.2) makes sense, since a centralized fiscal revenue system is conducive to effective transfer payments by central government,[2] while a decentralized fiscal expenditure system is conducive to effective service delivery by provincial governments.

Table 7.1 shows that the welfare spending system in China is extremely decentralized in terms of the provincial expenditure shares in the subtotals as well as in the total.[3]

Table 7.1. Welfare Spending Compound, 1998–2006 (in billions RMB)

|  | 1998 | | | 2002 | | | 2006 | | |
| --- | --- | --- | --- | --- | --- | --- | --- | --- | --- |
|  | Subtotal | Central | Provincial | Subtotal | Central | Provincial | Subtotal | Central | Provincial |
| Education | 133.81 (56.98%) | 12.33 (9.21%) | 121.48 (90.79%) | 264.50 (48.45%) | 21.03 (7.95%) | 243.47 (92.05%) | 478.04 (45.69%) | 29.52 (6.18%) | 448.52 (93.82%) |
| Health care | 41.45 (17.66%) | 0.86 (2.08%) | 40.62 (97.92%) | 63.51 (11.63%) | 1.73 (2.72%) | 61.78 (97.28%) | 132.02 (12.62%) | 2.43 (1.84%) | 129.60 (98.16%) |
| Social security | 59.56 (25.36%) | 2.51 (4.21%) | 57.06 (95.79%) | 217.90 (39.92%) | 14.18 (6.51%) | 203.73 (93.49%) | 436.18 (41.69%) | 35.62 (8.17%) | 400.56 (91.83%) |
| Total | 234.85 (100%) | 15.69 (6.68%) | 219.16 (93.32%) | 545.91 (100%) | 36.94 (6.76%) | 508.98 (93.24%) | 1,046.24 (100%) | 67.57 (6.46%) | 978.68 (93.54%) |

*Note:* Welfare spending is classified vertically by service types, and horizontally by government level. Percentages in the subtotal column are the shares of social services in the total, respectively, and percentages in the central and provincial columns are the shares of their expenditures in the subtotal.
*Source:* China State Statistical Yearbook (2003 and 2007).

According to fiscal federalism theory, a compound fiscal system can successfully equalize social services while also enhancing efficiency. This happens because decentralized spending arrangements provide an opportunity for lower levels of government to respond to local variations in preferences by purchasing different bundles of public goods and services (e.g., more parks and fewer police officers, or vice versa). The efficiency principle of fiscal equivalence then allows preferences to be optimized at the local level through "voting with one's feet," or allowing people to move to the jurisdiction that offers their preferred mix of goods and services (Fisher 2007, 130).[4] At the same time, centralized revenue collection facilitates redistribution for the sake of social equity because it makes central transfer payments possible. A centralized fiscal revenue system also can affect the ratio of costs to benefits by generating economies of scale. Thus, fiscal decentralization and centralization, just like the two sides of a coin, are complementary to each other within a compound fiscal system.

There is no guarantee, however, that fiscal federalism will eliminate fiscal disparities across sub-national units. In fact, during the period in which China's compound fiscal system emerged, provincial disparities in fiscal health have grown larger (see Figure 7.3), as indicated by the ratio of a region's negative deficit (expenditure minus revenue) to its revenue, expressed as a percentage. For provincial governments, a lower percentage indicates greater fiscal health, because it means that the shortfall between expenditure and revenue is small relative to overall revenue. Obviously, the less fiscal capacity the provincial government has, the higher will be its fiscal dependence upon central transfer payments. Based on the 2006 data on fiscal expenditure and revenue by province, regional disparities in fiscal health are mapped out in Figure 7.3. Specifically, eastern coastal regions such as Shanghai, Zhejiang, Jiangsu, Tianjin, Shandong, and Fujian show greater fiscal health, while western peripheral regions such as Tibet, Qinghai, Gansu, Ningxia, and Xinjiang show higher fiscal dependence.

## WELFARE SPENDING EQUALIZATION DETERMINANTS

Provincial disparities can be shown not only in terms of fiscal health but also in terms of fiscal equalization measurements. Based on per capita welfare spending data by province, Table 7.2 shows generally larger per capita expenditure disparities in 1998 than in 2006, as indicated by the coefficient of variation for the whole sample. Overall, provincial disparities of per capita welfare spending were significantly reduced between 1998 and 2006, with per capita health care expenditures showing more remaining provincial disparity than per capita expenditures for education and social security (see coefficients of variation in Table 7.2). Using the mean and national values of Table 7.2, the average growth rates of per capita welfare spending from 1998 to 2006 can be calculated for the

The Quest for Welfare Spending Equalization    127

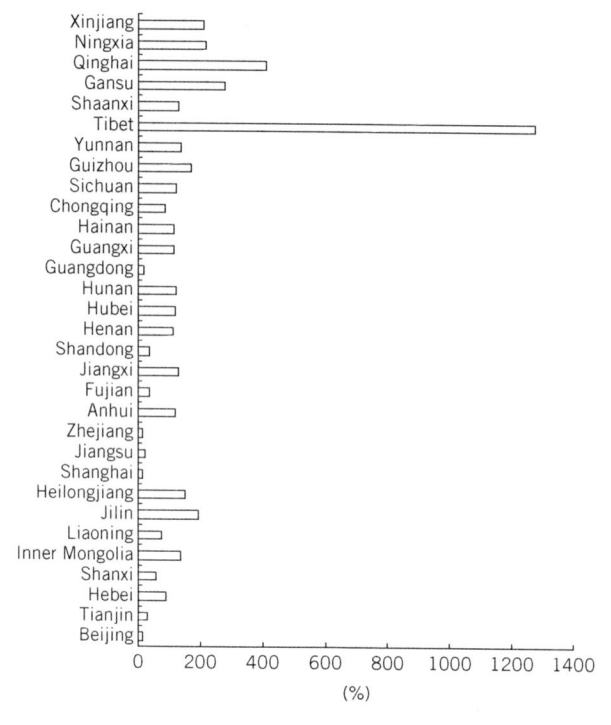

**Figure 7.3.** Provincial Disparity of Fiscal Health: Welfare Spending as a Share of GDP

provincial and national levels. Overall spending growth was well-balanced over the period, with a growth rate of 19.36 percent at the provincial level and 19.75 percent nationally, as was growth in education spending (16.50 percent provincially and 16.49 percent nationally), and somewhat less so growth in social security spending (26.41 percent growth in spending by provinces and 27.43 percent by national government). Growth in health care spending was more skewed, with a rate of 14.50 percent at the provincial level and 20.74 percent nationally.

Table 7.3 shows disparities in welfare spending size (welfare spending as a share of GDP) from 1998 to 2006. Generally, welfare spending size with respect to GDP is less diverse across provinces and more equalized through time than per capita welfare spending (see coefficients of variation in Tables 7.2 and 7.3). Specifically, the education and health care expenditure sizes are less diverse across provinces and more equalized through time than the per capita education and per capita health care expenditures (see coefficients of variation in Tables 7.2 and 7.3). By contrast, social security expenditure size is more diverse across provinces, but more equalized through time than the per capita social security expenditure (see coefficients of variations in Tables 7.2 and 7.3). Overall, welfare spending increased from 1998 to 2006, according to either measure. During that

## 128 CHINESE SOCIAL POLICY IN A TIME OF TRANSITION

Table 7.2. Per Capita Welfare Spending Disparities, 1998–2006

|      |          | Per capita total welfare spending (RMB yuan) | Per capita education expenditure (RMB yuan) | Per capita health care expenditure (RMB yuan) | Per capita social security expenditure (RMB yuan) |
|------|----------|---------|---------|--------|--------|
| 1998 | National | 188.17  | 107.21  | 22.24  | 47.72  |
|      | Mean     | 224.45  | 121.97  | 44.08  | 58.40  |
|      | S.D.     | 145.98  | 85.29   | 38.00  | 35.04  |
|      | C.V.     | 0.65    | 0.70    | 0.86   | 0.60   |
| 2002 | National | 424.99  | 205.91  | 49.44  | 169.64 |
|      | Mean     | 499.15  | 230.48  | 65.41  | 203.26 |
|      | S.D.     | 253.92  | 138.90  | 54.61  | 108.63 |
|      | C.V.     | 0.51    | 0.60    | 0.83   | 0.53   |
| 2006 | National | 795.94  | 363.67  | 100.44 | 331.83 |
|      | Mean     | 924.68  | 413.86  | 130.16 | 380.66 |
|      | S.D.     | 477.62  | 226.19  | 102.40 | 195.71 |
|      | C.V.     | 0.52    | 0.55    | 0.79   | 0.51   |

*Note:* S.D. denotes standard deviation; C.V. denotes coefficient of variation.
*Source:* China State Statistical Yearbook (1999 and 2007).

Table 7.3. Welfare Spending Size Disparities, 1998–2006

|      |          | Share of total welfare spending in GDP (%) | Share of education expenditure in GDP (%) | Share of health care expenditure in GDP (%) | Share of social security expenditure in GDP (%) |
|------|----------|------|------|------|------|
| 1998 | National | 2.96 | 1.69 | 0.52 | 0.75 |
|      | Mean     | 3.47 | 1.84 | 0.65 | 0.98 |
|      | S.D.     | 1.84 | 0.87 | 0.44 | 0.70 |
|      | C.V.     | 0.53 | 0.48 | 0.67 | 0.71 |
| 2002 | National | 4.54 | 2.20 | 0.53 | 1.81 |
|      | Mean     | 5.95 | 2.62 | 0.73 | 2.60 |
|      | S.D.     | 2.94 | 1.19 | 0.52 | 1.65 |
|      | C.V.     | 0.49 | 0.46 | 0.71 | 0.63 |
| 2006 | National | 4.96 | 2.27 | 0.63 | 2.07 |
|      | Mean     | 5.75 | 2.54 | 0.78 | 2.43 |
|      | S.D.     | 2.57 | 1.18 | 0.50 | 1.24 |
|      | C.V.     | 0.45 | 0.46 | 0.64 | 0.51 |

*Note:* S.D. denotes standard deviation; C.V. denotes coefficient of variation.
*Source:* China State Statistical Yearbook (1999 and 2007).

period, greater equalization was achieved in welfare spending size across provinces than in per capita welfare spending.

Although equalization is occurring, the data presented in Tables 7.2 and 7.3 provide grounds for arguing that greater fiscal equalization is needed to further reduce provincial disparities in welfare spending. The central question then becomes: How should this equalization be undertaken? Many fiscal disparity studies call for the establishment of a central grant system operated though a tax-sharing scheme to transfer fiscal revenue from the rich regions to the poor regions, but this approach runs the risk of trading away the fiscal and economic efficiencies gained by decentralization for the goal of fiscal equity (Buchanan 1950; Okun 1975). The alternative is to rely on economic growth alone to raise fiscal capacity in disadvantaged regions on the assumption that higher GDP in those areas will translate into more welfare spending. The analysis presented in the following sections explores the dynamics of these two approaches to fiscal equalization—one based on public spending (including central government transfers from richer to poorer areas) and the other based on economic development (growing the economy to boost fiscal capacity for welfare spending)—using multivariate regression and factor analysis.

## REGRESSION ANALYSIS

As a first step, it is useful to identify the factors that correlate with existing disparities in welfare spending across China's regions in order to better understand the phenomenon. Two measures of welfare spending are chosen as dependent variables in this part of the study. One is per capita welfare spending (PERSOEX), which may be seen as an outcome of policy because it roughly captures what the residents of a region actually receive. The other is welfare spending as a share of GDP (SOEXGDP), which may be seen as a measure of the welfare spending effort put forth by a region, or the size of the sacrifice (share of total economic resources) that each region makes to fund social welfare. The independent variables hypothesized to help explain variations in welfare spending are per capita GDP (PERGDP) as an indicator of economic development level; the total fiscal expenditure share in GDP (TOEXGDP) as an indicator of public sector size; and the welfare spending share in the total fiscal expenditure (SOEXTOT) as an indicator of social protection priority. Accordingly, multiple regression models are set up with a general form as follows:

$$\text{PERSOEX/SOEXGDP} = \text{Const.} + \beta_1 \text{PERGDP} + \beta_2 \text{TOEXGDP} + \beta_3 \text{SOEXTOT} + \varepsilon.$$

Such a regression model hypothesizes that variations across regions in welfare spending (measured on a per capita basis or as a share of GDP) are determined by

Table 7.4. Standardized Regression Coefficients in 1998 and 2006

|  | 1998 | | 2006 | | change (2006–1998) | |
| --- | --- | --- | --- | --- | --- | --- |
|  | **PERSOEX** | **SOEXGDP** | **PERSOEX** | **SOEXGDP** | **PERSOEX** | **SOEXGDP** |
| PERGDP | 1.031** | 0.001 | 1.270** | −0.001 | 0.752** | −0.003 |
| TOEXGDP | 0.860** | 1.068** | 1.032** | 1.033** | 0.896** | 0.783** |
| SOEXTOT | 0.247** | 0.306** | 0.349** | 0.352** | 0.748** | 0.650** |
| Adjusted R square | 1.000 | 1.000 | 1.000 | 1.000 | 0.996 | 0.999 |

*Note:* All requested variables are entered by method.
*Source:* China State Statistical Yearbook (1999 and 2007).

differences in per capita GDP (economic development level), public spending as a share of GDP (public sector size), and the share of total fiscal expenditure spent on social welfare (social protection priority).[5] Based on the 1998 and 2006 provincial statistical data in the transformed values of natural logarithm, three sets of multiple regression models are estimated: the 1998 models; the 2006 models; and the change models of the 2006 values minus those of 1998. The standardized regression coefficients thereof are shown in Table 7.4 with adjusted R squares.

It may be observed from Table 7.4 that per capita welfare spending is significantly determined by all the independent variables, while the welfare spending share in GDP is determined only by the total fiscal expenditure share in GDP (public sector size) and the welfare spending share in the total fiscal expenditure (social protection priority). Such a structural pattern of regression coefficients is not significantly changed from 1998 to 2006. Further, it seems plausible that economic development level (per capita GDP) is not conducive to welfare spending size (the welfare spending share in GDP) but does influence welfare spending equalization (per capita welfare spending). However, welfare spending size through time is significantly determined by public sector size (the total fiscal expenditure share in GDP) and/or social protection priority (welfare spending share in the total fiscal expenditure).

## EXPLORATORY FACTOR ANALYSIS

Because all of the independent variables can be linearly combined into one dimension with respect to each dependent variable, it is necessary to explore any potential structural relationship between independent and dependent variables. Thus, the Pearson correlations between all the variables are calculated and shown in Table 7.5. This reveals no positive correlation between all independent variables. On a bilateral basis, however, relationships do exist. Specifically, economic development level (per capita GDP) is negatively related with public sector size (the total fiscal expenditure in GDP) as well as social protection priority (the welfare spending share in the total fiscal expenditure) through time. From the perspective of fiscal equalization

The Quest for Welfare Spending Equalization   131

**Table 7.5.** Pearson Correlation Matrix, 1998 and 2006

|  | PERSOEX | SOEXGDP | PERGDP | TOEXGDP | SOEXTOT |
|---|---|---|---|---|---|
| | | | 1998 | | |
| PERSOEX | 1.000 | | | | |
| SOEXGDP | 0.365* | 1.000 | | | |
| PERGDP | 0.684** | −0.429* | 1.000 | | |
| TOEXGDP | 0.416* | 0.959** | −0.346 | 1.000 | |
| SOEXTOT | −0.263 | −0.077 | −0.197 | −0.356* | 1.000 |
| | | | 2006 | | |
| PERSOEX | 1.000 | | | | |
| SOEXGDP | 0.191 | 1.000 | | | |
| PERGDP | 0.636** | −0.636** | 1.000 | | |
| TOEXGDP | 0.326 | 0.941** | −0.484* | 1.000 | |
| SOEXTOT | −0.413* | 0.081 | −0.386* | −0.263 | 1.000 |
| | | | change (2006–1998) | | |
| PERSOEX | 1.000 | | | | |
| SOEXGDP | 0.759** | 1.000 | | | |
| PERGDP | 0.168 | −0.512** | 1.000 | | |
| TOEXGDP | 0.681** | 0.758** | −0.246 | 1.000 | |
| SOEXTOT | 0.348 | 0.621** | −0.485** | −0.039 | 1.000 |

*Note:* ** Correlation is significant at the 0.01 level (2-tailed), while * correlation is significant at the 0.05 level (2-tailed).
*Source:* China State Statistical Yearbook (1999 and 2007).

strategies, these relationships suggest that the three independent variables may be structured into two different bundles: an economic-development orientation associated with per capita GDP, and a public-spending orientation associated with the two public-spending variables—social protection priority (SOEXTOT), which is the welfare state indicator, and public sector size (TOEXGDP), which captures the overall role of government vis à vis the economy.

As for the dependent variables, although a weak positive correlation is shown in 1998 and no correlation is found in 2006, there is a strong positive correlation between the differences of dependent variables from 1998 to 2006. In other words, as one measure of spending goes up or down, the other tends to move in the same direction. This apparent correlation between the two welfare spending measures accords with the policy performance literature (Pollitt and Bouckaert 1999), which treats per capita welfare spending as a welfare policy outcome, and welfare spending share in GDP as a welfare policy output.[6] If this interpretation of the relationship is correct, changes in the output (welfare spending as a share of GDP) would be expected to produce changes in the same direction for the outcome (welfare spending per capita). As a matter of fact, the change case from

1998 to 2006 shows a significant correlation (with coefficient of 0.759) between per capita welfare spending and welfare spending size (see Table 7.5).

In addition, welfare spending size is significantly correlated with public sector size, while per capita welfare spending correlates with economic development level in both the 1998 and 2006 models. There is no significant positive correlation between per capita welfare spending and social protection priority, nor is there correlation between welfare spending size and social protection priority. However, there are significant positive correlations among the change terms between 1998 to 2006 with respect to per capita welfare spending, welfare spending size, and public sector size.

Finally, because the Pearson correlation matrix shows more, rather than fewer, significant correlations among dependent and independent variables, there appears to be an underpinning structure to the model, which needs to be spelled out through the method of factor analysis. Based on the Pearson correlations, factor analysis with rotation technique is conducted. The two-factor solutions shown in Table 7.6 are the result, as anticipated by the two-by-two conceptual relationships of independent variables to dependent variables discussed above.

By and large, according to Table 7.6, the 2006 structure of factor loading coefficients is not significantly changed from the 1998 structure, in which the first factor is significantly positively related to SOEXGDP and TOEXGDP but negatively to PERGDP, while the second factor is significantly positively related to PERSOEX and PERGDP, but negatively to SOEXTOT. We can, therefore, visually paraphrase the multiple regression models discussed above by means of a path diagram of the two-factor solutions, which is able to show any causal patterns of dependent and independent variables (see Figure 7.4).

The bold lines in Figure 7.4 denote positive causal linkages, and the dot-and-dash lines denote negative causal linkages. The first factor shows a positive linkage between public sector size and welfare spending size, as well as a negative linkage of economic development level to welfare spending size. These relationships suggest that regions with larger public sectors relative to the size

Table 7.6. Rotated Factor Loadings Matrix in 1998 and 2006

|  | 1998 | | 2006 | | change (2006–1998) | |
| --- | --- | --- | --- | --- | --- | --- |
|  | Factor 1 | Factor 2 | Factor 1 | Factor 2 | Factor 1 | Factor 2 |
| PERSOEX | 0.235 | 0.915 | 0.151 | 0.898 | 0.942 | 0.004 |
| SOEXGDP | 0.973 | 0.070 | 0.986 | –0.029 | 0.808 | 0.588 |
| PERGDP | –0.532 | 0.834 | –0.657 | 0.728 | 0.021 | –0.888 |
| TOEXGDP | 0.976 | 0.216 | 0.971 | 0.229 | 0.886 | 0.061 |
| SOEXTOT | –0.224 | –0.529 | –0.050 | –0.753 | 0.176 | 0.827 |
| Eigenvalue | 2.347 | 1.804 | 2.400 | 1.929 | 2.803 | 1.377 |

Note: All data by province are in the ln value. Extraction method is Principal Component Analysis, while rotation method is Varimax with Kaiser Normalization.
Source: China State Statistical Yearbook (1999 and 2007).

The Quest for Welfare Spending Equalization    133

```
┌──────────────────┐                              ┌──────────────────┐
│ Public Sector Size│─────┐                    ┌─▶│ Per capita welfare│
└──────────────────┘     ╲                    ╱   │ spending          │
                          ╲                  ╱    └──────────────────┘
┌──────────────────┐       ╲                ╱
│ Social protection│─ ─ ─ ─ ╳ ─ ─ ─ ─ ─ ─ ─
│ priority         │       ╱                ╲
└──────────────────┘      ╱                  ╲    ┌──────────────────┐
                         ╱                    ╲─▶│ Welfare spending │
┌──────────────────┐    ╱    ─ ─ ─ ─ ─ ─ ─ ─ ─ ─▶│ size             │
│ Economic         │───┘                          └──────────────────┘
│ development level│
└──────────────────┘
```

────────── positive linkage        — · · — · · —  negative linkage

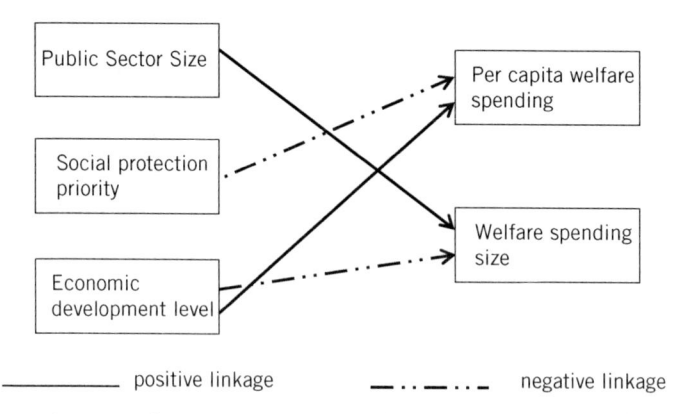

**Figure 7.4.** Path Diagram for Two-Factor Solutions Without Change Terms. *Note:* Based on data from Table 7.6

of their economies are likely to spend more on welfare relative to the size of their economies. This makes sense and points directly to the relatively orthodox hypothesis that disparities in welfare spending size across regions may be effectively addressed by increasing the size of government budgets in those areas. At the same time, factor 1's relationships also suggest that China's more economically developed regions can get away with spending a smaller percentage of their overall economic resources on social protection programs (welfare spending as a share of GDP), for the same reason that a rich family can spend a smaller percentage of its total budget on basics, such as food and shelter, than a poor family does. This finding gives rise to the hypothesis that increasing levels of regional economic development may be an inefficient way of trying to equalize welfare spending as measured by size or effort.

Looking at the second factor, it appears that, even with the smaller proportional effort that they typically give to social welfare, as seen in factor 1's relationships, China's more economically developed regions can still maintain higher levels of per capita welfare spending than the less developed regions (note the positive relationship between economic development and per capita welfare spending). Thus, we may hypothesize that pro-regional-development policies are a potentially good strategy for equalizing welfare spending as measured by per capita outcomes. Finally, the logic of the second factor's negative causal linkage between social protection priority and per capita welfare spending is difficult to discern. Regions in which welfare state functions command a larger share of the public budget appear to have lower per capita welfare spending. If those regions are also less wealthy, then the relationship makes more sense, both because of their relatively smaller capacity to raise local revenue, which would explain the lower per capita welfare spending, and because of their greater need for social services (due to poverty and unemployment), which would explain the higher social protection priority. The latter factor would also be explained by the presence of central transfer funds targeted to social welfare.

Based on these two sets of factor relationships, the first factor earns the label "public-spending (or welfare state) approach," because it appears to support the hypothesis that public sector expenditures are a better route toward equalizing welfare spending effort or output than is economic growth. In contrast, the second factor earns the label "economic-development (or pro-growth) approach," because it suggests that accelerating economic development will be more effective in equalizing welfare spending on a per capita basis than increasing the share of public spending on social protection. These factor solutions are based upon a principal component method with orthogonal rotation.

As noted above, the two dependent variables may be interpreted as outputs (welfare spending size, or SOEXGDP) and outcomes (welfare spending per capita, or PERSOEX), a relationship that can be seen in the correlation between these variables' change terms. To a great extent, any causal relationships among dependent and independent variables seem to be harmonized through time by the two factor solutions with change terms from 1998 to 2006.

Figure 7.5 shows the path diagram for the two-factor solutions with change terms from 1998 to 2006. That diagram shows positive linkages through time among public sector size, per capita welfare spending, and welfare spending size with respect to the first factor. The second factor demonstrates a positive linkage between social protection priority and welfare spending size but a negative linkage between economic development level and welfare spending size through time.

When change terms are used, the positive effect of economic development level on welfare spending equalization (per capita) through time drops out, as seen in Figure 7.5, leaving positive linkages between change in public sector size and changes in both forms of welfare spending measures, as well as a positive linkage between change in social protection priority and change in welfare spending effort. Therefore, the path diagram with change terms seems to accord

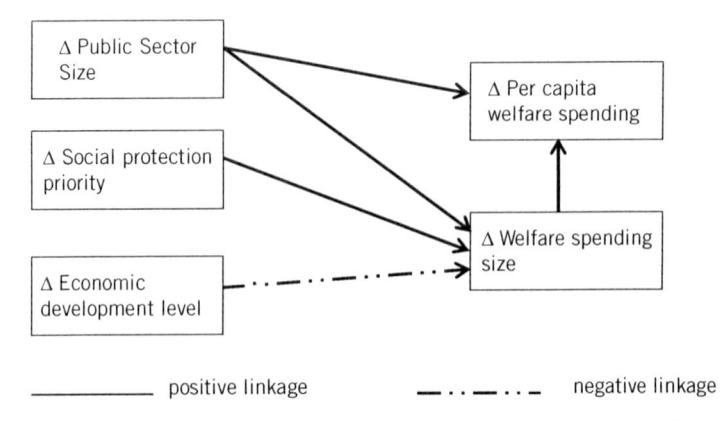

**Figure 7.5.** Path Diagram for Two-Factor Solutions with Change Terms. *Note:* Based on data from Table 7.6.

more closely with the public-spending approach and its related hypotheses rather than the economic-development approach to fiscal equalization.

The path diagram in Figure 7.5 offers a plausible account of the causal mechanisms of the public-spending-based, welfare-state approach. Per capita welfare spending is directly determined by public sector size and welfare spending size, while social protection priority has an indirect effect on per capita welfare spending through welfare spending size. The positive causal linkage from change in welfare spending size to change in per capita welfare spending suggests that the latter term is indeed the ultimate policy outcome, with welfare spending as a share of GDP a means to that end, rather than an end in itself. The apparently negative causal relationship between change in economic development level and change in per capita welfare spending, which operates via change in welfare spending size, is more difficult to interpret, but may reflect differences in either needs or priorities across regions, based on economic development level. For example, faster developing regions may have placed economic growth higher on their lists of priorities than social welfare (and vice versa for less rapidly developing regions). Alternatively, it may be that faster developing regions have lower unemployment rates and, therefore, fewer of the social problems associated with unemployment and less need for services (and vice versa for poorer regions).

## REGIONAL PATTERNS FOR EQUALIZATION

Factor analysis works not only for exploring association structures for all the variables discussed above, but also for demonstrating any location patterns for the observations in the reduced factor space. Such location values are called factor scores. Unlike the common factor model, in which each original variable is a linear function of common factors, each common factor is a linear function of original variables with respect to factor score. Usually, factor scores can be obtained through a regression method.

Based on the 2006 factor model, the factor scores of observations by province are calculated and shown in Figure 7.6. According to the two-factor solution discussed above, the horizontal $x$-axis denotes the public-spending approach to welfare spending equalization (factor 1), while the vertical $y$-axis shows the economic-development approach (factor 2). The scatter plot of factor scores by province shows a few important patterns. Three large coastal regions—Shanghai, Beijing, and Tianjin—set themselves apart from most of the others with their strong economic-development orientation (see Figure 7.6). Although these regions also have relatively high per capita welfare spending, thanks to considerable overall income, they score at the lower end of the public-spending scale.

In contrast, many of the western peripheral regions, such as Inner Mongolia, Xinjiang, Ningxia, Qinghai, Gansu, Guizhou, and Yunnan, display a consistent

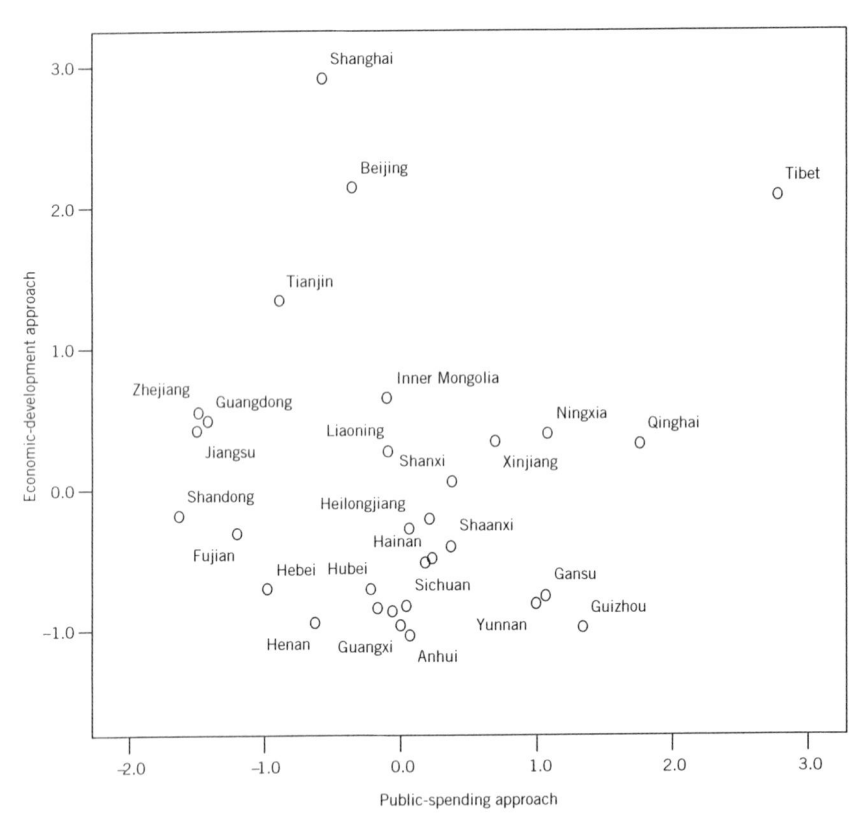

**Figure 7.6.** Scatter Plot of Factor Scores by Province, 2006

public-spending orientation, while varying quite a lot in their economic development profile (see Figure 7.6). With the combination of both higher welfare spending share in GDP and higher total fiscal expenditure share in GDP, this less-advantaged second group of regions has to make a larger effort to provide even moderate social welfare services to its residents. The autonomous regions in the second group reach a medium level of per capita welfare spending only through the help of central transfer payments.

Only Tibet scores highly on both clusters, suggesting a balanced approach.

## DISCUSSION AND CONCLUSION

This chapter argues for a rebalancing of the compound fiscal system to bring about welfare spending equalization, based on a fiscal federalism approach to the challenges posed by contemporary China's emerging market economy. While rapid, geographically concentrated economic growth has pulled China's wealthier, faster developing regions steadily away from its poorer regions in terms of fiscal capacity and outcomes, increasing transfers from central government to the poorer regions has helped keep the overall regional fiscal gap relatively steady over the past several decades. Modest progress toward fiscal equalization was even seen between the late 1990s and early 2000s, the period covered by the present study.

The analyses reported in this chapter used regional data on welfare spending, alongside several factors that determine welfare spending, to develop and then test competing hypotheses about the relative effects of public spending versus economic development on actual regional disparities in welfare spending. The results roughly support the view that fiscal equalization in the 1998–2006 period occurred largely through the route of public spending, as measured by variables that capture the share of GDP represented by public spending generally and the share of public spending represented by the social welfare budget (see Figure 7.5). Where economic development is concerned, the conclusions are less clear. The pathways illustrated in Figure 7.4 show a positive impact on welfare spending per capita, whereas the pathways illustrated in Figure 7.5 show the reverse effect, operating through a negative relationship between economic development and welfare size, which then feeds through to welfare per capita. The negative link shown in Figure 7.5 should not come as a surprise, given the simple fact that richer regions can provide an adequate level of social welfare services with less fiscal effort than poorer regions. This finding is not inconsistent with the direct and positive pathway from economic development to per capita welfare spending shown in Figure 7.4, because a region with a rapidly growing economy can hold its welfare effort (welfare spending as a share of GDP) constant, or even let it decline a bit, while at the same time spending more per capita on welfare services thanks to the automatic increases in revenue that accompany economic growth.

Based on the findings shown in Figure 7.5, it would be easy to jump to the conclusion that further increases in regional welfare-state spending, boosted by central transfers, are the only tool needed to address the problem of continuing fiscal disparities in China. This would be a mistake, however, because the models presented in this chapter did not—and could not—fully test the potential of economic development to reduce regional inequalities. In particular, this study did not test the hypothesis that a more geographically distributed approach to economic development—with strong support for economic growth in more rural, isolated regions—could have a large and significant leveling effect on fiscal conditions across the regions. That scenario has never been actualized and, therefore, its impacts on fiscal equalization cannot be known. The Chinese government has expressed its intention to steer economic development to less-advantaged areas; if successful, those efforts might register as significant influences on fiscal equalization in later iterations of this research.

The models illustrated in Figures 7.4 and 7.5 tell a complex, but incomplete story of the determinants of welfare state spending and their interrelationships.

Based on these preliminary findings, it is a story with the potential to mutually reinforce two central themes from the fiscal federalism literature: (1) the efficiency-enhancing effects of decentralized spending, which may have contributed to China's dramatic economic growth during the 1980s and 1990s (further research is needed to test this); and (2) the vital role of transfers from central government to balance inequities in regional fiscal capacity, which the model presented in Figure 7.5 strongly supports. If these propositions hold up under further research scrutiny, the case for a compound fiscal system based on fiscal federalism principles will be strengthened.

The compound model of fiscal federalism is further supported by the practical observation that social goods and services such as education, health care, social security, and affordable housing have both public and private characteristics, which make public financing (the welfare-state approach) complementary to private financing (through markets). Social security and health care, for example, may rely more or less on centralized public financing or private, individual, or workplace-based contributions, and different countries choose different combinations of these arrangements. Lane (2000) uses the terms "welfare state" and "welfare society" to capture the pure types at either end of this continuum, whereas Esping-Andersen (1997) has attempted to categorize whole countries and regions under his expanded typology (with market-based welfare regimes dominant in North America, state-based ones dominant in Northern Europe, and civil-society–based and production-oriented welfare regimes being the norm in Asian countries). In practice, however, most countries operate a mixed model with many complex parts.

This chapter affirms the possibility of effective equalization within an efficient economy. Specifically, just as the mixed economy of government and market is rationalized as offering the best opportunity to minimize the need for trade-offs between equality and efficiency, the compound fiscal federal system of centralized revenue collection and decentralized expenditure with transfers is rationalized for the same purpose. Operationally, the two approaches to welfare spending equalization formulated above—one based on public spending and the other based on economic development—provide preliminary empirical support for this interpretation. As a result of the exploratory factor analysis, the two-factor solutions without change terms distinguish what we have labeled the economic-development approach from the public-spending approach. Finally, the two-path diagram, with and without change terms (Figures 7.4 and 7.5), illustrates the harmonization of the market-based approach with the government-based approach. It is empirically confirmed that per capita welfare spending is regarded as a welfare policy outcome, while welfare spending size is seen as welfare policy output. In addition, the regional patterns for welfare spending equalization show that the coastal eastern regions are in closer correspondence with an economic-development–based approach, as one would expect, while the peripheral western regions must rely more heavily on a public-spending–based approach with considerable assistance from central government. Through time, the in-between regions are expected to demonstrate a catch-up effect by means of expanded public spending.

Looking ahead, China offers a remarkable test of the proposition that fiscal federalism embedded within a market economy can reconcile equality with efficiency and economic welfare with social welfare. Much depends on the ability of the state not only to share revenue with needier regions, but also to steer economic growth toward those regions. This two-pronged approach has potential to shrink the fiscal disparities that inevitably worsen social inequalities.

## ACKNOWLEDGMENTS

This research is funded by the project of "985" in China. The author would like to thank Karen Baehler, M. Ramesh, Zhi-yong Lan, and anonymous reviewers for their thoughtful comments and suggestions.

## NOTES

1 The term "equity" here refers to equal access to social services, whereas "equality" means that everyone is at the same level. For further discussion, see Frederickson (1990).
2 Central transfer payments are regarded as fiscal revenue redistribution to equalize fiscal capacity across regions, based upon regional fiscal needs.
3 Although not fundamental to this chapter's story, it is also interesting to note in Table 7.1 that the education expenditure share in the total decreased between 1998 and 2006 at a rate of 17.25%, and the social security share increased at a rate of 28.26%. The health care share fluctuated and decreased at a rate of 15.58%.
4 To make such a system operational, obstacles to internal migration must be removed. Depending upon how much movement is needed for people to find their ideal locality, "voting with one's feet" is likely to be disruptive of long-standing community bonds and geography-based identities.
5 In other words, economic development level can be the indicator of rich or poor regions, public sector size the indicator of the role of government in the region relative to the economy, and social protection priority the indicator of less or more welfare state orientation.
6 The policy performance evaluation literature studies the process that converts input to output and then to outcome. In the case of welfare policy, per capita welfare spending (outcome) is used to measure fiscal disparity, and increasing welfare spending size (output) is recommended to equalize fiscal disparity.

## REFERENCES

Adamovich, Ivan Baron, and Gerald Hosp. 2003. Fiscal federalism for emerging economies: Lessons from Switzerland? *Publius: The Journal of Federalism* 33(1): 1–21.

Bailey, S. 1991. Fiscal stress: The new system of local government finance in England. *Urban Studies* 28(6): 889–907.

Barry, Norman P. 1999. *Welfare*. 2nd ed. Buckingham: Open University Press.

Buchanan, James M. 1950. Federalism and fiscal equity. *American Economic Review* 40(4): 583–599.

Esping-Andersen, Gøsta, ed. 1996. *Welfare states in transition: National adaptations in global economies*. London: Sage.

Fisher, Ronald C. 2007. *State and local public finance*. 3rd ed. Thompson South-Western.

Frederickson, H. George. 1990. Public administration and social equity. *Public Administration Review* 50(2): 228–237.

Lane, Jan-Erik. 2000. *New public management*. London: Routledge.

Ma, Jun. 1995. Modeling central-local fiscal relations in China. *China Economic Review* 6(1): 105–136.

Martinez-Vazquez, Jorge, Baoyun Qiao, and Li Zhang. 2008. The role of provincial policies in fiscal equalization outcomes in China. *The China Review* 8(2): 135–167.

Mikesell, J. L. 1995. *Fiscal administration: Analysis and applications for the public sector*. 4th ed. Orlando, FL: Harcourt Brace.

Musgrave, R. A., P. B. Musgrave, and R. M. Bird. 1987. *Public finance in theory and practice*. Toronto: McGraw-Hill Ryerson.

Oates, W. E. 1972. *Fiscal federalism*. New York: Harcout Brace Jovanovich.

Oates, W. E. 1999. An essay on fiscal federalism. *Journal of Economic Literature* 37(3): 1120–1149.

Okun, Arthur M. 1975. *Equality and efficiency: The big tradeoff*. The Brookings Institution.

Olson, Mancur. 1969. The principle of "fiscal equivalence": The division of responsibilities among different levels of government. *American Economic Review* 59(2): 479–487.

Ostrom, V. 1991. *The meaning of American federalism: Constituting a self-governing society*. San Francisco: Institute for Contemporary Studies Press.

Pierson, P, ed. 2001. *The new politics of the welfare state*. Oxford: Oxford University Press.

Pollitt, C., and G. Bouckaert. 1999. *Public management reform: A comparative analysis*. Oxford: Oxford University Press.

Rieger, E., and S. Leibfried. 1998. Welfare state limits to globalization. *Politics & Society* 26(3): 363–390.

Rodden, Jonathan. 2003. Reviving Leviathan: Fiscal federalism and the growth of government. *International Organization* 57(4): 695–729.

Rudra, N. 2002. Globalization and the decline of the welfare state in less-developed countries. *International Organization* 56(2): 411–445.

Salamon, L. M. 1995. *Partners in public service: Government-nonprofit relations in the modern welfare state.* Baltimore: The Johns Hopkins University Press.

Savas, E. S., ed. 1977. *Alternatives for delivering public services.* Boulder, CO: Westview Press.

Stiglitz, J. E. 1988. *Economics of the public sector.* New York: W. W. Norton.

Wong, Christine P. W. 1991. Central-local relations in an era of fiscal decline: The paradox of fiscal decentralization in post-Mao China. *The China Quarterly* 128: 691–715.

World Bank. *World development indicators.* Washington, DC: World Bank.

# 8

# FINANCING MIGRANT CHILD EDUCATION

## Jing Guo

## INTRODUCTION

In addition to being the most highly populated country in the world, China has had more internal migration than any other country in the past three decades. The 2010 China census shows that 221.4 million in China left their registered places, an increase of 83 percent from the 2000 census data (National Bureau of Statistics of China 2011). The 1 percent population sample data in 2005 estimated that 12.5 percent of the total migrant population were children ages zero to 14 (Duan and Yang 2008).[1] Using this estimate, the migrant child population was over 27 million in 2010.

Migrant status was a major barrier for students enrolling in public schools in cities in the 1980s and 1990s (Shi 2002), mainly due to China's household registration system and a decentralized education financing system. Policies adopted in 1998 and 2003 (and reinforced in 2006 and 2008) made significant progress toward a more inclusive approach; however, local implementation of these policies has been hampered by financing issues.

This chapter describes China's migrant child education problem in the context of both educational funding and developmental issues (including international benchmarks), reviews major migrant child education policies from the past decade, and discusses policy implementation in different areas and regions. The analysis presented here identifies inter-governmental transfers as the missing dimension of the current policy and suggests that the central and provincial governments should take the lead in reforming mechanisms for financing migrant child compulsory education.

## THE HOUSEHOLD REGISTRATION SYSTEM

The household registration system was designed in the mid-1950s to provide population statistics and to regulate migration. At the time of its establishment in the mid-1950s, each individual was registered in the location where he or she lived, and the population was divided into two types of residents: rural and urban. If a parent was registered as a rural resident, her child would be as well, and likewise for a parent living in an urban area. As of 1953, the year of China's first census, the urban population accounted for only 14 percent of the country's total population (National Bureau of Statistics of China 2001).

During the pre-reform era between the 1950s and 1970s, China had a strictly planned economy, which strongly supported maximizing urban industrialization (Chan 1994; Cheng and Selden 1994; S. Liu, Li, and Zhang 2003). To promote the growth of urban centers at the time, the government began offering social benefits, such as employment, housing, medical care, food, and education to urban residents—none of which was available to rural residents. To keep governmental spending within a specified range and to guarantee full employment with benefits for all urban residents, the household registration system has been used to control population mobility.

In addition to controlling rural-urban migration, migration between cities also is strictly managed through the household registration system. According to national policy, whenever people want to move, they must obtain permission from both their current registered place and their prospective place of residence (Zhao 2001). Before China's economic reform, the combination of a centrally planned economy and restrictive migration policy made it very hard for people to find a job and to gain permission not only to move and but also to change their place of registration (Z. Liu 2005; Meng and Zhang 2001; Solinger 1999). Most people remained in the place where they were born, and their children inherited the same residence status.

Starting with China's social and economic reforms in the late 1970s, there has been a large influx of workers and their families from rural to urban areas (Liang 2001; Seeborg, Jin, and Zhu 2000), accompanied by a weakening of controls on population mobility. During the early reform period, basic housing and food supplies in cities were publicly managed and were provided though work units for urban residents, which made it almost impossible for rural residents to survive in cities. A critical household registration policy change came in 1984 when the State Council issued a directive allowing peasants to move to urban areas under the condition that they bring grain and food and pay for their own basic living expenses. That change, outlined in two important documents "The State Council Notification on the Question of Peasants Entering Towns" (1984) and "The Provisional Regulations on the Management of the Population Living Temporarily in the Cities" (1985)—allowed rural people to move to and work in a city where they could make more money than in their rural hometowns without changing their registration. As a result, a large number of people moved and have continued to move from economically underdeveloped rural areas, such as Heinan, Sichuan, Anhui, Hunai, and Jiangxi Province, to the more developed urban areas in eastern coast provinces, such as Jiangsu, Zhejiang, Fujian, Shandong, and Guangdong, as well as large metropolitan areas, such as Beijing and Shanghai (Shen and Huang 2003).

In the 1980s, migrants were predominantly single adults who temporarily worked in urban areas and eventually returned to their original places of residence. Since the early 1990s, however, more migrants have come to urban areas with their families, including their young children (Duan and Liang 2003; Zhou 2003). Rather than temporarily staying in cities, more and more migrant families attempt to find a way to settle and ultimately integrate into the destination city. However, given that a change in residence does not necessarily mean a change in registration, migrants' capacity to integrate is limited (Chan 1994). Migrant workers and their families who work and live in cities, but are not considered city residents, find themselves marginalized (Pan 2004).

The rules regarding a permanent change in residence registration status vary from place to place, and the degree to which migrant workers are marginalized varies accordingly. Some small towns and townships that are considered urban are open to rural migrants who have found a job and housing. Once they have secured a stable job and housing in those towns, migrants can apply for a change of registration. Some medium-sized cities and provincial capitals have lifted the limit on the number of rural migrants who can apply for permanent residency; however, given the requirements that must be met, such as maintaining a high income level, obtaining a certain type of job, and buying housing, not all migrants can apply for a change of registration. Migrant workers generally take low-paying jobs with no benefits, locking them into a low economic status and a position of social inferiority. Such jobs do not qualify them to change their place of registration to the destination city. Large cities such as Beijing and Shanghai still rigidly control the number of rural laborers granted permanency (Meng and Zhang 2001). Because most migrants move to larger cities and metropolitan areas with more restrictive policies, a large number of migrants cannot apply to change their registration status. The latest policy, "The State Council Notification on the Household Registration Reform" (2012), states that middle- to lower level cities are encouraged to have household registration reform initiatives for migrants, while larger cities still need to manage the size of their populations in accordance with economic development goals.

The practical obstacles to registration change have important implications for the children of migrants. Since the children of rural migrants remain registered as rural residents regardless of where they live or where they were born, they do not have access to many government-funded social services, including education, in the cities where their migrant parents live and work. As a result, many migrant parents choose not to bring their children with them to the city and instead leave them with grandparents or other relatives in the place of origin.

## THE DECENTRALIZED EDUCATION FINANCING SYSTEM

According to the 1986 Compulsory Education Law, which directs the development of primary and secondary education in China, all children between ages 6 and 15 are entitled to nine years of compulsory education, including six years of primary school and three years of middle school. Since the late 1980s, the top priority of China's educational development has been to enforce nine years of compulsory education across the country, with a special emphasis on rural and economically underdeveloped regions (Tsang and Ding 2005).

Starting in the early 1980s, the Chinese public finance system underwent a fundamental structural change from a centralized to a decentralized system. According to the earlier practice of *tong shou tong zhi* (unified collection and unified allocation) under the cenrtralized public finance system, a lower level county or provincial government submitted all its tax revenues to a higher level provincial or central government and received all its expenditures from the higher level government (Tsang 1996). Since the new practice of *fen zao chi fan* (eating from separate pots) was introduced in 1982, each level of government is now responsible for its own finances (Tsang 1996). Consequently, education finance in China has changed from a formerly centralized system with a narrow revenue base to a decentralized system with a diversified revenue base (Tsang 1996). Policy changes have made county-level governments take primary responsibility for financing social services, including compulsory education for registered local children (Guo 2006). In the past, county governments could receive reimbursement for educational expenditures from higher levels of governments, namely the provinces or the central government. Under the new policy, county governments must mobilize their own fiscal revenues and other financial resources to fund compulsory education, without subsidies from higher levels of governments. Figure 8.1 shows the structure of China's decentralized education financing system.

The decentralized education financing system, which is based on diversified revenue at the county level and below, aims to mobilize various resources, including non-governmental, non-budgeted resources, to support education. While total educational expenditures rose in the 1980s and 1990s, the governmental share in educational expenditures declined (Tsang 2000). For example, between 1990 and 1998, the percentage of all educational expenditures from government budgets dropped from about 65 percent to 53 percent. Other sources of funding included levies and surcharges, enterprise and school-raised funds, social contributions, and funding from private schools and other sources. Together these sources comprised over one-third of educational expenditures through the 1990s. The trend has continued since then, as shown in Figure 8.2.

While the decentralized system mobilized new education resources as the economy expanded, it also brought new inequalities in school funding between areas and regions. Because of the new public finance system, non-governmental and non-budgeted funding sources are now more closely tied to local economic

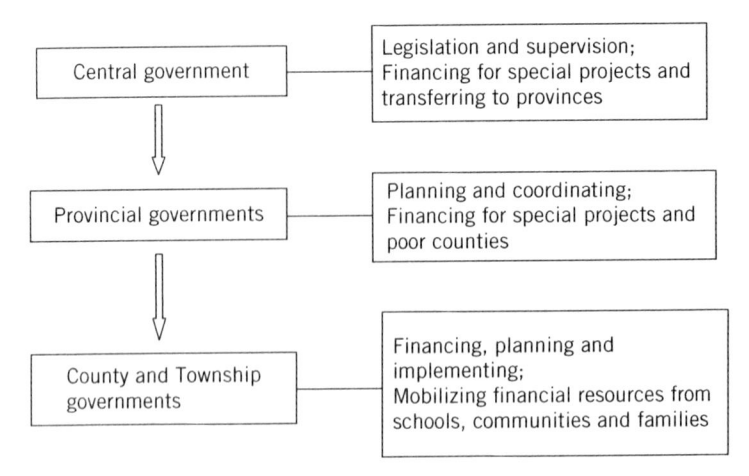

## 146 CHINESE SOCIAL POLICY IN A TIME OF TRANSITION

**Figure 8.1.** Decentralized Education Financing System in China

development. The new system has also reduced resource transfers from richer to poorer regions because each government is reponsible for education finance at its jurisdictionary level (Hannum and Wang 2006).

As a result, two of the prominent problems in Chinese compulsory education are inadequate funding in poor and rural areas and large financial disparities across areas and regions (Tsang and Ding 2005). Statistics show that in 1999 national per-student total spending was 701 RMB (US$88) at the primary level and 1,165 RMB (US$146) at the middle school level. Per-student

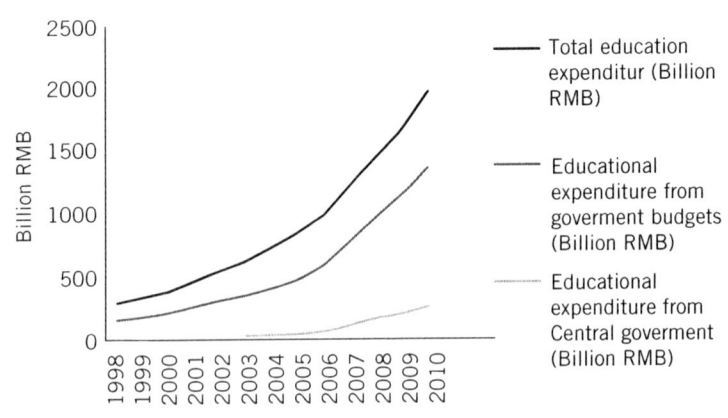

Data source: 1998–2010 Annual National Educational Expenditure Report by Ministry of Education of China, National Bureau of Statistics of China, and Ministry of Finance of China. Data on Educational Expenditure from Central government are available for 2003–2010.

**Figure 8.2.** China National Educational Expenditure, 1998–2010. *Source:* 1998–2010 Annual National Educational Expenditure Report by Ministry of Education of China, National Bureau of Statistics of China, and Ministry of Finance of China

total spending in urban areas and rural areas was 1,062 RMB (US$133) and 576 RMB (US$72), respectively—a ratio of 1.84 (Tsang and Ding 2005). The disparity between the most developed urban metropolitan areas and the less developed rural areas is even larger. For example, in 1999 the highest per-student educational spending was in Shanghai; it was ten times greater than the spending at the other end of the spectrum in Guizhou Province; the inequality ratio roughly doubled in the decade of 1990s as a result of education finance reform (Hannum and Wang 2006). With the overall increase of educational spending across the country in the past decade, the disparity remains. Table 8.1 shows per-student spending at primary school and middle school levels in 2007 and 2008 among several major migrant-sending and receiving provinces. Although the cost of delivering education in urban areas was higher than in rural areas, partly due to higher salaries, property costs, and living expenses, the gaps in funding far exceed the differences in costs. Even after taking legitimate disparities into consideration, educational funding for rural, economically underdeveloped areas was insufficient and highlighted the funding inequalities across areas and regions. Studies have shown that the imbalance between local governments' financial capacity and their responsibility has led to widening regional gaps in educational resources, teacher quality, and school facilities, especially if there is lack of effective central and provincial fiscal transfers (Guo 2006).

**Table 8.1.** Per-student Educational Spending across Regions in 2007–2008 (RMB)

| Region | Primary school | | | Middle school | | |
|---|---|---|---|---|---|---|
| | 2007 | 2008 | Increase (%) | 2007 | 2008 | Increase (%) |
| Total | 2207.04 | 2757.53 | 24.94 | 2679.42 | 3543.25 | 32.24 |
| Migrant receiving | | | | | | |
| Shanghai | 11498.99 | 13016.14 | 13.19 | 13122.69 | 15473.62 | 17.92 |
| Beijing | 7316.16 | 10111.51 | 38.21 | 10358.08 | 13224.85 | 27.68 |
| Zhejiang | 3734.35 | 4528.11 | 21.26 | 4795.31 | 5710.27 | 19.08 |
| Jiangshu | 3679.97 | 4306.54 | 17.03 | 3595.85 | 4464.21 | 24.15 |
| Shandong | 2396.58 | 2908.50 | 21.36 | 3387.00 | 4389.46 | 29.60 |
| Guanggong | 2053.92 | 2470.06 | 20.26 | 2742.77 | 3206.87 | 16.92 |
| Migrant sending | | | | | | |
| Hunan | 1905.43 | 2327.61 | 22.16 | 2660.86 | 3611.40 | 35.72 |
| Sichuan | 1681.05 | 2230.71 | 32.70 | 1995.44 | 2690.64 | 34.84 |
| Jiangxi | 1666.80 | 1795.53 | 7.72 | 2067.24 | 2513.38 | 21.58 |
| Anhui | 1644.73 | 2083.25 | 26.66 | 1793.39 | 2527.79 | 40.95 |
| Henan | 1392.91 | 1640.03 | 17.74 | 1909.95 | 2436.20 | 27.55 |

*Source:* Beijing Municipal Education Finance Expenditure Report 2009.

## CHALLENGES OF MIGRANT CHILD EDUCATION

Children have a right to a nine-year compulsory education, and it is the local government's responsibility to provide education funds for registered children. Theoretically, the place of origin governments at the county level should provide education funds for migrant children. However, once children move to urban areas with their parents, there is no mechanism that allows migrant children to take any educational funds from their place of origin to the destination cities. In addition, there is often a lack of funds in the place of origin because most migrant families have moved from poor, less developed rural areas.

The situation in the 1980s and early1990s caused severe hardship for migrant children. As a result of inadequate resources in the rural areas where they were registered and the laws that prohibited them from attending school in the urban areas where they actually lived, there was effectively no affordable schooling for these children. Children without local residence status could not attend the local public schools because that the public schools did not receive government funding for their education. Destination cities were not required to allocate education funds for the incoming migrant children. There were only two choices for migrant children: (1) urban public schools with surcharges, called *jiedu fei* (temporary studying fees); or (2) private migrant schools (*dagong zidi xuexiao*) (Chen 2004).

In response to the challenge of migrant children going unschooled, some urban public schools opened their doors on the condition that the migrant parents pay extra fees to supplement their children's education. However, financial hardship has prevented many migrant children from attending urban public schools. A study in 2000 that surveyed nearly two thousand migrant children who were enrolled in public schools in Beijing found that only about 15 percent of these children were from families with monthly household income higher than 1,000 RMB (US$140); about 20 percent were from families with a monthly income of less than 500 RMB (US$70) (Han 2001). Given the high cost of living in large cities such as Beijing, it was hard for those families to pay extra fees, estimated at 1,200 RMB (US$145) a semester, to send their child to a public primary school (Han 2001; Y. Li, Sun, and Yang 2003).

In lieu of paying fees to attend public school, the only other option has been attending private migrant schools, which charge lower fees. Starting in the mid-1990s, migrant workers created schools for their children that were funded by tuition and fees paid by migrant families (Chen 2004; Han 2001). Migrant schools were not supervised by the government and did not match the public school standards for education, curriculum development, and school building safety; thus most migrant schools were excluded from the formal school system in China. The topic of migrant school development is beyond the scope of the current chapter but deserves further attention from researchers.

In 2002, the Office of the National Working Committee on Children and Women under the State Council, China National Children's Center, and United

Nations Children Fund conducted a survey about migrant children's demography, health, education, and child rights protection in nine Chinese cities. Findings of the survey demonstrate that in these nine cities most migrant children enrolled in public schools. Among the migrant children who received schooling, on average four-fifths of them attended public schools (L. Zhang and Zhao 2003). Enrollment of migrant children in public schools was lower in large cities, such as Beijing, than in small cities. Possible reasons for the disparity are stricter requirements for registration status and higher education fees in large cities.

## MAJOR POLICIES FOR MIGRANT CHILD EDUCATION

Since the mid-1990s, a series of educational regulations and administrative policies have been developed regarding migrant child education. The trend has been a gradual shift from exclusive to inclusive arrangements. Two critical policies have been the Interim Measure of School Education for Temporary Migrant Children in 1998 (*Liudong ertong shaonian jiuxue zanxing banfa*), hereafter referred to as the 1998 Measure, and the Notice of Improve Education of Children of Rural Migrant Workers in 2003 (*Guowuyuan guanyu jinyibu zuohao jincheng wugong jiuye nongmingong zinv jiaoyu gongzuo de yijian de tongzhi*), hereafter called the 2003 Notice.

The State Education Committee and the Public Security Department jointly issued the 1998 Measure, which outlines two significant guidelines for migrant child education. One calls upon governments of destination cities to be primarily responsible for the education of migrant children. The other calls upon public schools in those cities to be primarily responsible for accommodating the education of migrant children. However, according to the 1998 measure, if a guardian, such as a grandparent, resides in the location where a child was initially registered, then that is where the child can attend public school. Only if there is no guardian available can a child of migrants apply to schools in the host city.

The 2003 Notice was issued by the State Council and inherited the same guidelines. The Compulsory Education Law in 1986 states that the nine-year compulsory education is a right for all school-age children; therefore, all migrant children should receive compulsory education, no matter where they live. The 2003 Notice specifically refers to "children of rural migrant workers," which is different from the term "migrant children" used in the 1998 Measure. The change in terminology acknowledges that migrant families who encounter financial difficulties and institutional barriers to their children's education are those who migrated from rural areas. Nearly 80 percent of the migrant population has moved from rural areas; the remaining 20 percent came from different cities or towns (Tsang and Ding 2005). Rural migrant workers are challenged not only by the barrier of institutional residence registration but also by economic barriers associated with low-paying jobs. The 2003 Notice not only reinforces the responsibility of urban public schools to educate rural migrant children in urban areas, but also supports the idea that migrant children should receive the same education as their peers. Both of these changes are steps toward a more inclusive education policy for migrant children.

Regarding the question of how migrant child education is financed, the 1998 Measure does not provide a clear answer, except in item 11, which says that public schools may charge migrant families extra fees for their children to attend school. The 2003 Notice, which requires equal treatment of all children regarding tuition and fees, aims to eliminate these extra fees. It also states that the governments and education authorities of destination cities have the responsibility to finance the education of migrant children and to provide subsidies for education fees to migrant children from poor families. The 2003 Notice lists three major principles of financing migrant child education. First, city government financial bureaus should subsidize public schools that accept a large number of migrant children. Second, city governments should budget part of their regular educational funds for migrant child education. Finally, city governments should encourage donations from companies, organizations, and individuals to help fund public schools.

Since 2003, the central government has issued several policies regarding migrant child education, including the State Council Directives on Issues of Migrant Workers in 2006, the new Compulsory Education Law in 2006, and the State Council Notice Regarding Tuition and Fee Waivers for Compulsory Education Age Children in Cities in 2008. These major statements reaffirm previous policy guidelines that urban city governments and urban public schools should take major responsibility for educating migrant children.

## MIGRANT CHILD EDUCATION POLICY IMPLEMENTATION

Under the guidelines of the Compulsory Education Law, the 1998 Measure, and the 2003 Notice, provincial and municipal governments started developing local measures to implement migrant child education policy. Given various financial capacities and policy preferences, the implementation varied. Although there is a lack of systematic review of all types of policy implementation, research has generated valuable information about how the policies are operating in large cities, such as Beijing and Shanghai, and eastern coast provinces, including Zhejiang Province, and the Yangzi River area, including Guangdong Province (B. Li 2009).

This section discusses two cases of migrant child education policy implementation: one in Beijing and the other in Zhejiang Province, where large migrant child populations are concentrated. The focus of this discussion is on how local governments finance the schooling of migrant children in urban public schools. Rather than exploring all types of policy implementation, this chapter aims to compare and contrast the Beijing and Zhejiang cases. Beijing, China's capital city, with its economic resources and development opportunities, is a major migration destination. The reform of social policies related to migrant families in Beijing will influence migration patterns in the future. The special significance of migrant child education policies in Zhejiang Province comes from its higher enrollment rate of migrant children, which was 96 percent in 2004 (Xinhuanet, 2004), and its specific financial reform, that is, the government financial guarantee mechanism, which seeks to improve compulsory education while implementing the new migrant child education policy (The People's Government of Zhejiang Province 2007).

## Beijing

According to the 2010 China census, Beijing's total population of 19.6 million included 7 million migrants from other provinces (National Bureau of Statistics of China 2011). The influx of migrants is the major reason for Beijing's population increase over the last decade. Migrants accounted for 35.9 percent of its total population in 2010, compared to 18.9 percent in 2000.

More recent figures are not available, but in 2000, 2 million of Beijing's 2.6 million migrants did not have a local Beijing household registration status. Estimates of how many migrant children were enrolled in the Beijing public schools varied from 79 percent (L. Zhang and Zhao 2003) to 96 percent (Wang 2003). One study reports that the enrollment rate of migrant children improved substantially after 1998 with the development of new policies (Wei and Du 2005). Since 1998, the parents of a migrant child who have lived in Beijing for more than six months and have already received temporary residence cards can apply to send their children to public schools.[2] Migrant child enrollment at present is likely concentrated in schools located in urban and rural joint areas in Beijing. In some schools, migrant students may account for up to two-thirds of student enrollment.

In Beijing, responsibility for financing education falls on district governments, of which there are 14, plus two counties. Since Beijing is one of four directly controlled municipalities under the central government in China, district governments are on the same level as county governments in other provinces. Fiscal disparities exist among these districts, and implementation of migrant child education in each district varies accordingly. Since 2002, the Beijing municipal government has required district governments to include enrolled migrant children in annual educational finance planning. Schools accepting a large number of migrant children can receive some financial subsidies from the municipal government. Nonetheless, because the per-migrant student subsidy is lower than the per-student spending in urban public schools (Wang 2003), the sum of subsidies and regular education funds in these districts is lower than the normal standard of public schools in Beijing. Accepting migrant children thereby decreases the overall resources available to a school and raises concerns about possible adverse effects on a school's quality and standards. Schools with larger migrant enrollments are further disadvantaged because subsidies for financing migrant child education are not a regularized part of the municipal government budgetary process, which means that schools cannot predict how much additional funding they will be able to obtain for enrolling migrant children every year. Subsidies from the municipal government have been used mainly for building and maintaining school facilities rather than for instruction, a fact that raises further concerns about the quality of instruction.

Until 2010, the financial responsibility to fund regular school operations and per-student spending for both locally registered and migrant children in Beijing lay on the shoulders of county and district governments. A new policy from Beijing, the Guide on 2010 Educational Subsidy Priority to Counties and Districts, required the 2010 budget for basic education funding to give priority to ensuring compulsory education by introducing a government financial guarantee mechanism and integrating migrant child education into city and district general educational planning (Beijing Municipal Commission of Education 2009).

## Zhejiang Province

Zhejiang Province is one of the most popular destinations for migrants. According to the 2010 China census, the total population of Zhejiang Province was 54.4 million, including 11.8 million migrants from other provinces, who accounted for 21.7 percent of the province's total population (National Bureau of Statistics of China 2011). To implement the 2003 Notice at the local level in a large province like Zhejiang, the key questions are how to define the responsibilities of government at different levels and how to balance the disparity in various regions. A notable feature of this case is Zhejiang's financial subsidy strategy for migrant child education (C. Liu 2007), which is embedded in the provincial strategies to reform and improve compulsory education finance (The People's Government of Zhejiang Province 2007).

The provincial government divides the province into five regions, according to level of socioeconomic development, and then applies a sliding-scale subsidy to local governments for supporting migrant child education. For the least developed regions, the provincial government provides 100 percent financial transfer to subsidize education for migrant children, while for the most developed regions, the provincial government provides only 20 percent. Regions at the other three levels of development receive 70 percent, 50 percent, or 30 percent (C. Liu 2007). With the subsidy from the provincial government, the county- or town-level governments, regardless of their local fiscal situation, obtain enough money to fund migrant child education and do not compromise the school's standards. In addition to these subsidies to public schools, governments at different levels, particularly the local level, support low-income migrant families by reducing education fees or providing scholarships.

Financing has been the most frequently cited challenge for implementing migrant child education policy. Although the 2003 Notice provides an overall guideline about financing migrant child education, how to implement it at local levels is not clearly defined—not an unusual feature in social policy development in China. The central government sets up the overall guidelines and principles, and provincial governments implement them in various ways, according to their special local needs and characteristics, a practice that often leads to significant disparities among various regions. A comparison between Beijing and Zhejiang suggests that the higher the fiscal transfer level, the stronger the ability of local governments of destination cities to fund migrant child education. For instance, in Zhejiang Province, where the fiscal transfer level is at the provincial rather than the county level, the ability to manage regional disparity becomes stronger because all regions have the capacity to fund migrant child education. In Beijing, which has little or no fiscal transfer at the city level, financing migrant child education in public schools lies heavily on the local levels of government, that is, the district and county level, putting large fiscal burdens on local governments where more migrants are concentrated.

## EDUCATION FINANCING IN INTERNATIONAL PERSPECTIVE

This section puts China's policies in an international perspective by asking who pays for education in other countries. The Organization for Economic Cooperation and Development (OECD) and the United Nations Educational, Scientific and Cultural Organization (UNESCO) collect comparable statistical data in the field of education. In particular, the OECD/UNESCO World Education Indicators (WEI) program aims to address the financing of education systems by examining spending and investment strategies in various developing countries, including Argentina, Brazil, Chile, China, Egypt, India, Indonesia, Jamaica, Jordan, Malaysia, Paraguay, Peru, the Philippines, the Russian Federation, Sri Lanka, Thailand, Tunisia, Uruguay, and Zimbabwe (UNESCO Institute for Statistics Organization for OECD and Development World Education Indicators Programme 2003).

The report states that, on average, WEI countries display current levels of investment in education relative to GDP on par with those of OECD countries and spend about 5.5 percent of their GDP on educational institutions. However, profound variations exist among those countries' social, economic, and political environments. Data show that spending on education varies widely among WEI countries—ranging from 1.2 percent of GDP in Indonesia to 9.9 percent in Jamaica, with China falling on the low side at 3.7 percent (UNESCO Institute for Statistics Organization for OECD and Development World Education Indicators Programme 2003). The Chinese government has set up a goal of increasing public spending on education. The newly published "National Long-term Educational Reform and Development Plan (2010–2020)" states that by 2012, the government aims to increase educational spending to 4 percent of GDP (State Council P.R. China 2010).

Besides overall education spending, it is important to examine the distribution of education funding across different education levels and the structure of funding sources across different government levels. Differences in costs per student by level of education can influence overall proportions of spending. An examination of how public resources are distributed across China's three levels of education shows that the expenditure on a tertiary student is 12–16 times that of a primary student, and that a secondary student receives more than twice the expenditure of a primary one. Among WEI countries, the ratio of spending on a tertiary student compared to a primary student ranges from 2 times in the Philippines, to 4 times in Chile, to more than 14 times in Brazil and China. In addition, the Chinese government spends the smallest portion of its education fund on primary education among these countries. All WEI countries, including China, have a larger demand for primary and lower secondary education than is the case for OECD countries, due to demographic pressures: WEI countries have an average 21 percent of the population aged 5–14, compared to 13 percent in OECD countries. Research suggests that a more equal distribution of resources across the three levels would help sustain economic growth; in particular, investment in universal primary education results in significant societal benefits. Given the huge education disparity between rural and urban areas in China, enhanced efforts to finance compulsory education for children in rural areas would dramatically affect the distribution of educational opportunities and would likely reduce education inequalities. Providing funds to migrant child education is one way to increase educational opportunity for children from rural areas.

Educational funding in China is highly decentralized by international standards. Even with overall increased education funding in recent years, the education expenditures from the central government remained as low as 6.9 percent in 2003 and 18.8 percent in 2010 (as shown in Figure 8.2). Regarding financing compulsory education, findings of a survey by the State Council Development Research Center show that local governments (i.e., county and town governments) provide about 87 percent of funds, while provincial and central governments account for only 11 percent and 2 percent, respectively (Lu 2004). Clearly, the central government contributes a very small percentage of education financing, particularly for compulsory education in China. Decentralized education finance has been an important policy issue among the WEI countries. Regional and local governments are more likely to govern and fund primary than tertiary education. Meanwhile, the WEI report states that intergovernmental transfers are commonly used to address fiscal imbalances. Local education authorities govern and fund public schools in their districts, but a considerable proportion of funding is the result of intergovernmental transfers from regional and central authorities (UNESCO Institute for Statistics Organization for OECD and Development World Education Indicators Programme 2003).

The WEI program suggests taking a developmental perspective, which considers education as an investment in the collective future of societies and nations, rather than simply in the future success of individuals. Through this lens, education is viewed as a strategy to promote economic prosperity, employment, and social cohesion. In Chinese society, education is highly valued as a means for individual mobility. At a social policy level, education is also an investment in the collective future of society because educated children will become the skilled labor force of the future. Because of the changing migration pattern from individual to family migration, many migrant children grow up in cities and are likely to stay there as adults (Duan and Liang 2003; Zhou 2003). This trend makes financing migrant child education essential for China's successful long-term social development and for China's urbanization process in particular.

## DISCUSSION AND CONCLUSION

Migrant child education is a national issue, and associated policies should take into account the large fiscal and educational disparities between regions in China. Development of the compulsory education in rural areas is one of the best ways to bridge the educational gap, and serving the needs of migrant children in cities is one way to improve the enforcement of compulsory education for children from rural areas. The central government has initiated a variety of strategies to enhance rural education development, such as financial subsidies to supply school buildings, free textbooks, and financial aid to students from poor families, as well as teacher training in rural areas (T. Zhang and Zhao 2006). The nature of the migrant child education problem lies in the structure of the household registration system, the challenge of population migration, and the rapid urbanization of China. Providing education for children who have already migrated to cities with their parents is an opportunity to provide equal education for children from rural areas. To achieve this goal, the government needs to change its mind-set from an administrative perspective that focuses on population migration control to a developmental perspective that focuses on investing in human capital. Educational statistics show substantial increases in educational funding as a percent of GDP in recent years in China, as shown in Figure 8.2. The national goal of increased education spending provides opportunities to discuss and reform education financing for migrant child education.

The national education development plan also highlights the importance of continuing to strengthen free compulsory education, including providing appropriate education for migrant children. Given China's ongoing urbanization, children of migrants today will be part of the urban labor force in the future. The better educated the labor force is, the more likely the economy will thrive. The potential impact of policy change on the size of the migrant child population needs further research. It should be noted that a person's decision to migrate is determined by a complex number of factors, such as his job opportunities, education, experience, and social network. A change in migrant child education policy itself will not necessarily lead to a dramatic increase in the migrant polulation.

The goals of expanding education and maintaining equitable access to education are inextricably linked to the funding of education. In the case of migrant child education, the central government needs to develop a financing mechanism to transfer education money to areas and regions where large populations of migrant children live and where local governments have less fiscal capability. Only the central government has the financial and legal power to provide financial transfers and to meet migrant children's educational needs across different areas and regions in the country. With the decentralized public finance system since China's fiscal reform, county-level governments depend even more on the central and provincial governments, especially in less developed areas.

The case of Zhejiang Province highlights the potential for provincial governments, which have more financial resources than lower levels of government, to establish financial transfers to support migrant child education as part of the regular budget. An examination of Zhejiang Province shows that these provincial subsidies can be varied according to the variation in the financial capacities of the county governments receiving the transfers. In accordance with the principle of decentralized financing, local governments still take primary responsibility for funding compulsory education, but the additional funds transferred from the central and provincial governments give local governments in different areas and regions the capacity to provide sufficient funds to public schools to meet the needs of all students, including migrant children without local household registration status.

In summary, through a review of major migrant child education policies and an examination of policy implementation, this chapter argues that financing is the critical element of current migrant child education policy in China. It suggests that higher level governments, that is, central and provincial governments, should take the lead in developing regularized fiscal transfers for migrant child compulsory education. It also calls for more research and discussion about policymaking, with an emphasis on a developmental perspective. A strong future research agenda, with more available data on migrant child populations and educational spending on migrant child education, is needed to follow and review the educational funding flows across different levels of government. The end result of this research should be better policy with appropriate financial sharing mechanisms between higher level (central and provincial) governments and lower level (county, city, and township) governments to ensure sufficient financing for migrant child education in urban areas.

## NOTES

1. Because the public report of the 2010 census data does not present migrant children by age, 2005 sample data are the latest available.
2. It should be noted, however, that having a temporary residence card does not indicate a change of household registration status.

# REFERENCES

Beijing Municipal Commission of Education. 2009. *2010 niandu dui quxian jiaoyu buzhu zhongdian touru fangxiang yu xiangmu zhinan [Guide on 2010 educational subsidy priority to counties and districts]*. Retrieved from http://www.bjedu.gov.cn/publish/main/19/2009/20091022113251071294823/20091022113251071294823_.html

Chan, K.-W. 1994. *Cities with invisible walls*. New York: Oxford University Press.

Chen, J. 2004. Beijingshi liudong ertong jiaoyu wenti chuntan [Migrant child education in Beijing municipal]. *Journal of Haidian Zoudu College, special issue*, 108–113.

Cheng, T., and M. Selden. 1994. The origins and social consequences of China's hukou system. *The China Quarterly 139*: 644–668.

Duan, C., and H. Liang. 2003. *Liudong ertong jiaoyu wenti zhuanti yanjiu [Special issue on migrant children education problem]*. Beijing: Office of the Women and Children Work Committee of the State Council and the China National Children's Center.

Duan, C. and K. Yang. 2008. Woguo liudong ertong zuixin zhuangkuang: Jiyu 2005 nian quanguo 1% renkou chouyang diaochao shuju de wenxi [The new update of migrant children in China: Based on the 2005 national 1% population sample data analysis]. *Population Research* 2008(6): 23–31.

Guo, G. 2006. Decentralized Education Spending and Regional Disparities: Evidence from Chinese Counties 1997–2001. *Journal of Chinese Political Science 11*(2): 45–60.

Han, J. 2001. Beijingshi liudong ertong yiwu jiaoyu zhuangkuang diaocha baogao [A report of migrant child compulsory education survey in Beijing]. *Youth Studies* 8:1–7.

Hannum, E., and J. Wang. 2006. Geography and educational inequality in China. *China Economic Review 17*(3): 253–265.

Li, B. 2009. Liudong ertong jiaoyu zhengce wei he zai difang yu ganga [Policy implementation difficulty at locals regarding migrant child education ]. *China Youth Daily* (December 19). Retrieved from http://article.cyol.com/home/zqb/content/2009-12/19/content_2990851.htm.

Li, Y., W. Sun, and Z. Yang. 2003. Beijingshi liudong renkou jiqi zinv jiaoyu zhuangkuang ciaocha yanjiu (Xia) [A survey research of education condition for migrants and their children in Beijing, Second part]. *Journal of Capital Normal University 2* (total No. 151): 110–114.

Liang, Z. 2001. The age of migration in China. *Population and Development Review 27*(3): 499–524.

Liu, Z. 2005. Institution and inequality: The hukou system in China. *Journal of Comparative Economic 33:* 133–157.

Liu, C. 2007. Zai zhongyang yu defang zhijian: Mingong zinv jiaoyu zhengce de caozuohua—Zhejiang sheng weili [Between the central and local governments: Education for children of rural migrant workers, A case of Zhejiang Province]. *Youth Studies 10*: 24–28.

Liu, S., X. Li, and M. Zhang. 2003. *Scenario analysis on urbanization and rural-to-urban migration in China*. Laxenburg, Austria: International Institute for Applied Systems Analysis.

Lu, X. 2004. Tongchou chengxiang fazhan, pojie "san nong" nanti [Coordinating urban and rural development, solving the "three rural" problem ]. *China Comment 4*: 20–22.

Meng, X., and J. Zhang. 2001. The two-tier labor market in urban China: Occupational segregation and wage differentials between urban residents and rural migrants in Shanghai. *Journal of Comparative Economic, 29*: 485–504.

National Bureau of Statistics of China. 2001. *China statistical yearbook (2000)*. Beijing: China Statistics Press.

National Bureau of Statistics of China, (2011, April 28th). *Major Figures of the 2010 National Population Census*. Retrieved from http://www.stats.gov.cn/tjfx/jdfx/t20110428_402722238.htm

Pan, Z. 2004. Zhongguo chengshi liudong renkou de fazhan kunjing yu shehui fengxian: Shehui paichi yu bianyuanhua de shengchan yu zaishengchan [China migrant population development problem and social risks: Social exclusion and marginalization]. *Zhanlue yu Guanli [Strategy and Administration] 1*: 87–91.

Seeborg, M. C., Z. Jin, and Y. Zhu. 2000. The new rural-urban labor mobility in China: Causes and implications. *Journal of Socio-Economics 29*: 29–56.

Shen, J., and Y. Huang. 2003. The working and living space of the "floating population" in China. *Asia Pacific Viewpoint 44*(1): 51–62.

Shi, B. 2002. Chengshi liudong ertong shaonian jiuxue wenti zhengce fenxi [A policy analysis of migrant children education problems in cities]. *Journal of China Youth College for Political Sciences 21*(1): 31–35.

Solinger, D. J. 1999. *Contesting citizenship in urban China: Peasant migrants, the state, and the logic of the market*. Berkeley, Los Angeles, London: University of California Press.

State Council P.R. China. 2010. National medium- and long-term educational reform and Development Plan (2010–2020).

The People's Government of Zhejiang Province. 2007. *Zhejiang sheng renmin zhengfu guanyu shishi yiwu jiaoyu jingfei baozhang jizhi gaige de tongzhi [Zhejiang People's Government Notice on compulsory education finance security reform]*. Retrieved from http://www.zhejiang.gov.cn

Tsang, M. C. 1996. Financial reform of basic education in China. *Economics of Education Review 15*(4): 423–444.

Tsang, M. C. 2000. Education and national development in China since 1949: Oscillating policies and enduring dilemmas. *China Review 2000*: 579–618.

Tsang, M. C., and Y. Ding. 2005. Resource utilization and disparities in compulsory education in China. *China Review*. Retrieved from http://www.tc.columbia.edu/centers/coce/pdf_files/a10.pdf

UNESCO Institute for Statistics Organization for OECD and Development World Education Indicators Programme. 2003. *Financing education: Investments and returns analysis of the world education indicators*. Retrieved from http://www.uis.unesco.org/TEMPLATE/pdf/wei/WEI_ExecSummary_Eng.pdf

Wang, W. 2003. Beijing liudong renkou zinv yiwu jiaoyu zhengce shishi fenxi [Beijing migrant child compulsory education policy analysis]. *Zhongguo jiaoyu xuekan [Journal of the Chinese Society of Education]* 10: 9–12.

Wei, H., and W. Du. 2005. *Zhong guo te shu xu qiu qun ti shi ling er tong yi wu jiao yu fa zhan yan jiu bao gao [Compulsory education development report regarding vulnerable school-age children in China ]*. Beijing: Beijing Academy of Educational Sciences.

Xinhuanet (2004, September 3). *Zhejiang jiang yiwu jiaoyu yanchang zhi 15 nian xueqian 3 nian dao gaozhong biye [Zhejiang province extends the compulsory education to 15 years from pre-school to high school]*. Retrieved from http://news.xinhuanet.com/edu/2004-09/03/content_1941326.htm.

Zhang, L., and S. Zhao (Eds.). 2003. *Survey report on the temporary migrant children in 9 cities of China*. Beijing: Office of the Women and Children Work Committee of the State Council and the China National Children's Center.

Zhang, T., and M. Zhao. 2006. Universalizing Nine-Year Compulsory Education for Poverty Reduction in Rural China. *International Review of Education* 52(3–4): 261–286.

Zhao, Z. 2001. Registered households and micro-social structure in China: Residential patterns in three settlements in Beijing area. *Journal of Family History* 26(1): 39–65.

Zhou, H. 2003. *Liudong renkou de jiatinghua jiqi yingxiang yinsu [Trend of family migration and its causes]*. Paper presented at the the national conference regarding the fifth national census.

# 9

# LABOR MIGRATION, CITIZENSHIP, AND SOCIAL WELFARE IN CHINA AND INDIA

Josephine Smart, Reeta Chowdari Tremblay, and Mostaem Billah

## INTRODUCTION

India and China have been the focus of a great deal of international interest in recent years for a variety of reasons ranging from politics to economics to culture. It is hard not to notice these two Asian countries, which rank at the very top worldwide for population size, at 1.3 billion (China) and 1.1 billion (India), respectively. The uninterrupted robust annual economic growth rate in China since the mid-1980s has created a nation that is playing an ever larger role in the world economy as a destination for foreign investments in manufacturing, an increasingly lucrative market for global consumer goods, and an active investor in the world arena in natural resources, land, and other strategic resources. While India's economic growth rate has been more modest at 5.6 percent per year for the period 1978–2007, compared to China's 9.9 percent per year average for the same period (Hong 2009), it has gained much international attention for its ambitious structural-adjustment program dubbed the New Economic Policy (NEP), which was introduced in 1991 in compliance with International Monetary Fund (IMF) directives (Sharma 2009, 76–77). Prior to the global recession, India was becoming a new frontier for foreign investments in manufacturing, information technology (IT), software development, and customer service call centers. Foreign investment of US$44.1 billion was expected in the year to March 2010 and US$52.1 billion the following year, about 35 to 40 percent of which was foreign direct investment.[1] For the first time in the history of India, agriculture accounted for a smaller share of gross domestic product (GDP) than manufacturing in 2010, at 5.42 trillion rupees and 5.69 trillion rupees, respectively (Cox 2009, 62).

One of the keys to the success of the economic reform policies first introduced in China in the late 1970s is the liberalization of people's mobility, which used to be tightly controlled as part of the state's effort to avoid mass rural-urban migration and its myriad associated problems, which are common in developing countries. This liberalization of individual mobility was informed by the foresight that a steady stream of workers would be needed in factories financed by foreign investments throughout the coastal regions in China. As the Chinese economy expands rapidly, the demand for migrant workers in all sectors financed by foreign and domestic investments grows in tandem. The magnitude of this post-reform mobility grew from 88.5 million in 1995 to 120 million in 2000 (Feng 2010, 222). By 2005, it was estimated that up to 147.5 million Chinese, or 11.3 percent of the total population in China, were migrant workers (Li and Li 2010, 189). A somewhat different set of figures on rural worker outflow in China reported 114 million in 2003, 118 million in 2004, and 126 million in 2005 (Hussain and Wang 2010, 135). Labor migration, in the case of China, is both an outcome and a driver of economic development. In absolute numbers, India surpasses China in reporting a total of 300.9 million internal migrants in 2001, compared to 220.9 million in 1991 and 200.6 million in 1981.[2]

This chapter compares labor migration in China and India as of the early 2000s to begin answering four broad questions: How are migration patterns different in the two countries? How do we explain the similarities and differences in labor migration? What are the likely impacts of these different patterns on migrant-sending (rural) communities in the two countries? What are the policy implications? Circumstantial evidence suggests that differences in migration policies may help explain some of the differences in economic development in the two countries. According to figures released by the State Council Poverty Alleviation Office (Beijing), the number of impoverished rural residents in China dropped from 94.23 million in 2000 to 35.97 million in 2009.[3] This impressive rate of rural poverty reduction in China is unheard of in India. The dedicated government policies in China since 2000 to support a "new socialist countryside" through rural tax reduction, rural school tuition waivers, rural health insurance, and a minimum livelihood guarantee program appear to have been instrumental in improving economic and social conditions in rural China (Lei 2010, 332–333). In addition, evidence suggests that the ongoing out-migration of rural workers contributes to and sustains rural development in significant ways.

In this chapter, we articulate the very different outcomes of rural migration in China and India through a critical comparative examination of state interventions (or lack of), conditions of social and economic disparity, and scale of long-term and return migration. Our findings suggest that the household registration (*hukou*) system in China, acknowledged widely as the ultimate root cause of urban-rural inequality,[4] may play a key role in securing return migration and advancing rural development via remittances, knowledge, and skill and technology transfer. In the absence of either a registration system or any government incentives for return migration in India, the rate of return migration among rural migrants has always been very low, and the overall contribution of out-migration to the rural economy and rural development has been limited at best.

## LABOR MIGRATION IN CHINA AND INDIA

The massive relocation of production from the United States, Canada, and Europe to China, India, and other newly industrialized nations since the 1980s has transformed the global economy and has set into motion a series of far-reaching global-local transformations that have attracted much attention from policymakers and academic researchers (Rees and Smart 2001). One of the readily observable impacts of this new regime of production on post-1978 China is the unprecedented scale of internal migration, which is now estimated to involve over 130 million people. A significant proportion of these migrants, known as *mingong, nonggong*,[5] labor migrants, or floating population, are engaged in manufacturing production in the rapidly industrializing coastal cities that were designated by the Chinese state as "special economic zones" in its 1978 economic reform policies (J. Smart and A. Smart 1991, 216–233). The concentration of foreign direct investment (FDI) in Guangdong, greater Shanghai, Zhejiang, and Jiangsu resulted in a most uneven geographical dispersal of labor migrants within China. Over 60 percent of the total migrant population within China is located along the southeastern coastal regions. In particular, the province of Guangdong remains the most favored destination for labor migrants; it was home to more than 35 percent of the total migrant labor force in 2002 (see Table 9.1, from Zhou 2005, 279).

Household registration (*hukou*) is a Chinese policy that has been in place since 1958. It was designed to avoid the massive rural-urban migration experienced by other developing countries, with some very negative impacts on local and national economies. Household registration is tied to key resource entitlements such as housing, employment, education, and health care. The structural inequality inherent in the *hukou* system that creates the urban-rural divide is referred to as "local citizenship" (A. Smart and J. Smart 2001) or "differential citizenship" (Wu 2010) because people without household registration in a particular loclity are not entitled to anything in that locality. Wong and Zeng (2008, 177) describe rural migrant workers as people who are "denied the legal, civil and social rights enjoyed by people with an urban hukou." This policy remains in effect today, but in modified form. Prior to 1978, rural residents required permission from their local government or administrative office to travel; this policy was loosened after 1978 to enable a more flexible response to rising labor demand in the rapidly industrializing regions along the coastal provinces after

Labor Migration, Citizenship, and Social Welfare in China and India   163

Table 9.1. Major Labor Migrant-Sending and Receiving Regions in China in 2002

| Migrant-sending provinces | Percentage of national total |
|---|---|
| Sichuan | 16.4 |
| Anhui | 10.2 |
| Hunan | 10.2 |
| Jiangxi | 8.7 |
| Henan | 7.2 |
| Hubei | 6.6 |
| **Migrant-receiving provinces** | |
| Guangdong | 35.5 |
| Zhejiang | 8.7 |
| Shanghai | 7.4 |
| Jiangsu | 6.0 |
| Beijing | 5.8 |
| Fujian | 5.1 |

*Source:* Zhou 2005:279, Table 2.1, original in Chinese.

the introduction of economic reforms. That liberalization of mobility has made possible the phenomenon of 130 million labor migrants now working within China in locations away from their home locality where their household registration is recorded. Large numbers of citizens were mobilized by state efforts to serve national interests on several occasions in modern Chinese history: the resettlement of Chinese scientific and industrial workers from the coastal urban centers into strategic interior locations to safeguard national interests in the event of war during the 1950s and 1960s; the major mobilization of urban residents into the countryside during the Cultural Revolution period from 1967 to 1977 for ideological "re-education;" and the more recent coordinated resettlement of Chinese citizens in western China and in border cities for strategic purposes both cultural and military (Whyte 2010, 7–19). Voluntary individual mobility tied to work migration in China is a reform driven phenomenon now entering its fourth decade.

In contrast to China, migration of all types has largely been a voluntary phenomenon in India since its independence in 1947, with minimum state intervention. Unlike China, where data about internal migration are collected by local authorities as part of the household registration system, the only available information about migrants in India comes from the Census and the National Sample Survey (NSS). The latest available Census information on migrants is from the 2001 Census.[6]

The Indian Census provides data on migrants based on two characteristics: place of birth and place of last residence. It also collects information on reasons for migration and the duration of residence at the place of enumeration. The reasons for migration are noted as employment, education, marriage, family moved, natural calamities, and others. Data are collected for three different migration distances: intra-district, inter-district, and inter-state, the first two defining the movement of individuals and households within the boundaries of a state, the third describing the movement from one state to another. Although the census of 1881 collected data on the place of birth, it is only since 1961 that intra-district migration, along with the four patterns—rural to urban, urban to rural, rural to rural, and urban to urban—has been measured. The 1971 census added the reasons for migration. Since 1961, data for the four patterns have been provided for each of the three distance classifications.

The NSS, on the other hand, collects data on migrants in relation to employment and defines a migrant by using the concept of usual place of residence (i.e., the place where the person has most recently stayed continuously for six months or more).

Despite a differing methodology for defining "migrant" and some scholars' assertions that the two data sets are not comparable, other studies point out that both data sets present a similar picture. Poor states like Bihar, Uttar Pradesh, Orissa, and Rajasthan are characterized by net out-migration or very low in-migration, whereas developed states, such as Maharashtra, Punjab, West Bengal, and Gujarat, tend to register a high rate of in-migration (Mukherji 2001).

In order to conduct a comparative study of India and China, it is essential to point out the limitations of the Indian data. To begin with, India's Census presents a very basic picture of people who change their residence. Neither the Indian Census nor the NSS data allow us to differentiate between seasonal, permanent, individual, family group, and return migrants (Srivastava and Sasikumar 2003). Furthermore, as Bhagat points out, if a rural mother delivers her baby in a nearby town, the child will be recorded as a migrant in the Indian Census because the place of birth is different from the place of residence. He notes that currently 34 percent of deliveries take place away from home, and that, according to a Government of India forecast, we can expect an 80 percent rate of institutional deliveries by the year 2010 (Bhagat 2005, 7). Bhagat draws our attention to the inability of the Census to capture migration that takes place due to unofficial civil wars (communal riots, social disturbances) and terrorism (Kashmiri Hindus' migration from the Kashmir Valley). Srivastva and Sasikumar also caution us about our exclusive reliance on macro data and point to the large gap between the conclusions one might draw from the macro data and the realities explored by field studies (A. Smart and J. Smart 1991, 216–233).

According to the 2001 Census, there were approximately 300.9 million people who changed their place of residence in India in the period 1991–2001 (see Table 9.2). Within this group, 20.5 million people migrated from rural to urban areas (see Table 9.3). This was a very small proportion (less than 4 percent) of the Indian rural population, which in turn accounts for over 60 percent of

Labor Migration, Citizenship, and Social Welfare in China and India

**Table 9.2.** Numbers of Internal Migrants Based on Place of Last Residence (POLR), India, 1971–2001 (in Millions)

| Census | Total Population of India (million) | Internal Migrants in millions (percentage) |
|---|---|---|
| 1971 | 548.1 | 159.7 (29.1) |
| 1981 | 659.3 | 200.6 (30.4) |
| 1991 | 814.3 | 220.8 (27.1) |
| 2001 | 991.9 | 300.9 (30.2) |

Sources: Census of India, Migration Tables from 1971 to 1991; D(i), D1 and D2 Table for the 2001 Census available on compact disk.

India's population. A total of 78 million people were identified in the 2001 Indian Census as migrants who moved intra-state, of which 60.6 percent moved from rural to rural locales. By comparison, only 16.1 million people moved inter-state. Migration in India was and continues to be dominated by rural to rural movements within the same state. This strong intra-state circulation of migrant flow in rural India differs from the strong inter-provincial flow of rural labor migrants to urban regions in post-1978 China.

There are many similarities and differences in labor migration patterns in China and India. Here are some of our main observations:

1. In absolute numbers, India identifies 300.9 million people, or 30.3 percent of its total population, as internal migrants (see Table 9.2), whereas in China

**Table 9.3.** Number of Migrants by Streams of Migration in India (0–9 Years Duration*), 2001

| | Migration Streams | Migrants (in millions) | Distribution within each migration stream (percentage) | Sex-ratio (males per 1,000 females) |
|---|---|---|---|---|
| **Intra-state** | Rural to rural | 48.8 | 60.6 | 257 |
| | Rural to urban | 14.2 | 17.6 | 842 |
| | Urban to rural | 5.2 | 6.5 | 651 |
| | Urban to urban | 9.8 | 12.1 | 796 |
| **Inter-state** | Rural to rural | 4.4 | 26.6 | 648 |
| | Rural to urban | 6.3 | 38.2 | 1480 |
| | Urban to rural | 1.0 | 6.0 | 984 |
| | Urban to urban | 4.4 | 26.6 | 970 |

*101 million migrants had moved at least 20 years back and they were not *included* in this table, which identified only those who moved within the 0–9 year range.
Sources: Census of India 2001, Migration Tables D2 Census available on compact disk; migrants unclassifiable by rural-urban streams are excluded.

**Table 9.4.** Number of Migrants, Percentage Distribution, and Growth Rates by Migration Type, India, 1971–2001

| Migration Type | Migrants in 2001 Census (in million) | Percentage distribution | Growth Rate (percent) 1971–1981 | 1981–1991 | 1991–2001 |
|---|---|---|---|---|---|
| Intra-district | 193.5 | 61.7 | 25.0 | 8.3 | 37.0 |
| Inter-district | 74.6 | 23.7 | 44.3 | 13.7 | 26.3 |
| Inter-state | 41.2 | 13.1 | 28.1 | 11.7 | 53.6 |
| International migrants | 5.2 | 1.5 | −9.1 | −6.1 | −13.3 |
| All migrants | 314.5 | 100.0 | 27.0 | 10.0 | 35.0 |
| Total population of India | 1028.6 | – | 25.0 | 24.0 | 21.4 |

*Source:* Census of India 1971, Part II- D(i) Migration Table; Census of India 1981, Part V-A & B (i); Census of India 1991,Vol. 2, Part 2, (Tables D1 and D2); Census of India 2001, Table D2, Compact Diskette, Registrar General and Census Commissioner, India, New Delhi.

the estimated number is around 130 million, or 10 percent of its total population. Unlike India, where freedom of mobility is a given and migration receives little state intervention, China's state policy maintains an effective and tight control over individual mobility through the policy of household registration and the practice of local citizenship. The liberalization of labor mobility since the introduction of economic reform in 1979 ushered in a new era of large-scale voluntary labor migration, which enabled China to become the "factory" for the world. Despite this liberalization of individual mobility, the household registration policy remains in effect, and people's entitlement to key resources (such as land allocation, health care, and education) is still fully embedded in the locality where they are registered. This household registration policy creates the conditions that strongly encourage labor migrants to return home upon the completion of their employment contract or when employment opportunity is no longer available or attractive in locations away from their home region. In other words, return migration is highly encouraged under the current policy regime in China.

2. The vast majority of Indian migrants, 85.3 percent, moved within their state of origin (both intra- and inter-district), while a much smaller proportion, 13.1 percent, or 41 million individuals, moved from one state to another in 2001 (see Table 9.4). In other words, Indian migrants typically travel small distances. In contrast, the flow of migrants in China is dominated by a net outflow of people from the interior and western provinces to the coastal provinces, in close correspondence with the status of economic development disparity within the country (see Table 9.1). A 2005 study found that over 60 percent of the total labor migrant population was located along the southeastern coastal regions (Zhou 2005, 279). This does not negate the reality of significant intra-provincial labor migration

Labor Migration, Citizenship, and Social Welfare in China and India 167

**Table 9.5.** Migrants by Sex and Streams of Migration in India, 2001

|  | All Migrants |  | Males |  | Females |  |
|---|---|---|---|---|---|---|
|  | Percentage of total | Percentage of subtotal | Percentage of total | percentage of subtotal | percentage of total | percentage of subtotal |
| **Total** | 100 |  | 100 |  |  |  |
| *Intra-district* | 60.44 | 100 | 44.8 | 100 | 66 | 100 |
| Rural-rural | 46.88 | 77.56 | 24.24 | 54.11 | 54.93 | 83.23 |
| Urban-rural | 2.61 | 4.31 | 3.35 | 7.48 | 2.34 | 3.55 |
| Rural-urban | 6.99 | 11.57 | 10.45 | 23.32 | 5.76 | 8.73 |
| Urban-urban | 3.96 | 6.55 | 6.76 | 15.08 | 2.97 | 4.5 |
| *Inter-district* | 25.27 | 100 | 30.08 | 100 | 23.56 | 100 |
| Rural-rural | 11.99 | 47.46 | 7.84 | 26.05 | 13.47 | 57.19 |
| Urban-rural | 1.45 | 5.74 | 1.84 | 6.13 | 1.31 | 5.56 |
| Rural-urban | 6.32 | 25.01 | 11.3 | 37.56 | 4.55 | 19.31 |
| Urban-urban | 5.51 | 21.79 | 9.1 | 30.24 | 4.23 | 17.95 |
| *Inter-state* | 14.29 | 100 | 25.13 | 100 | 10.43 | 100 |
| Rural-rural | 4.04 | 28.26 | 4.33 | 17.23 | 3.93 | 37.71 |
| Urban-rural | 0.71 | 4.94 | 1.15 | 4.58 | 0.55 | 5.25 |
| Rural-urban | 5.62 | 39.33 | 12.46 | 49.59 | 3.18 | 30.54 |
| Urban-urban | 3.93 | 27.47 | 7.18 | 28.58 | 2.77 | 26.53 |

*Source:* Census of India 2001, Table D2, Census available in CD.

from rural to urban settings, which reflects the existing uneven distribution of income and opportunity along the urban-rural divide within China.

3. Overall there were many more female migrants in India in all migration streams, with the exception of inter-state, rural-to-urban migration (see Table 9.3, sex ratio column). The proportion of Indian men migrating from one state to another, at 25.1 percent, was more than twice the corresponding proportion of women at 10.4 percent in 2001 (see Table 9.5). Inter-state migration only accounted for 13.1 percent of the total migrants in the 2001 Indian Census, whereas intra-state migration was at 85.4 percent of the total flow (see Table 9.4) and was dominated by female migrants, who accounted for almost two-thirds of the intra-district migrants (i.e., migrants who changed residence but stayed within their census district). A comparison between 1981, 1991, and 2001 Census data points to an increase in female migration and a declining trend of migration for males (Dev and Evenson 2003). In the 1981 Indian Census, 29.4 percent of the total migrants were males; in 1991, this proportion declined to 27.0 percent.

Women in India move primarily for marriage reasons and that probably explains why women migrate closer to their place of birth and why they also tend to live in their relocated community for extended periods (see Table 9.6). Out of the total

Table 9.6. Distribution of Internal Migrants by Sex and Duration of Residence at the Place of Enumeration by Percentage, 1981–2001

| Duration (Year) | 1981 Male | 1981 Female | 1991 Male | 1991 Female | 2001 Male | 2001 Female |
| --- | --- | --- | --- | --- | --- | --- |
| >1 | 8.5 | 3.7 | 5.0 | 2.2 | 4.5 | 2.1 |
| 1–4 | 26.1 | 17.0 | 21.5 | 15.3 | 18.0 | 13.9 |
| 5–9 | 16.6 | 14.7 | 15.3 | 14.9 | 13.2 | 13.6 |
| 10–19 | 20.8 | 23.6 | 20.6 | 24.7 | 18.0 | 23.9 |
| 20 + | 20.9 | 37.2 | 23.4 | 36.4 | 20.0 | 36.5 |
| Duration not stated | 6.7 | 3.6 | 14.1 | 6.3 | 26.1 | 9.9 |

*Source:* Census of India 1981, Series 1, Part V-A& B (i); Census of India 1991, Vol. 2, Part 1, Tables D1 and D2; Census of India 2001, Table D2, Census available in CD.

intra-district migration, 81 percent of women moved as a result of marriage, while an additional 7 percent migrated for family reasons. Due to the prevalence of the arranged marriage system in India, women migrants are not generally free agents. However, marriage may improve their situation; migration to urban areas normally provides females with an opportunity to improve their social and economic status. Once they have moved for marriage or family reasons, they might join the labor market. Several field studies indicate that it is females who tend to settle down more easily in the labor market as domestic servants or fruit/vegetable/flower vendors while men search for appropriate jobs. While males are waiting for longer periods for regular jobs, women tend to support their spouses (Premi 2001, 49–59). The demonstrated economic contribution by female migrants to their household accords with the observed tendency for families to out-migrate as a unit, and the tendency for single migrants who married subsequent to out-migration to bring their wife and children to their place of employment. This pattern suggests a likelihood of weakening ties to one's place of origin after out-migration in India.

Using the 55th and 64th rounds of the NSS data for the years 1999–2007, Amitabh Kundu and Lopamudra Ray Saraswati point to some very interesting recent trends and patterns of internal migration in India. They suggest that:

> the mobility of men, more specifically the adult men, which is often linked to the survival strategies of households seeking livelihoods, has gone down systematically over the past decades.... Poor and unskilled male labourers are finding it difficult to gain footholds in urban centres. Consequently, poverty induced migration has become a less important component in mobility overtime. (Kundu and Saraswati, 2012, 226)

In a growing economy, urban centers are expected to provide more and better opportunities for employment for migrants. However, in India, it appears to be the educated urban male population that is enjoying the greatest economic mobility opportunities. Kundu and Saraswati conclude:

> Urban centres have become less hospitable and less accommodating for the poor, restricting their entry and thereby increasing RU (rural-urban) economic inequality. This puts a question mark over the role of migration as an instrument for sharing the benefits of uneven growth across the states and districts and between rural and urban areas. (Kundu and Saraswati, 2012, 226)

In contrast, the sex ratio among internal migrants in China is more or less equal. The 2006 Chinese National Bureau of Statistics (NBS) survey, with a sample fraction of 0.907 percent, projected that a total of 122.6 million people resided in a location different from that of their permanent household registration; 66.3 million of these were female, and 56.3 million were male (National Bureau of Statistics of China 2007, 114, Table 4.9). Some of the women listed as internal migrants in China are not necessarily migrant workers, but rather brides who move with marriage. In a different NBS dataset (2004) pertaining specifically to rural migrants, it showed that nationwide 33.7 percent of rural migrants were female, suggesting a dominance of men among the floating population (Hussain and Wang 2010, 139–140). Furthermore, only 20 percent of the rural migrants emigrated with dependent(s) in 2003, 2004, and 2005 (Hussain and Wang 2010, 135). More recent data shows that 58 million children in rural China have one or both parents away working in the cities. Among rural children under six years of age, one-third have both parents working as migrant workers (China Today 2011). What these data suggest, confirmed by various studies of rural migrant workers since the mid-1980s, is that the majority of migrant workers leave their children and other dependents (parents and spouse) in their place of household registration. Even though they are working away from home, their economic and social ties to their home location are maintained through their children and other dependents.

## LONG-TERM IMPACT ON SENDING COMMUNITIES

Internal migration has mixed impacts on sending and receiving communities. In general, people tend to focus on the more positive aspects of labor-seeking migration, such as the perceived benefit of moderating any existing problem of unemployment or underemployment in the home region and the widely documented benefit of remittances as a source of valuable revenue to support remaining family members at home and to contribute to local infrastructure and economic development (Skeldon 1997, 61–117). In this comparative analysis, the data suggest that there is a substantive difference in the overall impact of migration on the sending communities in China and India.

## The India Case

Dev and Evenson compared the NSS data of the 49th and 55th round surveys and found that while rural-rural migration is still the predominant pattern in India, the proportion of migration represented by this stream "has dwindled between the two NSS surveys and this is true for both the sexes. There has been a marginal increase in urban-urban migration" (Dev and Evenson 2003, 5–6). Their study shows that migration rates have increased during the reform period since 1991, particularly in rural-to-urban and urban-to-urban migration. Comparing the 1991 and 2001 Census data, overall migration went up by 34.7 percent (see Table 9.4). The inter-state migration rate went up by a sharp 53.6 percent to bring the total number of inter-state migrants to 41.4 million in 2001. Intra-district migration went up by 37 percent between 1991 and 2001; inter-district migration increased by 26.3 percent. The only exception in this pattern of increase is a drop in international migration by 13.3 percent between 1991 and 2001. The New Economic Policy introduced in 1991 is likely to be an important contributing factor to the documented rise in migration flow in India in the 2001 Census. After 1991, the states of Bihar, Rajasthan, Orissa, Madhya Pradesh, and Uttar Pradesh have been hampered in their economic development due to the curtailment of public expenditure and reduction of subsidies. In contrast, due to the devaluation and convertibility of the rupee, states with large flows of remittances in foreign currencies, such as Punjab, Kerala, Gujarat, and Tamil Nadu, have benefited. In addition, these states, along with Delhi and Haryana, have found positive net in-migration as trade policy has increased foreign direct investment. As a result, the new economic policy accelerated rural-urban migration after 1991 (Kant 1999, 94).

The majority of migrants documented in the 2001 Census were intra-state migrants moving between rural locales: 90.7 million were intra-district rural-to-rural migrants, and 8.9 million were inter-district rural-to-rural migrants. Most of the intra-state migrants are females who move from their parental households to join their husbands' households after marriage. Though many of the relatively poor and underdeveloped states show large population mobility driven by economic necessity, the mobility of male population is also seen to be prominent in the relatively developed states like Maharashtra and Gujarat. Rapid migration of rural females within the boundaries of the states is prominent across most of the regions. Women tend to be short-distance migrants, and their role in migration diminishes as the distance between the place of origin and destination increases. When men migrate alone, the impact on the family unit and on women, children, and the elderly left behind can be quite significant.

In 1991, most of the migrants in urban centers tended to come from within the same state (40 percent within the same district and 35 percent from other districts). Only 25 percent of the migrants in urban centers came from outside the state. Even inter-state migrants tend to travel short distances to neighboring states. In other words, migrants who leave their state in search of employment do not necessarily or even usually travel to richer states if the distances are too large. Take the example of Bihar and Uttar Pradesh, two of the poorest states. Bihar sends most of its migrants to West Bengal (31.3 percent), ranked as the fifth poorest state, followed by Orissa (9.9 percent), ranked second poorest. Migrants from Uttar Pradesh go to Madhya Pradesh, another poor state (23.9 percent) and Bihar (16.6 percent). West Bengal migrants move to Bihar (29.9 percent), Assam (23 percent), and Orissa (17.4 percent)—the three poorest states. On the other hand, Punjab and Haryna (the richest states) appear to exchange migrants with each other. The migration data clearly reveal that the four highest performing states receive a majority of migrants from each other rather than from the poor performing states. For example, 55.4 percent of migrants in Karnataka arrive from Maharashtra. Tamil Nadu receives 31.56 percent of its migrants from Karnataka, 21.6 percent from Kerala, and 16.6 percent from Andhra Pradesh. In Gujarat, 55.9 percent of migrants arrive from the neighboring state of Maharashtra. It appears that strong regional factors determine the nature of internal migration. Proximity seems to be the major determinant. Language barriers and lack of skills might further explain the prevalence of short-distance migration in India.

Dev and Evenson add some interesting conclusions from their study of the 1993 and 1999–2000 NSS data. They point out that:

- Developed states have higher net in-migration compared to poorer states;
- The percentage of migrants who cited economic reasons for moving increased in urban areas and decreased in rural areas over the study period;
- Self-employed and regularly employed workers' migration rate increased as compared to casual laborers. Most of these migrants came from non-agricultural sectors;
- Migrants have higher workforce participation rates after migration compared to pre-migration rates, suggesting that migration tends to be successful in securing employment;
- Members of the richer classes migrate at higher rates than members of the poorer classes (Dev and Evenson 2003, 5–6).

## The China Case

Labor migration after the 1978 economic reform has had diverse impacts on the migrants themselves, their families, and their home communities (Gaetano and Jacka 2004; Murphy 2002; L. Zhang 2001; Zhou 2005). In a 2001 survey of 17 villages in Jiangxi province (a major labor migrant-sending province), Zhou and his graduate students from Sun Yat-sen University found that most young villagers (80–90 percent) had gone to Guangdong, Shanghai, or Zhejiang to work as labor migrants (Zhou 2005, 97). As a result, the villages were dominated by older people and children. This changing rural demographic throughout China is noted by other researchers. Since most or all of the young workers are away from their home villages, the land they are allocated by the government for farming is in need of labor from other people. In most cases, it is the aging parents who take up most of the extra day-to-day farming duties. During the seeding and harvest seasons, when short-term extra laborers are needed, many migrant workers take leave from their wage employment to return home to help. In a survey of labor migrants in the Pearl River Delta in the early 1990s, 83.6 percent of the surveyed labor migrants had a family member to work on their land during their absence, 3.8 percent hired someone to do it, 7.1 percent rented out their land, 0.7 percent left the land fallow, and 1 percent returned the land to the village administration (Zhou 2005, 103).

During the early phases of economic reform in the 1980s and early 1990s, most female labor migrants volunteered and were expected to remain home in the husband's village after marriage. They took on the farming and child-rearing duties, in addition to the care of the aging parents-in-law. In recent years, there is a trend among female labor migrants to keep their employment after marriage. Recent information released by the All-China Women's Federation shows that 58 percent of children in rural China have one or both parents away working in cities; of those under six years of age, one-third have both parents away as rural migrants (China Today 2011). As a result, many rural households today are made up of grandparents and grandchildren (known as "skip generation households") (Gaetano and Jacka 2004; Murphy 2002; Zhou 2005, 88).

Return migration is common in post-reform China. Some returnees utilize their urban and industrial experience to start a business or gain employment in nearby towns, as J. Smart has witnessed in various rural communities in Guangdong in her field visits since 1987. In a significant way, these returnees facilitate the modernization and diversification of local economies and the creation of new employment and growing consumption in rural China. Most returnees show a reluctance to return to agricultural work. Some experience a sense of dissonance between their urban/factory experience and worldview and their rural existence upon return migration. In general, returnees consider their labor migration in a positive light, that "the experience and knowledge of living and working in the cities has exposed the migrants to alternative values and life goals, broadening their perspective on life" (Murphy 2002, 215). In a survey of labor migrants in the Pearl River Delta in the early 1990s, 72.4 percent of labor migrants indicated that they did not intend to stay permanently in the location where they worked, only 15.5 percent indicated an interest in staying, and 12.1 percent were undecided (Zhou 2005, 104).

The reasons given to explain their strong intention to return to their home region were as follows: 26.0 percent attributed their intention as a reaction to the negative attitude among local permanent residents toward labor migrants; 15.0 percent indicated their duties to return home to get married; 39.9 percent pointed to the lack of (social and economic) security in labor migration; and

25.4 percent pointed to verbal and disciplinary abuses from employers or managers as the reason for their intention to return home eventually (Zhou 2005, 104). Other studies also point to a common awareness, supported by experience, among labor migrants of their "second class citizenship" as an "outsider" without local household registration in the Pearl River Delta (J. Smart and A. Smart 1991; A. Smart and J. Smart 1992, 47–61; 2001, 1853–1969; J. Smart 1995, 14–19; 1999, 407–445), Beijing and Shanghai (L. Zhang 2001), and other locations (Murphy 2002, 42–44; Zhou 2005, 192–194). The marginalization of labor migrants in their locations of work is a major factor that encourages their practice of maintaining active ties with their home community, as well as their desire to return home eventually instead of seeking permanent settlement in an urban location away from their designated home community in rural China (Nielsen and Smyth 2008; Wu and Webster 2010; Wu 2010, 55–81).

Most labor migrants maintain strong and active ties with their families and home communities. This is not surprising given that their livelihood resources (i.e., land) and dependents (children, parents, and spouse) remain in the home community. Remittances are sent regularly to cover the living costs of dependents, to pay for children's education, to finance construction or renovation projects to improve and modernize the living environment, and to cover the expenses of upgrading farm equipment and acquiring other new production technologies. Labor migrants also return regularly to visit with family and dependents on major holidays like Chinese New Year, to attend weddings or funerals, and to help out during the busy seasons in the agricultural cycle. When labor migrants return for a visit, they may bring appliances or entertainment technologies that were previously unknown in the village. Cultural shifts, such as modern conveniences like flush toilets, air conditioning, and supermarket shopping; new cultural icons of Hong Kong and Taiwan movie stars and singers; and broadened worldviews on education, skill, technology, and consumption are finding their way into the rural landscape throughout China via the returning labor migrants (Hussain and Wang 2010, 139–140; Murphy 2002, 88–117; Zhou 2005, 90–92).

## CONCLUSION: WHAT CAN WE LEARN FROM THIS COMPARATIVE ANALYSIS?

Labor migration has positive economic impacts on rural communities in China through injections of cash, knowledge, material culture, and technology to support economic revitalization and diversification. The remittances from labor migration that go toward the education of children are part of this generally positive impact on rural China. Living conditions have improved due to cash injections and knowledge transfer from labor migration. Naturally, some of the immediate and long-term impacts of labor migration on rural families and communities are negative and disruptive, and they should be recognized as such and taken into account in our consideration of the net impact of labor migration on rural China. One major negative aspect of labor migration is the separation of parents and children for extended periods measured in years, which is widely perceived to be a root cause of the rise in behavioral problems and poor academic performance among the younger generations from migrant-sending communities.[7]

Future economic development in the home communities in labor migrant-sending regions can be expected to improve with modernization and diversification as a direct result of labor migration. This positive prediction about rural development in China is based on the strong indication that most labor migrants intend to return home eventually and the fact that they maintain active ties with their home communities during their sojourns as labor migrants. These practices and intentions are shaped by multiple factors. First, there are the cultural primordial ties among kin, the moral economy of family and kinship groups, and the Confucian values of filial piety and reciprocity. Second, and more significant, there are the policies of the socialist political economy of China that promise a positive outcome of labor migration for rural communities in the country. In particular, the policy of household registration, the established practices of differential entitlement according to local citizenship, and the state-controlled differential resource allocation to urban and rural regions, which support uneven regional and urban-rural development, provide the necessary conditions to enable a steady supply of labor migrants to the locations where they are needed to support the national mandate of modernization, while at the same time discouraging these migrants from settling permanently in the cities so that the economic viability of rural China is maintained.

In contrast, internal migration in India does not appear to produce direct positive economic impacts of any meaningful size. Given that internal migration is largely from rural to rural areas within a state, positive impacts in terms of remittances and transfers of technology are most probably very slight, if any. Some field studies show that migrants do send remittances to their families in their place of birth, and that migrants are unwilling to accept adverse working conditions in their place of origin/previous residence, suggesting that they leave to seek greater well-being. But these factors may stimulate little more than a movement from destitution to adversity. Other field studies have noted a negative impact of internal migration. For example, some single males who migrate temporarily to cities bring back contagious diseases, such as HIV/AIDS, and infect their partners upon their return. When illiterate and semi-literate migrants move into the city to find jobs, they add to the existing ranks of the very poor and to the slum population (Mukherji 2001).

It is possible that some intra-state migration could be related to a movement from agrarian to industrial urban centers, a trend that may increase with the anticipated rise in foreign direct investment in India as a result of the 1991 New Economic Policy. The macro data so far suggest that there is very little migration from agrarian to industrial urban centers in India. The internal migrants, by their choice of destination, are not generally beneficiaries of the economies in the richer states. As yet, India lags behind China in terms of attracting foreign direct investment. China attracted US$67 billion in FDI in 2006 (National Bureau of Statistics of China 2007, 746, Table 18–16). India is catching up with a projected FDI injection of US$44.1 billion in 2010 (Li and Li 2010, 189). Globalization and liberalization appear to have negligible impact on the internal migrants in India, at least according to Indian Census data. If there is any impact, it is only in the highest performing states, which are all located in the western and southern parts of India—with close proximity to each other and a general tendency to exchange their migrant populations among themselves.

In West Bengal, the bargaining power of workers has improved due to the intervention of the Krishak Sabha and Panchayats (rural local communities). These organizations have helped workers in settling disputes and closing the gap between immigrant and non-immigrant, and male and female wages (Rogaly et al. 2001, 2002). The Krishak Sabha has negotiated between employers and local workers at the district level so that migrant wages do not undercut local wages and employment, thereby reducing friction with local laborers. Local government policies and practices also have important implications for migrant workers in eastern India by ensuring that agreed wage rates are paid and in a timely manner (Rogaly et al. 2002, 90–92).

Unlike China, labor migrants in India prefer to permanently settle at their new destinations rather than returning to their home state. The government of India does not have any policy or incentive program regarding internal migration that may influence the migrants' choice of returning or staying. In the case of China, there are specific government policies and incentives that increase the probability of migrant laborers returning, which in turn enhances rural economic development.

Internal migration clearly follows different patterns and appears to have quite different impacts on migrant-sending communities in China and India. What are the policy implications of these findings?

In the case of China, household registration is a key policy that requires further consideration. Many critics point to the inequity inherent in local citizenship within China under the current household registration system, and some suggest that the policy should be abolished to support a single set of citizenship rights for all people in China.[8] If the government of the People's Republic of China should ever abolish the household registration policy, which Wang (2010, 335–336) describes as the "great floodgate" that "remains an indispensable pillar of sociopolitical stability and economic development," the question must be asked: How would the abolition of *hukou* affect the future economic well-being and social stability of rural China? At least for labor migrant-sending communities and regions, abolishing the household registration policy would be likely to slow the pace of modernization and social and economic development in rural communities. It also may destabilize rural communities and further aggravate the already uneven social and economic outcomes within the country.

In the case of the world's second-largest nation, it would appear that the Indian state cannot count on current migration pathways to alleviate regional disparities and must seek other solutions instead. Given the prevailing patterns of internal migration and foreign direct investment, it would appear that further liberalization of the Indian economy will most likely widen rather than narrow the gaps between the rich and the poor, both individually and regionally, and aggravate differences between the "have" and "have-not" states. This study confirms the extent of poor governance and weak infrastructure in India's poorest regions, so that for many potential migrants the choice is between the frying pan and the fire. Indian policymakers need to consider programs that can stimulate the types of internal migration—and perhaps return migration—that will produce net benefits for both sending and receiving communities.

## ACKNOWLEDGMENT

Josephine Smart wishes to thank SSHRC, the University of Calgary, Chiang Ching Kuo Foundation, and the Centre of Asian Studies (University of Hong Kong) for supporting fieldwork in the Pearl Delta River region from the mid-1980s to present.

## REFERENCES

Bhagat, Ram. 2005. Conceptual issues in measurement of internal migration in India. Paper presented at *XXVth IUSSP International Conference*, Tours, France, July 2005.

*China Today*. 2011. Vol. 60, No. 2 (Beijing), p. 10.

Cox, Simon. 2009. An imperfect storm. In *The world in 2010*, 62. London: The Economist.

Dehejia, Vivek. 2012. From the Prime Minister's Twitter Feed, a Puzzling View of Foreign Investment. India Ink: Notes on the World's Largest Democracy, http://india.blogs.nytimes.com/2012/07/20/image-of-the-day-july-20/ (accessed July 20, 2012).

Dev, S. Mahendra, and Robert E. Evenson. 2003. *Rural development in India: Rural, non-farm and migration.* Stanford Center for International Development Working Paper No. 187.

http://www.stanford.edu/group/siepr/cgi-bin/siepr/?q=system/files/shared/pubs/papers/pdf/credpr187.pdf

Economist, The. 2010. *Pocket world in figures*. London: Profile Books.

Feng, Wang. 2010. Boundaries of inequality: Perceptions of distributive justice among urbanities, migrants, and peasants. In *One economy, two societies: Rural-urban inequality in contemporary China*, ed. M. K. Whyte, 219–240. Cambridge, MA: Harvard University Press.

Gaetano, Arianne M., and Ramara Jacka, eds. 2004. *On the move: Women in rural-to-urban migration in contemporary China*. New York: Columbia University Press.

Hong, Zhao, 2009. An energy comparison of the Asian giants: China and India. *Asian Affairs XL*(III): 377–390.

Hussain, Athar, and Youjuan Wang. 2010. Rural-urban migration in China: Scale, composition, pattern and deprivation. In *Marginalization in urban China: Comparative perspectives*, eds. F. Wu and C. Webster, 133–152. Hampshire, UK: Palgrave Macmillan.

Wu, Jieh-Min. 2010. Rural migrant workers and China's differential citizenship: A comparative institutional analysis. In *One economy, two societies: Rural-urban inequality in contemporary China*, ed. M. K. Whyte, 55–84. Cambridge, MA: Harvard University Press.

Jones, Richard Palmer, and Kunal Sen. On India's poverty puzzles and the statistics of poverty. www.uea.ac.uk/~280/other/measuringPovertyinIndia.doc.

Kant, S. 1999. Spatial implications of India's new economic policy. *Tijdschrift voor economische en sociale geografie* 90(1): 80–96.

Kundu, A., and S. Gupta. 2000. Declining population mobility, liberalization and growing regional imbalances, the Indian case. In *Inequality, mobility and urbanization* ed. A. Kundu, 257–274. New Delhi: Manak Publications.

Kundu, A., and L. Ray Saraswati. 2012. Migration and exclusionary urbanisation in India. *Economic and Political Weekly* 47(26–27): 226.

Lei, Guang. 2010. Bringing the city back in: The Chinese debate on rural problems. In *One economy, two societies: Rural-urban inequality in contemporary China*, ed. M. K. Whyte, 311–334. Cambridge, MA: Harvard University Press.

Li, Limei, and Li Si-ming. 2010. The impact of variations in urban registration within cities. In *One economy, two societies: Rural-urban inequality in contemporary China*, ed. M. K. Whyte, 188–215. Cambridge, MA: Harvard University Press.

Martin, Philip. 2009. *Human development research paper #32: Migration in the Asia-Pacific region: Trends, factors, impacts*. New York: United Nations Development Programme.

Metha, Asha Kapur, Sourab Ghosh, Deepa Chatterjee, and Nikhla Menon, eds. 2003. *Chronic poverty in India*. New Delhi: K. K. Agencies.

Mukherji, Shekhar. 2001. Low quality migration in India: The phenomena of distressed migration and acute urban decay. Paper presented at the 24th IUSSP Conference, Brazil.

Murphy, Rachel. 2002. *How migrant labor is changing rural China*. Cambridge: Cambridge University Press.

National Bureau of Statistics of China. 2007. *China Statistical Yearbook 2007*. Beijing, China Statistics Press.

Naughton, Barry. 2007. *The Chinese economy: Transitions and growth*. Cambridge, MA: MIT Press.

Nielsen, Ingrid, and Russel Smyth, eds. 2008. *Migration and social protection in China*. Singapore: World Scientific.

Premi, K. Mahendra. 2001. Who migrates to Delhi. *Demography India* 30(1): 49–59.

Rees, Martha, and Josephine Smart, eds. 2001. *Plural globalities in multiple localities: New world borders*. Lanham, MD: University Press of America.

Rogaly, B., J. Biswas, C. Daniel, R. Abdur, R. Kumar, and A. Sengupta. 2001. Seasonal migration, social change and migrants rights, lessons from West Bengal. *Economic and Political Weekly* 36: 4547–4558.

Rogaly, B., C. Daniel, R. Abdur, R. Kumar, A. Sengupta, and J. Biswas. 2002. Seasonal migration and welfare/illfare in Eastern India: A social analysis. *Journal of Development Studies* 38(5): 89–114.

Sharma, Shalendra D. 2009. *China and India in the age of globalization*. New York: Cambridge University Press.

Sinclair, Terry, Yue Ximing, Bjorn A. Gustafsson, and Li Shi. 2010. How large is China's rural-urban income gap? In *One economy, two societies: Rural-urban inequality in contemporary China*, ed. M. K. Whyte, 87–104. Cambridge, MA: Harvard University Press.

Skeldon, Ronald. 1997. *Migration and development: A global perspective*. Essex, UK: Addison Wesley Longman.

Smart, Alan, and Josephine Smart. 1992. Capitalist production in a socialist society: The transfer of manufacturing from Hong Kong to China. In *Anthropology and the global factory: Studies of the new industrialization in the late twentieth century*, eds. M. Blim and F. Rothstein, 47–61. Westport, CT: Bergin and Garvey.

Smart, Alan, and Josephine Smart. 2001. Local citizenship: Welfare reform, urban/rural status, and exclusion in China. *Environment and Planning A* 33:1853–1969.

Smart, Josephine. 1995. Capitalist production under socialism in the People's Republic of China (PRC) since 1978. *Anthropology of Work Review* XVI(3–4): 14–19.

Smart, Josephine. 1999. The global economy and South China development in post-1978 China: Relevance and limitations of the flexible accumulation approach. *Urban Anthropology* 28(3–4): 407–445.

Smart, Josephine, and Alan Smart. 1991. Personal relations and divergent economies: A case study of Hong Kong investment in South China. *International Journal of Urban and Regional Research* 15(2): 216–233.

Smart, Josephine, and Alan Smart. 1993. Obligation and control: Employment of kin in capitalist labor management in China. *Critique of Anthropology* 13(1): 7–31.

Srivastava, Ravi, and S. K. Sasikumar. 2003. An overview of migration in India, its impact and key issues. Paper presented at the Regional conference on migration, development and pro-poor policy choices in Asia, Dhaka, Bangladesh.

Tremblay, Reeta Chowdhari. 2003. Globalization and Indian federalism. In *Indian federalism in the new millennium*, eds. B. D. Dua and M. P. Singh, 335–350. New Delhi: Manohar Publishers.

Wang, Fei-ling. 2010. Renovating the great floodgate: The reform of China's hukou system. In *One economy, two societies: Rural-urban inequality in contemporary China*, ed. M. K. Whyte, 335–364. Cambridge, MA: Harvard University Press.

Webster, Chirs, and Yanjing Zhao. 2010. Entitlement to the benefits of urbanization: Comparing migrant and peri-urban "peasants." In *Marginalization in urban China: Comparative perspectives*, eds. F. Wu and C. Webster, 59–71. Hampshire, UK: Palgrave Macmillan.

Whyte, Martin King. 2010. The paradoxes of rural-urban inequality in contemporary China. In *One economy, two societies: Rural-urban inequality in contemporary China*, ed. M. K. Whyte, 1–25. Cambridge, MA: Harvard University Press.

Wong, Linda, and Gongcheng Zheng. 2008. Getting by without state-sponsored social insurance. In *Migration and social protection in China*, eds. I. Nielsen and R. Smyth, 155–183. Singapore: World Scientific.

Wu, Fulong. 2010. Property rights, citizenship and the making of the new poor in urban China. In *Marginalization in urban China: Comparative perspectives*, eds. F. Wu and C. Webster, 72–89. Hampshire, UK: Palgrave Macmillan.

Wu, Fulong, and Chris Webster, eds. 2010. *Marginalization in urban China: Comparative perspectives*. Hampshire, UK: Palgrave Macmillan.

Zhang, Jijiao. 2004. *Chengshi de shiying*. Beijing: Commercial Press.

Zhang, Li. 2001. *Strangers in the city: Reconfiguration of space, power, and social networks within China's floating population*. Stanford, CA: Stanford University Press.

Zhou, Daming. 2005. *Kwang Shengcun*. Guangzhou: Zongshan University Press.

# 10
# ETHNIC MINORITIES AND TRILINGUAL EDUCATION POLICIES

Bob Adamson, Feng Anwei, Liu Quanguo, and Li Qian

## INTRODUCTION

China has a relatively long history of bilingual education in secondary schools dating from 1903, when English or other foreign languages first entered the curriculum. This provision was extended to primary schools in 2002 with the inclusion of English as a compulsory subject from grade three. A consequence of the compulsory English policy was the expectation that primary schools in ethnic minority areas would shift from bilingual to trilingual education by adding English to a curriculum that typically included both the local ethnic minority language and Putonghua, the national standard version of Mandarin Chinese. Given the diversity of contexts in which ethnic minority groups live, several different models of trilingual education have emerged across the country.

China has 55 officially recognized ethnic minority groups, estimated to be using between 80 and 120 languages (State Language Commission 1995). Over 300 other groups have applied but have not been granted official recognition (Poa and LaPolla 2007). China's ethnic minorities are mostly located close to national borders, in areas accounting for 64 percent of the national territory and 8.49 percent of the national population (People's Daily 2011). Five autonomous regions make up the largest areas where such groups live: Xinjiang, Guangxi, Tibet, Inner Mongolia, and Ningxia. The places inhabited by ethnic minority groups tend not to have enjoyed the benefits of national economic growth to the same extent as other parts of the country. However, the natural scenery and cultural resources available in these areas have attracted investors and visitors. The resulting growth of business and tourism has opened many remote regions to stronger national and international connections and has reinforced the perception among ethnic minority groups that seizing economic opportunities will require proficiency in Mandarin Chinese and English.

Nearly 50 percent of the country's ethnic minorities have mastered Mandarin Chinese—either the official standard form (Putonghua) or a local dialect—to some degree of proficiency (Huang 2000). However, the current situation in schools is not propitious for trilingualism. As a result of the remoteness of many groups, educational provision tends to be limited, standards of literacy tend to be low, and the majority of teachers tend to be relatively poorly trained for the demands of trilingual education. As a result of these disadvantages, ethnic minority students generally perform worse in the Chinese academic system than students from the Han majority.

The authors of this chapter form part of a research network that has been exploring different models of trilingual education in ethnic minority regions of China since 2009. The research has involved documentary analysis, interviews with key stakeholders, surveys, and field trips to a representative sample of primary and secondary schools. The selected schools are located in major cities, towns, and more remote rural areas; they have different mixes of ethnic minority and majority Han students; and they are supported by communities with different socioeconomic statuses. The research agenda of this network seeks to fill an important gap in knowledge caused by the scarcity of multilevel, comparative work aimed at mapping different forms of language policies across the country and assessing their impact. One relatively small-scale study by Adamson and Feng (2009) examined the tensions behind trilingual education policies by comparing the implementation of policies for three minority groups: the Zhuang, the Uyghur, and the Yi people. It found that ethnic minority languages are at a disadvantage compared with Chinese and English, and that additive trilingualism (the learning of three languages without mutual detriment) would be facilitated by strategies such as supporting the development of written scripts in the minority languages and provision of space in the school curriculum for all three languages; the barriers to additive trilingualism include the low social status ascribed to minority languages because of their lack of associated economic and political capital. That study raises the questions of social equity that lie at the heart of language policies affecting ethnic minority groups (Mohanty 2009; Adamson and Xia 2011).

The research network extends from the south of China, around the west and across the north of the country, encompassing Guangdong, Yunnan, Sichuan, Guangxi, Guizhou, Tibet, Gansu, Qinghai, Xinjiang, Inner Mongolia, and Jilin. The topography covered includes industrial cities, mountainous regions, grasslands, and deserts. The network covers considerable political and linguistic diversity both between and within minority groups. Politically, some ethnic groups (such as those in Xinjiang and Tibet) are associated with "separatist" tendencies and social disharmony; others are seen as well-assimilated, living in relative peace with their Han neighbors. Although ethnic minority languages vary considerably in development and vitality, they can be categorized into three broad types (Zhou 2000, 2001). Type 1 groups possess both the spoken and traditional written form of the language in wide usage and have had regular bilingual education since 1949. Type 1 groups include Uyghurs and Kazaks, living mainly in Xinjiang, Tibetans in Tibet and Qinghai, Mongolians in Inner Mongolia, and Koreans in Jilin. Type 2 groups have functional writing systems of only limited use and have had only occasional bilingual education since 1949. This type consists of Dai, Jingpo, Lisu, Lahu, Miao, Naxi, Va, and Yi minority groups, living mainly in the southwestern regions of the country. The remaining 42 minority group communities belong to Type 3 and are defined as having had no fully functional writing systems before the founding of the People's Republic of China in 1949, and limited or no bilingual education since then. A complication with the categorical system lies in the fact that any relatively large ethnic minority group, for example the Tibetans (Denwood 1999), may include several mutually unintelligible dialects.

Given the various complexities of this situation, the goals of trilingual education must be seen as ambitious. The characteristics of different ethnic minority languages, as outlined above, make the teaching of some languages more difficult than others. Putonghua, the form of Mandarin Chinese that is the second language for minority students, is officially defined as having "Beijing speech as its standard pronunciation, the northern Chinese dialect, and modern Chinese literary classics written in vernacular Chinese as its grammatical norm" (National Linguistics Work Committee 1996, 12). It is often linguistically distant from the minority languages in terms of syntax, vocabulary, pronunciation, and written form. English, the third language, might be considered even more linguistically distant, especially when one considers the lack of exposure to English in remote areas. While governments at different levels in all regions where minority groups live have taken strong measures to ensure vigorous promotion of Mandarin Chinese, the attention paid to the ethnic minority language shows significant variations across and even within groups. The high-stakes national college entrance examination, for example, is administered in Chinese and six minority languages, namely Tibetan, Uyghur, Mongolian, Korean, Kazakh, and Kirghiz (Mackerras 1994). This is a strategic decision, as the speakers of these six minority languages are located in the key border trading areas in China. Meanwhile, the teaching of English tends to be very piecemeal in ethnic minority regions, being dependent upon the resources available locally (Adamson and Feng 2009).

This chapter provides an overview of trilingual education policy in China, using a framework (adapted from Adamson and Morris 2007) that covers four vital dimensions of policy: design, implementation, outcomes, and sustainability. The chapter does not purport to be a definitive evaluation of trilingual education, as evidence of outcomes is relatively scarce, but it points out some emergent trends based on the results of the research network initiatives referred to above, as well as secondary sources of evidence. In light of these trends and the rationales for trilingual education, the chapter offers a series of policy recommendations for furthering the development of sustainable trilingual education in China.

## DESIGN

Trilingual education emerged through policy accretion; no single act of coherent, centralized policymaking can be credited. Since 1949, the central government's language policies in education have consistently stressed the propagation of Mandarin Chinese for its role in the development of mass literacy and nation-building (Adamson 1998). Policies toward ethnic minorities and their languages have oscillated between suppression and support, depending on the prevailing political climate (Lam 2005; Adamson and Feng 2009). Minority languages have been suppressed during periods when extreme leftist ideology prevailed, revolutionary action was stressed over economic prosperity, and ethnic minority groups were subjected to a policy of assimilation (Feng 2007). Likewise, the status of English has varied in China: at times such as the period of cooperation between China and the Soviet Union in the 1950s, English received little attention; at other times, such as the era of the Open Door Policy instituted by Deng Xiaoping in 1978, English has been enthusiastically promoted (Adamson 2004). It was thus a confluence of factors that resulted in what effectively amounts to a trilingual education policy in 2002. This was a period when generally supportive policies toward ethnic minorities coexisted with pressure to introduce English into primary school education (see Ministry of Education 2001a, 2001b, 2001c).

Table 10.1 summarizes how the broad policy emphasis has shifted for the three languages since 1949. The complexities of the case of ethnic minority languages are simplified in this figure to general trends. The decentralized nature of education policymaking, as promulgated in the educational reforms of 1985 (Lewin, Little, Xu, and Zheng 1994), means that a variety of policies emerged across China. For instance, in the Xinjiang Uyghur Autonomous Region, many areas have a policy that calls for Mandarin Chinese to be prioritized and the Uyghur language to be downplayed. This policy is apparently designed to foster a sense of national unity and to counterbalance Uyghurs' strong sense of cultural identity, which has given rise to tensions between them and Han residents (Adamson and Feng 2009). In contrast, in the Zhuang Autonomous Region in Guangxi, southern China, local language policies focus on Mandarin Chinese because the Zhuang have become well integrated with the Han (Gu 1999; Tan 1999) and, in general, do not attach great importance to the preservation of their language (Adamson and Feng 2009). The Yi, in the southwestern areas of the country, unlike many of the Zhuang, do have a strong sense of identity but also

**Table 10.1.** Roles of Ethnic Minority Languages, Mandarin Chinese, and English in Education Policies in the PRC

| Dates | Ethnic Minority Languages | Mandarin Chinese | English |
|---|---|---|---|
| 1949 | Egalitarian respect; codification; new written scripts developed for some languages | Nation-building: *lingua franca* for patriotic and political education | Russian as main foreign language in secondary schools; English for science and technology |
| 1957 | Instability; value of ethnic minority languages questioned | | |
| 1961 | | Mandarin Chinese for culture and revolution | English as main foreign language in secondary schools; developing cultural and scientific knowledge |
| 1966 | Suppression of ethnic minority languages | Mandarin Chinese for revolutionary ideas | English abandoned, then used for political propaganda |
| 1977 | Egalitarian respect; codification of ethnic minority languages resumed | Mandarin Chinese for classical and contemporary culture | English as main foreign language in secondary schools; developing trade; cultural and scientific knowledge |
| 1987 | | Mandarin Chinese for modernization and national culture | |
| 1991 | Promotion of bilingualism: Mandarin Chinese and ethnic minority language | | |
| 2002 | | | English as main foreign language in primary and secondary schools; developing trade; cultural and scientific knowledge |

*Sources:* Lam 2005; Lai Au Yeung 1994; Adamson 2004.

appreciate the opportunities for social and economic advancement afforded by competence in Mandarin Chinese, and therefore have developed policies that support both languages (Adamson and Feng 2009). In all cases, the teaching of English is problematic, largely because of the shortage of qualified teachers at the primary level, especially in the rural areas.

## IMPLEMENTATION

The broad framework for policy design described in the previous section includes central government support—or lack of support—for ethnic minority languages and national mandates regarding the teaching of Mandarin Chinese and English at the primary school level, combined with decentralized school financing arrangements and devolved control of various other education-related functions. The predictable result has been a potpourri of different local methods for turning the goals of bilingual or trilingual education into action.

Studies undertaken by the groups in the research network have identified four principal models of trilingual education being implemented across different regions of China. Table 10.2 gives a summary of these models.

**Table 10.2** Key Features of the Four Models Found in the Trilingualism-in-China Project

| Models | Aims | Key Features | Likely Outcomes |
|---|---|---|---|
| Additive | • To maintain L1 and ethnic identity<br>• To foster real trilingualism | • Strong ethno-linguistic vitality<br>• Using L1 as medium of instruction (MoI) as minority pupils dominate<br>• Strong presence of L1 culture in school environment<br>• Given favourable conditions, L2 and L3 are promoted robustly as school subjects | • Strong competence in L1 and strong sense of ethnic identity<br>Where favourable conditions exist, it is likely to develop:<br>• strong performance in all school subjects<br>• additive trilingualism |
| Balanced | To develop both L1 and L2<br>To promote ethnic harmony | • Mixed Han and minority groups<br>• Using both L1 and L2 as MoI<br>• Strong presence of L1 and L2 cultures in school environment<br>• L3 could be introduced according to state policies | • Strong competence in L1 and L2<br>• Strong performance in school subjects<br>• Likely to foster additive trilingualism |
| Transitional<br>a) L2 as MoI but L1 taught<br>b) L1 as MoI in early years to change to L2 as MoI | • To eventually shift to L2 as MoI<br>• To assimilate pupils into the mainstream | • May be mixed Han and minority groups or a single minority group where ethno-linguistic vitality is weak<br>• L2 emphasised in classrooms<br>Pupils' L1 is only deemed useful as a stepping stone | • Acquiring competence in L2 at the expense of L1 (leading to subtractive bi- or trilingualism)<br>• Unlikely to foster trilingual competence |
| Subtractive | • To aim usually covertly for monolingualism<br>• Linguistic and cultural assimilation | • Claiming to be minority school with mixed minority groups or a single minority group of pupils<br>• L2 is the only MoI and L1 is ignored | • Acquiring competence in L2 at the expense of L1 (leading to subtractive bi- or trilingualism)<br>• Little chance to develop trilingual competence |

The first model focuses strongly on the ethnic minority language. In this model, the ethnic language tends to have strong vitality, being widely used and supported by the community. Where favorable conditions exist with regard to resources and regional policies, the other two languages are equally robustly promoted by being allocated sufficient time in the curriculum for the students to acquire a high degree of competence in Chinese (L2) and a developing competence in English or another foreign language (L3). This model is likely to produce additive trilingualism, by which we refer to complementary competencies in L2 and L3 that pupils acquire in school and in society while maintaining a high standard of their L1 and their ethnic identity. This model is found, for example, in schools where Korean students dominate in Yanbian and Changchun in Jilin Province. For the purpose of comparison with other models, we call it an Additive Model.

The second model is a balance between Chinese and the minority language. The balance is evident in terms not only of the medium of instruction but also of the ethnicity of the teachers and students. In one school visited by the research team in Inner Mongolia, the ratio of Han teachers to Mongolian teachers was 30:70, and of Han students to Mongolian students was 60:40. As well as using both languages as the medium of instruction, the school encourages a bilingual environment through the use of both Chinese and Mongolian notices. The playground language was also bilingual. English is taught as a school subject and the teacher used either Mongolian or Chinese to explain difficult teaching points, depending on the preferred language of the students in the class and the ethnicity of the teacher. The second model is more nuanced than the first model, as the school and the local community display more ethnic diversity. The ethnic language is supported, while the educational needs of the students to learn through a familiar language is respected. The bilingual pupils are likely to perform well in other school subjects, including English, their L3. Again, for comparison, we label it a Balanced Model.

The third model often exists in two different forms. First, in some mixed communities such as towns and cities where there is a substantial minority population (see Dong and Narisu, forthcoming), the medium of instruction can be the reverse of the first model, that is, Chinese is used as the medium of instruction. However, the dominant ethnic minority language in the region is taught as a school subject to all students in the school, irrespective of their own ethnicity or mother tongue. This might be seen as an attempt to maintain the minority language, but there is little role for the minority language to play in later years of schooling. Second, in many remote village schools in which one minority group dominates, the minority language is used as the medium of instruction for the first two to three years with Chinese taught as a major school subject. Starting from Year 3 or Year 4, all school subjects are taught in Chinese. In both cases, English is again taught as a school subject, with Chinese being used when necessary in those lessons.

The two forms are placed under Model 3 because they have one feature in common, that is, to transit to using Chinese as the medium to teach all school subjects. The second transitional form of bilingual education is widely seen in many Type-2 and Type-3 communities (Zhou 2001) that possess a weak degree of ethnolinguistic vitality. In some Type-1 communities such as Inner Mongolia and Xinjiang, as the transitional model privileges Chinese, there is concern to preserve the ethnic minority language and to propagate it among non-native speakers. This model is especially applicable in regions where there is a significant Han population but the ethnic minority language also possesses a strong degree of vitality. However, while the cultural value of the ethnic minority language might be acknowledged, its vitality is often insufficient for it to be used as the predominant language in the school. The third model, in these two forms, is therefore termed a Transitional Model.

A fourth model is represented by schools that proclaim to be an ethnic minority language school but, in reality, do not use the minority language as the medium of instruction nor even teach it as a school subject. Such schools also claimed to be bilingual, in the sense that Chinese and English are studied as languages in the curriculum and Chinese serves as the medium of instruction. In these cases, the bilingual label reflects the curriculum content, while the trilingual label reflects the ethnic profile of the students. The outcome is almost inevitably the loss of pupils' L1 and eventually their ethnic identity. This is a Subtractive Model.

It can be seen that these four models form a continuum, moving from the predominance of the ethnic minority language at one end to the predominance of Chinese at the other. In all the models cited, English is only taught as a school subject with some schools in cities or towns providing it earlier and in better quality than those in remote areas, even though in some parts of the PRC—most notably the richer areas of eastern China—English is used in some schools as the medium of instruction for teaching a certain percentage of school subjects (Hu 2007; 2008) and immersion programs in English are also mushrooming in these areas (Qiang, et al. 2011). The medium of instruction used to teach English in minority regions follows the line of the continuum.

In addition to these major models, other practices are found for students from specific contexts—often those that are deemed politically sensitive. For example, in Xinjiang, minority and Han schools are sometimes merged as *Min Han Hexiao* (Tsung 2009); another practice is Tibetan and Xinjiang *Neidiban*—classes usually located in schools in relatively developed inland cities in other provinces but attended by Tibetan or Xinjiang secondary students away from their minority communities (see Adamson and Feng, forthcoming, for more detailed explanations).

## OUTCOMES

Little research has been undertaken to date on the trilingual competence of ethnic minority students who have studied under the four models outlined in the previous section. However, there are a number of indications that the outcomes of strong forms of trilingual education as defined above are usually positive while the outcome of weak forms are often disappointing. In areas where resources are scarce, students are, not surprisingly, poor in English when compared to the performance of many Han students. For instance, Wu (2000) reported at the turn of the millennium that the majority of Uyghur students at tertiary institutions had never taken any English lessons and had to start from scratch. Seven years later, Olan (2007) conducted a survey among 618 minority students at the prestigious Xinjiang University and found that 62 percent of them had had no English learning experience at all.

One policy response at the tertiary level has been a form of affirmative action. Universities in Xinjiang have exempted Uyghurs from passing the College English Test Level 4, which is the current national standard, although they are required to pass the Chinese Proficiency Test for admission and graduation (Yang 2005). Ethnic minority students elsewhere receive favorable treatment from some universities when the English language component of the entrance examinations for tertiary education is assessed—the required standards of proficiency are lower than those for majority Han students. This form of affirmative action to mitigate social inequalities is not without problems. First, although the ethnic minority students gain entry with lower English scores, they do not usually receive similar dispensation when it comes to graduation, resulting in large numbers failing to graduate (Adamson and Xia 2011). Second, those who do graduate can find themselves stigmatized by the affirmative action label when it comes to applying for a job or for graduate school (Sunuodula and Feng 2011).

The handicaps afflicting many ethnic minority students arise from their lower language competence in Chinese and English as they move through secondary schooling and attempt to access tertiary education (Jiang et al. 2007; Tsung 2009). These handicaps have a deleterious effect on ethnic minority groups' attitudes toward their own languages: Mandarin Chinese and English tend to be preferred for the social mobility and economic returns they offer (Postiglione et al. 2007). This phenomenon is not universal, however. Korean and Russian minority groups attach considerable importance to their own language. They usually used the strong form of trilingual education and they also have a higher percentage of the population with tertiary education qualifications than other groups do, including the Han (Zhou 2001).

The mixed results for ethnic minority languages reflect the complexities of the political, demographic, and linguistic diversity of these groups. Policies vary along a continuum from strong support to bare acknowledgment of the existence of an ethnic minority language on the part of either the Han-dominated communities or the minority people themselves. Economic factors also come into play. When proficiency in the ethnic minority language can bring financial benefits, as is the case with the Koreans in the northeastern regions, there tends to be greater concern for teaching that language in schools, and outcomes tend to be optimized.

Three major justifications can be discerned for trilingual education. The interplay of these justifications, in turn, translates into three policy goals that evaluators should use as criteria for assessing the performance of various language programs and approaches. The first is the fostering of mother tongue literacy and cultural identity through the learning of the ethnic minority language. The second is the cultivation of a sense of national unity and of opportunities for social and economic advancement through the learning of Mandarin Chinese. The third is to broaden students' worldviews and facilitate their contribution to national economic development through their learning of English as an international language. Of the four major model of trilingual education described above, it appears that the model most likely to achieve these goals would be the first and the second. These two models seek to provide students with a good foundation in their mother tongue while incrementally strengthening their competence in Mandarin Chinese and introducing them to English at apposite stages in their cognitive and linguistic development. The challenge is to provide the pre-requisite conditions to replicate and sustain effective models in different contexts across the nation, an issue to which we now turn.

## SUSTAINABILITY: TOWARD POLICY RECOMMENDATIONS

In pursuing sustainable language policy and sustainable curriculum design and implementation, two major considerations need to be borne in mind: the goals of trilingual education and the grassroots reality. Though goals set a general direction, schools can move toward them only within the limits of their capacity. Drawing on Vygotsky's (1978) notion of a zone of proximal development that determines a person's capacity to learn, schools (as learning organizations) have constraints on their potential for developing effective strategies to support the implementation of trilingual education. This suggests the need for a simultaneously bottom-up and top-down approach to curriculum design and implementation to ensure both national and local relevance and sustainability.

Such an approach is facilitated by China's tripartite education structure, which makes possible a national curriculum, local curriculum, and school-based curriculum (Meng 2003). The multilevel approach, if fully implemented, should result in a customized, integrated curriculum in each school that is oriented toward trilingual education and multiculturalism, but is tailored to match local characteristics and is rooted in the reality of that school and its community. Such an approach does not imply stasis or provincialism. Trilingual education opens up opportunities for enhancing students' ethnic, national, and international identities, and for enabling students to explore values and ways of living that go beyond their quotidian cultural and linguistic experiences. To achieve this—and following the principles of social constructivism espoused by Vygotsky—curriculum content should be pitched to match students' needs, interests, and abilities; integrated according to themes; focused on students' experiences; and oriented toward involving students as active participants in learning activities (Liu 2007).

Rebalancing the tripartite structure toward more robust school-based curriculum design would allow for more fine-grained customization of trilingual education. The proportions of the three languages in the curriculum, for example, should differ across regions according to regional circumstances. Generally speaking, in an ethnic minority dominated region or prefecture, students in urban and suburban schools display good proficiency in Mandarin Chinese and English; therefore, for them, the proportion of mother tongue instruction can be increased. Those inhabiting rural and mountainous areas often demonstrate high proficiency in the ethnic minority language, but their Mandarin Chinese and English are comparatively weak, so the proportion of Chinese and English teaching can be increased in those areas. Schools with a mixture of different ethnic minority groups and schools that teach ethnic minority languages with no written script would need to enhance their provision of trilingual education as far as their resources and capacity permit, and this work would need to be supported more rigorously by regional or national projects.

For any policy to be coherent, there must be clarity of purpose, and goals need to be made explicit. First, with respect to ethnic minority languages, the following goal could be set: that students develop cultural literacy through learning their mother tongue, which means getting to know the history, achievements, and distinctive characteristics of their own ethnic minority groups, as well as acquiring grammar, vocabulary, and communicative competence. However, this goal might not be embraced wholeheartedly by the stakeholders in minority regions unless there is obvious economic capital associated with competence in the minority language. The extension of trade relations between groups with the same or similar languages within China and across the national border, based on the Korean model, has the potential to raise the status of minority languages, thereby ensuring community support for their presence in the primary school curriculum. Tourism in Lijiang, Yunnan, has also helped boost the status of the Naxi language. What is often neglected is the cognitive and affective benefits of minority language maintenance as shown by the experimental study in the Dong dominated area in Guizhou (Finifrock 2010) as well as many other studies conducted in other parts of the world (e.g., Cenoz and Jessner 2000; Hoffmann and Ytsma 2004) . The message can only be conveyed more effectively to stakeholders in minority education in China through more research in different regions.

Second, learning Mandarin Chinese would help students cultivate socioeconomic literacy and a positive sense of national identity, which are important goals for policymakers in central government. Third, the goal of learning English would be to equip students with linguistic tools for academic and career development, and a worldview to act as global citizens.

Within this framework, a coherent trilingual education policy could delineate the roles and statuses of the different languages. As the language that is most familiar to most students in remote areas, the ethnic minority language can facilitate their cognitive development, build up their confidence in claiming their ethnic identity and scaffold learning across the curriculum, at all stages of schooling. Once children have developed sufficient competence in their mother tongue or first language and continue to maintain it throughout schooling, they are better able not only to acquire a second language but also to transfer their cognitive abilities to other school subjects that require strong cognitive skills (Bialystok and Cummins 1991; Cummins 1981, 1984a, 1984b). This transfer of abilities at primary level would facilitate competence in Mandarin Chinese as a medium for learning across the secondary curriculum and into tertiary education. Competence in both the mother tongue and Mandarin Chinese can then influence the development of proficiency in English, thereby completing the final stage of the path toward additive trilingualism (Herdina and Jessner 2002).

A prerequisite for achieving this vision of additive trilingualism is teacher education. Educators in ethnic minority areas tend to be poorly equipped to handle the complexity of trilingual education. There is a pressing need for both pre-service and in-service training to support the policy goals. While pre-service training requires the development of research-and-theory-based curriculum and pedagogical approaches which cannot be dealt with within the confines of this chapter, in-service training could feature seminars and workshops to promote strong models together with school-based training that takes into account the current educational situation of each ethnic minority area to enable trainees to integrate theory with practice to ensure relevance. School-based training (rather than generic, centralized programs) should encourage teachers, through the use of self-reflection, to focus on improving the quality of trilingual education in their own contexts, and to become increasingly autonomous in managing their own professional development.

## CONCLUSION

Although China's trilingual education policy emerged almost accidentally, as a confluence of diverse policy strands, it opens the possibility for a more coherent future plan that balances students' needs for identification with their ethnic culture; integration into the social, economic, and political life of the nation; and engagement with the opportunities of internationalization. To date, the implementation of trilingual education in different parts of the country has varied in focus and effectiveness, reflecting the haphazardness of the policy's genesis and the different political, economic, and social conditions that prevail. After a decade of trilingual education policy development, it is a good moment to take stock. If it is well-designed and effectively implemented, trilingual education can be a force for social justice, with the potential to reduce marginalization by giving ethnic minority groups the means to sustain and improve their social, economic, and political status.

Of course, the gap between goals and realities is huge. It would be totally unrealistic to assume that current conditions will permit the achievement of fully functional trilingualism throughout China. Indeed, some ethnic minority languages are in serious danger of extinction, and their survival will require a wide range of interventions, of which the development of trilingual education in schools forms just one component. Where conditions permit, priority should be accorded—initially—to the ethnic minority language and then to Mandarin Chinese, with a view to the students becoming competent bilinguals with proficiency in English that is comparable to their Han majority peers. Schools could move toward these targets according to their capacity, provided that they received structural support, training, and resources from education authorities and other stakeholders. Governments at all levels, especially the central government, are the key players in this policy domain. In addition to calling attention to the great importance of developing effective trilingual education, government leaders need to take decisive steps to support the policy, especially in areas where ethnic minority languages are under threat of extinction. Educational departments should accept responsibility for aiding the implementation in line with local conditions. Communities must work with schools to ensure the vitality of both their own ethnic minority languages and Mandarin Chinese. School leaders and teachers need to work together to find the most effective methods for fostering trilingualism in their students. To achieve such aims, only a concerted effort can bring about sustained progress.

## ACKNOWLEDGMENTS

The research undertaken by the network has been funded by various sources, including the institutions in which the team members work. We would like to acknowledge the generous funding received from the Hong Kong Institute of Education, Bangor University, and the Hong Kong Research Grants Council (General Research Fund 840012).

## REFERENCES

Adamson, B. 1998. English in China: The junior secondary school curriculum 1949–1994. Unpublished Ph.D. thesis, University of Hong Kong.

Adamson, B. 2004. *China's English: A history of English in Chinese education.* Hong Kong: Hong Kong University Press.

Adamson, B., and A. Feng. 2009. A comparison of trilingual education policies for ethnic minorities in China. *Compare* 39(3): 321–333.

Adamson, B., and A. Feng. Forthcoming. Models for trilingual education in the People's Republic of China. In *Minority languages and multilingual education*, eds. V. Zenotz, D. Gorter, and J. Cenoz. Clevedon: Multilingual Matters.

Adamson, B., and P. Morris. 2007. Comparing curricula. In *Comparative education research approaches and methods*, eds. M. Bray, B. Adamson, and M. Mason, 263–282. Hong Kong and Dordrecht: Comparative Education Research Centre & Springer.

Adamson, B., and B. Xia. 2011. A case study of the College English Test and ethnic minority university students in China: Negotiating the final hurdle. *Journal of Multilingual Education* 1(1).

Bialystok, E., and J. Cummins. 1991. Language, cognition and education of bi-lingual children. In *Language processing in bilingual children*, ed. E. Bialystok, 222–232. Cambridge: Cambridge University Press.Cenoz, J., and Jessner, U. 2000. *English in Europe: the acquisition of a third language*. Clevedon: Multilingual Matters.

Cummins, J. 1981. The role of primary language development in promoting educational success for language minority students. In *Schooling and language minority students: A theoretical framework*, ed. California State Department of Education, 3–49. Los Angeles: National Dissemination and Assessment Center.

Cummins, J. 1984a. Wanted: A theoretical framework for relating language proficiency to academic achievement among bilingual students. In *Language proficiency and academic achievement*, ed. C. Rivera, 2–19. Clevedon: Multilingual Matters.

Cummins, J. 1984b. *Bilingualism and special education: Issues in assessment and pedagogy*. Clevedon: Multilingual Matters.

Denwood, P. 1999. *Tibetan*. Amsterdam: John Benjamins.

Dong, F., and Narisu (forthcoming). Four models of Mongolian nationality Schools in the Inner Mongolia Autonomous Region. In *Trilingualism and trilingual education in China*, eds. A. Feng and B. Adamson. Dordrecht: Springer.

Feng, A. 2007. Intercultural space for bilingual education. In *Bilingual education in China: Practices, policies and concepts*, ed. A. Feng, 259–286. Clevedon: Multilingual Matters.

Finifrock, J. 2010. English as a third language in rural China: Lessons from the Zaidang Kam-Mandarin Bilingual Education Project, *Diaspora, Indigenous, and Minority Education*, 4(1), 33–46.

Gu, Y. S. 1999. An historical view on mutual assimilation between Zhuang and Han. *Guangxi Minzu Yanjiu (Research in nationalities in Guangxi)* 3: 46–50, 75 (in Chinese).

Herdina, P., and U. Jessner. 2002. *A dynamic model of multilingualism: Perspectives of change in psycholinguistics*. Clevedon: Multilingual Matters.Hoffmann, C., and Ytsam, J. (eds.) 2004. *Trilingualism in family, school and community*. Clevedon: Multilingual Matters.

Hu, G.W. 2007. The juggernaut of Chinese–English bilingual education. In *Bilingual education in China: Practices, policies and concepts*, ed. A. Feng, 94–126. Clevedon: Multilingual Matters.

Hu, G. W. 2008. The misleading academic discourse on Chinese–English bilingual education in China. *Review of Educational Research, 78*, 195–231.

Huang, X. 2000. *On the vitality of ethnic languages.* Beijing: Minzu University of China Press (in Chinese).

Jiang, Q. X., Q. G. Liu, X. H. Quan, and C. Q. Ma. 2007. EFL education in ethnic minority areas in Northwest China: an investigational study in Gansu Province. In *Bilingual education in China: Practices, policies and concepts*, ed. A. Feng, 240–255. Clevedon: Multilingual Matters.

Lai Au Yeung, W. Y. W. 1994. The Chinese Language curriculum in the People's Republic of China from 1978–1986: Curriculum change, diversity and complexity. Unpublished Ph.D. thesis, University of Hong Kong.

Lam, A. S. L. 2005. *Language education in China: Policy and experience from 1949.* Hong Kong: Hong Kong University Press.

Lewin, K. M., A. W. Little, H. Xu, J. W. Zheng. 1994. *Educational innovation in China: Tracing the impact of the 1985 reforms.* Harlow: Longman.

Liu, Q. 2007. Construction and development of a multicultural curriculum: A case study of multicultural curriculum development of Leishan Miao Nationality (in Chinese). Chongqing: Southwest University.

Mackerras, C. 1994. *China's minorities: Integration and modernisation in the twentieth century.* Hong Kong: Oxford University Press.

Meng, F. L. 2003. *A study of local curriculum development in multicultural settings* (in Chinese). Lanzhou: Northwest Normal University Press.

Ministry of Education. 2001a. *Guiding ideas to promote the English curriculum in primary schools by the Ministry of Education* (in Chinese). Beijing: Ministry of Education.

Ministry of Education. 2001b. *Standard of English courses for 9-year compulsory education and general senior secondary schools (for experimental purposes)* (in Chinese). Beijing: Beijing Normal University Press.

Ministry of Education. 2001c. *Guidelines for improving the quality of undergraduate teaching* (in Chinese). Beijing: Ministry of Education.

Mohanty, A. K. 2009. Multilingual education: A bridge too far? In *Social justice through multilingual education*, eds. T. Skutnabb-Kangas, R. Phillipson, A. K. Mohanty, and M. Panda, 3–15. Clevedon: Multilingual Matters.

National Linguistics Work Committee. 1996. *Collection of state language and script policies, 1949–1995* (in Chinese). Beijing: Yuwen Press.

Olan, M. 2007. An investigation of the status quo of minority college students learning English. *Xinjiang Daxue Xuebao* 35(2): 156–160.

People's Daily. 2011. *China has over 2.9 million ethnic minority cadres: Report.* http://english.people.com.cn/90001/90776/90785/7439871.html (accessed July 3, 2012).

Poa, D., and R. J. LaPolla. 2007. Minority languages of China. In *The vanishing languages of the Pacific rim,* eds. O. Miyaoka, O. Sakiyama, and M. E. Krauss, 337–354. Oxford: Oxford University Press.

Postiglione, G., B. Jiao, and Manlaji. 2007. Language in Tibetan education: The case of the Neidiban. In *Bilingual education in China: Practices, policies and concepts,* ed. A. Feng, 49–71. Clevedon: Multilingual Matters.

Qiang, H., X. Huang, L. Siegel, and B. Trube. 2011. English emersion in mainland China. In *English language in education and societies across Greater China,* ed. A. Feng, 169–188. Clevedon: Multilingual Matters.

State Language Commission. 1995. *100 questions in language orthography work* (in Chinese). Beijing: Yuwen Press.

Sunuodula, M., and A. Feng. 2011. Learning English as a third language by Uyghur students in Xinjiang: A blessing in disguise? In *English language in education and societies across Greater China,* ed. A. Feng, 260–283. Clevedon: Multilingual Matters.

Tan, D. Q. 1999. Multiple identity, mutual integration. *Guangxi Minzu Yanjiu (Research in nationalities in Guangxi)* 4: 28–34 (in Chinese).

Tsung, L. 2009. *Minority languages, education and communities in China.* Hampshire, UK: Palgrave Macmillan.

Vygotsky, L. F. 1978. *Mind in society: The development of higher psychological principles.* Cambridge, MA: Harvard University Press.

Wu, X. Q. 2000. Exploration and practice in English provision for Xinjiang minority students who start "from scratch." *Wai Yu Jie (Foreign Language World)* 77(1): 41–43 (in Chinese).

Yang, J. 2005. English as a third language among China's ethnic minorities, *The International Journal of Bilingual Education and Bilingualism* 8(6): 552–567.

Zhou, M. L. 2000. Language policy and illiteracy in ethnic minority communities in China. *Journal of Multilingual and Multicultural Development* 21(2): 129–148.

Zhou, M. L. 2001. The politics of bilingual education and educational levels in ethnic minority communities in China. *International Journal of Bilingual Education and Bilingualism* 4: 125–149.

# 11
# *DANWEI*, FAMILY TIES, AND RESIDENTIAL MOBILITY OF URBAN ELDERLY IN BEIJING

Zhilin Liu and Yanwei Chai

## INTRODUCTION

Dramatic changes have taken place in Chinese cities amid profound reforms from a centrally planned economy to a market-oriented economy (Ma and Wu 2005). Urban housing marketization, which was a crucial part of the reform agenda, has reduced direct government involvement in housing and has led to the emergence of a private urban housing market. Instead of receiving welfare housing from the state, urban residents are now expected to seek housing according to their preferences and budgets, with various forms of government support available in some circumstances. In the meantime, Chinese cities have undertaken dramatic spatial restructuring, often through massive inner-city redevelopment and commercial land development in the suburbs. Both institutional and spatial transformation has led to the rise of home ownership and residential mobility in urban China.

The patterns and determinants of residential mobility in transitional urban China have attracted much scholarly attention since the 1990s (e.g., Huang and Deng 2006; Li 2003, 2004; Li and Siu 2001a, 2001b; Wu 2004a). On one hand, the literature shows that individual housing choices based on preferences and budgets become more observable in an emerging housing market. On the other hand, institutional factors reflecting the transitional nature of China remain vital to the housing system. Many studies conclude that variables such as work unit type, seniority, and party membership are significant in explaining individual housing access and status in transitional urban China (Bian and Logan 1996; Li 2005).

Indeed, the work unit, or *danwei*, attracts the most attention as the socialist institution where urban residents work, live, and receive welfare; the work unit (*danwei*) also determines access to housing and other welfare benefits.

This argument, while correct, conceptualizes *danwei* only as a formal institution of welfare allocation but neglects the spatial dimension of *danwei* as a type of urban community. The importance of a spatial dimension, however, has been a core insight in geographical research on the Chinese *danwei* phenomenon. Bjorklund (1986) argued two decades ago that *danwei* should be understood as a fundamental spatial concept and that *danwei* is a basic territorial unit of Chinese socialist urban space to which people are bound to develop a sense of place attachment. *Danwei* also can be understood as a social network and an informal institution with its own social norms. Although institutional sociologists often stress the importance of such networks, norms, and informal institutions when researching market and transitional economies (Nee 1998, 2005; Granovetter 1974; Greif 1994), urban housing research in China has yet to explore informal institutional constraints faced by individuals when making residential decisions.

This chapter attempts to address this gap in the literature by investigating the ways in which informal factors affect the residential mobility of the urban elderly population in Beijing. Little research has been conducted that focuses on specific age cohorts in Chinese housing, including the elderly population, though some studies using statistical models have noted the age factor in mobility (e.g., Li 2004). In contrast, numerous empirical studies have revealed unique patterns and mechanisms of elderly migration both across and within cities in Western countries, shedding light on the urban spatial restructuring process of post–World War II Western cities (Longino 1990). Elderly migration and relocation decisions are deterred by neighborhood attachment and are driven by amenities, health care facilities, and the need for family support (Hunt, Feldt, and Marans 1983; Litwark and Longino 1987; Liaw, Frey, and Lin 2000). Given the different institutional context, it is interesting to explore whether or in which ways these factors are relevant in Chinese cities. In particular, special attention should be paid to how the Chinese urban elderly population has responded to or has been impacted by large-scale institutional and spatial transformations.

We also argue that the urban elderly population is composed of important age cohorts whose life experience provides a new perspective on the path-dependent urban transformation in China. Glen Elder (1975, 179) suggests that "cohorts represent a link between social change and life course patterns, between historical time and life time." Different age cohorts face unique social landscape and time-spatial contexts and are provided with different sets of opportunities and constraints, thus causing their life histories to bear unique historical inscriptions. Cohort membership provides "a proxy for exposure to historical change" (Elder 1994, 6). From this perspective, today's urban elderly population in China can be understood as encompassing the age cohorts that have lived through two systematic changes in urban China during the last six decades, as suggested by Lawrence Ma (2002). Born in the 1920s and 1930s, members of these cohorts entered the labor force in the late 1940s and 1950s, during the formation of a state-controlled socialist welfare system, and retired in the 1980s and 1990s, when the socialist system was being broken down by reform.

This chapter focuses on housing experiences of the elderly in the city of Beijing, while bearing in mind the historical-cohort effect of institutional and societal changes that have taken place throughout the past three decades. Our key proposition is that, although marketization has weakened, if not replaced, the influence of socialist institutions on residential mobility, elderly mobility is still constrained by informal factors such as social networks, neighborhood attachment, and family ties. We stress the changing meaning of *danwei* in the life experiences of individuals, highlighting its spatial dimension as a type of urban community that provides mature social networks, strengthened neighborhood bonds, and convenient access to public facilities. We also explore the effects of traditional Chinese family values when the elderly make residential decisions. Our analysis is based on in-depth interviews with 39 senior residents aged 65–85, living in different types of residential communities in Beijing. Interviews were conducted during March 2005–March 2006, and information was collected on interviewees' life histories and housing experiences. The interviews were supplemented with on-site observations and small questionnaire surveys with 153 senior residents regarding current housing and life quality.

## ELDERLY MIGRATION AND RESIDENTIAL MOBILITY

There is a great volume of Western literature on the patterns and mechanisms of elderly migration both within and across metropolitan areas in the post–World War II era. For instance, U.S. literature has studied the migration of elderly populations toward "Sun Belt" areas like Florida and California in the 1960s and 1970s (Lee 1980), noting that migration directions started changing or reversing in the late 1980s (Golant 1990). This migration trend led to growing elderly populations in small Sun Belt and non-metropolitan areas in the West (Longino 1982; Frey 1992). Similar trends of elderly migration toward rural areas were confirmed in other Western countries such as Canada and Britain (Liaw and Knaroglou 1986; Rogers, Watkins, and Woodward 1990). Within metropolitan areas, outward moves of urban elderly outnumbered inward residential mobility, while such trends differed by socioeconomic status (Wiseman and Virden 1977).

In addition to known socioeconomic determinants of residential mobility such as gender, age, and income, there are other determinants that are unique to elderly migration (Litwark and Longino 1987). Cantor (1975) finds that elderly people tend to be neighborhood-bound because of their reliance on the social interactions and social support provided by the neighborhood. Oh (2003) argues that local social bonds—measured by friendship, social cohesion, trust, informal social control, and accessibility of local services—increase the residential satisfaction of elderly residents, which directly deters intentions to move out of a neighborhood. When elderly people relocate, they are often attracted to destinations with better health care facilities or natural environments and amenities, otherwise known as "amenity migration" (Hunt, Feldt, and Marans 1983). Meanwhile, family ties play a growing role in elderly migration. In Japan, the elderly often make residential moves to live with or be near family members (Otomo 1981). The locations of adult children also affect elderly migration decisions in the United States, but this is mainly due to needs for family care and support (e.g., Litwark and Longino 1987; Liaw Frey, and Lin 2000).

China became "an aging society before being affluent" in the end of last century, largely due to the country's one-child policy that was adopted in the 1970s (Cai and Wang 2006; Zhang and Goza 2006). According to the fifth national population census conducted in 2000, 7.1 percent of the country's total population was aged 65 and older, which placed China within the United Nations' definition of an aging society (at least 7 percent of total population aged 65 and older) (National Bureau of Statistics of China 2000; Cai and Wang 2006). By 2005, the national household survey showed that the elderly proportion had reached 8.6 percent (DPES-NBSC 2005), and this increased to 8.86 percent in the 2010 census (NBSC, 2011). Beijing has one of the highest aging rates among all Chinese cities. The share of the aged population in Beijing increased from 8.4 percent in 2000 to 10.8 percent in 2005 (BSB and BST-NBSC 2006), compared to 7.1 percent and 8.6 percent nationwide, respectively.

Scholars have written much about the challenges that the aging trend imposes on Chinese society and policymaking. Most studies focus on areas such as elder care, social security, and health care (e.g., Zhang and Goza 2006; Zhan et al. 2006; Wong 2008; Li, Feldman, and Jin 2004; Zhan 2005). Some studies examine the life quality and daily activities of the elderly with specific interests in rural China (Zhang, Li, and Feldman 2005; Liu and Guo 2007, 2008). Existing literature on elderly migration in China typically focuses on inter-provincial rather than intra-city migration (e.g., Ma and Chow 2006; Meng et al. 2004) and the co-residence patterns of elderly parents and adult children (e.g., Logan and Bian 1999; Chen 2005).

Nonetheless, a few studies have revealed a lower rate of residential mobility of elder people compared to other age cohorts. Based on a survey of Beijing residents, Li (2004) concludes that the mobility rate for people over 60 is only 3 percent, as compared to the average 4.9 percent mobility rate of the general population. According to a national survey of the elderly population, senior citizens on average have lived in the same sub-district (*jiedao*) for 27.6 years (China Research Center on Aging 2003). This figure increases by age cohort, rising from 23.1 years for those aged 60–64 to 40.5 years for those aged 85 and older (see Table 11.1).

Lower residential mobility has led to a relative concentration of the elderly in certain areas in Beijing. As of the 2000 population census, sub-districts (*jiedao*) with the highest shares of aged population were in the four inner-city districts

200  CHINESE SOCIAL POLICY IN A TIME OF TRANSITION

Table 11.1. Average Years of Living in Current Residence of Urban Elderly in China

| Age Cohorts* | 60–64 | 65–69 | 70–74 | 75–79 | 80–84 | 85+ | Average |
|---|---|---|---|---|---|---|---|
| Male | 22.7 | 24.6 | 29.5 | 32.3 | 34.5 | 38.5 | 26.5 |
| Female | 23.6 | 27.7 | 30.2 | 34.1 | 37.2 | 41.7 | 28.8 |
| Total Average | 23.1 | 26.2 | 29.9 | 33.2 | 36.1 | 40.5 | 27.6 |

* In China, people aged 60 years and older are considered "elderly population" as the official retirement age is 60 years old.
Source: China Research Center on Aging 2003.

(where typical *hutong*-courtyard communities are located) and surrounding sub-districts inside the Third Ring Road (where most socialist *danwei* compounds are located) (see Figure 11.1). This phenomenon contradicted the general trend of outward population moves from the urban core in the past decade (Zhou and Ma 2000). What were the underlying mechanisms of lower mobility of the urban elderly population in Beijing, despite overall increases in residential mobility in emerging urban housing markets? What factors drive decisions when urban elderly residents decide to move? These are the questions we seek to answer in the following sections of this chapter.

## METHODOLOGY

Unlike most housing research on urban China, which has adopted statistical methods, we employ qualitative interviews as a major methodology for this

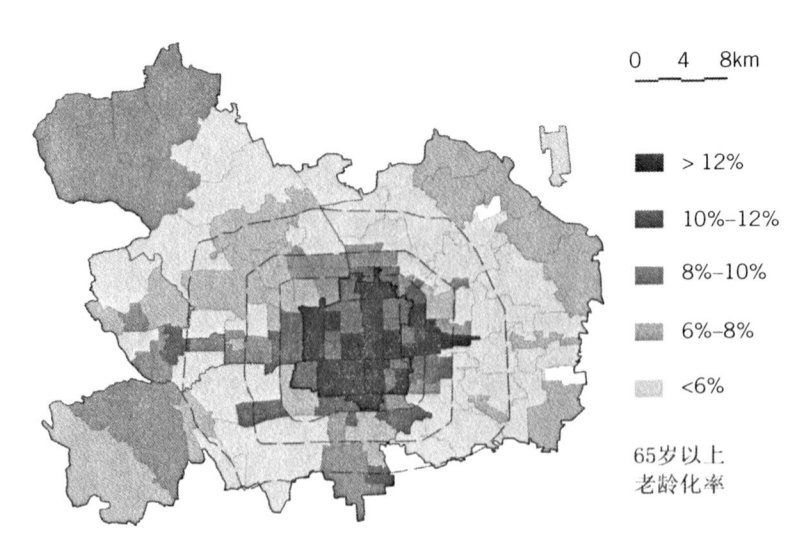

Figure 11.1. Share of Population Aged 65 and Older in Total Population, by Sub-district (*Jiedao*), Metro-Beijing. *Data Source*: NBSC 2000: The Fifth National Population Census

*Danwei*, Family Ties, and Residential Mobility of Urban Elderly   201

research. This method has proven useful in answering "how" and "why" questions in exploratory research when past research has been limited, and qualitative methods have been widely applied to aging studies (e.g., Zhang and Goza 2006) and in elderly migration research (e.g., McHugh and Mings 1996). In March 2005–March 2006, we conducted in-depth interviews with 39 senior residents living in different types of residential communities in Beijing. Most interviewees were born during 1926–1940 and were aged 65–80 when the interviews were conducted, with the oldest interviewee born in 1923 and the youngest born in 1941. Semi-structured interviews were designed and conducted in a way to build life-history records of each interviewee and his or her family, as well as to understand interviewees' recent housing experiences since the market reform. Life histories included housing events, career events, other major life events, and historical-societal events.

Respondents for qualitative interviews came from six residential communities in Beijing. These communities include one *hutong*-courtyard community in the historical inner-city districts of Beijing, three typical *danwei* compounds located in districts surrounding the historical inner city, and two commercial housing

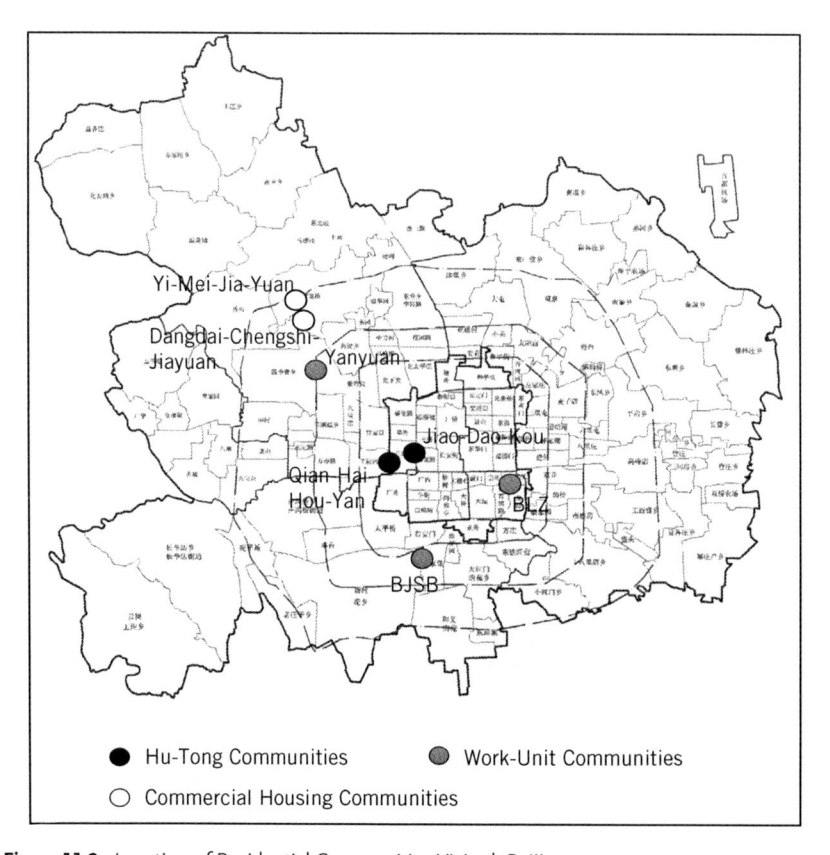

**Figure 11.2.** Location of Residential Communities Visited, Beijing

communities in suburban areas (see Figure 11.2). Selection of residential communities was based on the concentric model of residential spatial structure of Beijing developed by Zhang, Liu, and Li (2003). The three *danwei* compounds include one typical government agency residential compound in the southern part of central Beijing (BMSB), one residential compound of a major university in northwestern Beijing (YY) that represents a typical public organization (*shi-ye danwei*), and a residential compound of a typical state-owned enterprise (BLZ). During the field research, a questionnaire survey of 153 senior residents was conducted as a supplemental data source to capture level of satisfaction and future plans for residential moves of seniors living in three different types of communities.

Empirical analysis using qualitative interviews and questionnaires focuses on informal constraints on seniors' residential mobility by *danwei* and by traditional norms. First, the life history of a typical case of serior residents living in *danwei* compounds are analyzed and compared with that of seniors living in *hutong*-courtyard and commercial housing communities to highlight the interlocking of individual life histories with the paths of the *danwei* system over the last six decades. Second, recent housing experiences of "*danwei* elderly" are further analyzed to investigate the role of informal social networks and social supporting systems that have developed in *danwei* compounds. Third, we explore the ways in which traditional Chinese norms exercise informal constraints on elderly residents' mobility decision.

## *DANWEI* IN URBAN CHINA: WORKPLACES, WELFARE INSTITUTIONS, AND URBAN COMMUNITIES

*Danwei* is the key to understanding the Chinese urban transformation in both socialist and post-socialist eras. The nature, function, and role of *danwei* in housing and welfare are among the central debates in urban research on China in various disciplines, including sociology and geography (e.g., Bjorklund 1986; Lu 1993; Li and Li 1999; Li 1993; Logan and Bian 1993; Huang and Deng 2006; Huang 2004; Li 2005; Bray 2005). *Danwei* literally refers to the units where employees work, or work units. Functionally, however, *danwei* is much more complex than simply a workplace, and literature suggests the more complex and multifaceted nature of *danwei* in urban China.

From a sociological perspective, *danwei* represents an organizational basis of economic production, social organization and control, and welfare provision in socialist Chinese cities (Li and Li 1999). *Danwei* is the basic unit of economic production and distribution, which functions as the fundamental instrument of the state to mobilize all resources into industrial development. Sociologists have stressed *danwei* as the socialist institution of welfare allocation. This welfare system originated from the rationing system during the Yan'an Period in the 1940s and was fully established in the late 1950s and 1960s (Lu 1993; Bray, 2005). Employees not only worked in *danwei* but also were described as those that "belonged to *danwei*." They received all sorts of welfare from the *danwei*, including public housing, health care, child care, and pension. In exchange for secure jobs and welfare, individuals became dependent on the unit for which they worked, and job mobility between different units was highly limited (Li 1993).

From a geographical and planning perspective, *danwei* is more than a socialist institution or an organizational unit of economic production and social control. *Danwei* should be understood as a fundamental spatial concept (Bjorklund 1986). That is, *danwei* is a basic territorial unit of the socialist urban space in China, often a self-governed territory—called the *danwei* compound (or the *danwei dayuan*)—characterized by mixed land use and physically separated by tall, firm walls from the outside world (Bray 2005).

Figure 11.3 illustrates a typical *danwei* compound of a state-owned enterprise in Beijing. Enclosed in the compound are two separated but connected sections: the production quarter, with factory plants and management offices; and the living quarter, with buildings for public housing and basic service facilities. Most employees live in public housing flats in the compound, regardless of their rank, political status, income, or family life cycle. A variety of services are provided, including shops, health clinics, a child care center, elementary and middle schools, a vocational school, and even a post office. With these basic services, a *danwei* compound would sufficiently function as the basic daily activity space of its employees (Chai and Liu 2003). The urban space of socialist China is composed of many *danwei* compounds of various sizes and functions, from which urban residents seek not only jobs and income but welfare and overall livelihoods as well.

## *DANWEI* AS A WELFARE INSTITUTION IN THE SOCIALIST ERA: FROM A LIFE HISTORY PERSPECTIVE

Literature on housing specifically emphasises the nature of *danwei* as the building block of the socialist welfare system that determines individual housing opportunities (Logan and Bian 1993). Under the *danwei*-based welfare system, urban housing is considered a welfare good that is owned and provided by the state and allocated to residents through a centralized redistributive system. The central government controlled the housing funds, while municipal governments and *danwei* assumed construction and allocation responsibilities. As a direct distributor of resources, *danwei* usually allocated housing (of varying size and quality) to employees based on factors such as occupational rank, seniority, and family size (Wang and Murie 1999).

As discussed earlier, the life paths of today's urban elderly populations are interlocked with the formation and transformation of the *danwei* system in

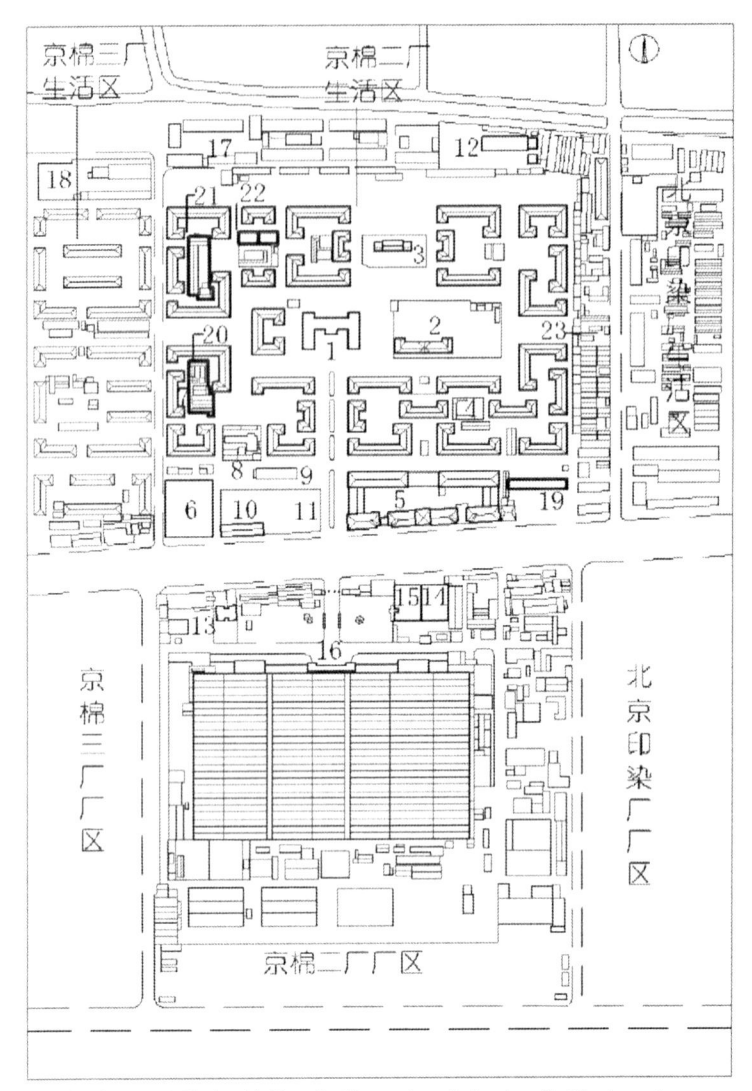

1- Auditorium and Dining Hall;   2- Elementary School;   3- Kindergarten;
4- Garden House;   5- Single Employee Dormitory;   6- Balizhuang Sub-district Corporation;   7- Family Flats;   8- Textile Industry Vocational School;
9- Retail Service Centers;   10- Post Office;   11- Sports Quad;
12- High School;   13- Child Care Center;   14- Bathrooms;   15- Garage;
16- Administrative Office;   17- Reserved Land;   18 - Middle School;
19- Family Flats;   20- Dormitory;   21- Factory owned by the sub-district;

**Figure 11.3.** Layout of a Typical *Danwei* Compound of a State-owned Factory, Beijing

urban China. The *danwei* system as a welfare institution was powerful enough to have dominated the housing careers of most of the senior residents whom we interviewed. Due to space limitations, we only present life-history tables of three interviewees, currently living in a typical *danwei* compound (Case No. WXY05, see Table 11.2), a *hutong*-courtyard community (Case No. HT02, see Table 11.3), and a commercial housing community (Case No. DD01, see Table 11.4). Life-history tables present major life-course events, job and housing careers, and major historical-societal events.

## Case No. WXY05

Mr. Liu was born in 1928 in rural Beijing, was married in 1945, and joined the army in 1952 during the Korean War. After leaving the army in 1956, he began working as a staff member in a national university in Beijing. The *danwei* system was formally established in Chinese cities during this period (Chai and Liu 2003). Mr. Liu's life history, as shown in Table 11.2, reflects the interlocking of his housing career with the *danwei*-based welfare allocation system.

Over the 50 years that he worked in the university, Mr. Liu and his family lived in five different dormitories or apartments, of which the first four were public rental housing owned and allocated by the work unit. All four residential moves between the five places were short-distance and were conducted between residential quarters within the *danwei* compound.

Western housing literature often stresses major life-course events such as marriage and childbirth in residential relocation decision. In the case of Mr. Liu, the allocation of the first three residential units somewhat coincided with the birth of a child, but the moves did not result from individual decision making based on family life cycle stages, as is often seen in market economies. Rather, the moves appear to be the result of favors bestowed by the *danwei*, where welfare housing allocation took account of employees' needs according to the number of family members and the status of crowding. Similarly, interviews with senior residents who had worked for state-owned enterprises revealed similar mechanisms of *danwei*-controlled housing allocation. The *danwei* would have surveyed "whether current housing was sufficient for the employee's family, how many children the employee had, whether both employee and spouse worked in the *danwei*, and other considerations" to determine an employee's priority on the list (Interview notes, retired employee in a state-owned enterprise, No.BLZ01).

## Case No. HT02

Ms. Hu was born in Beijing in 1947, and began working as a government employee in 1967, when the *danwei* system was fully developed. By that time, however, housing shortages had already appeared, as the state allocated most capital funds into economic production rather than improving living condition for residents following the "first production, second consumption" strategy (Wang and Murie 1999). The housing career of Ms. Hu and her husband also reflected the strong influence of the *danwei* system, though in a much different manner from that of Mr. Liu in the previous case. In contrast to Mr. Liu, Ms. Hu worked in a government agency that had fewer resources and less capacity to provide better housing for its employees. Ms. Hu had had to live with parents-in-law for 17 years, before

**Table 11.2.** Life History and Housing Career: Case No. WXY05 (Mr. Liu, Currently Living in *Danwei*-Compound Community)

| Year | Societal events | Life-course events | Job Career | Housing Career | |
|---|---|---|---|---|---|
| 1928 | | Born in rural Beijing | N/A | Privately-owned rural housing in the village | Born in rural Beijing |
| 1945 | | Married | | | |
| 1947 | | Eldest son born | | | |
| 1952 | Korean War | Joining the army; Second son born | Military | | Working in *Danwei* |
| 1956 | *Danwei* Sys. established | Back from army | University staff | | |
| 1957 | | Eldest daughter born | | Shared unit in a one story bungalow, allocated from *danwei* | Housing allocated by *danwei* |
| 1958 | | | | One-story temporary building, allocated by *danwei* | |
| 1960 | | Second daughter born | | | |
| 1963 | | Youngest son born | | | |
| 1964 | | | | One-story bungalow housing | |
| 1967 | Cultural revolution | | | Rented a unit of a one story bungalow housing; allocated by *danwei* | Short-distanced moves in *danwei* compounds |
| 1969 | | Second son departed | | | |
| 1974 | | Youngest son departed | | | |
| 1978 | Reform and open policy | Eldest son married and departed; Youngest son moving back | | | |
| 1981 | | Second son moving back | | | |
| 1982 | | Second son married and departed | | | |
| 1996 | | | Retired | Rented apartment unit from *danwei* | |
| 1998 | Housing marketization | | | Bought *danwei* apartment; privatized public housing | Bought privatized public housing; tenure transition |
| 2005 | | | | | |

her husband was allocated a two-bedroom unit by the automobile maintenance factory (a state-owned enterprise, SOE B) in 1986.

## Case No. DD01

Mr. Li was born in Hubei Province in 1937, migrated to Beijing in 1958, and started working as a staff member in a high school (*Danwei* A, see Table 11.4) in 1960, where he met his future wife, a colleague at the time. As they were both employees of the high school, Mr. Li and his wife received a one-bedroom unit in the staff dormitory upon their marriage. Mr. Li has since made two job changes, but his wife continued working for the same high school until retirement in 1993. Similarly to Mr. Liu, Mr. Li and his family had made a series of short-distance

**Table 11.3.** Life History and Housing Career: Case No. HT02 (Couple Currently Living in *Hutong*-Courtyard Community)

| Year | Societal Events | Life-Course Events | Husband Job Career | Husband Housing Career | Wife Housing Career | Wife Job Career |
|---|---|---|---|---|---|---|
| 1945 | | Husband born | N/A | Living with parents | N/A | N/A |
| 1947 | | Wife born | | | Living with parents | |
| 1949 | PRC founded | | | | | |
| 1956 | *Danwei* system established | | | | | |
| 1960 | | Husband started working | SOE A | | | |
| 1963 | | Husband job change | Government agency A | | | |
| 1967 | | Wife started working | | | | Government agency A |
| 1969 | | marriage | | Living with husband's parents | | |
| 1970 | | Eldest daughter born | | | | |
| 1972 | | Wife job change | | | | Government Agency B |
| 1973 | | Second daughter born | | | | |
| 1978 | Reform and open policy | | | | | |
| 1979 | | Husband job change | SOE B | | | |
| 1986 | | | | Renting public housing: A two-room unit, 20 sq.m, in a one-story bungalow in a hutong-courtyard, allocated by husband's *danwei* | | |
| 1993 | First-wave national privatization of public housing | Wife retired | | | | retired |
| 1998 | Housing marketizaiton | | | | | |
| 1999 | | Eldest grandsonborn | | | | |
| 2000 | | Husband retired | retired | | | |

residential moves until they bought an apartment in a co-op housing project organized by the wife's *danwei*. Such *danwei*-bound housing careers undertook dramatic change in the early 2000s. The residential quarters of *Danwei* A's compound were demolished and redeveloped, and thus Mr. Li's family was forced to move out of the *danwei* compound. As the 1998 housing marketization agenda prohibited continuous welfare housing allocation by *danwei*, such redevelopment drove Mr. Li—a *danwei* employee eventually abandoned by the *danwei* system—to become a real "consumer" of the housing market and, finally, a property owner.

# 208 CHINESE SOCIAL POLICY IN A TIME OF TRANSITION

Table 11.4. Life History and Housing Career: Case No. DD01 (Couple Currently Living in a Suburban Commercial Housing Community, Relocated from a *Danwei* Compound)

| Year | Societal Events | Life-Course Events | Husband Job Career | Husband Housing Career | Wife Housing Career | Wife Job Career |
|---|---|---|---|---|---|---|
| 1937 | | Husband born | N/A | He-Bei Province | N/A | N/A |
| 1939 | | Wife born | | | Henan Province | |
| 1949 | PRC founded | | | | | |
| 1956 | Danwei system established | | | | | |
| 1958 | | Both migrated to Beijing | | Living with parents | Living with parents | |
| 1960 | | Both started working | *Danwei* A | Staff dorm | Staff dorm | *Danwei* A |
| 1968 | | Marriage | | Renting public housing: one-bedroom staff apartment, allocated by wife's *danwei* | | |
| 1969 | | Eldest son born | | | | |
| 1970 | | Second son born | | Renting public housing: 1.5-bedroom staff apartment, allocated by wife's *danwei* | | |
| 1973 | | Husband job change | *Danwei* B | | | |
| 1976 | | | | Renting public housing: two-bedroom staff apartment, allocated by wife's *danwei* | | |
| 1978 | Reform and open policy | | | | | |
| 1979 | | Husband job change | *Danwei* C | | | |
| 1993 | | | | Bought co-op housing from Wife's *danwei* | | |
| 1994 | | Wife retired | | | | Retired |
| 1999 | | Husband retired | Retired | | | |
| 2000 | | Eldest son married | | | | |
| 2002 | | Granddaughter born | | Renting private housing (temporary due to redevelopment) | | |
| 2003 | | | | Bought commercial housing with redevelopment compensation | | |

## Cross-case Comparison: *Danwei*-bound Housing Career

The job and housing careers of today's senior residents started when the *danwei* system was established in socialist urban China, with the following decades seeing gradual integration of individual life histories into the trajectory of the *danwei* system. The life histories described in the above three cases demonstrate this interlocking process, which was particularly powerful in the socialist era. *Danwei* as a welfare institution exercised a stronger influence on employees' housing tenure and residential mobility than either their family life cycle stage or other individual attributes.

The *danwei* system gradually broke down as China steadily departed from the socialist planning economy. In the early stage of urban housing reform, *danwei* continued to affect housing access for urban residents (Logan, Bian, and Bian 1999; Huang and Clark 2002; Li 2005). More dramatic changes took place in the late 1990s. It is notable that Mr. Liu's last residential relocation took place in 1998, when he finally purchased an apartment from his university, marking a tenure transition from public renting to partial ownership. This was made possible by the massive privatization of public housing in the 1990s. In 1998, a more comprehensive package of housing marketization was adopted, in which work units (*danwei*) were prohibited from providing in-kind welfare housing to employees (Wang 2001). The private real estate industry was encouraged to expand and replace the public sector as the major provider of housing. Thus, the urban housing reform, despite being an incremental and complicated process, eventually led to the dismantling of *danwei*-based welfare housing and the emergence of an urban housing market system.

In the wake of these changes, the intriguing question for the aged cohorts—whose life paths have been so closely bound with *danwei* as their workplace, source of housing and welfare, and lifetime living space—becomes to what degree the *danwei* system retains its role in people's life experiences. More specifically, to what extent have the sociological dimensions of *danwei* (as a socialist welfare institution) and the spatial dimensions of *danwei* (as a territorial unit of urban space) strengthened or weakened during the transitional period? In particular, what does the term "living in *danwei*" mean for the urban elderly population, particularly when they face mobility decisions in the emerging housing market?

## EVOLVING MEANING OF *DANWEI*: FROM WELFARE INSTITUTION TO URBAN COMMUNITY

The current debate mainly concerns the extent to which *danwei* persists as a formal institution of housing welfare allocation. Our interviews, however, show that there is greater complexity in the informal role of *danwei* as an urban community in which senior residents have lived for decades. Our small-sample questionnaire survey reported a low tendency of senior respondents to move out of *danwei* compounds (77.4 percent among all 53 samples unwilling to relocate).[1] When asked about their reasons for not moving, interviewees often stressed the importance of familiarity with the living environment and the sense of "belonging to" the *danwei* community, in addition to other main reasons such as "lack of affordability."

For example, Mr. Qin, a retired worker in a state-owned enterprise, continues to live in his old employee's flat despite the lack of maintenance and facilities. He explains his decision as follows:

"We all came to work here in our twenties, and now, I am in my seventies.... This work unit has about 10,000 employees, and we are all familiar with each other. If I move to another place, I do not know anybody there, nobody in the neighborhood, and nobody in the property management office.... If I need help with anybody like Mr. Zhang, Mr. Liu, Mr. Wang, I know them all. It is convenient. If I move to the suburb, I do not know anybody, and they do not know me, and do not care about me." (Interview notes, retired employee of a state-owned enterprise, No. BLZ01)

The above quote indicates that as residents "living in *danwei*" gradually have developed a strong sense of place attachment toward the *danwei* compounds as an urban community (as argued in Bjorklund 1986), this attachment has reduced their aspirations for residential relocation. Such sense of place attachment is first of all built upon senior residents' dependence on neighbors (and also lifelong colleagues, in most cases) for social interaction and support.

Interviewees living in other types of *danwei* compounds echoed the impact of the sense of place attachment:

"It is safer and convenient to live in own *danwei* compound. And if anything happens, like if you get sick, it is easy to find help by making a phone call." (Interview notes, retired employee of a government agency, No. TYJ02)

"I am satisfied here now and do not want to move. It is not bad here, [as] I am familiar with neighbors, and the environment is good too." (Interview note, retired employee of a public organization, No. YDY20)

This holds true even when relocation is feasible for these residents, or when there is the possibility of living with their children:

"My son has apartment housing and he wants me to live with him. But I do not want to move as long as I can manage it. First of all, I do not want to bother them, and secondly, I am not used to commercial housing communities. There is a cold and detached feeling in that neighborhood." (Interview notes, retired employee of a public organization, No. YDY19)

Another benefit of "living in *danwei*" is that, due to their prime location, *danwei* compounds provide convenient access to public services, in particular, the community health care services and major hospitals that are critical for urban elderly residents.

"I am satisfied with this place. Transportation is convenient, with good provision of gas and other utilities. It is convenient to go shopping or go to hospitals. It is important to live with convenient transportation and especially access to hospitals." (Interview notes, retired employee of a public organization, No. ZGY 06)

Compared to new commercial housing communities, where public service delivery is often inadequate and slow, "living in *danwei*" renders substantive values for elder residents.

"You may say that housing is cheap in Tongxian[2] costing only a hundred thousand *yuan*,[3] [but] who would want to move there? ... First, I would have to transfer three buses [to come to the city to see the doctor] if I get sick... it is not convenient even though there are supermarkets or clinics. [But] If I live here, it is close to major hospitals in the city.... There is even an emergency-care and ambulance station in the community. If I dial 120, it takes less than two minutes for the ambulance to come...."(Interview notes, retired employee of a state-owned enterprise, No. BLZ01)

To summarize, interviews of elderly residents in different types of *danwei* compounds shed light on the growing influence of the informal power of the *danwei* system on individual housing experience. First, although marketization created better housing opportunities, the urban elderly populations in Beijing retained their strong sense of attachment toward *danwei* communities as their primary channel of social interaction and social support, rather than merely as an institutional channel of welfare housing opportunities. Second, such attachment is also built on convenient access to community facilities and infrastructure associated with "living in *danwei*." This informal power of the *danwei* contributes to the reluctance of urban elderly residents to relocate from *danwei* communities on the basis of housing quality alone.

The association of *danwei* with good social networks and convenient access to public services also surfaces during interviews with elderly people living in commercial housing units. For instance, Mr. Li, a retired high school teacher now living in a suburban commercial housing community, expressed his nostalgia for the social environment that he would have enjoyed in an "old *danwei* community":

"We elderly people do not pursue new housing. I like my old place better... My old colleagues are all there.... It is convenient just to live in *danwei*, with better health care service provision. If my wife gets sick, I can call upon somebody [to help] and drive us to the hospital, which is just nearby. Here, it is even hard to find a taxi, and to whom I can turn for help?" (Interview notes, senior residents having relocated from a *danwei* compound to a commodity housing apartment, No. DD01)

## EFFECTS OF FAMILY TIES: PROVIDING CHILD CARE SUPPORT FOR ADULT CHILDREN

Another informal social mechanism that affects mobility decisions of the elderly in urban Beijing concerns traditional norms and family values. Literature on elderly migration patterns across Chinese provinces has given much attention to traditional family values. Chinese people value the tradition of co-residence among aged parents, adult children, and grandchildren. Chen (2005) concludes that the elderly make inter-provincial migrations toward the residences of their adult children in response to child care support needs and their own needs for family care. Yang and He (2004) argue that family ties in the traditional Chinese system often mean that the elderly generation will try to minimize the burden on their adult children and make efforts to provide support for their adult children.

The effects of family ties rooted in the Chinese culture are also seen in the housing decisions of elderly residents in Beijing. On one hand, family ties may deter the residential mobility of the elderly, despite a desire to live with their children and grandchildren, as reflected in interviews with senior residents currently living in *hutong* communities and *danwei* compounds. Generational differences in lifestyle contribute to this reluctance to move in with adult children. One interviewee named Mr. Yang stated:

> "Although we maintain close relationships with them, different generations have their own lifestyle." (Interview notes, retired employee of a public organization *danwei*, No. ZGY06)

More deeply, this is a sacrifice that elderly people often make to avoid creating financial and psychological burdens on their adult children. It may help to explain why 60 percent of the Chinese urban elderly population prefer not to live with their children, according to a national survey (China Research Centre on Aging 2003). Responses from interviewees revealed the willingness of elderly people to sacrifice their desire to live with their children and grandchildren—a traditional norm rooted in the Confucius tradition—while choosing rather to live alone to allow their children to maintain their own lifestyle.

> "Even if you want to live with them, maybe they do not like this idea? Even if my daughter likes it, what about my son-in-law? Even if my son likes it, what about his wife? Also two generations have different habits, and we cannot accept their lifestyle—always they talk about mortgage, fashion, and eating outside." (Interview notes, retired employee of a public organization *danwei*, No. ZGY06)

*Danwei*, Family Ties, and Residential Mobility of Urban Elderly 213

**Table 11.5.** Descriptive Results from Small Questionnaire Survey: Whether Respondents Have Made Residential Moves since Age 60

|  | Number of Sample | Percentage |
|---|---|---|
| All Sample with Valid Answer | 140 | 100% |
| No, Have Not Moved Since | 90 | 64.3% |
| Yes, Have Moved Since | 50 | 35.7% |
| *Reason: Redevelopment* | 9 | 18.0% |
| *Reason: Allocation by Danwei* | 9 | 18.0% |
| *Reason: Live with Children* | 12 | 24.0% |
| *Reason: Buy Own Housing* | 11 | 22.0% |
| Other Reasons | 9 | 18.0% |

Data source: small sample survey of senior residents in Beijing, 2006

On the other hand, family ties may encourage the residential mobility of urban elderly in other situations. In the small questionnaire survey, senior residents were asked whether they had made a residential move since they were 60 years old and, if yes, the main reasons for such moves. As shown in Table 11.5, for respondents who have moved since age 60, to live with children is the main reason for such moves, accounting for a higher percentage than other reasons such as buying own commercial housing, receiving welfare housing by *danwei*, or forced relocation due to redevelopment. Senior respondents specifically cited "to take care of grandchildren," "to take care of my children," along with "to take care of each other" as explanations for "relocation to live with children."

Such behavior patterns indicate an important role for Chinese family norms in the elderly's residential decisions after retirement. These norms are not merely about receiving family care support from children (as seen in Western countries), but are also about offering child care support to their adult children and grandchildren.

> "My granddaughter was born in 2000, and somebody had to take care of her. My wife's health condition was not very good, and she had to have enough rest and sleep. So, I had to move to my daughter's house to take care of the baby, and my wife stayed home alone. In 2002, I moved back." (Interview notes, retired employee of a public organization *danwei*, No. CHCY05)

This reflects the unique Chinese ethic in which elder generations feel responsible for supporting younger generations (Yang and He 2004). Contrary to younger elderly populations in the United States who generally migrate toward Sun Belt regions in search of leisurely amenities and better living environments, the elderly population in Beijing often base their relocation decisions on the provision of household and child care support for their adult children.

Co-residence with children and grandchildren often brings the elderly a mixture of joy and pain. On one hand, taking care of grandchildren brings "a lot of fun and [a] feeling of accomplishment" (interview notes, retired employee of a public organization *danwei*, No. YDY02). On the other hand, child care is a challenge to those who have moved away from familiar *danwei* compounds when adjusting to a new neighborhood, as shown in the following interview note:

> "I moved to YDY mainly to take care [of] my grandson, who is seven now.... But still I am not used to living here [in this community], and when I do grocery shopping, I still go to that supermarket near where I used to live." (Interview notes, retired employee of a public organization *danwei*, No. YDY02)

These types of residential moves tend to be temporary. The elderly are more likely to move back to their original locations after a few years of child care support because, as the above interviewee pointed out, "from the bottom of my heart, I prefer going back to my old place; so when my grandson grows older, I will move back" (Interview notes, retired employee of a public organization *danwei*, No.YDY02). Other interviewees living in commercial housing communities echoed this preference.

> "I came here mainly to take care of this kid – my granddaughter. Her parents do not have time.... About the future, we will see. She is growing up every day, and it is not convenient for so many people to live under the same roof. If our health condition is still good, we will move back (to our old place)." (Interview notes, senior resident living in a commercial housing community, No. YM01)

## CONCLUSION

The findings reported here from in-depth interviews challenge conventional wisdom that *danwei* is only a formal socialist institution of welfare provision in transitional urban China. While we agree with existing literature on the enduring role of *danwei* in housing, we argue that *danwei* itself has transformed and is in need of reinterpretation. Although our qualitative interviews examined only the elderly age cohort, we nevertheless demonstrated that *danwei* now represents a form of social networking and support that is valued by senior residents, along with the more traditional amenity values. *Danwei* is more than just a symbol of welfare resources. The strong sense of neighborhood attachment and social belonging held by elderly people contributes to their reluctance to move away from "old *danwei* compounds." We argue that the informal aspect of "living in *danwei*" is critical and merits further investigation in order to better understand the dynamics of urban social transformation in China.

Second, when elderly people move away from *danwei* compounds, their decisions may be based on involuntary and constrained processes, rather than free market choice. Scholars have written about the involuntary mobility of urban residents that is caused by inner-city housing redevelopment by local governments (Wu 2004b). Our research has complemented these findings by pointing out that family ties and norms are important drivers of residential mobility for the urban elderly, as demonstrated by the cases in which older people make residential moves within Chinese cities with the purpose of offering child care support, rather than seeking care from adult children. In 1996, China passed the Senior Rights and Interests Protection Law, which is currently under amendment. Most likely, the amendment will further emphasize the responsibility of adult children in elder care—that is, to uphold the traditional values of the Chinese family through a formalized legal framework of elder care and protection of rights. The impact of this policy change on the residential patterns of the urban elderly is difficult to predict, but it may contribute to the further erosion of *danwei* communities if more older people move to live with their children and grandchildren.

Our qualitative studies suggest the need for a new theoretical framework for understanding the housing experience of urban residents in the emerging Chinese market economy. Currently, theoretical debates center on the dichotomy between the rise of individual preferences (which are reflected by socio-democratic indicators) and the persistence of socialist institutions in the transitional era. However, it is important to note that individual choices are bound not only by formal institutional constraints, such as welfare allocation policies or regulations, but also by informal social networks and norms (Nee and Ingram 1998). Such informal institutional constraints often affect the preferences and capacity of residents more directly than formal constraints. In addition, individual preferences may reflect a hybrid of economically rational, market-based components (such as the value placed on easy access to hospitals, transportation, and other services) and socially rational components (such as attachment to networks of mutual support).

This research has implications for welfare policy targeted at elderly people, as well as the ongoing "community building" movement toward reforming urban governance and public service delivery in Chinese cities. Indeed, in the process of rapid urban spatial restructuring, *danwei* "has retained a significant if diminishing role within the urban scene, even adapting to take advantage of opportunities that have arisen through reform" (Bray 2005). While the market economy gradually takes shape with the dismantling of the socialist welfare system, *danwei* compounds remain and have strengthened their spatial characteristics as urban communities with strong neighborhood bonds and better accessibility to public facilities and services.

Overall, if these patterns persist, residential mobility—or lack thereof—is likely to create a relatively stable landscape of aging communities in the urban core. This overall stability may incorporate temporary episodes of mobility for elderly people who are needed as caretakers of their grandchildren in the outskirts of the city. Whether the patterns described in this chapter persist depends on the ongoing process of market development and urban restructuring, as well as the evolution of cultural norms. What is clear in the near future is that, despite the overall improvement of living conditions and the rapid reform of formal institutions, cultural norms are unlikely to change immediately, which means that urban elderly residents will continue to be caught between the informal but powerful demands of family members and the equally powerful desire to remain in the *danwei* community. If the "residualization" of urban elderly in *danwei* compounds continues, municipal governments will need to meet the challenge with improved provision of services and facilities for the elderly who choose to age in place.

Indeed, a recent "community building" agenda in Beijing has given attention to providing community-based services and assistance for elderly residents (including retired *danwei* employees). In the *Provisional Guiding Directory of Basic Community-Based Public Services in Beijing*, the Office of Municipal Steering Group of Societal Development specified nine forms of services and assistance that would be coordinated and provided by community-level residential committees, including assistance to family-based elder care, community-based elderly care centers, assistance with transportation arrangements, and community-based medical services. These basic services used to be provided through the *danwei*-based welfare system in the socialist era and are now being transferred into the community-based divisions of municipal government. Although basic social services, including elderly care and welfare, were often neglected during the rapid transition toward a market economy, the current campaign to build "a harmonious society" appears to have refocused attention on this important government function.

Social services need to serve elderly people where they live, and therefore the effective delivery of such services requires a deeper understanding of the formal and informal factors that drive residential patterns. We hope that the results of our research will spur further examination of mobility and stasis among the urban elderly generally, and the specific role that *danwei* communities continue to play in this emerging story.

## ACKNOWLEDGMENT

This research has been funded partially by the Natural Science Foundation of China (Grant No. 40801056) and the Social Science Foundation of China (Grant No. 11AZD085).

## NOTES

1 In fact, the questionnaire survey revealed a high percentage of respondents unwilling to make further residential moves in the near future (77.4% in *danwei* compounds, 81.6% in *hutong* communities, and 87.8% in commercial housing communities).
2 Tongxian is an outer suburban district of Beijing, which is now called "Tongzhou District".

## REFERENCES

Beijing Statistical Bureau and Beijing Survey Team of National Bureau of Statistics of China. 2006. *Data report on 2005 Beijing 1% population sample survey*. National Bureau of Statistics of China Website. http://www.stats.gov.cn/tjgb/rkpcgb/dfrkpcgb/t20060317_402311329.htm (accessed February 1, 2013).

Bian, Y., and J.R. Logan. 1996. Market transformation and the persistence of power: The changing stratification system in urban China. *American Sociological Review* 61(5): 739–758.

Bjorklund, E. M. 1986. The danwei: Socio-spatial characteristics of work units in China's urban society. *Economic Geography* 62: 19–29.

Bonaguidi, A., and V. T. Abrami. 1992. The metropolitan aging transition and metropolitan redistribution of the elderly in Italy. In *Elderly migration and population redistribution: A comparative study*, eds. A. Rogers, W. H. Frey, R. Rees, et al., 143–162. London: Belhaven Press.

Bray D. 2005. *Social space and governance in urban China: The danwei system from origins to reform*. Stanford: Stanford University Press.

Cai, F., and M. Wang. 2006. Challenge facing China's economic growth in its aging but not affluent era. *China & World Economy* 14(5): 20–31.

Cantor, M. H. 1975. Life space and the social support systems of the inner city elderly of New York City. *The Gerontologist* 15: 23–27.

Chai, Y., and Z. Liu. 2003. The transformation of work unit system in China: Its implication to individual daily life and urban spatial restructuring. *Komaba Studies in Human Geography* 16 (Special Issue: Human Activity Systems in Chinese Cities): 55–78. The University of Tokyo, Japan.

Chen, F. 2005. Residential patterns of parents and their married children in contemporary China: A life course approach. *Population Research and Policy Review 24*: 125–148.

China Research Center on Aging (CRCA). 2003. *Data analysis from the Sample Survey of Urban and Rural Elderly Population in China [Zhongguo chengxiang laonian renkou zhuangkuang yicixing chouyang diaocha shuju fenxi]*. Beijing: China Standard Press.

DPES-NBS (Department of Population and Employment Statistics, National Bureau of Statistics of China). 2005. *China population statistical yearbook 2005*. Beijing: China Statistics Press.

Elder, G. H., Jr. 1975. Age differentiation and the life course. *Annual Review of Sociology 1*: 165–190.

Elder, G. H., Jr. 1994. Time, human agency, and social change: Perspectives on the life course. *Social Psychology Quarterly 57(1)*: 4–15.

Frey, W. H. 1992. Metropolitan redistribution of the US elderly: 1960–1970, 1970–1980, and 1980–1990. In *Elderly migration and population redistribution: A comparative study*, eds. A. Rogers, W. H. Frey, R. Rees, et al., 123–142. London: Belhaven Press.

Golant, S. M. 1990. Post-1980 regional migration patterns of the USA elderly population. *Journal of Gerontology 45(3)*: 135–140.

Granovetter, M. 1974. *Getting a job*. Cambridge, MA: Harvard University Press.

Greif, A. 1994. Culture beliefs and the organization of society: A historical and theoretical reflection on collectivist and individualist societies. *Journal of Political Economy 102*: 912–950.

Huang, Y. 2004. The road to homeownership: A longitudinal analysis of tenure transition in urban China. *International Journal of Comparative Sociology 28(4)*: 774–795.

Huang, Y., and F. Deng. 2006. Residential mobility in Chinese cities: A longitudinal analysis. *Housing Studies 21(5)*: 625–652.

Huang, Y., and W. A. V. Clark. 2002. Housing tenure choice in transitional urban China: A multilevel analysis. *Urban Studies 39(1)*: 7–32.

Hunt, M. E., A. G. Feldt, and R. W. Marans et al. 1983. Retirement communities: An American original. *Journal of Housing for the Elderly 1*: 262–275.

Lee, E. S. 1980. Migration of the aged. *Research on Aging 2*: 131–135.

Li, H. 1993. China's danwei phenomenon and the mechanisms of conformity in urban communities *[Zhongguo danwei xianxiang yu chengshi shequ de zhenghe jizhi]*. *Sociological Research 5*: 23–32.

Li, H., and L. Li. 1999. Resources and exchange: The dependence structure in *danwei* organization. *Sociological Research 4*: 44–63.

Li, S.-M. 2003. Housing tenure and residential mobility in urban China: A study of commodity housing development in Beijing and Guangzhou. *Urban Affairs Review 38(4)*: 510–534.

Li, S.-M. 2004. Life course and residential mobility in Beijing, China. *Environment and Planning A* 36(1): 27–43.

Li, S.-M. 2005. China's changing urban geography: A review of major forces at work. *Issues and Studies* 41(4): 67–106.

Li, S.-M. 2005. Residential mobility and urban change in China: What have we learned so far? In *Restructuring the Chinese city: Changing society, economy and space*, eds. L. J. C. Ma, and F. Wu, 175–191. London and New York: Routledge.

Li, S.-M., and Y. M. Siu. 2001a. Commodity housing construction and intra-urban migration in Beijing—An analysis of survey data. *Third World Planning Review* 23(1): 39–60.

Li, S.-M., and Y. M. Siu. 2001b. Residential mobility and urban restructuring under market transition: A study of Guangzhou, China. *Professional Geographer* 53(2): 219–229.

Li, S.-M., and Z. Yi. 2005. *The road to homeownership under market transition: Beijing 1980–2001* (Occasional paper No. 61). Hong Kong: Centre for China Urban and Regional Studies Hong Kong Baptist University.

Li, S. Z., M. W. Feldman, and X. Y. Jin. 2004. Children, marriage form, and family support for the elderly in contemporary rural China: The case of Songzi. *Research on Aging* 26(3): 352–384.

Liaw, K. L., W. H. Frey, and J. P. Lin. 2000. Location of adult children as an attraction for black and white elderly migrants in the United States. *QSEP Research Report* 349: 1–15.

Liaw, K. L., and P. Kanaroglou. 1986. Metropolitan elderly out-migration in Canada, 1971–1976: Characteristics and explanation. *Research on Aging* 8(2): 201–231.

Litwark, E., and C. F. Longino. 1987. Migration patterns among the elderly: A development perspective. *The Gerontologist* 25(3): 266–272.

Liu, L. J., and Q. Guo. 2007. Loneliness and health-related quality of life for the empty nest elderly in the rural area of a mountainous county in China. *Quality of Life Research* 16:1275–1280.

Liu, L.-J., and Q. Guo. 2008. Life satisfaction in a sample of empty-nest elderly: A survey in the rural area of a mountainous county in China. *Quality of Life Research* 17: 823–830.

Logan, J. R., and F. Bian. 1993. Family values and coresidence with married children in urban China. *Social Forces* 77(4): 1253–1282.

Logan, J. R., Y. Bian, and F. Bian. 1999. Housing inequality in urban China in the 1990s. *International Journal of Urban and Regional Research* 23(1): 7–25.

Longino, C. F. 1982. Changing aged non-metropolitan migration patterns, 1955 to 1965 and 1965 to 1970. *Journal of Gerontology* 37(2): 228–234.

Longino, C. F. 1990. Geographical distribution and migration. In *Handbook of aging and the social sciences*, 445–463. San Diego, CA: Academic Press.

Lu, F. 1993. The origins and formation of the unit (danwei) system. *Chinese Sociology and Anthropology* 25(3).

Ma, A., and N. W. S. Chow. 2006. Economic impact of elderly amenity mobility in southern China. *Journal of Applied Gerontology* 25(4): 275–290.

Ma, L. J. C. 2002. Urban transformation in China, 1949–2000: A review and research agenda. *Environment and Planning A 34*: 1545–1569.

Bonaguidi, A., and V. T. Abrami. 1992. The metropolitan aging transition and metropolitan redistribution of the elderly in Italy. In *Elderly migration and population redistribution: A comparative study*, eds. A. Rogers, W. H. Frey, R. Rees, et al., 143–162. London: Belhaven Press.

Ma, L.J.C., and F. Wu. 2005. Restructuring the Chinese city: Diverse processes and reconstituted spaces. In *Restructuring the Chinese city: Changing society, economy and space*, eds. Ma, L.J.C., and F. Wu, 1–20. London and New York: Routledge.

McHugh, K. E., and R. C. Mings. 1996. The circle of migration: Attachment to place in aging. *Annals of the Association of American Geographers* 86(3): 530–550.

Meng, X., X. Jiang, J. Song, H. Wan, Y. Chen, Z. Han, and Y. (2004). The floating elderly population in Beijing: Characteristics and determinants. *Population Research (renkou yanjiu)* 28 (6): 53–59.

National Bureau of Statistics of China (NBSC). 2000. The Fifth National Population Census. http://www.stats.gov.cn/tjsj/ndsj/renkoupucha/2000pucha/html/t0301.htm (accessed August 20, 2008).

National Bureau of Statistics of China (NBSC). 2003. *China statistical yearbook 2003*. Beijing: China Statistics Press.

National Bureau of Statistics of China (NBSC). 2011. *First communique of main data results from the 2010 Sixth National Population Census*. Released April 28, 2011. http://www.stats.gov.cn/tjgb/rkpcgb/qgrkpcgb/t20110428_402722232.htm (accessed May 23, 2011).

Nee, V. 1998. Norms and networks in economic and organizational performance. *American Economic Review* 88(2): 85–89.

Nee, V. 2005. A new institutional approach to economic sociology. In *The handbook of economic sociology*, 2nd ed., eds. S. Neil and R. Swedberg, 49–74. New York and Princeton: Russell Sage Foundation and Princeton University Press.

Nee, V., and P. Ingram. 1998. Embeddedness and beyond: Institutions, exchange, and social structure. In *The new institutionalism in sociology*, eds. M. C. Brinton and V. Nee, 19–45. New York: Russell Sage Foundation.

Office of Municipal Steering Group of Societal Development. 2010. *Provisional guiding directory of basic community-based public services in Beijing* (Document OMSGSD [2010] No. 7), September 1, 2010.

Oh, J-H. 2003. Social bonds and the migration intentions of elderly urban residents: The mediating effect of residential satisfaction. *Population Research and Policy Review* 22: 127–146.

Otomo, A. 1981. Mobility of elderly population in Japanese metropolitan areas. *Journal of Population Studies* 4: 23–28.

Rogers, A., F. Watkins, and J. A. Woodward. 1990. Interregional elderly migration and population redistribution in four industrialized countries: A comparative analysis. *Research on Aging* 12(3): 251–293.

Wang, Y. 2001. Urban housing reform and finance in China: A case study of Beijing. *Urban Affairs Review* 36(5): 620–645.

Wang, Y., and A. Murie. 1999. *Housing policy and practice in China.* Macmillan: Basingstoke.

Wiseman, R. F., and M. Virden. 1977. Spatial and social dimensions of intra-urban elderly migration. *Economic Geography* 55: 324–337.

Wong, L. 2008. The third sector and residential care for the elderly in China's transitional welfare economy. *Australian Journal of Public Administration* 67(1): 89–96.

Wu, F. 1996. Changes in the structure of public housing provision in urban China. *Urban Studies* 33(9): 1601–1627.

Wu, F. 2001. China's recent urban development in the process of land and housing marketization and economic globalization. *Habitat International* 25(3): 273–289.

Wu, F. 2004a. Intraurban residential relocation in Shanghai: Modes and stratification. *Environment and Planning A* 36(1): 7–25.

Wu, F. 2004b. Residential relocation under market-oriented redevelopment: The process and outcomes in urban China. *Geoforum* 35(4): 453–470.

Yang, S., and C. He. 2004. The ethic of responsibility and the family support in Beijing: An analysis based on the data from the survey carried out in 1999 for the demand of the aged in Beijing [Zeren lunli yu chengshi jumin de jiating yanglao]. *Journal of Peking University (Philosophy and Social Sciences)* 41(1): 71–84.

Yu, Z. 2006. Heterogeneity and dynamics in China's emerging urban housing market: Two sides of a success story from the late 1990s. *Habitat International* 30: 277–304.

Zhan, H. J. 2005. Aging, health care, and elder care: Perpetuation of gender inequalities in China. *Health Care Women International* 26(8): 693–712.

Zhan, H. J., G. Liu, X. Guan, and H. Bai. 2006. Recent developments in institutional elder care in China: Changing concepts and attitudes. *Journal of Aging Social Policy* 18(2): 85–108.

Zhang, W. J., S. Z. Li, and M. W. Feldman. 2005. Gender differences in activity of daily living of the elderly in rural China: Evidence from Chaohu. *Journal of Women & Aging* 17(3): 73–89.

Zhang, W., W. Liu, and Y. Li. 2003. Residential spatial structure and housing location preferences of urban residents in the city of Beijing. *Geographical Research (dili yanjiu)*. 22(6): 751–759.

Zhang, Y., and F. W. Goza. 2006. Who will care for the elderly in China? A review of the problems caused by China's one-child policy and their potential solutions. *Journal of Aging Studies 20*: 151–164.

Zhou, Y., and L .J. C. Ma. 2000. Economic restructuring and suburbanization in China. *Urban Geography 21*(3): 205–236.

# 12

# MARRIAGE, PARENTHOOD, AND LABOR OUTCOMES FOR WOMEN AND MEN

Yuping Zhang and Emily Hannum

## INTRODUCTION

In the wake of China's transition from state-socialism to a market economy, many researchers have sought to track social inequalities—including those based on gender—in the labor market. Some scholars argue that the market system creates incentives to base employment decisions on proxies for productivity, such as human capital, rather than on ascribed traits such as gender, and that returns to human capital will increase as the employment system more efficiently rewards talent (for a review, see Cao and Nee 2005). On the other hand, past inequities in access to education and unequal access to political connections place women at a disadvantage in a system that increasingly rewards human capital and, by many estimates, still rewards political connections. Privatization and the profit motive may have created incentives for discrimination based on gender. Moreover, one significant change that accompanied economic reform was the withdrawal of many policies to promote gender equality at work.

In earlier work, we analyzed a five-city urban labor survey conducted in 2001 to investigate the scope of the gender gap in wage employment and earnings and possible explanations for the gap (Zhang et al. 2008). We evaluated the potential contributions of human capital and family responsibilities to observed gender gaps, and showed that, although men enjoyed advantages in human capital and political capital, these advantages did not explain the gender gap. Instead, results pointed to the importance of family-work conflict: female disadvantages in employment and income existed only for wives and mothers, overall and controlling for other background characteristics. This situation was likely tied to the fact that wives and mothers in the 2001 sample spent much more time than husbands and fathers doing household chores, even net of controls for potential earnings.

In this chapter, we replicate our earlier analysis of wage employment and income with more recent data from the China Health and Nutrition Survey (CHNS 2006).[1] The CHNS is a multi-province data set that includes provinces from different geographic regions and at different levels of economic development. Unlike the urban labor survey we used in the prior study, the CHNS encompasses both rural and urban areas. Also unlike the earlier data, the CHNS contains detailed information on women's fertility history, which provides a better measurement of childbearing status than the data we used in the earlier work. Building on our earlier analysis with this broader and more recent data set, we argue that, in both rural and urban areas, female disadvantage in wage employment and earnings needs to be reconceptualized as being concentrated among those who are experiencing family-work conflict: wives and mothers.

## FAMILY-WORK CONFLICTS AND GENDER GAPS IN LABOR OUTCOMES

### Comparative Perspectives

In comparative perspective, our argument is not a new one. Scholars have viewed the conflict between family and work responsibilities as a major cause of gender disparities in labor market outcomes in the United States and many other industrialized and developing countries. A number of studies have found persistent wage penalties for motherhood (Anderson, Binder, and Krause 2003; Avellar and Smock 2003; Budig and England 2001; England 2005; Lundberg and Rose 2000; Waldfogel 1997). For example, using National Longitudinal Survey of Youth data in the United States, Budig and England (2001) used pooled information from 1982 to 1993 on women who were ages 14–21 in the initial wave in 1979 and found a wage penalty of 7 percent for each child. The penalty is larger for married women than for unmarried women. A cross-cohort comparison that also used National Longitudinal Survey of Youth data found that the penalty had not diminished over time, even after controlling for human capital and other unobserved heterogeneity (Avellar and Smock 2003).

Research has highlighted similar issues for wives and mothers in employment and earnings in European countries (Davies, Elias, and Pierre 2003; Sigle-Rushton and Waldfogel 2004). For example, Trappe and Rosenfeld (2000) found that in the former West Germany, being a parent had positive effects on men's earnings, but strong negative effects on women's wages. In the former

East Germany, some young women balanced family and employment by taking jobs below their qualifications, and this reduced their earnings (Trappe and Rosenfeld 2000).

Sources of the mother penalty include women's career breaks after childbirth, segregation into low-status and part-time jobs, shorter work hours, and, importantly, a disproportionate share of family responsibilities in the context of dual-earner couples (Arun, Arun, and Borooah 2004; Cohen and Huffman 2003; Jacobs 1989, 2001; Jacobs and Gornick 2002; Reid 2002). Women's household responsibilities, particularly after marriage or childbirth, are often greater than men's. Gupta (1999) tested the impact of changes in marital status on men's housework hours using U.S. National Survey of Families and Households data from 1987 and 1992. He showed that men decrease their hours spent on routine housework as they enter marriage or cohabitation, but for women, entering marriage or cohabitation means more housework hours. Thus, wives and mothers face barriers to productivity in the workplace not experienced by single women, married men, or fathers.

Research in East Asia outside China also illustrates the close relationship between families and women's labor force participation and labor outcomes. In these countries, urban women's participation in the labor market has risen in recent years (Brinton 2001). For example, in South Korea, economic activity rates among 25–29-year-old women rose from 38 percent in 1980 to 58 percent in 2000; in Japan, corresponding figures were 49 and 70 percent (Hannum and Fuller 2004, Figure 1). Despite these increases, in some East Asian countries, specifically Japan and South Korea, many women drop out of the labor force at marriage or childbirth, then reenter in middle age. In Taiwan, where work and day care arrangements are more flexible, the trend of women's participation across the life course is more like that in the West, where many remain in the labor force after marriage and childbirth (Brinton 2001; Yu 2005, 2006).

In East Asian countries, the income of women lags behind that of men. In Taiwan, estimates suggest that full-time employed women earn about 69.8 percent of men's earnings; in South Korea, full-time employed women earn only about 54.6 percent of men's earnings (Brinton 2001, 16). The gender wage gap is particularly wide for older workers (Brinton 2001; Brinton and Lee 2001; Yu 2001, 2002). Research on why these gaps emerge has considered discriminatory attitudes, but has also placed a high degree of emphasis on the difficulty of balancing family and work life, especially for mothers (Yu 2001). Importantly, women's increasing level of economic activity in East Asia does not appear to have accompanied increases in men's domestic roles: housework and childrearing remain primarily women's work (Tsuya and Bumpass 2004). These studies indicate that in various cultural settings, marriage and parenthood have significant negative relationships with women's labor market employment and earnings. One of the major causes of women's disadvantage appears to be their disproportionate share of family responsibilities.

## Research in China

*Gender gaps in urban areas.* In some ways, China's record of female employment and earnings stands out quite favorably in comparison to its East Asian neighbors. Economic activity rates for 25–29-year-olds in China were 87 percent in 1980 and 92 percent in 2000, higher than in South Korea or Japan (Hannum and Fuller 2004, Figure 1). Similarly, while an earnings gap between men and women exists, it is moderate in scope (Bian et al. 2000; Maurer-Fazio and Hughes 2002; Shu and Bian 2003; Xie and Hannum 1996; Zhou 2000; Zhang et al. 2008). For example, in national, city-based surveys for 1988 and 1997, women earned 80 to 82 percent as much as men (Parish and Busse 2000, 227). Zhang et al. (2008) found similar results for women ages 25–44, using data collected from five large cities in 2001.

Interestingly, as China has transitioned to a market-oriented society in recent decades, concerns have been raised that women's status in the urban workplace may be deteriorating. Part of this concern may be characterized as a story of discrimination. For example, Summerfield (1994) argued that the main threat to urban women in the wake of economic reforms occurred through discrimination in hiring and policies taken under consideration to reduce the pressure of surplus labor. This argument states that managers, faced with numerous applicants for each position and with a growing awareness of the need to minimize costs, choose male applicants over equally qualified women, citing costs of maternity and child care benefits as the reason (Stockman 1994; Summerfield 1994).

Consistent with this argument, attitude research indicates that women's perceptions of discrimination are on the rise among cohorts of women seeking jobs in the years after market reforms (Parish and Busse 2000). In addition, in the 1990s, women appeared to be disproportionately represented among the ranks of the laid-off, a new phenomenon in the reform era. One press account cites Ministry of Labor statistics from 1997 indicating that women accounted for only 39 percent of China's workforce, but nearly 61 percent of its laid-off population (Rosenthal 1998). Still other research suggests that even within the workforce, women and men experience significantly different career trajectories. In urban Tianjin, women experience slower wage growth than men, and they have to retire earlier (Bian et al. 2000). In a multi-city study, Cao and Hu (2007) showed that married urban women were more likely to face terminations, more likely to change jobs for family reasons, and less likely to experience career-advancing job changes. Moreover, urban occupational gender segregation increased dramatically after the early 1980s (Shu 2005).

Somewhat surprising in light of the changing settings in which women and men work, as well as the changing perceptions of discrimination, is evidence suggesting that the earnings gap between men and women has been relatively stable between the pre-reform and reform periods and across different cohorts (Bian et al. 2000; Maurer-Fazio and Hughes 2002; Shu and Bian 2003; Zhou 2000). This stability suggests that male-female gaps cannot be traced to phenomena that are new in the reform period. Part of the story may be the different skills that women and men bring to the job. Most important, scholars have highlighted human capital differences between men and women, as human capital has become ever more important for employment and income. Returns to education in urban China have increased rapidly, with one recent study suggesting that returns were as high as 10.2 percent per year of schooling by 2001 (Zhang et al. 2005, 749). While studies suggest that returns to education are higher for women than for men, past educational disparities mean that the human capital stock of adult women nationwide remains lower than that of men (Hannum 2005; Hannum and Xie 1994; Zhang et al. 2005).

Recent studies have highlighted the important role of human capital in explaining the gender gap in earnings over time and space in urban China (Bian et al. 2000; Shu and Bian 2003). Bian et al. (2000) also note that in the change from first job to current job, women's slower wage growth is attributable in part to their lower rates of college education. Further, educational differences may play a role in gender differences in whether individuals are employed at all. Maurer-Fazio's (2007) work indicates that the more education a worker has, the better his or her protection against layoff and the better his or her chance of being reemployed.

Interestingly, conflicts between family responsibilities and work have received relatively little attention outside discussions of employers' discrimination based on perceptions of family-work conflicts. A few studies of urban labor market outcomes have included marital status and parenthood as control variables, though not as an analytic focus (Shu and Bian 2003; Matthews and Nee 2000). One exception is a study by Maurer-Fazio and Hughes (2002), which found that married Chinese women experience much larger wage disadvantages than do their unmarried counterparts. In our earlier work using the China Urban Labor Survey/China Adult Literacy Survey (Zhang et al. 2008), we found that although urban women were significantly disadvantaged by various measures of human capital and political capital as compared to men, these disadvantages did not explain the observed gender gap in employment and earnings. Instead, gender gaps were closely related to family status. In the cities surveyed, it was only among married women and mothers that we found a gender gap in employment and income.

Parish and Busse (2000) suggest that whereas the socialist social contract encouraged formal work for all citizens, a new non-work norm for women with small children may be emerging. This norm is manifested in data showing that declines, albeit moderate declines, in market work through 1995 were concentrated among young women. The authors suggest that part of the shift was voluntary, as young women chose to stay home to care for children. Direct documentation of gender role attitudes in China, however, is limited. (For a significant exception, see Shu's [2004] study of gender attitudes and their variation with education.) The trend documented by Parish and Busse (2000) might also be framed as a rising incompatibility between home and work responsibilities, as socialist institutions that alleviated some of women's traditional family burdens, such as day care centers and canteens in urban work units, have disappeared, while investment of private resources in homes and children has grown.

*Rural women's participation in wage employment.* The above mentioned studies focus on urban labor markets. With the rapid development of rural labor markets, other studies have focused on rural women's opportunities in wage employment (Parish et al. 1995; Matthews and Nee 2000; Benjamin et al. 2001; Rozelle et al. 2002; Zhang et al. 2003; Shen and Deng 2008). Matthews and Nee (2000), using the China-Cornell-Oxford survey of rural China in 1989 and 1990, found that in more developed regions, especially places with growth of local industry, women had more opportunities to shift out of agriculture. In turn, those women who were engaged in wage employment made significant contributions to household income and enhanced their power and status within the family. However, rural women who work for wages still experience disadvantage, compared to men. Analyzing data from eight provinces in 1995, with retrospective data to 1988, Rozelle and colleagues (2002) found that gender wage gaps were substantial and rising in rural areas. On average, wages for men were about 29 percent higher than those for women (or 25 percent when measured as the difference in logs), but by 1995 the wage gap had increased to 45.7 percent (or 38 percent, as measured in logs). The authors speculate that a traditional ideology discriminating against women that is stronger in rural than in urban areas is at play, but found no evidence that the disparities or trends therein could be linked to policy shifts.

These studies emphasize mostly the increasing demand for labor with economic growth and the impact that policy changes might have on women's labor force participation and gender wage gaps. Parish and his colleagues (1995) focused on how family structure relates to women's opportunities for wage employment. Using data from the Chinese General Social Survey, a study of 10 counties conducted in the spring of 1993, the authors found that women remained in farming more than men, their incomes were lower than those of men, and that single women lost some of the better jobs once they were married. Though women have less education, at higher education levels, women are almost as likely as men to get non-agricultural jobs and to be well paid (Parish et al. 1995).

## Summary

Overall, research outside China has highlighted the central role of family-work conflict for understanding gender-based employment and income gaps. Recent trends in China suggest that while income gaps are moderate, they are not dissipating in urban areas, and appear to be worse and possibly increasing in rural areas. Whether gaps indeed differ in urban and rural areas and the relevance of family-work conflicts for understanding gender differences in employment and income attainment have been little studied. In this study, we estimate the gender gap in wage employment and earnings among people ages 25–52, test whether the gap is worse in rural than in urban areas, and consider evidence about various explanations for observed gaps. We focus on family-work conflict explanations.

## DATA

This article uses data from the China Health and Nutrition Survey (CHNS), a panel study that was drawn from nine provinces, including both urban and rural populations, using a multistage, random cluster sampling procedure. These provinces are geographically diverse and at different levels of economic development. Counties in each province were first stratified by income, and four counties were randomly selected. In addition, the province capital and a lower income city were selected when feasible. The first wave was collected in 1989 by the Chinese Academy of Preventative Medicine and the Institute of Nutrition and Food Hygiene, in collaboration with the Carolina Population Center at the University of North Carolina. The subsequent waves were collected about every two years since then (Carolina Population Center).

This study uses the 2006 wave of the CHNS and draws on the household survey, an adult individual survey that provides information on education, employment, and wage income, and an ever-married women survey that records marriage and fertility history for all the women under age 52 who were ever married. From the 2006 sample, we drew a subsample of those ages 25–52, from both urban and rural areas. We set the lower age limit at 25 to make sure that our sample is not biased by the non-working status of those who are still in school. Among those who are older than 52, there are not enough cases who are not currently married and who have never had children for us to make comparisons, since the impact of marital and parental status on labor market outcomes is the focus of this study. After eliminating cases with missing data on relevant variables, 5,135 cases are included in the analysis.

### Measurement

*Demographic variables.* The central analytical variable is the respondent's gender. *Gender* is coded 0 for male and 1 for female. We also report *age* in the descriptive statistics. Opportunities for wage employment may be quite different between urban and rural areas. We control for a measure of residency, *rural*, which is coded as 0 if a person lives in an urban area, and coded as 1 if a respondent is from a rural area.

*Labor market outcomes.* Two measures are used for labor market outcomes. *Wage employment status* reflects whether a person is employed and has a wage income. It is determined by whether the participant reported a wage income. Those who reported wage income are coded as 1, with 0 assigned to those who did not. Our focus on wage employment is based on the consideration that for those who are engaged in farming or other self-employed activities, it is hard to separate the income of one household member from that of another and to separate income from labor from income from land, capital and entrepreneurship. Because the focus of this study is labor market participation and outcomes, we treat those who do not report wage income, most of whom are engaged in farm work, as not engaging in wage labor.

Among those who are wage earners, we employ the *annual wage income* variable calculated in the CHNS. According to CHNS documentation (Carolina Population Center), this variable was calculated by using average monthly non-retirement wage times months worked, and if information for number of months worked was missing, 12 months was assumed. To this annualized wage income, bonuses and other cash or in-kind income was added. If a person has more than one job, wages and other income from all jobs are included. In multivariate analysis, logged annual wage income is used.

*Family characteristics.* Family structure is measured by marital status and the number of children a person has ever had. *Married* is a dummy variable indicating if a person is currently married or not (0 = no, 1 = yes). The non-married category includes those who are single and never married, as well as those who are divorced or widowed. Using detailed information on fertility history, we created *number of children* a woman has ever had, regardless of whether the children are still living in the household. We then attributed this number to husbands of the women in the ever-married woman survey. This construction takes into consideration the possible impact of having children on a person's labor market outcomes, even though the child (or children) may already be grown up.

Another measure of family characteristics is *annual household income*. This measure is calculated in the CHNS as the sum of all sources of income and revenue minus expenditures. The sources of household income include business, farming, fishing, gardening, livestock, non-retirement wages, retirement income, subsidies, and other income (Carolina Population Center). In multivariate analysis, we use *other household members' income* (without the person's own wage income), which is constructed by subtracting the person's wage income from the total household income. Logged income is used in multivariate analysis.

*Human capital.* Human capital is measured by the *years of schooling* that a respondent has completed. Considering that the human capital that a person accumulates after entering the labor market is also important in understanding current wage employment status and wage income, we also created a *potential work experience* variable, which is constructed by subtracting age at school completion from current age. We acknowledge the limitations of such an approximate construction, for it ignores the fact that women may have more potential experience if they left school earlier, as well as the problem that women are more likely to experience a break in work experience due to childbearing.[2] However, this construction of experience is standard in the literature, and, more pragmatically, is the only option in the CHNS data. In multivariate analysis, both potential work experience and its squared term are used. Because potential work experience is calculated from age and is highly correlated with age, we allow potential experience to serve as an indirect measure of age, and we do not include a direct measure of age in the models.

## ANALYSIS

### Descriptive Results

Table 12.1 presents the descriptive statistics by residency and gender, to examine the overall gender gap in human capital, labor market outcomes, and family characteristics. Women make up 52.8 percent of the total sample, 52.7 percent of the urban subsample, and 52.9 percent of the rural subsample. The average age is 40.9, with urban women on average a little younger than their male counterparts, while rural women are about the same age as rural men. The total sample has an average of 8.8 years of formal schooling. The urban subsample has higher education than the rural subsample, and within each subsample, women have significantly less education than men, with rural women having the least education. There is no gender difference in potential experience among urban people, and rural women have longer potential experience than rural men. The rural difference probably reflects the fact that rural women have less education, considering the construction of the measure.

Overall, in this sample, 42 percent of respondents have wage employment. Among those living in urban areas, 59.8 percent of men and 46.2 percent of women are wage earners, while the percentages are much lower for those living in rural areas, with 47.8 percent wage earners among men and only 26.7 percent among women. Again, these figures reflect only those who are employed and have wage income. Within each subsample, there are significant gender differences in wage employment status that favor men. On average, among wage earners, urban women earn 69 percent as much as men, while the comparable figure for rural women is about 71 percent. These figures are much lower than we found in the previous study using urban labor data in 2001, where women on average earned 79 percent of men's income, but this discrepancy is a function of the extreme gender gap in earnings of a few individuals at the top of the earnings distribution in the CHNS.[3]

Considering the family structure measures, we find that marriage and childbearing are prevalent, with rural women more likely to be married than rural men. Among the urban subsample, 88.3 percent of men and 89.8 percent of women are married, while for the rural subsample, 90.2 percent of men and 96 percent of women are married. Also, women are more likely to have ever had children, and they have more children on average when compared to men, for both the

Table 12.1. Descriptive Statistics by Residency and Gender

|  | Total | Urban Male | Urban Female | Rural Male | Rural Female |
|---|---|---|---|---|---|
| Rural | 0.68 | | | | |
| Female (%) | 52.83 | | | | |
| Age | 40.89 (7.22) | 41.04 (7.62) | 40.74 (7.69) | 40.81 (7.40) | 40.98 (7.47) |
| **Human Capital** | | | | | |
| Years of Schooling | 8.79 (3.61) | 10.31 (3.22) | 9.67 *** (3.64) | 9.09 (3.09) | 7.46*** (3.72) |
| Potential Experience (Years) | 25.11 (8.94) | 23.72 (8.48) | 24.07 (9.29) | 24.72 (8.29) | 26.53*** (9.24) |
| **Labor Market Outcomes** | | | | | |
| Wage Employment (%) | 41.99 | 59.81 | 46.23*** | 47.77 | 26.70*** |
| Annual Individual Wage Income | 13,495.37 (18,192) | 17,947.78 (24,269.27) | 12,361.10 *** (8,933.93) | 13,731.05 (19,233.65) | 9,784.41*** (13,965.04) |
| **Family Structure** | | | | | |
| Married (%) | 91.90 | 88.28 | 89.81 | 90.20 | 96.00*** |
| Ever Had Children (%) | 82.22 | 76.18 | 82.38*** | 78.43 | 88.10*** |
| Number of Children | 1.30 (0.89) | 1.03 (0.75) | 1.12*** (0.73) | 1.31 (0.95) | 1.50*** 0.91 |
| Annual Household Income | 23,910.24 (29,936.38) | 30,101.96 (30,434.77) | 28,852.07 (29,525.41) | 21,848.78 (30,746.97) | 20,753.62 (28,476.28) |

*Notes:* Significant t-test or chi-square test of difference by gender. \*\*\*p<.01. Standard Deviation in parentheses.
N = 5,135; females make 52.68% of urban subsample and 52.91% of rural subsample.

urban and rural subsamples. About 82.4 percent of women and 76.2 percent of men in the urban subsample have ever had children, while among rural women, 88 percent have ever had children, as have about 78 percent of rural men.

Next, we examine more closely the gender gap in labor market outcomes by family structure. Figure 12.1 presents wage employment by marital status and gender, for urban and rural areas. Among unmarried people, women and men have almost the same employment rate. The gender gap in wage employment status exists only among those who are married, for both urban and rural subsamples. The proportion tests show significant gender differences for both the urban and rural subsamples, as indicated in the figure. Among married people, urban men enjoy a 15 percentage point higher wage employment rate compared to urban women, and the difference reaches 22.4 percentage points between rural men and rural women.

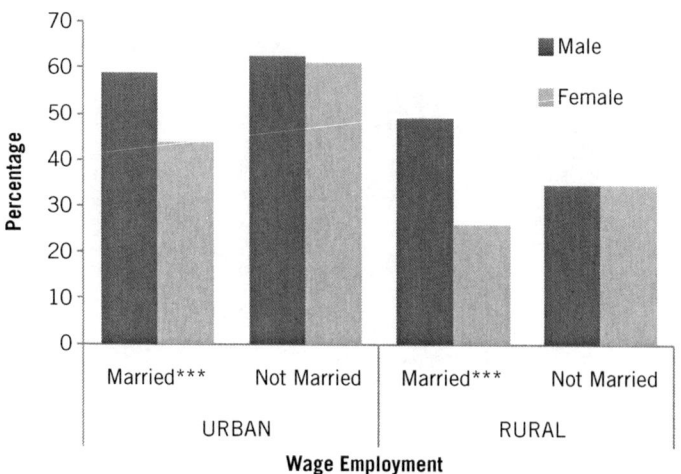

# Marriage, Parenthood, and Labor Outcomes for Women and Men 233

**Wage Employment**
Note: Significant proportion test of difference by gender. ***p.<0.01

Figure 12.1. Wage Employment by Marital Status and Gender, Urban and Rural Areas

Looking at the results in another way, marriage has no association with urban men's wage employment, but it has a strong negative association with employment for women. Compared with wives, unmarried urban women are almost 40 percent more likely to have wage employment. Even more strikingly, in the rural subsample, marriage shows opposing associations for men and women: married men have a higher rate of wage employment compared with men who are not married, but married women have a lower rate of wage employment than women who are not married. Rural unmarried women are about 38 percent more likely to have wage employment than rural wives, though there are only a very small number of rural women who are not currently married. In some sense, this shows that, at least for rural women who remain in rural areas, the normative pathway is marriage rather than wage employment.

Figure 12.2 compares men's and women's wage employment by parenthood status, and shows a similar trend to that just described. For the urban subsample, the gender gap in wage employment among people who have no child is relatively small, but there is a larger gender gap that is significant at the .05 level among parents. For urban men, fatherhood has no association with wage employment, but urban mothers have lower employment rates compared to women who have no children. In the rural subsample, we see a gender difference in wage employment among both parents and those who have no children. Rural mothers' chance of having wage employment is only half of that of rural fathers. Among rural people who have no child, women's chance of being a wage earner is about 62 percent of the chance for men. Rural fathers have a higher rate of employment compared with rural childless men. However, rural women with children appear to have slightly reduced chances of being wage earners than rural childless women.

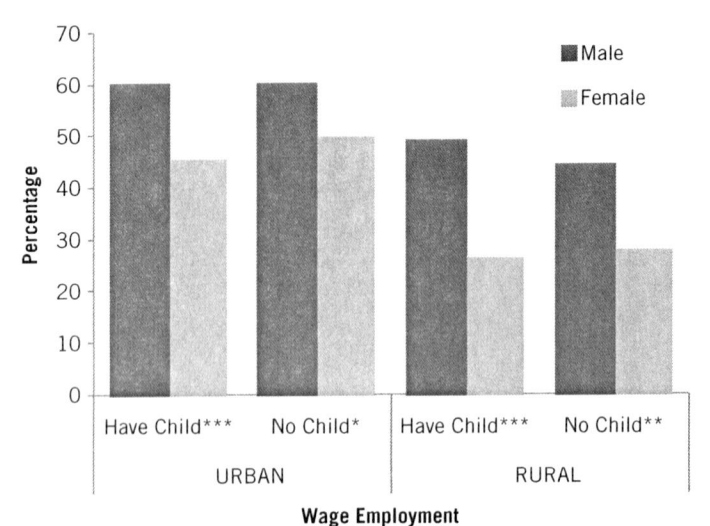

**Figure 12.2.** Wage Employment by Parental Status and Gender, Urban and Rural Areas

We turn next to an analysis of wages. Table 12.2 shows annual wage income by family structure and gender. There are significant gender gaps in annual wage income in both the urban and rural subsamples. However, these gaps exist only among people who are currently married and who are parents. There is no significant difference in annual wage income between men and women who are not currently married, or those who have no children. In the rural subsample, we see that women who are not married actually have higher wage income than unmarried men, on average, though the difference is not significant. However, wives are making significantly less than husbands: urban married women make 35 percent less than married men, and rural married women make 32 percent less than rural married men. For both urban and rural people, mothers are making only about 69 percent of the annual wage income of fathers. Among people who have no child, we still see wage differences that favor men, but these differences are not statistically significant when no other factors are considered.

Comparing wage income in another way, on average, married men earn more than unmarried men for both urban and rural subsamples, though the differences are not significant. For women, the association between marital status and wage income is in just the opposite direction. Married women earn significantly less than single women. Urban wives' wage income is 19 percent lower than that of urban single women, and rural wives' wage income is about 35 percent lower than that of rural single women.

The association between parenthood and wage income is different for urban and rural subsamples. Among urban people, those who have no child have higher wage income for both women and men. Urban women who have no child

Marriage, Parenthood, and Labor Outcomes for Women and Men    235

**Table 12.2.** Annual Wage Income by Family Structure and Gender, Urban and Rural Areas

|  | URBAN || RURAL ||
|  | Male | Female | Male | Female |
| --- | --- | --- | --- | --- |
| Annual Wage Income |  |  |  |  |
| Total | 17,947.78 | 12,361.10*** | 13,731.05 | 9,784.41*** |
|  | (24,269.27) | (8,933.93) | (19,233.65) | (13,965.04) |
| By Marital Status |  |  |  |  |
| Married | 18,434.33 | 11,984.58*** | 13,916.20 | 9,507.16*** |
|  | (25,534.10) | (8,721.84) | (19,790.15) | (13,374.10) |
| Not Married | 14,491.63 | 14,729.71 | 11,330.72 | 14,742.92 |
|  | (11,456.62) | (9,929.45) | (9,169.15) | (21,809.14) |
| By Parenthood |  |  |  |  |
| Ever Had Child | 17,277.13 | 11,867.47*** | 14,539.72 | 9,896.54*** |
|  | (18,440.69) | (8,460.01) | (21,360.82) | (13,782.86) |
| No Child | 20,091.47 | 14,471.99 | 10,944.16 | 8,978.93 |
|  | (37,267.36) | (10,531.80) | (8,572.03) | (15,310.68) |

*Notes:* Significant t-test of difference by gender. **p<.05, ***p<.01.
Standard deviation in parenthesis. N = 2,144 (individuals who reported wage income).

on average earn significantly more—18 percent more—than urban mothers. However, in rural areas, people who have children enjoy higher wage income, on average, than do people who have no child. Rural fathers earn significantly more than rural childless men, and rural mothers have a slightly higher wage than childless women.

These descriptive findings are consistent with the hypothesis that marriage and parenthood have different effects on women's and men's labor market outcomes. However, age and other compositional differences between individuals in different family structures might be contributing to the patterns found in the descriptive data. In order to account for other potential compositional differences across these groups and to test urban-rural pattern differences, we turn to multivariate analysis in the next sections.

## Analysis of Wage Employment

Table 12.3 shows a logistic regression analysis of wage employment status. Robust standard errors are reported to correct for household clustering. All models control for provinces with dummy variables. Model 1, which includes only gender and residency, is a baseline model. It shows that, for the whole sample, women's odds of wage employment are 57 percent (1-exp[-0.838]) lower than men's. In model 2, we add an interaction of gender and residency, to test whether there are additional barriers for rural residents, especially rural women. As expected,

Table 12.3. Logistic Regression of Wage Employment Status

| | (1) | (2) | (3) | (4) | (5) | (6) | (7) |
|---|---|---|---|---|---|---|---|
| Female | −0.838*** | −0.590*** | −0.681*** | −0.536*** | −0.672*** | −0.114 | −0.471*** |
| | (−16.242) | (−6.569) | (−12.278) | (−5.613) | (−12.027) | (−0.515) | (−4.308) |
| Rural | −0.703*** | −0.509*** | −0.418*** | −0.307*** | −0.378*** | −0.417*** | −0.374*** |
| | (−9.996) | (−5.646) | (−5.733) | (−3.243) | (−5.156) | (−5.698) | (−5.107) |
| Rural x Female | | −0.377*** | | −0.220* | | | |
| | | (−3.445) | | (−1.890) | | | |
| Years of Schooling | | | 0.200*** | 0.199*** | 0.196*** | 0.197*** | 0.194*** |
| | | | (15.470) | (15.390) | (15.174) | (15.121) | (15.061) |
| Potential Work Experience | | | −0.046** | −0.046** | −0.031 | −0.048** | −0.023 |
| | | | (−2.435) | (−2.429) | (−1.588) | (−2.495) | (−1.164) |
| Experience Squared | | | 0.001*** | 0.001*** | 0.001* | 0.001*** | 0.001 |
| | | | (2.584) | (2.576) | (1.891) | (2.595) | (1.473) |
| Other Household Members' Income | | | 0.004 | 0.005 | 0.004 | 0.004 | 0.007 |
| | | | (0.255) | (0.264) | (0.200) | (0.211) | (0.428) |
| Married | | | | | 0.289** | 0.346** | |
| | | | | | (2.256) | (2.257) | |

|  |  |  |  |  |  |
|---|---|---|---|---|---|
| Number of Children |  |  | −0.201*** (−4.206) |  | −0.107** (−2.082) |
| Married x Female |  |  |  | −0.620*** (−2.712) |  |
| Number of Children x Female |  |  |  |  | −0.155** (−2.084) |
| Constant | 0.809*** (7.283) | 0.674*** (5.734) | −0.912*** (−2.724) | −0.980*** (−2.905) | −1.121*** (−3.316) | −1.144*** (−3.318) | −1.086*** (−3.213) |
| N | 5,135 | 5,135 | 5,135 | 5,135 | 5,135 | 5,135 |
| Pseudo R² | 0.065 | 0.066 | 0.125 | 0.125 | 0.129 | 0.126 | 0.128 |

*Note:* *** p<0.01, ** p<0.05, * p<0.1 All models control for provinces.

rural men have lower odds of wage employment compared to urban people, and a significant interaction tells us that rural women have even lower odds of having wage employment, when no other factors are considered.

Model 3 adds controls for education, potential work experience and its squared term, and a measure of family economic situation, the other household members' income. Higher education increases the odds of wage employment. These factors reduce the gender gap, but women's odds are still 49 percent (1-exp[-0.681]) lower than men's.

We add back in a gender-residency interaction term in model 4. After controlling for education and other household members' income, the interaction term is no longer significant at the .05 level, though it is marginally significant. Rural people still face disadvantage in employment compared with urban residents, but the extra disadvantage for rural women appears to be, in some part, a function of their human capital and family economic situation. The disadvantage dissipates when these characteristics are taken into consideration.

Model 5 incorporates family structure measures: marital status and parental status. On average, married people are more likely to be wage earners than non-married people, while people with children are less likely to have wage employment than childless people. In order to test the hypothesis that family responsibilities affect women and men differently, in the next two models, we include in turn interactions between gender and marital status and gender and number of children.[4]

In model 6, with the interaction of marital status and gender, we see that married men are more likely to be employed than unmarried men. However, for women, marriage reduces their odds of being employed by about 24 percent (1-exp[0.346–0.620]). At the same time, among unmarried people, there is no gender difference in employment, controlling for human capital and family economic situation measures. Model 7 tests the relationships between parenting status and men's and women's wage employment. Here, unlike in our earlier work, we find that having children has a negative effect on men's employment. However, consistent with the earlier study, women are particularly negatively affected: compared with women who have no children, with each additional child, women reduce their odds of wage employment by 27 percent (1-exp[-0.107–0.155]). Also unlike our earlier study, among people who have no child, there is still a gender gap in wage employment. We also see that in all models, rural residents have a significantly lower chance of having wage employment compared with people living in urban areas.[5]

### Analysis of Wage Income

Finally, we turn to an analysis of the gender gap in wage income. Table 12.4 shows ordinary least squares (OLS) models of wage income, and, for the last two models, we also present Heckman estimation results that account for the non-random selection process into employment.[6] In the Heckman models,

**Table 12.4.** OLS and Heckman Models of Logged Annual Wage Income

| | (1) | (2) | (3) | (4) | (5) | | (6) | |
|---|---|---|---|---|---|---|---|---|
| | OLS | OLS | OLS | OLS | OLS | Heckman | OLS | Heckman |
| Female | −0.376*** | −0.317*** | −0.316*** | −0.314*** | −0.045 | −0.029 | −0.198*** | −0.195*** |
| | (−9.853) | (−6.222) | (−8.647) | (−8.647) | (−0.374) | (−0.244) | (−2.740) | (−2.710) |
| Rural | −0.369*** | −0.325*** | −0.190*** | −0.182*** | −0.192*** | −0.183*** | −0.181*** | −0.179*** |
| | (−8.462) | (−6.435) | (−4.759) | (−4.521) | (−4.784) | (−4.565) | (−4.490) | (−4.453) |
| Rural x Female | | −0.103 | | | | | | |
| | | (−1.372) | | | | | | |
| Years of Schooling | | | 0.108*** | 0.107*** | 0.107*** | 0.103*** | 0.106*** | 0.105*** |
| | | | (13.254) | (13.029) | (13.143) | (12.231) | (12.331) | (12.892) |
| Potential Work Experience | | | 0.016 | 0.016 | 0.014 | 0.015 | 0.018 | 0.018* |
| | | | (1.565) | (1.544) | (1.384) | (1.446) | (1.589) | (1.797) |
| Experience Squared | | | −0.000 | −0.000 | −0.000 | −0.000 | −0.000 | −0.000 |
| | | | (−1.254) | (−1.235) | (−1.158) | (−1.217) | (−1.059) | (−1.432) |
| Married | | | | 0.072 | 0.163* | 0.161* | | |
| | | | | (0.974) | (1.817) | (1.796) | | |
| Number of Children | | | | −0.043 | | | −0.025 | 0.003 |
| | | | | (−1.186) | | | (−0.070) | (0.088) |

(Continued)

Table 12.4. (Continued)

|  | (1) | (2) | (3) | (4) | (5) |  | (6) |  |
|---|---|---|---|---|---|---|---|---|
|  | OLS | OLS | OLS | OLS | OLS | Heckman | OLS | Heckman |
| Married x Female |  |  |  |  | −0.300*** | −0.302** |  |  |
|  |  |  |  |  | (−2.419) | (−2.441) |  |  |
| Number of Children x Female |  |  |  |  |  |  | −0.103* | −0.102* |
|  |  |  |  |  |  |  | (−1.730) | (−1.726) |
| Constant | 9.588*** | 9.559*** | 8.148*** | 8.123*** | 8.036*** | 8.103*** | 8.175*** | 8.141*** |
|  | (155.787) | (150.215) | (50.022) | (49.280) | (46.405) | (45.203) | (44.881) | (50.198) |
| N | 2,144 | 2,144 | 2,144 | 2,144 | 2,144 | 5,135 | 2,144 | 5,135 |
| Adjusted R² | 0.117 | 0.118 | 0.243 | 0.243 | 0.244 |  | 0.248 |  |

Note: *** p<0.01, ** p<0.05, * p<0.1 All models control for provinces.

logged annual wage income is the dependent variable in the main equation. In the selection equation, wage employment status is the dependent variable, and other household members' income is a predictor, along with all variables in the main model except the interaction terms. With this specification, we assume that family economic circumstances affect employment, but do not directly affect wages, once employed. Heckman estimation results show that the error terms of the selection equation and the wage income equation are significantly correlated. Robust standard errors are reported to correct for household clustering. All models control for provinces.

Model 1 includes only gender and indicator of rural residency. The model reveals strong gender and urban/rural differences. In model 2, we add the interaction term between gender and residency. There is no additional disadvantage for rural women. It seems that once they are selected into wage labor, rural and urban women face similar barriers. Model 3 incorporates controls for education years and potential work experience. Years of formal education are positively related to wage income, but controlling for human capital measures does not explain the gender wage gap. Women's wage income is still about 27 percent (1-exp[-0.316]) lower than men's. In model 4, marital status and number of children are added. On average, marital status and number of children are unrelated to people's wage income.

Similar to the wage employment model, we gain more insights from the family variables in interaction models. Model 5 and 6 test interactions between gender and marital status (model 5) and gender and number of children (model 6). Model 5 reveals that for men, marriage has a weak positive effect on their wage income. In contrast, for women, marriage is associated with a reduction in income by 13 percent (1-exp[0.163-0.300]). In fact, in this model, gender is only significant in the interaction with marital status. Among people who are not married, there is no gender gap in wage income. Model 6 includes an interaction term between number of children and gender. The result shows that compared to men who have no child, having children has no effect on a father's wage income. However, each additional child is associated with 12 percent (1-exp[0.025-0.103]) decrease in women's wage income, though this result is only marginally significant. Among people who have no child, there is still a gender gap in wage income. The main trend of effects is the same across OLS and Heckman selection models,[7] with only a slight change in the magnitude of the coefficients. Again, as shown in wage employment analysis, rural residency has a negative effect on wage income in all the models.

## DISCUSSION AND CONCLUSIONS

Much of the discussion of gender and labor market outcomes in China in the reform era has focused on elements of the transition to markets, particularly issues such as rising returns to education and new discrimination against women, especially in the urban marketplace. This research, using CHNS data from 2006, shows that women remain disadvantaged in education. However, this disadvantage does not appear to explain away gender differences in participation in wage employment or wage income.

In our previous study using urban labor data from five large cities in 2001, we found that there were no gender differences in employment and income among unmarried and childless people, but that the gaps were concentrated among wives and mothers. In this study using more recent, multi-province data including both urban and rural people, we found some similar patterns: the multivariate analysis results show that for both urban and rural residents, among unmarried people there is little gender gap to be explained in employment and wage income, and that in relative terms, women experience a more negative employment and income trajectory than do men, with marriage and childbearing. However, unlike the results of the previous study, among childless people in the CHNS, there do persist gender differences in employment and income. This discrepancy may have to do with the broader geographic scope of the sample for the CHNS, which includes less-developed areas than the urban labor survey from 2001.

Beyond the earlier study, our results show that rural residence has more negative implications for the employment of women than men, though this penalty is partially attributable to the human capital disadvantages of rural women. For those women who are employed in wage labor, there is no additional penalty beyond that experienced by men for rural residence. However, there is some evidence that the association between family structure and income differs in rural and urban communities. Descriptive findings show different wage implications of parenthood in rural and urban communities, which is likely due to the different selectivity of parenthood in these types of communities. There is probably less voluntary childlessness and less voluntary delay of childbearing in rural areas. However, both areas show a concentration of women's relative disadvantage among parents.

Our findings suggest that future research on gender disparities in labor market participation and earnings will benefit from incorporating family characteristics into analyses, especially considering the prevalence of marriage and childbearing. Moreover, the small percentage of women who are not married, especially among rural women, suggests that singlehood is a non-normative path and is likely highly selective of women who place career ahead of family. We have tried to partially address selectivity in the workforce decisions in this study, but this issue needs further careful consideration in future research designs.

Many previous studies have attributed the part of gender difference in employment and income that cannot be explained to discrimination. Our findings that gaps are exacerbated among the married and parents, together with evidence in our earlier work (Zhang, Hannum, and Wang 2008) that showed that marriage and parenthood were associated with much greater increases in housework responsibilities for women than for men, suggest that part of this discrimination may well happen in the private sphere, at home. A key issue for further research on gender and labor markets in China is whether the impact of marriage and childbearing on women's labor outcomes can be traced to overtly discriminatory practices that have, by some accounts, emerged in the reform era, or to more subtle factors at home and work that condition women's preferences and choices. Family-work conflict is a daily reality that shapes women's and men's opportunities and experiences in the labor market, and it should be a larger part of the study of the gender gap in labor market outcomes in China.

In the years since the establishment of the People's Republic of China, gender inequalities in the family and in the labor market have been the focus of many laws and policies. Recently, the government issued new policies aiming at the gender discriminations that reemerged with economic reform. Most notably, the Law on the Protection of Women's Rights and Interests (1992) requires that women enjoy equal rights with men in politics, education, employment, social security, assets, marriage and family, and other domains. The Employment Promotion Law (2007) contains detailed provisions on equal rights between women and men in employment and the labor market. The findings from this study are useful for the policy community by providing needed insights on recent progress toward, or regress from, gender equality in labor outcomes.

## NOTES

1  We thank the National Institute of Nutrition and Food Safety, China Center for Disease Control and Prevention, Carolina Population Center, the University of North Carolina at Chapel Hill, the NIH (R01-HD30880, DK056350, and R01-HD38700) and the Fogarty International Center, NIH, for financial support for the CHNS data collection and analysis files from 1989 to 2006 and both parties plus the China-Japan Friendship Hospital, Ministry of Health, for support for CHNS 2009 and future surveys.
2  In our earlier work, we did use direct measures of experience for women and men (Zhang et al. 2008).
3  The average wage income of the top 5 percent of urban men is 60 percent more than that of the top 5 percent of urban women. The gender gap among the top 5 percent of rural people is not that extreme, but the top 5 percent of rural women wage earners make only 68 percent of the incomes of the top 5 percent of rural men wage earners. After taking out the top 4 cases in both urban and rural subsamples, the female-to-male wage ratio becomes 77 percent among urban people, and 73 percent for rural residents.
4  We do not add these together, because of the high association between marriage and parenthood.

5  In order to test whether there is an urban/rural difference in the effects of family structure on wage employment, we tried a three-way interaction between ever having a child, gender, and rural, and between married, gender, and rural in separate models. However, these interaction terms were not significant.
6  Because the selection process that decides women's employment status is non-random and is related to income outcome, the Heckman procedure first estimates a probit selection model to take into consideration the existence of difference between employed and unemployed. A dummy variable indicating whether or not a person is employed is used as dependent variable for the probit model. The residual from the selection model, which reflects the characteristics that are related to employment, is then used as an additional independent variable in the second-stage substantive analysis as a selection bias control factor. Because this control factor catches the effect of characteristics that relate to the employment decision, the substantive analysis with income as a dependent variable produces unbiased coefficients of other predictors (Heckman 1979; Winship and Mare 1992; Smits 2003; Louis et al. 2003).
7  In selection equations, other household members' income is statistically significant until human capital is included in the main equation.

## REFERENCES

Anderson, Deborah, Melissa Binder, and Kate Krause. 2003. The motherhood penalty revisited: Experience, heterogeneity, work effort, and work-schedule flexibility. *Industrial and Labor Relations Review* 56(2): 273–294.

Arun, Shoba, Thankom Arun, and Bani Borooah. 2004. The effects of career breaks on the working lives of women. *Feminist Economics* 10(1): 65–84.

Avellar, Sarah, and Pamela Smock. 2003. Has the price of motherhood declined over time? A cross-cohort comparison of the motherhood wage penalty. *Journal of Marriage and Family* 65(3): 597–607.

Benjamin, Dwayne, Loren Brandt, and John Giles. 2001. *The evolution of income inequality in rural China*. Working Paper April 2001. Department of Economics and Institute for Policy Analysis. Toronto: University of Toronto.

Bian, Yanjie, John Logan, and Xiaoling Shu. 2000. Wage and job inequalities in the working lives of men and women in Tianjin. In *Re-Drawing boundaries: Work, households, and gender in China*, eds. Barbara Entwisle and Gale Henderson, 111–133. Berkeley: University of California Press.

Brewster, Karin L., and Ronald R. Rindfuss. 2000. Fertility and women's employment in industrialized nations. *Annual Review of Sociology* 26(1): 271–296.

Brinton, Mary. 2001. Married women's labor in East Asian economies. In *Women's working lives in East Asia*, ed. Mary Brinton, 1–37. Stanford: Stanford University Press.

Brinton, Mary, and S. Lee. 2001. Women's education and the labor market in Japan and South Korea. In *Women's working lives in East Asia*, ed. Mary Brinton, 125–150. Stanford: Stanford University Press.

Budig, Michelle, and Paula England. 2001. The wage penalty for motherhood. *American Sociological Review* 66(2):204–225.

Cao, Yang, and Chiung-Yin Hu. 2007. Gender and job mobility in postsocialist China: A longitudinal study of job changes in six coastal cities. *Social Forces* 85(4): 1535–1560.

Cao, Yang, and Victor Nee. 2005. Remaking inequality: Institutional change and income stratification in urban China. *Journal of the Asia Pacific Economy* 10(4): 463–485.

Carolina Population Center at University of North Carolina at Chapel Hills. http://www.cpc.unc.edu/projects/china/design/.

Christofides, Louis N., Qi Li, Zhenjuan Liu, and Insik Min. 2003. Recent two-stage sample selection procedures with an application to the gender wage gap. *Journal of Business and Economic Statistics* 21(3): 396–405.

Cohen, Philip, and Matt Hoffman. 2003. Individuals, jobs, and labor markets: The devaluation of women's work. *American Sociological Review* 68(3): 443–463.

Davies, Rhys, Peter Elias, and Gaelle Pierre. 2003. *Estimates of family gap in pay*. Female Employment in National Institutional Contexts Project Working Paper. www.warwick.ac.uk/ier/fenics/papers/Davies%20Elias.doc (accessed November 15, 2007).

England, Paula. 2005. Gender inequality in labor markets: The role of motherhood and segregation. *Social Politics: International Studies in Gender, State and Society* 12(2): 264–288.

Fong, Vanessa L. 2004. *Only hope: Coming of age under China's one-child policy*. Stanford: Stanford University Press.

Gupta, Sanjiv. 1999. The effects of transitions in marital status on men's performance of housework. *Journal of Marriage and the Family* 61(3): 700–711.

Hannum, Emily. 2005. Market transition, educational disparities, and family strategies in rural China: New evidence on gender stratification and development. *Demography* 42(2): 275–299.

Hannum, Emily, and Bruce Fuller. 2004. Commentary: Educational stratification in Asia. *Inequality Across Societies: Families, Schools and Persisting Stratification. Research in Sociology of Education* 14: 275–284.

Hannum, Emily, and Jihong Liu. 2005. Adolescent transitions to adulthood in China. In *Studies on the transition to adulthood in developing countries*, eds. Jere Behrman, Cynthia Lloyd, Nellie Stromquist, and Barney Cohen, 270–319. Washington, DC: National Academy of Science Press.

Hannum, Emily, and Yu Xie. 1994. Trends in educational gender inequality in China: 1949–1985. *Research in Social Stratification and Mobility* 13(1): 73–98.

Heckman, James. 1979. Sample selection bias as specification error. *Econometrica* 47(1): 153–161.

Hirao, Keiko. 2001. Mothers as the best teachers: Japanese motherhood and early childhood education. In *Women's working lives in East Asia*, ed. Mary Brinton, 180–203. Stanford: Stanford University Press.

Hughes, James, and Margaret Maurer-Fazio. 2002. Effects of marriage, education and occupation on the female/male wage gap in China. *Pacific Economic Review* 7(1): 137–157.

Jacobs, Jerry. 2001. Evolving patterns of sex segregation. In *Sourcebook of labor markets: Evolving structures and processes*, eds. Ivar Berg and Arne Kalleberg, 535–550. New York: Kluwer Academic/Plenum.

Jacobs, Jerry. 1989. *Revolving doors: Sex segregation and women's careers*. Stanford: Stanford University Press.

Jacobs, Jerry, and Janet Gornick. 2002. Hours of paid work in dual-earner couples: The United States in cross-national perspective. *Sociological Focus* 35(2): 169–187.

Lundberg, Shelly, and Elaina Rose. 2000. Parenthood and the earnings of married men and women. *Labor Economics* 7(6): 689–710.

Matthews, Rebecca, and Victor Nee. 2000. Gender inequality and economic growth in rural China. *Social Science Research* 29(4): 606–632.

Maurer-Fazio, Margaret. 2007. In books one finds a house of gold: Education and labor market outcomes in urban China. In *Education and reform in China*, eds. Emily Hannum and Albert Park, 260–276. New York: Routledge.

Maurer-Fazio, Margaret, and James Hughes. 2002. The effects of market liberalization on the relative earnings of Chinese women. *Journal of Comparative Economics* 30(4): 683–708.

Parish, William, and Sarah Busse. 2000. Gender and work. In *Chinese urban life under reform*, eds. Wenfang Tang and William Parish, 232–272. Cambridge: Cambridge University Press.

Parish, William, Xiaoya Zhe, and Fang Li. 1995. Nonfarm work and marketization of the Chinese countryside. *The China Quarterly* 143: 697–730.

Reid, Lori. 2002. Occupational segregation, human capital, and motherhood: Black women's higher exit rates from full-time employment. *Gender and Society* 16(5): 728–747.

Rosenthal, Elisabeth. 1998. In China, 35+ and female = unemployable. *New York Times*. October 13, p. A1.

Rozelle, Scott, Xiao-yuan Dong, Linxiu Zhang, and Andrew Mason. 2002. Gender wage gaps in post-reform rural China. *Pacific Economic Review* 7(1): 157–180.

Shen, Jie, and Xin Deng. 2008. Gender wage inequality in the transitional Chinese economy: A critical review of post-reform research. *Journal of Organizational Transformation and Social Change* 5(2): 109–127.

Shu, Xiaoling. 2004. Education and gender egalitarianism: The case of China. *Sociology of Education* 77(4): 311–336.

Shu, Xiaoling. 2005. Market transition and gender segregation in urban China. *Social Science Quarterly* 86(S1): 1299–1323.

Shu, Xiaoling, and Yanjie Bian. 2003. Market transition and gender gap in earnings in urban China. *Social Forces* 81(3): 1107–1145.
Sigle-Rushton, Wendy, and Jane Waldfogel. 2004. Motherhood and women's earnings in Anglo-American, Continental European, and Nordic Countries. Paper presented at the Conference on Cross-National Comparisons of Expenditures on Children, Princeton, NJ, January 2004.
Smits, Jeroen. 2003. Estimating the Heckman two-step procedure to control for selection bias with SPSS. http://home.planet.nl/smits.jeroen (accessed November 15, 2007).
Stockman, Norman. 1994. Gender inequality and social structure in urban China. *Sociology* 28(3): 759–777.
Summerfield, Gale. 1994. Economic reform and the employment of Chinese women. *Journal of Economic Issues* 28(3): 715–732.
Trappe, Heike, and Rachel Rosenfeld. 2000. How do children matter? A comparison of gender earnings inequality for young adults in the former East Germany and the former West Germany. *Journal of Marriage and the Family* 62(2): 489–507.
Parish, William L., Xiaoye Zhe, and Fang Li. 1995. Nonfarm work and marketization of the Chinese countryside. *The China Quarterly 143* (Sept.): 697–730.
Tsuya, Noriko, and Larry Bumpass, eds. 2004. *Marriage, work and family life in comparative perspective: Japan, South Korea and the United States*. Hawai'i: University of Hawai'i Press.
Tsuya, Noriko, and Minja Kim Choe. 2004. Investments in children's education, desired fertility, and women's employment. In *Marriage, work and family life in comparative perspective: Japan, South Korea and the United States*, eds. Noriko Tsuya and Larry Bumpass, 76–94. Hawai'i: University of Hawai'i Press.
Waldfogel, Jane. 1997. The effect of children on women's wages. *American Sociological Review* 62(2): 209–217.
Winship, Christopher, and Robert Mare. 1992. Models for sample selection bias. *Annual Review of Sociology* 18: 327–350.
Xie, Yu, and Emily Hannum. 1996. Regional variation in earnings inequality in reform-era urban China. *American Journal of Sociology* 101(4): 950–992.
Yu, Wei-hsin. 2001. Family demands, gender attitudes, and married women's labor force participation: Comparing Japan and Taiwan. In *Women's working lives in East Asia*, ed. Mary Brinton, 70–95. Stanford: Stanford University Press.
Yu, Wei-hsin. 2002. Jobs for mothers: Married women's labor force reentry and part-time, temporary employment in Japan. *Sociological Forum* 17(3): 493–523.
Yu, Wei-hsin. 2005. Changes in women's postmarital employment in Japan and Taiwan. *Demography* 42(4): 693–717.
Yu, Wei-hsin. 2006. National contexts and the dynamics of married women's employment: The cases of Japan and Taiwan. *The Sociological Quarterly* 47(2): 215–243.

Zhang, Junsen, Yaohui Zhao, Albert Park, and Xiaoqing Song. 2005. Economic returns to schooling in urban China, 1988 to 2001. *Journal of Comparative Economics* 33(4): 730–752.

Zhang, Linxiu, Alan de Brauw, and Scott Rozelle. 2003. Labor market liberalization, employment and gender in rural China. Paper presented at International Association of Agricultural Economists 2003 annual meeting, August 2003, Durban, South Africa.

Zhang, Yuping, Emily Hannum, and Meiyan Wang. 2008. Gender-based employment and income differences in urban China: Considering the contributions of marriage and parenthood. *Social Forces* 86(4): 1529–1560.

Zhou, Xueguang. 2000. Economic transformation and income inequality in urban China: Evidence from panel data. *American Journal of Sociology* 105(5): 1135–1174.

# 13

# IMPLICATIONS OF THE COLLEGE EXPANSION POLICY FOR SOCIAL STRATIFICATION

Wei-Jun Jean Yeung

## INTRODUCTION

In 1999, China implemented one of the most important educational policies in recent years—college enrollment expansion. Since then, overall college enrollment has dramatically increased, from 1,080,000 in 1998 to about 5.5 million in 2006, and 6.3 million in 2009. The extent to which the incremental quota for college enrollment has been equally allocated across gender, ethnic, and socioeconomic status (SES) and how much the overall inequality in access to college education has changed since the policy's implementation remain open questions. College education provides valuable human capital that has long-lasting consequences for the life opportunities of individuals and the international competitiveness of the country. It is important to understand the impact of the new policy on different subgroups, as the policy may either equalize or intensify inequality among subgroups in China.

The question addressed in this chapter is whether the college expansion policy has reduced educational inequality in China in terms of family SES, gender, and ethnicity. How the relationships between social origins and educational attainment change as China undergoes rapid economic changes is of great interest to social scientists and policy makers alike. I first provide a historical background for China's higher education and the college expansion policy and some descriptive analysis to examine changes at an individual level for different birth cohorts by gender, region, residence, and ethnic origins, based on data from the Chinese General Social Survey (CGSS) collected in 2005 and 2006. I examine college enrollment rates by birth cohorts and compare the within-birth-cohort inequalities in college education across interested subgroups, such as by gender, ethnicity, and family socioeconomic status among each birth cohort. These analyses will depict the evolution of inequality in access to college education over time. Then I present multivariate analysis to see how the impact of these family and individual characteristics on college attendance vary before and after the college expansion policy.

This chapter is among the first studies to use individual-level data to examine the impact of this important change in China's higher education policies on educational inequality. Given the timing of the reform and data availability, it may be premature to assess the impact of the college expansion policy on contemporary China's social stratification thoroughly. Preliminary results from this study, however, will add significant evidence to extant research that often uses small-scale convenience samples or census data aggregated at the provincial or regional level.

## BACKGROUND ON HIGHER EDUCATION IN CHINA

Opportunities for higher education in China have fluctuated dramatically since 1949 in response to various political shifts. The period between 1949 and 1959 was characterized by rapid economic development and the beginning of the rushed growth policy of the Great Leap Forward. Educational opportunities expanded rapidly in this period. By the early 1960s, there was virtually universal enrollment in primary education in China. Due to the dominant ideology of the time, the emphasis of higher education was on educating those from working-class backgrounds (Parish 1984). This period was followed by a time of economic contraction in the 1960s, with declining opportunities for high school and college education. During the Cultural Revolution (1966–1976), widespread social and political upheaval resulted in nationwide social and economic disarray, and dramatic disruptions in higher education occurred. Intellectuals were denounced, colleges were closed, the national examination system for admissions was discontinued, and thousands of teachers and administrators were persecuted. Mao initiated the Down to the Countryside Movement, forcing about 16 million senior and junior high school graduates, the so-called "intellectual youths," to go to the country and work as farmers (to be "reeducated"). Admissions to undergraduate and graduate studies were stopped for 6 years and 12 years, respectively. College education was stripped of funds, which were redistributed to basic education in villages and towns (Whyte and Parish 1984). In the early 1970s, only a limited number of selected students, mostly peasants and working class rather than those with high academic achievements, were allowed to attend college to "reform" the higher education sector (Wu 2008). In 1971, there was a plan to consolidate, close, and reconstruct 106 of 417 institutions of higher education (Tsang 2000, Table 1.)

# Implications of the College Expansion Policy for Social Stratification 251

After Mao's rule ended, Deng reiterated the importance of science and technology for China's economic modernization and proclaimed that higher education was to be a high national priority to cultivate the talents needed for national development. Education reform thus began as a complement to the move toward a market-oriented socialist economy. Educational funds were directed toward cities again and toward higher education. In 1977, the national college entrance examination was resumed, with no limit on the age or family background of the examinees, thus signaling a new era in China's educational system. Since then, college admission has become primarily merit-based and highly competitive, and the uniform entrance examination system remained firmly in place until recently. The examination was designed by the Ministry of Education, and all students across the country took the same examination. Only in recent years have many provinces been allowed to design their own examinations. The number of vocational colleges, technical schools, evening colleges, and other types of colleges has also increased dramatically since the initiation of economic reform (Liu 2004).

In 1985, to ease the transition to a market economy, the Chinese government issued initiatives such as nine years of compulsory education, the expansion of vocational education, and a shift of financial responsibilities from the central government to local levels (Cheng 1994). Major decentralization occurred in the form of administrative and financial devolution. Local government and higher education institutions were given more autonomy. The proportion of tuition funded by the central government declined over time (Bai 1998; China Statistical Yearbook 1985–1995). The corresponding increase in tuition paid by households created an unequal burden on those households due to their varying levels of financial resources, with particularly stark inequalities emerging between students in urban versus rural areas. According to a study by the World Bank, if tuition covers 24 percent of the average cost of college education, it will account for 56 percent of the annual income of a family in the city where there is one wage earner, and 109 percent for such a family in a rural area (Tsang and Min 1997; World Bank 1997).

Since the mid-1990s, the Chinese government has reoriented its emphasis on higher education from quantity to quality, pushing forward the development of science and technology in order to enhance China's overall capacity and international competitiveness. During the ninth five-year plan (1996–2000), the government put forward the "211 Higher Education Development Project" in 1994, which prioritized the improvement of the quality of about 100 higher education institutions so that these universities could rank among the top universities in the world. In addition, in 1998, the Chinese government launched a special "985 Project" which gave 10 of China's leading universities, including Peking, Tsinghua, and Fudan, three-year grants in excess of 30 billion RMB to improve the quality of education that they provide (Ma 2009). Much of the increased spending in higher education is thus directed toward elite schools.

Although China's literacy rate grew impressively from 60 percent in the 1960s to 90.9 percent in 2001,[1] disparities increased in secondary and higher education (Ministry of Education, China 2002). Between 1994 and 1997, there was a widening of educational inequality between urban and rural counties in aspects such as school expenditure, quality of teachers, and physical conditions in schools. Tuition fees for both high school and college have also increased significantly, making these forms of education inaccessible to a substantial segment of the population.

## COLLEGE EXPANSION IN THE LATE 1990S

In 1999, the State Council approved the Plan of Revitalizing Education in the 21st Century proposed by the Ministry of Education to expand college enrollment. This measure was part of the eleventh five-year plan, which stressed the importance of prosperity for all and the need to create a "harmonious society." The plan includes various strategies, such as encouraging colleges to set up multiple campuses and instituting a private college system. The plan also includes calls for an increase in education expenditures, especially in tertiary education. The plan set a target for China to reach by 2010 the tertiary enrollment ratio of 15 percent, defined as "mass higher education" by Martin Trow (1973). This policy was proposed during the Asian financial crisis as part of an economic stimulus package by Tang Min, then chief economist of the Asian Development Bank Mission in China. Although the immediate driver of college expansion was economic, this policy is consistent with the national strategy to bring China to modernity through education, particularly in science and technology. The purposes of the expansion are: (1) to enhance international competitiveness with a more skilled labor force; (2) to drive economic growth through boosting domestic consumption on tuition and industries related to an expanded education system; and (3) to meet public demands for higher education.

To give a comparative view of higher education in China, Figure 13.1 shows college enrollment ratios during the period 1990–2005 in China, as compared to selected countries in both the Western industrialized world and Asia.[2] As can be seen, China's college enrollment rates lag substantially behind those of other countries, slowly increasing from less than 3 percent in 1990 to about 5 percent in 1995, and then to 7 percent immediately prior to the college expansion policy of 1998. These rates were not only much lower than those in Western industrialized countries, but were also lagging behind those of many Asian countries. For example, on the eve of the Chinese college expansion policy, college enrollment rates were about 70 percent in the United States, 60 percent in Canada, 65 percent in Australia, and 50 percent in France. Even compared to many other countries with lower income, China's college enrollment rates are significantly lower, paralleling those in countries such as India and Bangladesh. In 1998, the college

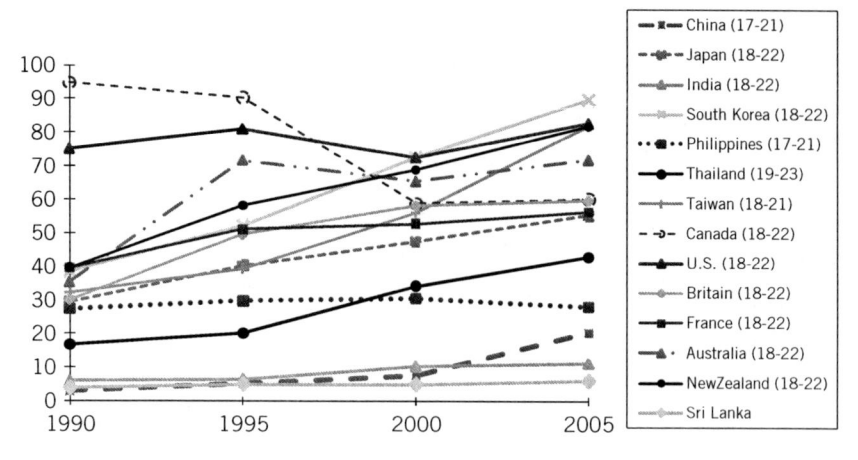

# Implications of the College Expansion Policy for Social Stratification 253

**Figure 13.1.** Gross College Enrollment Rate in Different Countries, 1990–2005. *Sources:* UNESCO Statistical Yearbook, World Bank Database, China State Bureau of Statistics

enrollment rate was about 68 percent in South Korea, 51 percent in Taiwan, 31 percent in Thailand, and 30 percent in the Philippines. After the college expansion policy, the college enrollment rate in China rose dramatically to 20.3 percent in 2005. However, even with this rapid increase, Chinese college enrollment rates remain significantly lower than those of all the countries included in Figure 13.1, except India and Sri Lanka.

Figures 13.2 and 13.3 depict historical college enrollment trends based on data from the China Statistical Yearbook. Figure 13.2 shows the number of newly enrolled college students per year, compared to those enrolled in other levels of schooling from 1990 to 2005. Expansion in basic education occurred much earlier than that in higher education. Figure 13.3 focuses on college enrollment trends by gender during this period of time. As seen, there was an unprecedented increase in the annual intake from about 1 million in 1998 to over 5 million students in 2005. This figure also shows an increase for both males and females and

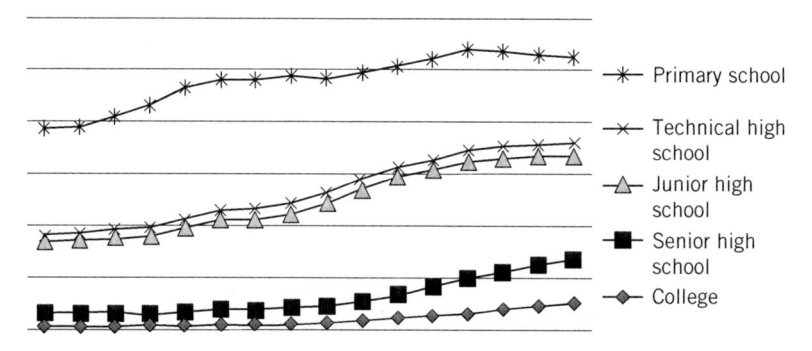

**Figure 13.2.** Number of Newly Enrolled Students by Level, 1990–2005 (in 10,000). *Source:* China Statistical Yearbook, 2006

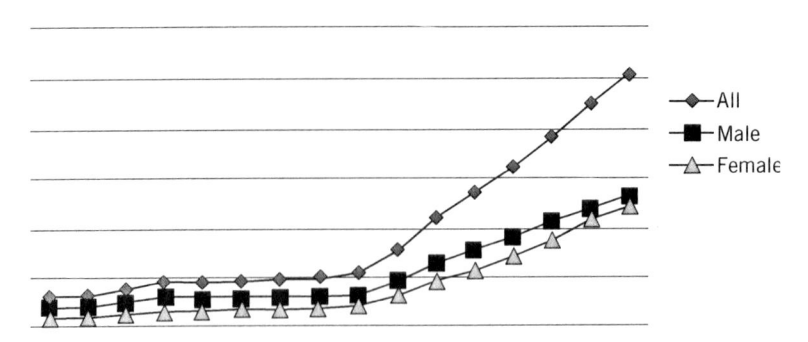

Figure 13.3. Number of Newly Enrolled Students (in 10,000) 1990–2005, by Gender. *Source:* China Statistical Yearbook 2006

a narrowing gender gap in recent years. In terms of total number of students, the 3.4 million college students in 1998 had increased to 15.6 million in 2005 (China Statistical Yearbook 2006).

Total education spending on higher education increased sixfold from 1998 to 2005 in infrastructure, teachers, and administration (China Statistical Yearbook 1999–2005). Despite the increase in total spending on higher education, the government's contribution to total expenditures declined from 64 percent before the college expansion policy (in 1998) to 42.5 percent in 2005 (China Statistical Yearbook 1999–2005). Before college expansion, the Chinese government had been the main funding source of higher education institutions. After 2000, private funding has covered more than 50 percent of total education expenditures (National Bureau of Statistics of China 2005). In contrast, the contribution from nongovernment resources such as private investment in schools, tuition, or donations has increased rapidly. In many areas, banks were heavily involved in lending to public universities. A study estimated that 150–200 billion yuan were loaned to higher education institutes in 2006 (Ru, Lu, and Li 2005). College tuition increased substantially from accounting for 14 percent of the total spending on higher education before expansion policy to more than 30 percent in 2005; it is mostly self-financed by students (China Statistical Yearbook). The increase in tuition was dramatic, amounting to $10,000 yuan or more per year in an average university when living expenses are taken into account. This presents a major financial burden for many households (Fleisher et al. 2004), especially at a time when no credit mechanism for borrowing has been established for poor families.

Moreover, an increased regional disparity in both quantity and quality of higher education has resulted from the college expansion. Government policies have granted eastern, coastal provinces more resources to undergo greater reforms than were possible in inland or more rural and remote areas. In addition, a high proportion of the new resources had gone to the elite schools included in the "211 project" and "985 project," which tend to be located in regions with high economic development such as Beijing and Shanghai (Min 2004).

## Implications of the College Expansion Policy for Social Stratification 255

The process of marketization of higher education brought greater emphasis on competition and efficiency. Many smaller or specialized educational institutes were merged to become more comprehensive universities. Since 1999, the Chinese government began to allow the establishment of private universities that are funded without government financing. Many public universities were also allowed to establish independent colleges, which share some of their infrastructure but are not eligible for government funding (hence they are classified as private institutions). By 2007, nearly 300 private universities were estimated to qualify for accreditation and about as many independent colleges (Ministry of Education 2007). These private universities and colleges often charge a higher tuition than the public universities.

Along with increased enrollment and government expenditure, the college entrance examination system has also undergone reform in recent years. Some colleges are now allowed to design their own admission policies. Some institutions, mainly the elite colleges, are now allowed to admit students based on recommendations by high school principals and students' skills, such as communication skills, in addition to test scores. These changes are controversial and have been reported in the mass media to have resulted in corruption seeping through the college admission system.

Rapid college expansion has brought some unintended consequences to Chinese society, including a dramatic increase in unemployment rates among college graduates (Bai 2006), as the labor market for the highly educated could not keep pace with the college expansion. Almost one in five of the 5 million graduates were still unemployed one year after graduation in 2007. This dire situation has since worsened. According to the Education Ministry, more than one-quarter of the 6.3 million Chinese college graduates in 2009 were still unemployed six months after graduation (Roberts 2010).

There are also concerns that the quality of higher education has declined. This is partly a result of the fact that the increase in student enrollment was not matched by an increase in the number of faculty members, and because private universities and colleges are more profit driven and less concerned about the quality of education. It has been reported that the ratio of faculty to students has increased from 1:11 in 1998 to 1:20 in 2003 in many universities; in some it has even reached 1:30 or 1:40 (Chen 2004). Another concern is that the escalating cost of college education is making higher education a greater financial burden to many Chinese families, which reduces access for many disadvantaged students (Jacob 2006).

To recap the trend before and after college expansion policy, Figure 13.4 shows the proportion of senior high school graduates who progressed to higher education between 1980 and 2008. In 1980, only 5 percent of senior high school graduates progressed to colleges. Since then, there has been a rapid increase. By 1985, this rate had increased to 31 percent, and by 1995, to 46 percent. The largest jump occurred between 1998 (43 percent) and 1999 (61 percent), when

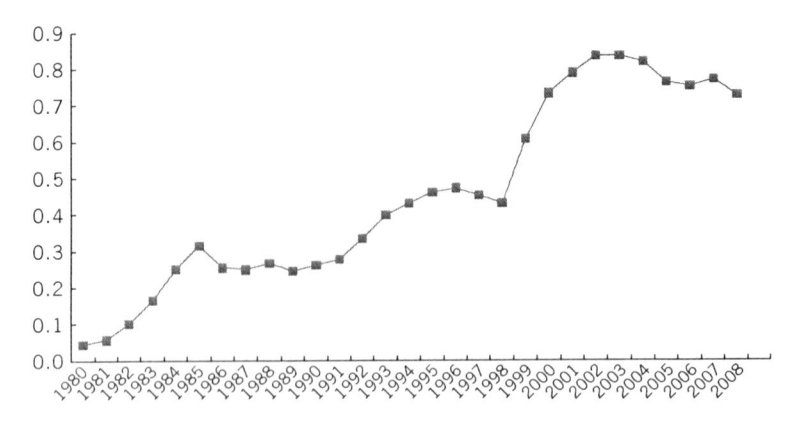

**Figure 13.4.** Progression Rate from Senior High Graduates to College. *Source:* China Statistical Yearbook

college expansion policy began. This was followed by a sustained rapid growth in the subsequent 6 years to over 80 percent, then a gradual decline to 73 percent in 2008, after college expansion slowed down. In the eleventh five-year program (2006–2010), the Chinese government announced its intention to control the scale of college expansion and to shift the emphasis to improving the quality of college education.

## HAS THE COLLEGE EXPANSION POLICY REDUCED EDUCATIONAL INEQUALITY IN CHINA?

There are two competing hypotheses regarding whether college expansion policy has reduced education inequality in China among groups differentiated by socioeconomic status, gender, and ethnicity. First, college expansion would be expected to reduce inequality if education serves as a great equalizer of life opportunities between children from advantaged and disadvantaged families, as argued by scholars such as Cremin (1951) and Downey (2004, 2008). This theory, known as human capital theory, posits that education potentially serves as an efficient instrument to reduce wage inequality (Ashenfelter and Rouse 2000). The conventional wisdom in development promotes education as an effective way to reduce social inequalities, although the emphasis in the developmental literature is more on increasing basic education rather than higher education.

A competing hypothesis is that China's college expansion policy will *exacerbate* inequality if access to college education becomes more unequal to subgroups. Given that college tuition in China has substantially increased and has become increasingly self-financed since the college expansion policy, higher education may become unattainable for individuals with disadvantaged socioeconomic family backgrounds.

Existing micro-level empirical evidence in this field is mixed. Research in other countries tends to suggest that education expansion does not reduce the relative position of social groups. That is, there is little change in the "education queue" among individuals with different socioeconomic backgrounds after an education expansion (Mare 1981; Halsey et al. 1980; Shavit and Blossfeld 1993; Smith and Cheung 1986) because elites manage to maintain their advantages by getting more education than the masses (Walters and Watters 2000). This tends to support the maximum maintained inequality (MMI) hypothesis, which predicts that there will be a persistence of intergenerational educational inequality and that the effect of family background will continue despite educational reform and economic development (Raftery and Hout 1993; Mare 1981; Halsey et al. 1980; Shavit and Blossfeld 1993; Smith and Cheung 1986). A recent study based on 13 countries found patterns in contrast with the persistent inequality theory presented by Shavit and Blossfeld (1993) (Tam and Ganzeboom 2009).

Literature on gender differences in educational attainment has revealed a global catch-up trend for female education, though returns to education vary across countries (Goldin, Katz, and Kuziemko 2006). For example, returns to education for female college graduates in Korea and Taiwan tend to be lower than for males. In terms of ethnicity differences, research in South Africa shows that despite education expansion, education disparities played an important role in maintaining race-based differences in occupational status (Treiman et al. 1996; Powell and Buchmann 2002).

## DATA

Analysis in this chapter is based on data from the 2005 and 2006 Chinese General Social Survey (CGSS) conducted by Renmin University and University of Hong Kong Science and Technology (HKUST). This study covers households in both rural and urban areas in 30 provinces/districts (excluding Tibet, Taiwan, Hong Kong, and Macau). The 2005 and 2006 waves each cover about 10,000 households. The study collects data on basic socioeconomic and demographic data for respondents and family members, including family composition, education, ethnicity, health, and psychological well-being, as well as community administration data for the residence where the respondent resided at the time of the interview. These data allow us to examine trends of college enrollment among subgroups of the population across birth cohorts.

## ANALYSIS SAMPLE

For this study, I combined the samples in the 2005 and 2006 waves of the Chinese General Social Survey (CGSS), resulting in a sample of 16,000 individuals who were born between 1971 and 1985 (including the main respondent and other family members). The two surveys use the same sampling frame, and there is no overlap of the sample drawn in each wave. Given that the interviews were only one year apart, combining the samples from both waves allows us to have a bigger sample for the specific birth cohorts that we are interested in investigating here.

I include five three-year birth cohorts in my analysis, consisting of those who were born between 1971 and 1983. The two cohorts born in 1971–1973 and in 1974–1976 would have been at college attendance age (assumed to be 18–22 years) before the college expansion policy began in 1999. They serve as a baseline benchmark to be compared to cohorts who were exposed to the college expansion policy. Some members of the cohort that consists of those born in 1977–1979 (age 22–20 in 1999) would have been potentially affected by the policy. The other two younger cohorts, those who were born in 1980–1982 (age 19–17 in 1999) and in 1983–1985 (age 14–16 in 1999), were also at college attendance age during the college expansion years, 1999–2006.

## RESULTS

CGSS data confirm the trend of dramatic increases in college enrollment that we saw in the census data earlier. Figure 13.5 shows the proportion of individuals who have attended college in each of the five birth cohorts. A more detailed analysis using the year of birth of the respondents, rather than birth cohort indicators, shows a similar increasing trend. Among members of the oldest cohort who were born in 1971–1973 and were at college attendance age before the college expansion, 9.6 percent had ever attended college by the time of the interview in 2005 or 2006. In contrast, twice as large a proportion of the youngest cohort, born in 1983–1985 and at college attendance age during the college expansion years, attended colleges. The rate increased by 62 percent from the 1974–1976 cohort to the 1983–1985 cohort. The proportion of individuals who had attended postgraduate school remains consistently low during this period, hovering around half a percent (data not shown).

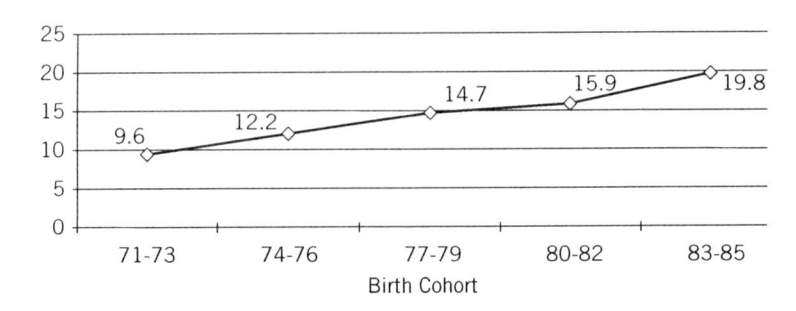

**Figure 13.5.** Percent of College Attendance, by Birth Cohort

Implications of the College Expansion Policy for Social Stratification 259

## SUBGROUP COMPARISON OF COLLEGE ATTENDANCE

Figure 13.6 shows the trend of college attendance by urban/rural *hukou* (household registration) origin. As can be seen, stark disparity has existed historically between the urban and rural areas. For the oldest cohort, 22 percent of those with urban origin had attended college, compared to 2.2 percent of those with rural origin. Enrollment rates increased over time for both, to 46 percent for those with urban *hukou* origin and 7.1 percent for those with rural origin for the youngest cohort. Even though the rate of increase from the 1974–1976 cohort to the youngest cohort is faster for those with rural origin than for those with urban origin, the gap in enrollment rates between the two groups has widened over time.

Figure 13.7 shows the trend by gender. The rate increased for both genders, though faster for females than for males. For the oldest cohort, 11 percent of males versus about 8 percent of females had ever attended college. The gender gap narrowed from 3.2 percent in the oldest cohort to about 2.2 percent for the youngest cohort. Figure 13.8 shows the trend by ethnicity. For the oldest cohort, the proportions of Han who had attended college were significantly higher than the minorities (10 percent for Han and 6 percent for others). For the youngest cohort, the rates were about 20.6 percent and 11.6 percent for Han and minority groups, respectively. The rate of increase between 1983–1985 and 1974–1976 was faster for minorities (93 percent) than for Han (61 percent), though the gap between the two groups has increased over this period of time. Figure 13.9 shows the pattern by father's party membership. As seen, more than twice as large a proportion of the youth in the oldest cohort whose father was a party member attended college (about 20 vs. 8 percent). This gap widened over the period being

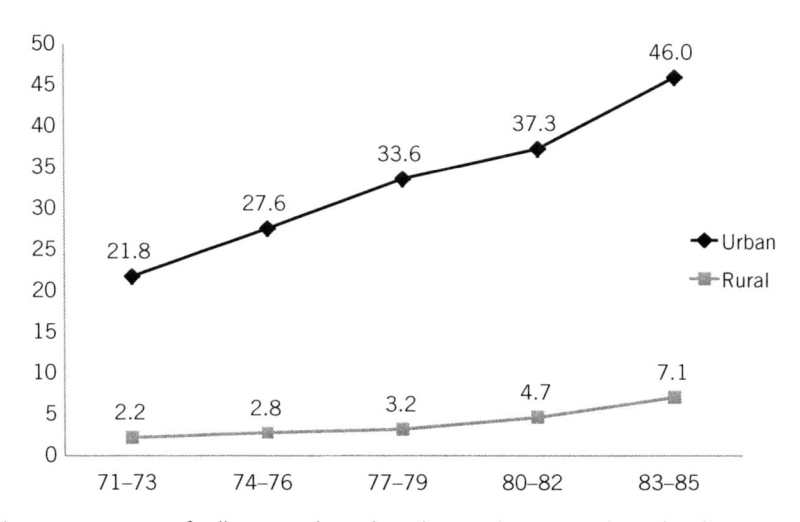

**Figure 13.6.** Percent of College Attendance, by Father's *Hukuou* Status, by Birth Cohort

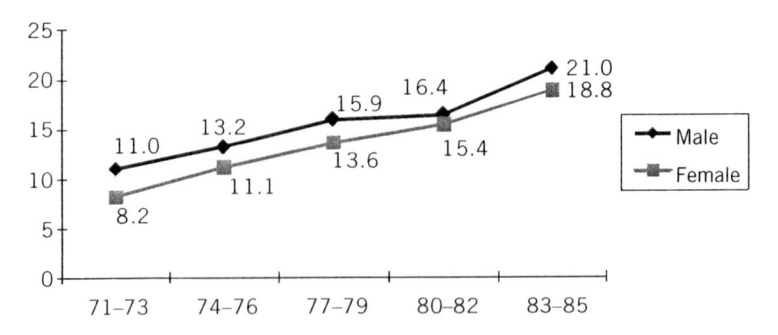

## 260 CHINESE SOCIAL POLICY IN A TIME OF TRANSITION

**Figure 13.7.** Percent of College Attendance, by Gender, by Birth Cohort

studied; although it decreased somewhat in the most recent cohort, there is still a substantial gap (25 vs. 16 percent).

## Multivariate Analysis

Next, I conduct multivariate logistic regression analysis to estimate the impact of individual characteristics, family background, and cohort indicators on the probability of college attendance and the progression from senior high school to college. These predictors include gender, rural residence, ethnicity, family income, and whether either parent is a Communist Party member. Unfortunately, data on household income prior to college-attending years are not available in CGSS; the income variable used here is measured at the time of the interview and thus is a poor proxy of the level of financial resources available to a youth while growing up. I also include a control for region, indicating whether each youth resided in the northeast, central, or western region. Then, to examine whether the impact of these individual and family background factors change significantly before and after the college expansion policy, I add to the model several interaction terms between the birth cohort indicator and the independent variables. For these models, I create a dummy variable indicator of "whether before or after the expansion." The younger three cohorts were treated as the "before policy" group (i.e., those at college-attending age before the college expansion policy), whereas the last two cohorts were treated as the "after policy" group.[3]

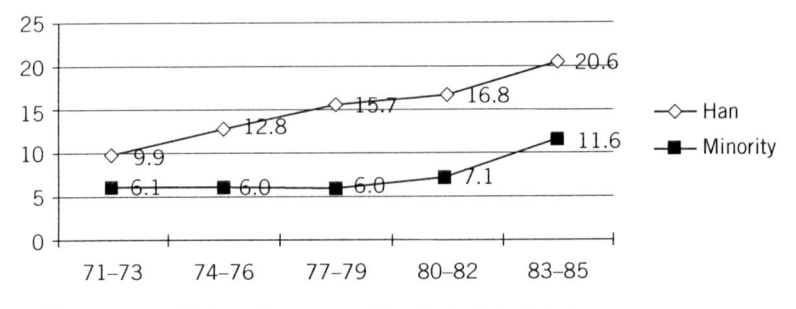

**Figure 13.8.** Percent of College Attendance, Ethnicity, by Birth Cohort

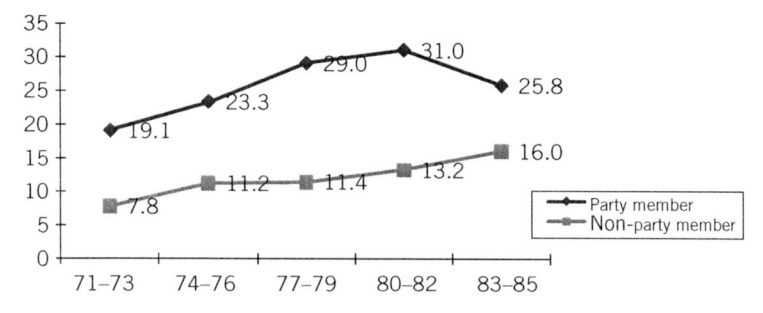

## Implications of the College Expansion Policy for Social Stratification 261

**Figure 13.9.** Percent of College Attendance, by Father's Party Membership, by Birth Cohort

| Cohort | Party member | Non-party member |
|---|---|---|
| 71–73 | 19.1 | 7.8 |
| 74–76 | 23.3 | 11.2 |
| 77–79 | 29.0 | 11.4 |
| 80–82 | 31.0 | 13.2 |
| 83–85 | 25.8 | 16.0 |

Table 13.1 presents logit estimates, with models 1 and 2 for the probability of ever having attended college, and models 3 and 4 for the probability of having progressed from high school to college. We include individual and family background covariates as predictors in the first model, then we add several interaction terms between the before/after policy dummy variable with these main independent variables.[4] Results show that, if we divide the sample into before and after the expansion, the odds of youth attending college after college expansion policy is on average slightly more than 3 times as high (exp(.331)) as before the policy change.[5] All the individual and family background variables are significant predictors, as expected. Several of the interaction terms are also significant (model 2). Controlling for other family background, the odds of males going to college are 50 percent higher (odds ratio = 1.5) than that for females before reform; after the expansion, the male advantage declines to 10 percent (odds ratio = 1.1). Rural residents are dramatically disadvantaged compared to urban residence. The odds of rural youth attending college are only 5.7 percent (exp(-2.88)) that of urban youth before reform, increasing to about 9 percent after the reform. This increase is statistically significant, despite a wide remaining gap. Regarding ethnicity, before reform, when other family characteristics are held constant, the odds of Han attending college are 35 percent higher than minority groups. After the reform, the odds increase drastically to 3.4. Children whose parents are Communist Party members are 30 percent more likely to attend college than those whose parents are not party members. There is no significant difference in the impact of parents' party membership before and after the reform.

Parents' education and household income are also positively related to the odds of attending college. A more detailed analysis controlling for other covariates shows that, compared to the lowest income quartile, the odds for those in the third quartile attending college are about 5 times as high, and those in the highest income quartile are about 11 times as high (results not shown). I also examine the nonlinear effect of household income, using the log of household income. Table 13.1 shows that before college expansion, doubling the household income

## 262 CHINESE SOCIAL POLICY IN A TIME OF TRANSITION

Table 13.1. Logit Estimates of the Probability of Ever Attended College and of Progressing from Senior High School to Colleges

| VARIABLES | (1) Ever Attended College | (2) Ever Attended College | (3) Progressing from HS to College | (4) Progressing from HS to College |
|---|---|---|---|---|
| Male | 0.287*** | 0.412*** | 0.192** | 0.267*** |
|  | (0.076) | (0.092) | (0.081) | (0.100) |
| Rural | −2.581*** | −2.878*** | −1.576*** | −1.746*** |
|  | (0.118) | (0.180) | (0.126) | (0.188) |
| Han | 0.370** | 0.302 | 0.133 | −0.009 |
|  | (0.148) | (0.173) | (0.170) | (0.224) |
| Parent party member | 0.208** | 0.141 | 0.115 | −0.019 |
|  | (0.093) | (0.108) | (0.097) | (0.114) |
| Father educ (ref = no edu) Elem-Junior High | 0.321** | 0.308** | −0.118 | −0.067 |
|  | (0.149) | (0.150) | (0.171) | (0.173) |
| High School & up Region (ref = northeast) | 1.092*** | 1.072*** | 0.342 | 0.412** |
|  | (0.158) | (0.159) | (0.179) | (0.181) |
| Region 3 |  |  |  | −0.018 |
|  |  |  |  | (0.095) |
| Region 3 |  |  |  | 0.179 |
|  |  |  |  | (0.109) |
| Log (family income) | 0.397*** | 0.414*** | 0.170*** | 0.187*** |
|  | (0.058) | (0.0601) | (0.057) | (0.062) |
| After Expansion (AE) | 0.524*** | 0.331*** | 0.434*** | 0.252** |
|  | (0.076) | (0.0989) | (0.085) | (0.107) |
| AE * male |  | −0.317** |  | −0.186 |
|  |  | (0.156) |  | (0.167) |
| AE *rural |  | 0.498** |  | 0.341 |
|  |  | (0.229) |  | (0.251) |
| AE * Han |  | 0.924*** |  | 0.548 |
|  |  | (0.336) |  | (.364) |
| AE * partymem |  | 0.255 |  | 0.369 |
|  |  | (0.197) |  | (0.205) |
| AE * logfamin |  | −0.054 |  | −0.033 |
|  |  | (0.034) |  | (0.037) |
| Constant | −6.191*** | −6.039*** | −2.389*** | −2.569*** |
|  | (0.608) | (0.613) | (0.601) | (0.605) |
| Observations | 10,633 | 10,663 | 4,526 | 4,536 |
| Log pseudolikelihood | −3293 | −3282 | −2502 | −2499 |

Robust standard errors in parentheses.
*** $p<0.01$, ** $p<0.05$.

increases the odds of attending college by 41 percent, whereas after the expansion, the odds increase by a smaller margin: 36 percent. This difference, however, is not statistically significant at the 5 percent level.

### Transition from Senior High School to College

Models 3 and 4 present estimates of the probability of progressing to college, controlling for completion of senior high school. The overall odds of such a transition after college expansion are 30 percent higher (exp(.263)) than those before the reform. A notable difference in this set of estimates is that most interaction terms are not statistically significant, indicating that the impact of these characteristics after college expansion is not significantly different from that before the policy change. The fact that other interaction terms are not significant when controlling for completion of senior high school suggests that the different impact of characteristics observed in the "ever attended college" models occurs before high school graduation. Perhaps the college expansion policy raised individuals' expectations of attaining a higher education, leading fewer people to drop out of high school.

## DISCUSSION

China has surpassed Martin Trow's definition of "mass higher education" since 2002. Between 1999 and 2005, the college expansion policy gave five times as many people per year the opportunity to attend college, benefiting all socioeconomic and demographic subgroups, despite its uneven impact. Results presented here reveal a complex picture of the consequences of college expansion policy for China's social stratification. It appears that the policy has reduced some inequality among certain subgroups but has increased the gap among other groups. In particular, opportunities for females have increased more rapidly than males. This pattern partly reflects a decreased gender gap in parental investment in their offspring's education. Many female single children have gained greater opportunity to receive higher education than in the past. Results also show a small improvement in the odds of attending college for rural youth relative to their urban counterparts, although the gap remains appallingly large. In this sense, college expansion policy has had an equalizer function that helps reduce disparities in life opportunities between these subgroups (Cremin 1951; Downey 2004, 2008). Nevertheless, there is still a long way to go, for stark disparities remain by urban/rural origin, ethnicity, family socioeconomic status, and across regions. Urban/rural *hukou* origin is the dominant determinant of attaining a college education. The odds of rural youth attending college after the policy change, though improved, are still less than 10 percent the odds for urban youth. The quota for admission and financial support to rural students should be increased. Recent reports of a declining proportion of rural students in elite universities such as

Peking and Tsinghua University and the higher cut-off entrance examination scores for students from rural areas compared to urban areas underscore the unjust distribution of resources for rural youth, especially for the opportunity to attend top educational institutions (Zhang and Liu 2005; Fish 2010).

Family background, such as parents' education, household income, and parents' party membership, remains highly predictive of college attendance, resulting in staggering inequalities among subgroups. There is also continued large regional disparity. These findings support the maximum maintained inequality (MMI) hypothesis that there will be a persistence of intergenerational educational inequality, with the effect of family background continuing, despite educational reform and economic development; this study provides evidence that elites will manage to maintain their advantages by getting more education than the masses, as predicted by Walters (2000). There is no evidence, however, that the college expansion policy has exacerbated the impact of these family characteristics, with one exception. The increased gap in the odds of attending college between minority groups and Han during the expansion years is a cause for concern. According to Jacob (2006), minority student enrollment as a percent of total university enrollment increased from 3.5 percent in the 1960s to 3.8 percent in 1980 to 6.6 percent in 1990, but then declined to 6.1 percent in 2000.

It is likely that minority students have been disadvantaged during the college expansion years. Even though minority students receive preferential treatment on the entrance examinations, it is often not enough to compensate for their lack of linguistic, cultural, and political advantages to compete with Han students. In addition, the fact that minority groups live in predominantly rural and remote areas compounds their disadvantages and creates higher obstacles to college enrollment for minority students (Andreas 2004). Future research needs to examine the opportunity structure in different regions for Han and ethnic minority groups over time.

It is somewhat surprising that we do not find college expansion policy exacerbating the inequality for economic groups, given our expectation that higher education may have become unattainable for individuals with disadvantaged socioeconomic family backgrounds due to the tuition hike. This finding may be a result of our poor proxy for family financial resources before college-attending years, or it may indicate that subsidies to youth from lower income families did indeed help to close the educational attainment gap. It may also be due to limitations in the analyses, such as exploratory analysis that does not examine the subgroups in sufficient detail or data that cover only seven years after the expansion policy began. I do not distinguish colleges of different quality in this chapter. Further examination of circumstances for youth from the top and bottom of the income distribution, and from different types of colleges, is needed in order to better understand the complex relationship between family income and college attendance over time.

Results presented here should therefore be taken as suggestive and interpreted with caution. The results suggest that the college expansion policy may have significantly raised people's educational expectations and led more people to complete high school education. The raised aspirations may have a longer term positive impact on China's human capital development.

Although college enrollment has expanded at a faster pace than the labor market can absorb, thus creating the unintended consequences of high unemployment rates among college graduates, this situation should improve as China's economy transitions from export-oriented, labor-intensive industries to more service-oriented and high-technology industries that demand high human capital. In the short run, the Chinese government has taken steps to:

- review college curricula toward the goal of offering more flexibility and specialty training to respond to market demand;
- help college students find employment by creating new skilled jobs and improving employment information and guidance systems;
- encourage college graduates to work in rural areas, in smaller townships, or in the western region;
- provide financial support to graduates to start their own businesses; and
- invest more in small and medium enterprises.

These are reasonable strategies for ameliorating the dire situation. Relaxing and eventually abolishing the *hukou* system to equalize development and social safety nets provided in urban and rural areas and to allow greater mobility in the labor market will be important for alleviating the regional mismatch between the supply and demand of labor.

As noted in the international comparative analysis, despite the rapid increase in college enrollment, Chinese college attendance rates remain very low by international standards, even significantly lower than some low-income countries such as the Philippines and Thailand. The decisions to expand higher education and subsequently to slow down the pace are steps in the right direction, if not in magnitude, especially in view of the declining working-age population in the next few decades. Although China needs to prepare its labor force for a rapidly growing economy, enhancing the human capital of a population does not take place overnight. Fortunately, the Chinese government now has the financial capacity to increase education investment, but China's impressive economic growth has not yet been accompanied by a similarly rapid growth in education. For example, the average duration of schooling was still only 6.6 years in 2000 (up from 3.7 years in 1980), and the increase in public spending on education at that point in time was still relatively small. In 1999–2000, China's government expenditure on education accounted for only 1.9 percent of its gross domestic product (GDP), lower even than developing countries such as Thailand (5.5 percent) and India (4 percent) (UNESCO 2000). In the last decade, the Chinese government has significantly increased its investment in human resources.

As of 2009, education expenditures increased to 3 percent of GDP. Average years of schooling increased to 7.5 years by 2011 (UNESCO 2010). Access to higher education, however, remains unequal and unattainable for many of those with disadvantaged family backgrounds during this period. Continued and more equal investment in human capital is necessary for sustained economic growth and social stability. In particular, resources and opportunities for those with limited family resources, in rural and inland areas, and for minority groups should be increased significantly. The National Talent Development Plan passed in 2010 to increase national investment in human resources in the next decade will help transform China's growth model.

Clearly, the impact of the college expansion policy on social stratification in China will be long lasting, but it is too early to tell the nature of that impact. Its short- and long-term influence on China's development and on the well-being of various subgroups should be carefully monitored.

## NOTES

1  Literacy levels reached 94.3 percent in 2010 (UNESCO, 2012).
2  The age groups based on which the gross college enrollment ratios were calculated vary somewhat across countries, as indicated in the parentheses in Figure 13.1.
3  An alternative cut-off is used where the cohort born between 1977 and 1979 is included in the "after policy" group. Results are similar, though the effect of time change is slightly weaker. Given that there may be a lag effect of the policy, I choose to include only the older two cohorts in the "after policy" group.
4  We added one interaction term at a time to the model first. The results vary only marginally and not qualitatively; therefore we present the model with all interaction terms added here.
5  A more detailed analysis shows that compared to the oldest cohort, the odds of subsequent cohorts attending colleges are 1.3, 1.5, 1.8, and 3 times as high, without adding the interaction terms (data not shown).

## REFERENCES

Andreas, Joel. 2004. Leveling the little pagoda: The impact of college examinations, and their elimination, on rural education in China. *Comparative Education Review* 48(1): 1–48.

Ashenfelter, Orley, and Cecilia Rouse. 2000. Schooling, intelligence, and income in America. In *Meritocracy and economic inequality*, eds. Kenneth Arrow,

Samuel Bowles, Steven Durlauf. 89–117. Princeton, NJ: Princeton University Press.

Bai, Limin. 1998. Monetary Rewards *vs* the National Ideological Agenda: Career Choice Among Chinese Students. *Journal of Moral Education 27*(4): 525–541.

Bai, Limin. 2004. The metamorphosis of China's higher education in the 1990s. In *Education and change in the Pacific Rim: Meeting the challenges,* ed. Keith Sullivan, 241–265. Oxfordshire, UK: Triangle Books.

Bai, Limin. 2006. Graduate unemployment: Dilemmas and challenges in China's move to mass higher education. *The China Quarterly 185*: 128–144.

Chen Xi, Nuli. 2004. Nian quanguo putong gaoxiao biyesheng jiuye gongzuo (Making efforts to solve problems of employment for graduates in regular universities). httn://www.tech.net.cn/ (accessed September 17, 2004).

Cheng, K. M. 1994. Issues in Decentralizing education: what the reform in China tells us. *International Journal of Education Research 21*(8): 799–808.

China Statistical Yearbook 1985–1995. National Bureau of Statistics of China.

China Statistical Year Book. 2006. National Bureau of Statistics of China.

China Statistical Year Book. 2007. National Bureau of Statistics of China.

Cremin, Lawrence. 1951. *The American common school: An historic conception.* New York: Teachers College Press.

Downey, Douglas B. 2008. Black/white differences in school performance: The oppositional culture explanation. *Annual Review of Sociology 34*: 107–126.

Downey, Douglas B., Paul von Hippel, and Beckett Broh. 2004. Are schools the great equalizer? Cognitive inequality during the summer months and the school year. *American Sociological Review 69*: 613–635.

Fish, I. S. 2010. School of hard knocks: China's Ivy League is no place for peasants. *Newsweek,* August 21, 2010. http://www.newsweek.com/2010/08/21/the-rural-poor-are-shut-out-of-china-s-top-schools.html.

Fleisher, B. M., H. Li, S. Li, and X. Wang. 2004. *Sorting, selection, and transformation of the return to college education in China.* IZA Discussion Paper No. 1446. Bonn, Germany.

Freeman, Richard B. 2009. *What does global expansion of higher education mean for the U.S?* NBER Working Paper #14962. Cambridge, MA, USA.

Goldin, C., L. F. Katz, and I. Kuziemko. 2006. The homecoming of American college women: The reversal of the college gender gap. *Journal of Economic Perspective 20*(4): 133–156.

Halsey, A. H., A. Heath, and J. M. Ridge. 1980. *Origins and destinations: Family, class and education in modern Britain.* Oxford: Oxford University Press.

Hout, Michael. 2004. Maximally maintained inequality revisited: Irish educational mobility in comparative perspective. In *Changing Ireland, 1989–2003,* eds. Maire NicGhiolla Phadraig and Elizabeth Hilliard. Dublin: Liffey Press.

Hout, Michael. 2006. Maximally maintained inequality and essentially maintained inequality: Crossnational comparisons. *Sociological Theory and Methods* 21(2): 237–252.

Jacob, W. J. 2006. Social justice in Chinese higher education: Regional issues of equity and access. *International Review of Education* 52: 149–169.

Lewin, K., A. Little, H. Xu, and J. Zheng. 1994. *Educational innovation in China: Tracing the impact of the 1985 reform.* Harlow, UK: Longman.

Liu, Jingming. 2004. *Chinese education in the era of social transformation* (in Chinese). Shenyang: Liaoning Education Press.

Ma, Luting. 2009. A review of the development of higher education in China in the past 60 years and a projection (in Chinese). *Beijing Education* 10: 4–9.

Mare, Robert D. 1981. Change and Stability in Educational Stratification. *American Sociological Review* 46: 72–87.

Min, Weifang, 2006. Historical perspectives and contemporary challenges: The case of Chinese universities. Center on Chinese Education, Teacher's College at Columbia University. Available at http://www.tc.columbia.edu/centers/coce/pdf_files/c8.pdf

Ministry of Education of the People's Republic of China. 2002. http://www.moe.edu.cn/publicfiles/business/htmlfiles/moe/moe_568/index.html.

Parish, William L. 1984. Destratification in China. In *Class and social stratification in post-revolution China*, ed. James L. Watson, 84–120. New York: Cambridge University Press.

Powell, Troy A., and Claudia Buchmann. 2002. Racial inequality of occupational status in South Africa: The effect of local opportunity structures on occupational outcomes. Paper presented at the International Sociological Association Research Committee on Stratification (RC28) Conference, April 2002, Oxford, UK.

Raftery, Adrian E., and Michael Hout. 1985. Does Irish education approach the meritocratic ideal? *Economic and Social Review* 16: 115–140.

Raftery, Adrian E., and Michael Hout. 1993. Maximally maintained inequality: Expansion, reform, and opportunity in Irish education. *Sociology of Education* 66: 41–62.

Robert, Dexter. 2010. A dearth of work for China's college grads. *Bloomberg Businessweek Magazine,* http://www.businessweek.com/magazine/content/10_37/b4194008546907.htm (accessed September 1, 2012).

Ru, X., Lu Xueyi, and Li Peilin. 2005. *Analysis and forecast on China's social development: 2006.* Beijing: Social Sciences Academic Press.

Shavit, Yossi, and Hans-Peter Blossfeld, eds. 1993. *Persistent inequalities: A comparative study of educational attainment in thirteen countries.* Boulder, CO: Westview Press.

Smith, Herbert L., and P. P. L. Cheung. 1986. Trends in the effects of family background on educational attainment in the Philippines. *American Journal of Sociology* 91(6): 1387–1408.

Tam, Tony, and Harry B. G. Ganzeboom. 2009. Is persistent inequality a mirage? Educational opportunity over the long haul in 13 societies. Paper presented at the International Sociological Association (ISA) Research Committee 28 (RC-28) on Social Stratification and Mobility, Spring 2009 Meeting, Beijing, China.

Treiman, D. J., Matthew McKeever, and Eva M. Fodor. 1996. Racial differences in occupational status and income in South Africa, 1980 and 1991. *Demography* 33: 111–132.

Trow, Martin. 1973. Problems in the transition from elite to mass higher education. In *Policies for higher education, conference on future structures of post-secondary education*, 63. Paris: OECD.

Tsang, M. 2000. Education and national development in China since 1949: Oscillating policies and enduring dilemmas. In *China Review*, eds. Lau Chung-Ming and Jianfa Shen, 579–618. Hong Kong: Chinese University Press.

Tsang, M., and Y. Ding. 1992. Expansion, efficiency, and economies of scale of higher education in China. *Higher Education Policy* 5(2): 61–66.

UNESCO, World Education Report, 2000. http://www.unesco.org/education/information/wer/index.htm

UNESCO. 2012. UNESCO Institute for Statistics. http://www.uis.unesco.org/literacy/Pages/default.aspx?SPSLanguage=EN (accessed July 6, 2012).

Walters, S., and K. Watters. 2000. Adult education in southern Africa in the last twenty years. *International Journal for Lifelong Education* 20(1–2): 100–113.

Winship, C., and R. D. Mare. 1981. Change and stability in educational stratification. *American Sociological Review* 46: 72–87.

Whyte, Martin King, and William L. Parish. 1984. *Urban Life in Contemporary China*. Chicago: University of Chicago Press.

World Bank. 1997. *China: Management and Finance of Higher Education*. Washington DC: Author.

Wu, Yuxiao. 2008. Cultural capital, the state, and educational inequality in China, 1949–1996. *Sociological Perspectives* 51: 201–227.

Zhang, Yu-Lin, and Liu Bao-Jun. 2005. Social professional classes and higher education opportunities: A study on the distribution of a scarce social capital (in Chinese). *Journal of Beijing Normal University (Social Science Edition)* 3::25–31.

Zhou, Xiuegang, Phyllis Moen, and Nancy B. Tuma. 1998. Educational stratification in urban China, 1949–1994. *Sociology of Education* 71: 199–228.

# 14

# THE EVOLVING RESPONSE TO HIV/AIDS

Zunyou Wu, Sheena G. Sullivan, Yu Wang,
Mary Jane Rotheram, and Roger Detels

## INTRODUCTION

In March 2006, the State Council of the People's Republic of China promulgated the first legislation directly aimed at controlling HIV/AIDS: the AIDS Prevention and Control Regulations (State Council of P.R. China 2006b). These regulations, together with the Five-Year Action Plan to Control HIV/AIDS (2006–2010) (State Council of P.R. China 2006a), were an important step in the development of government policy related to the care and prevention of HIV/AIDS. Although bold, these regulations were passed more than 20 years after the first case of HIV infection was identified. The development of a coherent policy was the result of a long and unsystematic process that involved initial missteps, considerable domestic and international education, debate, iterative trial-and-error learning, and scientific studies. The new legislation resulted from communication and coordination among many agencies, including administrators, service providers, politicians, the scientific community, and policymakers. In this chapter, we describe the influence of scientific studies and other factors on the development of HIV/AIDS policy in China and provide a timeline of important milestones in the development of the current policy (Figure 14.1). This review is intended as a general overview of progress in China and does not attempt to provide a detailed account of province-to-province variation in the evolution and implementation of HIV prevention and control strategies. Originally published in 2007 (Wu et al., 2007), this review has been updated to include recent developments—which demonstrate the Chinese government's continued commitment to HIV/AIDS—and to reflect on

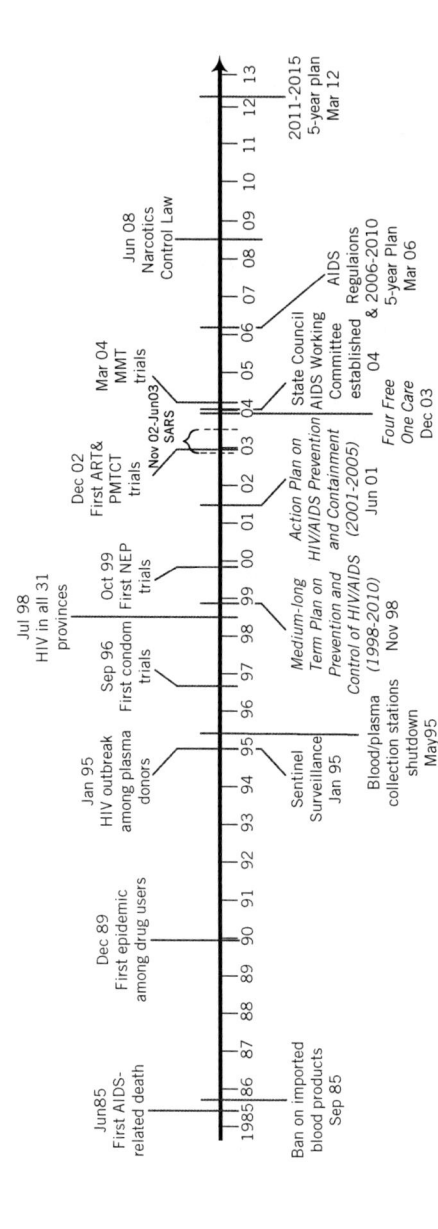

**Figure 14.1.** Timeline of Significant Events in China's HIV/AIDS Policy Development, 1985–2011. ART = antiretroviral therapy; MMT = methadone maintenance treatment; NEP = needle exchange program; PMTCT = prevention of mother-to-child transmission

## OVERVIEW OF THE EPIDEMIC

China's first AIDS case was identified in 1985 in a dying tourist (Settle 2003). In 1989, the first indigenous cases were reported as an outbreak among 146 infected heroin users in Yunnan Province, near China's southwest border (Ma, Li, and Zhang 1990). Between 1989 and the mid-1990s, HIV steadily spread from Yunnan into neighboring areas and along the major drug trafficking routes, then from injecting drug users (IDUs) to their sexual partners and children. In the mid-1990s, the occurrence of a second major outbreak in commercial plasma donors in the east-central provinces became apparent. Plasma donors were paid to donate blood, the plasma was removed, then the red blood cells were reinfused to prevent anemia. Reuse of tubing and mixing during collection and reinfusion led to thousands of new infections (Wu, Rou, and Detels 2001; Zhuang et al. 2003). At the same time, HIV was also spreading through sexual transmission. By 1998, HIV had reached all 31 provinces and was in a phase of exponential growth (Figure 14.2) (State Council AIDS Working Committee Office and UN Theme Group on HIV/AIDS in China 2004), which by 2011 had culminated in an estimated 780,000 infections, including 154,000 AIDS patients (Ministry of Health of the People's Republic of China 2012).

### Early Control Strategies

Initially, the Chinese government focused its preventive strategies on stopping HIV from entering the country. Regulations were introduced requiring foreigners who intended to stay one year or more and Chinese residents returning from

the goals of the 2006 Action Plan, as well as the plans set out in the AIDS Action Plan for the 12th Five-Year Program period (2011–2015) released in March 2012.

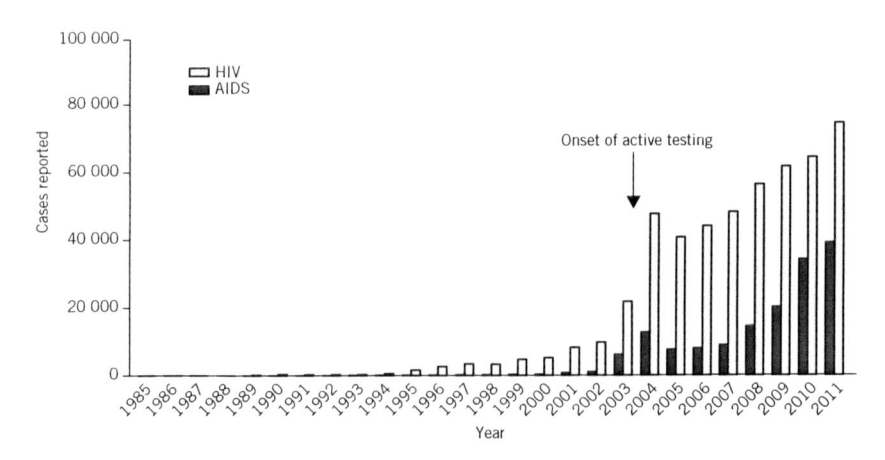

**Figure 14.2.** Reported HIV/AIDS Cases by Year, 1985–2011

overseas to have an HIV test (National People's Congress Standing Committee 1985a, 1985b; Frontier Health and Quarantine Law of the People's Republic of China 1988). All imported blood products were banned (Ministry of Health of China and General Office of Customs of China 1986; Ministry of Health of China 1986, 1987). There were attempts to stop transmission within the country as well—for example, laws against drug use (Standing Committee of the National People's Congress 1990) and prostitution (Standing Committee of the National People's Congress 1991) were strengthened, allowing authorities to isolate HIV-positive individuals (Frontier Health and Quarantine Law of the People's Republic of China 1988). In much the same way as in other countries, traditional public health methods of containment and isolation of infectious disease cases proved ineffective (Wu, Rou, and Cui 2004). Containment policies occurred in the context of rapid social and economic change, in which there were increases in drug use and changing sexual mixing patterns. These early policies did little to stop transmission of HIV; in fact, they probably promoted concealment of risk activities and made detection of HIV reservoirs more difficult (Li et al. 2003; Xue 2005; Husain 2004).

## Information and Communication Networks

The attitudes of government officials shifted substantially over time, a result of increasing exposure to scientific evidence that Chinese were becoming infected, the dramatic devastation caused by HIV/AIDS in other countries, and research in China that showed that HIV transmission could be reduced with targeted interventions.

As early as the mid-1990s, Chinese officials began to organize study tours to learn from the successes and failures of other countries in combating HIV/AIDS and to bring back information about strategies for HIV/AIDS control that could be adapted for China. Tour groups, including officials from the Ministries of Health, Public Security, Justice, Education and Finance, Commissions of Development and Reform, Population and Family Planning, as well as law- and policy-makers from the State Council, visited many places, including Australia, the United States, Brazil, Thailand, Europe, and Africa. These tours provided an opportunity for officials to learn from their counterparts in other countries, as well as promoting relationships among different Chinese government sectors that participated in the study tours.

Workshops that involved key government agencies were also held within China to further foster cross-sector communications. The organization of Chinese government services is traditionally hierarchical and departmentalized, not directly cultivating cooperation and collaboration across sectors. This tradition made the organization of multifaceted responses appropriate for HIV/AIDS control difficult. The WHO Global Programme on AIDS and subsequently UNAIDS, as well as other UN agencies in Asia and the Pacific, such as the UN Drug Control Programme (now the UN Office of Drugs and Crime [UNODC]), had played important roles in working with the government of China to organize and facilitate cross-sector discussions.

One workshop in particular was pivotal in pushing policies to support interventions targeting high-risk groups in China. Held in 1997 and organized by the Chinese Academy of Preventive Medicine (renamed the Chinese Center for Disease Control and Prevention [CDC] in 2002) and the University of California at Los Angeles, the workshop drew together scholars from sociology, ethics, public health, and education, as well as government officials and representatives of international agencies such as the WHO, UN, and World Bank. This workshop was the first open discussion of evidence-based but controversial intervention strategies that targeted those at high risk for HIV infection who were also highly stigmatized—for example, sex workers, IDUs, and men who have sex with men (MSM). Although controversial—pitting scientific, evidence-based prevention approaches against conservative, moralistic attitudes—the consensus acknowledged the possible benefit of implementing new prevention strategies.

Members of these various workshops and study tours have been responsible for identifying effective strategies that have increasingly been at the forefront of HIV control policy in China. They have also contributed to the development of strategic documents, including the Medium-and Long-Term Strategic Plan for HIV/AIDS (1998–2010) (Ministry of Health et al. 1998), the various Action Plans on HIV/AIDS Prevention and Containment and the AIDS Regulations (State Council of P.R. China 2006b). Other key documents warned of the potential epidemic in China and might have influenced the attitudes of policymakers. *China's Titanic Peril*, published by the UN in 2002, made the unsubstantiated prediction that China could have 10 million HIV-infected persons by 2010, a figure that had been repeatedly misused in discussions of China's HIV future. *A Joint Assessment of HIV/AIDS Prevention, Treatment and Care in China,* developed jointly by the State Council AIDS Working Committee Office and the UN Theme Group on HIV/AIDS in China (2004), estimated that China had 840,000 people living with HIV/AIDS (PLHA). This figure was revised down to 650,000 in 2005 in light of more representative data collection and more appropriate estimation methods (Ministry of Health of China, UNAIDS, and WHO 2005). Although this figure represented a prevalence of about 0.05 percent, it was substantially higher than previous government estimates (300,000 in State Council of P.R. China 1998) and provided the impetus for the immediate scaling up of prevention and control strategies.

## SCIENTIFIC EVIDENCE FOR INNOVATIVE POLICIES

Concurrent with educational activities and network building for government officials, Chinese researchers identified the key risk groups, documented and predicted the course of the epidemic, observed successful programs in other countries, and tested the effectiveness of behavioral interventions. HIV-related research projects were conducted by universities, hospitals, and community agencies, both independently and as collaborative projects with other domestic and international institutions. Most research and surveillance commissioned by the Chinese government is conducted by the National Center for AIDS/STD Control and Prevention (NCAIDS) at the China CDC. At the local level, almost all HIV research and intervention—whether conducted by the China CDC or other research organizations—is conducted in collaboration with provincial and county CDCs, township hospitals, and village health workers. Results from research initiated by China CDC administrators, particularly that commissioned by the Ministry of Health, are diffused and implemented faster than would be results from research done outside the existing government structure.

## Reduction of Transmission via Injecting Drug Use

Drug use was the main driver of the epidemic until 2006, when it was superseded by sexual transmission. As of the end of 2011, drug use was thought to account for 28 percent of infections (Ministry of Health of the People's Republic of China 2012). Ministry of Public Security data suggest that the number of registered drug users has risen steadily from 70,000 in 1990 to 1.16 million in 2006 (NNCC 2006) and 1.34 million in 2009 (UNODC, UNAIDS 2011). The total number, including unregistered drug users, is thought to be much higher. There are no recent estimates, and those last made suggested 3.5 million (Kulsudjarit 2004), while the UNODC World Drug Report estimated that in 2005, 0.3 percent of the 16–64-year-old population (i.e., 2.45 million people) were opiate abusers (UNODC 2012). The most commonly used drug is heroin, with 69 percent of drug users registered as heroin users in 2011 (UNODC 2012). Amphetamines have become more common, particularly in urban areas (UNODC 2012). Many opiate users begin heroin use by smoking, but later find it more cost-effective to inject because of the stronger effect gained from injecting a smaller amount. Sharing injection equipment is common (Yap et al. 2002).

National policymakers shifted their position in the mid-2000s and publicly acknowledged the extent and pattern of increasing drug use, which has led to a rapid increase in treatment options for drug users. The 1990 Regulations on the Prohibition Against Narcotics (Standing Committee of the National People's Congress 1990) had stipulated a three-tier system of increasing duration and severity of punishments for drug users. First-time offenders were either fined or sent for short-term voluntary detoxification (Zhao et al. 2004; Qian et al. 2006). Relapsing patients were sent for compulsory rehabilitation for three to six months. Those with multiple relapses were detained in a reeducation-through-labour center for one to three years. In reality, implementation of this policy varied enormously between administrative units, and the relapse rate was extremely high (Humeniuk and Ali 2005; H. Liu, Grusky et al. 2006; Zou 2002).

The government has since taken a new stance toward treatment of drug users. In June 2008 it passed the Narcotics Control Law (People's Republic of China 2008), which has revised the treatment process for drug use and now requires drug users to undergo up to three years of community-based detoxification—including methadone maintenance treatment (MMT), if available—and to be provided with vocational training and employment assistance. This law abolishes the use of reeducation-through-labour treatment and compulsory detoxification; however, drug users who fail to comply with community-based treatment can be interned in "direct forced isolation treatment" for one to three years. The new drug policy recognizes drug addiction as a chronic brain disease that requires treatment (Y. Liu et al. 2010). This shift of attitude toward harm reduction, rather than harsh penalties to control drug use, has evolved from increasing recognition that the previous punitive system was failing to adequately curb the drug use epidemic, amid growing evidence from within China that harm reduction strategies, such as MMT and needle exchange programs (NEPS) were able to yield more positive results.

### Needle Social Marketing and Needle Exchange Programs

Needle exchange programs are not a strategy officially sanctioned by the Ministry for Public Security, since such strategies appear to condone drug use. Thus, when this strategy was first introduced it was called needle social marketing—increasing the commercial availability and accessibility of needles in combination with health education about safe injecting practices and, in some cases, provision of free needles (Yap et al. 2002). Since 2001, the State Council has officially advocated needle social marketing as an HIV prevention measure (Ministry of Health 2001). Evidence from research and study tours to countries such as Australia (Bowtell 2006) that run successful needle exchange programs prompted the Ministry of Health to support the first such programs in Yunnan Province and Guangxi Zhuang Autonomous Region in 1999. In 2000–2002, a larger intervention trial of NEPs was conducted in four counties of Guangdong Province and Guangxi, funded by the World AIDS Foundation. Cross-sectional data gathered at follow-up indicated that participants in intervention communities were almost three times less likely to have shared needles in the past month than those in control communities (OR = 0.36; 95 percent CI = 0.25–0.52). Furthermore, rates of infection with hepatitis C virus were lower in the intervention arm than in the control arm (51 percent versus 84 percent, $p = 0.001$) as were HIV rates, although they did not reach statistical significance (18 percent versus 24 percent, $p = 0.391$) (Wu 2002).

The results of the trial were used to develop national policy guidelines in 2002, and needle exchange programs have been included in the second Five-Year Action Plan. The program has been substantially scaled up from 93 sites in 2002 to 913 sites in 19 provinces by the end of 2011, though the number of active sites may vary from year to year (Ministry of Health of the People's Republic of

China 2010, 2012). The scale-up has been focused in rural areas, and in many places additional services are offered to IDUs, including condom distribution, voluntary counseling and testing, antiretroviral therapy, and educational information about drug use and HIV (Liu 2006). Coverage has improved, but has suffered recent setbacks: the proportion of drug users able to access sterile injection equipment the last time they injected was reported at 66 percent in 2011, down from 73 percent in 2010 (Ministry of Health of the People's Republic of China 2012). Needle exchange programs remain controversial and are not explicitly mentioned in the 12th Action Plan.

## Methadone Maintenance Treatment Programs

A large body of international research has demonstrated the efficacy of methadone maintenance treatment (MMT) programs for the treatment of drug addiction and subsequent reduction in HIV risk behaviors (Sullivan et al. 2005; Gossop et al. 2002; Gibson, Flynn, and McCarthy 1999; Marsch 1998). Acknowledging this evidence, the Chinese government called for such practices to mitigate HIV transmission in 2001 (State Council of P.R. China 2001). A plan was developed to trial methadone maintenance treatment, under the governance of the Ministries of Health and Public Security and the State Food and Drug Administration. Technical and clinical support were provided by a secretariat based within the National Center for AIDS/STD Prevention and Control and the Yunnan Institute for Drug Abuse. Between March and June 2004, eight pilot clinics were opened in five provinces (Wu 2004, 2005). Inclusion in the program required: (1) several failed attempts to quit the use of heroin; (2) at least two terms in a detoxification center; (3) age of at least 20 years; (4) being a registered local resident of the area in which the clinic is located; and (5) being of good civil character. Those testing HIV positive needed only to fulfill criteria 4 and 5. To monitor the progress of the clinics, demographic, medical, drug use, and other information about the patients were collected. These data were evaluated at 3, 6, and 12 months and indicated substantial reductions in heroin use, drug-related crime, and unemployment among the clients who stayed in the program.

Based on these successes, the pilot was expanded to reach 128 clinics by the middle of 2006, at which point the 2006–2010 Action Plan (State Council of P.R. China 2006a) was issued, calling for the widespread expansion of the program. At the same time, a revised implementation protocol (Secretariat of the National Working Group for Community-Based Methadone Maintenance Treatment 2006) was developed, which relaxed eligibility and exclusion criteria to encourage greater access. A rapid expansion of the program began, which has culminated in 738 clinics being operational, serving more than 140,000 clients by the end of 2011 (344,000 cumulative clients) (Ministry of Health of the People's Republic of China 2012). Although this falls short of the targets set out in the 2006–2010 Action Plan of having methadone available to no less than 40 percent and 70 percent of drug users by the end of 2007 and 2010, respectively (Objective 6)

(State Council of P.R. China 2006a), it represents a significant achievement for supporters of harm reduction in China. Services offered at the clinics have been broadened, and some now also provide HIV and hepatitis testing, antiretroviral therapy to eligible AIDS patients, group activities, and skills training for employment. The use of methadone maintenance treatment has been incorporated into the new Narcotics Control Law (People's Republic of China 2008) signifying the now strong support for the program from the Ministry of Public Security. The program is not without problems, however, and poor retention remains a critical challenge (Sullivan 2011).

## Sexual Transmission

Until 2006, drug users accounted for most known HIV infections (34 percent). Sexual transmission, however, has rapidly overtaken drug use as the primary mode of infection, escalating from 33 percent of infections in 2006 to 76 percent by 2011, as well as comprising 82 percent of new infections in 2011. Overall, sexually transmitted infections represent 64 percent of estimated cases (46 percent through heterosexual sex and 17 percent among men who have sex with men) (Ministry of Health of the People's Republic of China, 2012). As with drug use, sexuality is not openly discussed and is therefore not easily targeted by health promotion campaigns, nor has it traditionally been taught in schools, although this is changing (Cai et al. 2008). Even among university students, levels of AIDS knowledge and risk perception are alarmingly low (Zhang et al. 2004; Li et al. 2004). On the other hand, attitudes toward sex are becoming increasingly more liberal, and premarital, extramarital, and same-sex sex are becoming more common (Zhou et al. 2009; Zhang et al. 1999; Chen et al. 2000). Although they are widely available, condoms are rarely used (F. Y. Wong et al. 2009; Yang et al. 2005).

## Commercial Sex Work

Commercial sex work is illegal in China; hence, brothels are illegal, and commercial sex workers operate out of entertainment establishments (e.g., karaoke bars), hotels, hair-dressing salons, or on the street. The traditional strategy for controlling HIV transmission through sex work has been development of stricter laws to prevent the risk behaviors (Standing Committee of the National People's Congress 1991), accompanied by raids on suspected sex establishments by public security officials. Those apprehended are subject to compulsory education on law and morality, testing and treatment for sexually transmitted diseases, and forced participation in productive labor (Husain 2004). Under the Frontier Health and Quarantine Law (Standing Committee of the National People's Congress 1987), those knowingly infected with HIV who continue to practice prostitution are subject to more severe penalties and criminal liability for creating a risk for spreading a quarantinable disease (Frontier Health and Quarantine Law of the People's Republic of China 1998; Gil et al. 1996). Detention ranges from six months to a maximum of five years for those sex workers who know they have a sexually transmitted disease (Hong 2010). Until recently, health education in this system was uncommon.

In 1996–1997, following the success seen in neighboring Thailand (AIDS Weekly Plus 1996), the China CDC conducted the first intervention projects to promote safer sex behaviors to prevent HIV and other sexually transmitted diseases among commercial sex workers working at entertainment establishments in Yunnan (Wu et al. 2007). These projects showed the feasibility of such programs, which included condom use to control the spread of HIV and other sexually transmitted diseases in commercial sex workers, and have been officially promoted since 1998 (Ministry of Health of China 1998). Between 1999 and 2001, the World AIDS Foundation supported a five-site trial of a behavioral intervention among commercial sex workers who worked in entertainment establishments (Rou et al. 2007). The intervention included condom promotion, establishment of clinics for sexually transmitted diseases to provide checkups, and outreach for health education and counseling. HIV-related knowledge improved substantially, and the rates of bacterial sexually transmitted diseases fell. The rate of condom use at last intercourse increased from 55 percent to 68 percent, and fewer commercial sex workers agreed to sex without a condom when requested to by a client who offered more money (40 percent down to 21 percent). The prevalence of gonorrhea fell from 26 percent at baseline to 4.4 percent after intervention, and the prevalence of chlamydia dropped from 41 percent to 26 percent.

The findings from this trial were used to draft national guidelines for interventions among sex workers in China. The provision of condoms at entertainment establishments is now an official requirement under the AIDS Regulations, and the 12th Action Plan will require 95 percent of hotels to have condoms or condom vending machines by 2015. Condom promotion and HIV education campaigns targeting youth and migrant workers have also been scaled up, with the aim of reaching 80 percent of target groups and 90 percent of high-risk groups. In 2011, 81 percent of sex workers surveyed had been reached by prevention programs, and 87 percent reported using condoms with their most recent client, but only 38 percent reported having had an HIV test in the last month (Ministry of Health of the People's Republic of China 2012).

## Men Who Have Sex with Men

Unlike prostitution and drug use, homosexuality has never been banned in China, but it was listed as a psychiatric disorder until 2001, and public acts of homosexual sex are punishable as hooliganism. Although it is becoming increasingly tolerated in the cities, in general, homosexuality is highly stigmatized, and social pressure to marry and have a family is enormous (Choi et al. 2003). As a result, many men who have sex with men conceal their sexual orientation and many marry, while continuing to engage in sex with other men, thereby putting their wives and other partners at risk (H. Liu, Yang, et al. 2006; Qian, Vermund, and Wang 2005; Choi et al. 2004). Behavioral surveys suggest low levels of HIV knowledge, perceived risk, and testing, and high rates of sexually transmitted diseases (Jiang et al. 2006; W. C. Wong et al. 2006; Choi et al. 2006).

The government had initiated few interventions for men who have sex with men, leaving such programs to advocacy groups, nongovernmental organizations (NGOs), and researchers (Zhang and Chu 2005). However, the proportion of new HIV infections estimated to occur among men who have sex with men has risen considerably—from 7 percent in 2005 to 12 percent in 2007 (State Council AIDS Working Committee Office and UN Theme Group on HIV/AIDS in China 2007), 32 percent in 2009, and 42 percent in 2011—making men who have sex with men a key high-risk group (Ministry of Health of the People's Republic of China 2010, 2012). The number of sentinel surveillance sites focused on this group has increased from 3 sites in 2005 to 9 sites in 2007 to 56 sites in 2009. To better understand the epidemic among men who have sex with men, the government commissioned a nationwide survey in 61 cities, the preliminary results of which indicated that the prevalence of HIV, syphilis, and herpes simplex virus-2 were all high at 9 percent, 11 percent, and 11 percent, respectively (Xu et al. 2010). Guidelines for conducting interventions among men who have sex with men have been developed, and collaborative structures have been established between government agencies and NGOs working in this field. Various programs have been conducted, including condom promotion, counseling and testing, peer education, sexually transmitted infection services, and follow-up and outreach (State Council AIDS Working Committee Office and UN Theme Group on HIV/AIDS in China 2007). These programs had reached 77 percent of 37,190 men surveyed in 2011, while the percentage of MSM who had been tested for HIV and who were aware of their result had increased from 33 percent in 2007 to 36 percent in 2009 to 50 percent in 2011 (Ministry of Health of the People's Republic of China 2010, 2012).

## INFLUENTIAL FORCES

### Changes in Government

In 2003, a new administration, led by President Hu Jintao, Premier Wen Jiabao, and Vice Premier and Health Minister Wu Yi, substantially accelerated the commitment to and implementation of evidence-based HIV policies. Under this administration, a number of initiatives have been introduced: the China Comprehensive AIDS Response (China CARES), which assists 127 high prevalence counties in providing care and support to PLHA; the "Four Free and One Care" policy (see Box 14.1); and the formation of a State Council AIDS Working Committee responsible for developing a comprehensive policy framework (e.g., the Notice on Strengthening HIV/AIDS Prevention and Control) (State Council AIDS Working

## Box 14.1. "Four Free and One Care" Policy for AIDS Control

1. Free ARV drugs to AIDS patients who are rural residents or people without insurance living in urban areas;
2. Free voluntary counseling and testing (VCT);
3. Free drugs to HIV-infected pregnant women to prevent mother-to-child transmission, and HIV testing of newborn babies;
4. Free schooling for AIDS orphans;
5. Care and economic assistance to the households of people living with HIV/AIDS.

Committee Office and UN Theme group on HIV/AIDS in China 2004). New policies, supported by expanding budgets, have been introduced (Figure 14.3), permitting a substantial acceleration in program development, testing, and scale-up.

## Media

The media have exerted substantial influence over the timing and course of HIV control in China by bringing news of HIV to the attention of the public, administrators, and policymakers. In 1996, the *Southern Weekend* newspaper ran a front-page story and devoted another two pages to AIDS in China. This coverage was the first time that any comprehensive exposure of the HIV/AIDS epidemic in China had been published by the Chinese press. From 1999, the international and subsequently the national media reported on the thousands of infected plasma donors in Henan and neighboring provinces who lacked access to services. Although the government had acted quickly when the tragedy

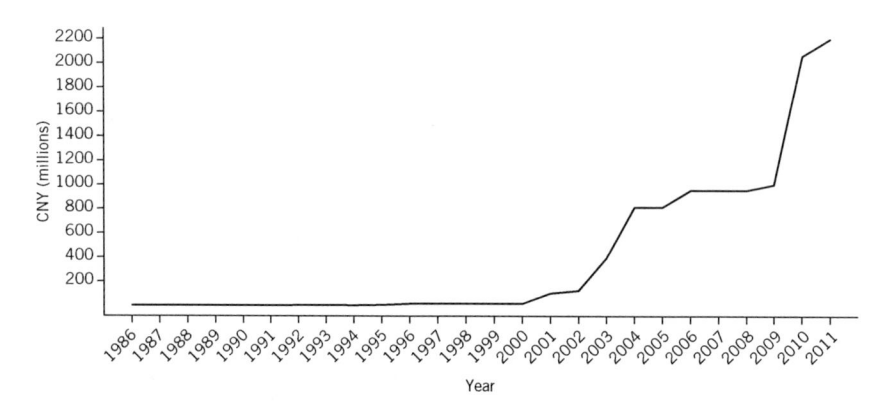

**Figure 14.3.** Chinese Central Government Spending on HIV/AIDS by Year, 1985–2011. (Funding increased substantially in 2011 to meet the shortfall from reduced Global Fund monies.). CNY = Chinese Yuan

became apparent in 1995 by shutting down collection stations and, later, introducing new laws and regulations on the collection and management of blood and blood products (Wu, Rou, and Detels 2001; Standing Committee of the National People's Congress 1998; State Council of P.R. China 1996), the provision of HIV testing, prevention, and care for donors in the local areas was slower. It was stimulated only by the attention of the media to the plight of the infected plasma donors. Since these initial reports, the HIV/AIDS situation in China has received a great deal of attention from the local and international media.

### Severe Acute Respiratory Syndrome

The challenge of managing the severe acute respiratory syndrome (SARS) epidemic in 2003 is often credited with further motivating the government to take aggressive policy action on HIV-related issues. SARS showed not only how infectious diseases could threaten economic and social stability but also the effect of China's policies on international health problems (Xue 2005). Policymakers announced a change of focus from purely economic goals to increasing the focus on health and social well-being and, as a result, increased support for public health agencies. In controlling SARS, contact between the government and international agencies such as the WHO, the UN, and the U.S. Centers for Disease Control and Prevention was essential and further stimulated stronger international collaboration for HIV/AIDS prevention and treatment. Intervention strategies necessary for SARS control have been translated into HIV/AIDS prevention—for example, real-time electronic case reporting.

## PROGRAM SCALE-UP

### Case Finding

The first step in understanding the extent of an epidemic is having the ability to identify cases. National sentinel surveillance has been implemented since 1995 but was initially limited to high-risk areas and to STD clinic attendees, sex workers, drug users, and long-distance truck drivers (Sun et al. 2007). Surveillance has gradually been expanded to 1,888 sites, and now also includes male migrants, young students, pregnant women, and men who have sex with men.

Around the same time, voluntary testing and counseling services were made available in some communities but, even when available, were rarely utilized. Reluctance to seek HIV testing was likely due to multiple causes, for example, cost, inaccessibility of services, absence of any treatment, lack of publicity or advocacy for testing, low or no perceived risk, and stigma associated with using testing services (Choi et al 2006; UNAIDS 2003; Herek 1999; Wu et al. 2005). In 2003, the government began addressing the structural barriers. The high cost was addressed by making free HIV testing available for the poor (Koralage 2004), and later under the Four Free and One Care policy, antiretroviral treatment was made freely available for all through the Chinese health system. By the end of 2011, the number of screening laboratories had expanded to 14,305, including 339 laboratories able to do confirmatory HIV tests. Free HIV testing has been made available and has been expanded from 365 counties in 15 provinces in 2002 to all counties and 3,037 sites in 2006 and to 14,571 sites in 2011 (Ministry of Health of the People's Republic of China 2012). The AIDS Regulations have introduced penalties for health units not providing free testing on request.

The rapid expansion of testing infrastructure has largely been prompted by the introduction of provider-initiated routine testing campaigns to identify infected individuals and put them in contact with treatment services. Client-initiated testing was failing to identify the majority of infected individuals, so campaigns to screen high-risk groups, including drug users, commercial sex workers, prisoners, and former plasma donors, were commissioned to link patients to treatment services (Wu et al. 2006). The campaigns resulted in a substantial increase in the number of individuals who knew their HIV status, with an additional 60,000 PLHA identified. This in part explains the rapid rise in reported HIV cases in the early twenty-first century (see Figure 14.2). However, even with this effort, only 326,000 of the estimated 740,000 PLHA living in China at the end of 2009 (Ministry of Health of the People's Republic of China 2010) had been identified, and many were tested late—13,227 of the 68,249 newly tested PLHA had AIDS in 2009 (National Center for AIDS/STD Control and Prevention 2010). Routine testing among high-risk groups continues.

## Educating the Public

Testing campaigns were accompanied by community-level social marketing to raise HIV awareness and to reduce HIV-related stigma (Wu et al. 2006). The AIDS Regulations have outlined requirements for local governments at the county level and above, as well as for educational establishments, businesses, health providers, customs and border control, and the media to promote HIV/AIDS education and social marketing. A number of schools now include sex, drug, and HIV education for their pupils, especially in high-risk areas, such as Yunnan, Guangxi, and Guangdong. Basic awareness among youth is around 88 percent (Ministry of Health of the People's Republic of China 2012).

An important part of HIV education is targeting behavior to reduce stigma toward PLHA. Stigma is well recognized as a major barrier to HIV control, because it prevents people from seeking services for testing and treatment, and discourages people from practicing safer behaviors (UNAIDS 2003; Malcolm et al. 1998; Yang et al. 2004). To address the issue, senior political figures have been involved in anti-discrimination campaigns and have publicly demonstrated that HIV cannot be transmitted through casual contact. For example, on World AIDS Day, December 1, 2003, Premier Wen Jiabao publicly shook hands with AIDS patients in Beijing Ditan Hospital (Watts 2003). The day before the 2004 World AIDS Day, President Hu Jintao and other senior government leaders visited AIDS patients and called for the elimination of bias against this group (China Daily 2004). During the Chinese New Year celebrations in 2005, Premier Wen Jiabao visited the homes of HIV-infected villagers in Henan Province. These actions had a tremendous impact on the general community and have now been backed up by policy changes. The AIDS Regulations have made it illegal to discriminate against people living with HIV/AIDS and their families in terms of their rights to schooling, employment, health services, and participation in community activities. Furthermore, the AIDS Regulations and the 2004 revision of the Law on the Prevention and Treatment of Infectious Disease include language to protect the identity and disease status of those with an infectious disease, with disciplinary action recommended for those individuals or institutions violating these laws. Although there had been language in previous regulations to protect the rights of people living with HIV/AIDS, these new laws provide them with a stronger basis from which to defend their rights. In mid-2010 a court agreed to hear China's first case of discrimination against a teacher who was denied employment because he is HIV-positive (BBC News 2010).

## Antiretroviral Treatment for Persons with AIDS

In 2001 and 2002, the number of AIDS patients being identified through treatment services began to increase. As many as 69,000 of these people were the rural poor who had been infected when they sold their blood and plasma in the mid-1990s and who were unable to access or afford much needed antiretroviral treatment (Ministry of Health of China, UNAIDS, and WHO 2005). Observing the successes in other nations, such as Brazil (Teixeira, Vitoria, and Barcarolo 2004), a free antiretroviral treatment program was piloted in late 2002 in Shangcai County, Henan Province, one of the most severely affected areas. Patients were provided with a combination of zidovudine (AZT) or didanosine (ddI) + lamivudine (3TC) + nevirapine (NVP). On the basis of the improved health status and survival of the initial cohort, the program was scaled up in early 2003, mainly through the China CARES program (Zhang et al. 2005).

The provision of free antiretroviral treatment to rural residents and the urban poor became policy in 2003 under the Four Free and One Care policy (see Box 14-1) (Watts 2003). The National HIV/AIDS Clinical Taskforce took the lead in establishing the program and set up a database to monitor it. As of the end of 2011, 126,448 patients (76 percent of those eligible) were being treated at one of 3,124 facilities, and retention rates were around 87 percent (Ministry of Health of the People's Republic of China, 2012). Research to inform further expansion and improvement of the program is ongoing, and it now includes pediatric care and drug resistance testing (Zhang, Haberer, Zhao, et al. 2007; Zhang, Au, et al. 2007). The first-line treatment regimen has suffered a high drop-out rate (at least 8 percent), primarily due to side effects, difficulty with adherence, and progression of the disease (Zhang et al. 2005). Moreover, the five-year treatment failure rate is around 50 percent, and drug resistance has been reported (Zhang,

Haberer, Wang, et al. 2007; Luo et al. 2009). Second-line treatment became available in 2007. Although this has alleviated some of the problems with the treatment programs, challenges remain.

## Prevention of Mother-to-Child Transmission

After reports of successful intervention in other developing countries (WHO Technical Consultation UNFPA/UNICEF/WHO/UNAIDS Inter-Agency Task Team on Mother-to-Child Transmission of HIV 2000), a feasibility trial of prevention of mother-to-child transmission was piloted in late 2002, concurrent with the antiretroviral treatment pilot, with financial and technical support from UNICEF. Mothers testing HIV-positive were offered counseling, the option of abortion or antiretroviral treatment, and, where available, cesarean delivery, to reduce the likelihood of mother-to-child transmission. Free formula milk for 12 months was provided for infants (Wu and Sullivan 2006).

Based on this pilot program, national guidelines were developed to guide prevention of mother-to-child transmission in the country. The provision of such services has been ratified by the AIDS Regulations. Services have been scaled up, prioritizing the most heavily affected areas first, to cover at least 90 percent of infected pregnant women by 2010 (State Council of P.R. China 2006a). However, this target was not reached, as only 74 percent of pregnant women received treatment to prevent mother-to-child transmission in 2010–2011 and 7 percent of children born to HIV-positive women in 2011 were infected (Ministry of Health of the People's Republic of China, 2012).

## Monitoring the Scale-up

With so many interventions being expanded at the same time, it became crucial to have a single reporting system for monitoring both the course of the epidemic and the response to it. Thus, a single monitoring and evaluation system was established, guided by a protocol, in 2007 (Mao et al. 2010). Provinces provide up-to-date information on the epidemic through online reporting. Targets are set annually for the roll-out of interventions, and this system permits evaluation of these targets.

## **CHALLENGES AHEAD**

China has now made impressive progress in the development and implementation of effective intervention strategies. The country is currently in a transition stage in its HIV policy development. It is increasingly adopting approaches that are based on scientific evidence and has encouraged the pilot testing of controversial methods of risk reduction, including methadone maintenance treatment, needle exchange programs, and the targeting of men who have sex with men and sex workers.

Although there has been considerable scale-up of programs, there have been issues with policy enforcement, timeliness and quality of services. China has a strong central government, but provincial and lower levels of government enjoy a great deal of autonomy, which has resulted in a mixed response and inconsistent enforcement of HIV/AIDS policy. For example, Yunnan Province has shown strong support for implementation and advocacy of harm-reduction strategies that reduce HIV transmission among its many drug users, whereas Henan Province had been slower to respond to the needs of former plasma donors in the early stages of the epidemic (Watts 2006). Moreover, the distribution of HIV in China is not even; it is concentrated in areas with high drug use (e.g., Yunnan, Guangxi, Xinjiang, Sichuan) and in areas where people were infected through unsafe blood/plasma donation (Henan, Anhui, Hebei, Shanxi and Hubei). Between provinces, the number of cases ranges dramatically, with, for example, less than 100 cases reported from Tibet and well over 50,000 in neighboring Yunnan (see Figure 14.4). In provinces with an extremely low prevalence, it can be difficult for officials to see the need for or cost-effectiveness of HIV prevention and control.

Conflicts of interest between departments, such as Health and Public Security, have also made coordination of services to reach high-risk groups that engage in illegal behavior difficult (Davis 2004). For example, despite greater support for services for sex workers and drug users, there continues to be a "Strike Hard" campaign against these groups, hindering prevention efforts. The central government has called for greater cooperation between relevant departments—including Public Security, Justice, Education, Civil Affairs, and Health—but implementation of this policy at the local level varies.

The problem is further exacerbated by inadequate resources and trained personnel. Many rural areas—where the majority of China's HIV-positive population reside—do not have the equipment needed to monitor patients' $CD4^+$ cell counts and viral load, or lack the skills or reagents to use it. Human resource capacity is a major constraint on China's ability to deliver HIV prevention and care. Many health workers and educators have poor HIV knowledge and hold their own biases and stigmas toward those at risk or infected with HIV (Wu et al. 1999; Hesketh et al. 2005; Li et al. 2006). A substantial proportion of the funds allocated to HIV prevention and control is being spent on establishing training centers and in building the capacity of health workers so that they can deliver better services. But many of those willing to work in rural areas do not have formal medical qualifications to begin with, which limits their abilities to understand the complexities of treating HIV patients (Yip 2006). Furthermore, health services rely heavily on user-fees, which often encourages health workers to perform additional, chargeable services, which many PLHA cannot afford (Zhang et al. 2006).

With an estimated 780,000 PLHA (0.06 percent) and an ever greater number of people at risk of infection, the government has embarked upon a formidable task. Providing accessible testing and treatment services not only requires financial resources but, in many cases, requires reorganization and supplementary funding of existing local health services infrastructure, especially in rural areas where most of China's HIV-positive individuals reside (Ministry of Health of China 2005). In particular, rural areas do not have adequately trained staff capable of providing effective treatment and prevention services, as well as the laboratory and clinical infrastructure necessary to monitor treatment. The problem of inadequate human resources is not limited to health departments—in rural areas, there are few adequately trained technical and management personnel at all levels and across all sectors. The combination of insufficiently trained staff, inadequate technical resources, and a largely remote, poorly educated, rural population represent a challenge to implementing effective programs.

A major step has been the government's promotion of involvement from nongovernmental organizations (NGOs), which has been reinforced in the 12th Action Plan. NGOs are a relatively new concept in China (China Daily 2006). Many of the larger domestic groups are actually government-funded, and those not affiliated with the government are required to go through a complicated registration procedure to be officially endorsed (He 2005). The presence of international NGOs is also increasing. The ability of NGOs to work with high-risk groups, especially those engaging in behaviors considered illegal or immoral, and to provide care and outreach where overstretched health services cannot has been recognized (Chen and Liao 2005) and has been a valuable tool in the response to the epidemic among men who have sex with men. However, Chinese NGOs still suffer from poor capacity, unstable funding, and difficulties with registration and legal status and can find it difficult to work with government agencies (Anna 2010; Chen 2001; Xu, Zeng, and Anderson 2005). The private sector has also been encouraged to undertake prevention and education activities (People's Daily 2005).

## CONCLUSION

What has allowed the mobilization of multiple sectors within China to address the control of HIV/AIDS? First, over a 15-year period, there was a long series of educational workshops, conferences, collaborative projects, and networking among members at multiple levels of the government and administrative structural hierarchies. At local, national, and international forums, officials from multiple sectors were able to meet each other, share a common knowledge base, and debate the appropriateness of different interventions. Personal relationships were formed that facilitated the consideration and examination of previously unrecognized policy options for detection, prevention, and care. In a non-linear process, a consensus slowly evolved, identifying policy options. Second, political officials, policymakers, administrators, and service providers

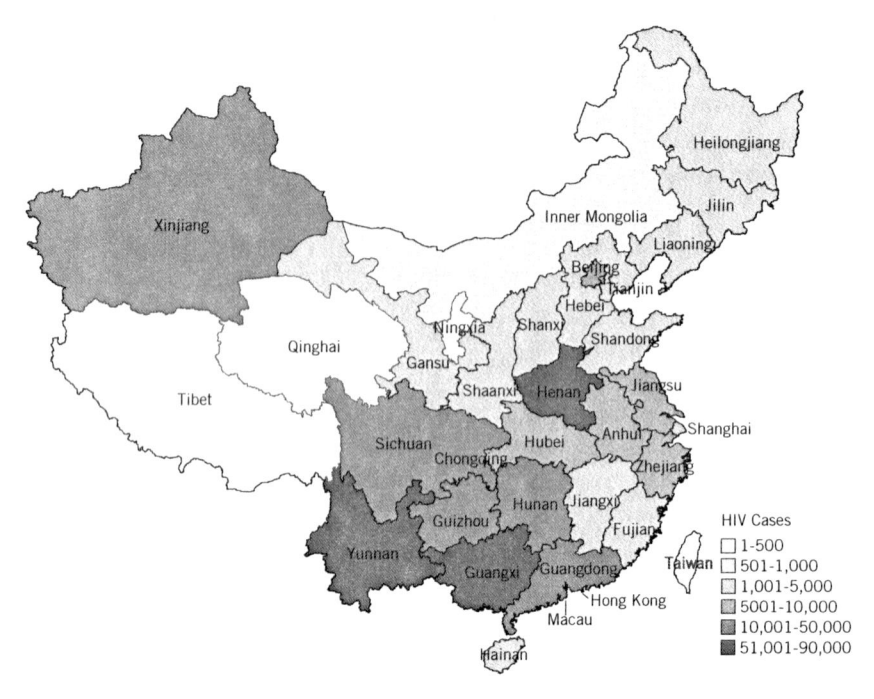

288  CHINESE SOCIAL POLICY IN A TIME OF TRANSITION

**Figure 14.4.** Cumulative Reported HIV Cases by Province, 1985–2011

were increasingly willing to recognize the relevance of a significant body of scientific research suggesting effective intervention strategies that could change the course of the epidemic. Third, major policy recommendations regarding behavioral interventions were preceded by small pilot projects that demonstrated feasibility or efficacy in those populations at highest risk. Fourth, once the evidence base was documented, both the policymakers and politicians publicly demonstrated their support for HIV prevention and care, as well as passing legislation to enforce and broadly disseminate health practices (e.g., routine HIV testing and access to care).

These processes occurred in a context of ongoing influences from the media and international donor agencies, with some contribution from advocacy groups within China. The SARS epidemic demonstrated the potentially disastrous effect of a fast-moving infectious disease and, simultaneously, allowed the HIV community to acquire new tools to fight the epidemic (e.g., real-time data collection of new cases). However, the mobilization of resources, scientific evidence, and administrative drive did not occur until there was enthusiastic political commitment. The pace of implementing innovative strategies for HIV detection, prevention, and care accelerated with the commitments made by the government of Hu Jintao, starting in 2003.

After a slow start and reluctance to recognize the existence of risk activities in its population and of the HIV epidemic, China has responded to international influences, media coverage and scientific evidence to take bold steps to control the epidemic, using scientifically validated strategies. The country has faced the challenge of scaling up these programs and of convincing all levels of government to implement these innovative strategies and policies. This vigorous response, incorporating research findings into policy formulation, can be informative to other countries facing similar challenges in responding to the HIV/AIDS epidemic.

## ACKNOWLEDGMENTS

We thank Wendy Aft for endlessly editing the many drafts of this manuscript, and Professor Zuo-Feng Zhang for helpful suggestions.

Reprinted from Wu, A., S. G. Sullivan, Y. Wang, M. J. Rotheram-Borus, and R. Detels. Evolution of China's response to HIV/AIDS. *The Lancet 369*: 679–690, Copyright (2007), with permission from Elsevier.

## CONFLICT OF INTEREST STATEMENTS

Prof. Zunyou Wu is the Director of the National Center for AIDS/STD Control and Prevention in the China CDC. Prof. Yu Wang is the Director of the China CDC. Both have been directly involved in HIV/AIDS research and policy development in China.

## REFERENCES

*AIDS Weekly Plus*. 1996. Thailand condom campaign reduced AIDS infections by fifty percent. August 19.
Anna, C. 2010. NGOs in China say threatened by new donor rules. *The Associated Press*. March 12.
BBC News. 2010. China court accepts first HIV job discrimination case. August 31.
Bowtell, W. 2006. Australia. In: T. Yamamoto and S. Itoh (Eds.), *Fighting a rising tide: The response to AIDS in East Asia*, 1st ed. pp. 19–52. Tokyo: Japan Center for International Exchange.
Cai, Y., H. Hong, R. Shi, X. Ye, G. Xu, S. Li, et al. 2008. Long-term follow-up study on peer-led school-based HIV/AIDS prevention among youths in Shanghai. *International Journal of STD & AIDS* 19(12): 848–850.
Chen, G. 2001. China's nongovernmental organizations: Status, government policies, and prospects for further development. *The International Journal of Not-for-Profit Law* 3(3). Available at http://www.icnl.org/research/journal/vol3iss3/art_2.htm (last accessed 18/3/2013).

Chen, H. T., and Q. Liao. 2005. A pilot study of the NGO-based relational intervention model for HIV prevention among drug users in China. *AIDS Education and Prevention* 17(6): 503–514.

Chen, X. S., X. D. Gong, G. J. Liang, and G. C. Zhang. 2000. Epidemiologic trends of sexually transmitted diseases in China. *Journal of the American Sexually Transmitted Diseases Association* 27(3): 138–142.

*China Daily*. 2004. Hu visits AIDS patients in Beijing. November 30.

*China Daily*. 2006. NGOs act as bridge between government and people. February 23.

Choi, K. H., D. R. Gibson, L. Han, and Y. Guo. 2004. High levels of unprotected sex with men and women among men who have sex with men: A potential bridge of HIV transmission in Beijing, China. *AIDS Education and Prevention* 16(1): 19–30.

Choi, K .H., H. Liu, Y. Guo, L. Han, J. S. Mandel, and G. W. Rutherford. 2003. Emerging HIV-1 epidemic in China in men who have sex with men. *The Lancet* 361 (9375): 2125–2126.

Choi, K. H., H. Lui, Y. Guo, L. Han, and J. S. Mandel. 2006. Lack of HIV testing and awareness of HIV infection among men who have sex with men, Beijing, China. *AIDS Education and Prevention* 18(1): 33–43.

Davis, S. 2004. Restrictions of AIDS Activists in China. *Human Rights Watch* 17(5): 1–57.

Frontier Health and Quarantine Law of the People's Republic of China. 1988.

Gibson, D. R., N. M. Flynn, and J. J. McCarthy. 1999. Effectiveness of methadone treatment in reducing HIV risk behavior and HIV seroconversion among injecting drug users. *AIDS* 13(14): 1807–1818.

Gil, V. E., M. S. Wang, A. F. Anderson, G. M. Lin, and Z. O. Wu. 1996. Prostitutes, prostitution and STD/HIV transmission in mainland China. *Social Science and Medicine* 42(1): 141–152.

Gossop, M., J. Marsden, D. Stewart, and S. Treacy. 2002. Reduced injection risk and sexual risk behaviors after drug misuse treatment: Results from the National Treatment Outcome Research Study. *AIDS Care* 14(1): 77–93.

He, Z. 2005. Helping NGOs develop strength. *China Daily*. May 28.

Herek, G. M. 1999. AIDS and stigma. *American Behavioral Scientist* 42(7): 1102–1112.

Hesketh, T., L. Duo, H. Li, and A. M. Tomkins. 2005. Attitudes to HIV and HIV testing in high prevalence areas of China: Informing the introduction of voluntary counselling and testing programmes. *Sexually Transmitted Infections* 81(2): 108–112.

Hong, H. (on behalf of the National Center for HIV/AIDS Prevention and Control). 2010. 2010 National Composite Policy Index (NCPI) report. Available at http://www.unaids.org/en/dataanalysis/knowyourresponse/ncpi/2010countries/china_2010_ncpi_en.pdf (accessed November 26, 2012). http://en.chinagate.cn/reports/2008-07/10/content_15989177.htm (accessed June 25, 2008).

Humeniuk, R., and R. Ali. 2005. The first methadone clinic in Beijing. *Drug and Alcohol Review* 24(3): 285–287.

Husain, L. 2004. *Policing AIDS in China: Official discourses, change, continuity, and unofficial voices.* Leeds East Asia Papers: 1991–2005, Series No.66. Department of East Asia Studies, University of Leeds, UK: Leeds East Asia Papers.

Jiang, J., N. Cao, J. Zhang, Q. Xia, X. Gong, H. Xue, et al. 2006. High prevalence of sexually transmitted diseases among men who have sex with men in Jiangsu Province, China. *Journal of the American Sexually Transmitted Diseases Association* 33(2): 118–123.

Koralage, N. 2004. China to offer free HIV testing and treatment. *British Medical Journal* 328(7446): 975.

Kulsudjarit, K. 2004. Drug problem in southeast and southwest Asia. *Annals of the New York Academy of Science* 1025: 446–457.

Li, X., C. Lin, Z. Gao, B. Stanton, X. Fang, Q. Yin, et al. 2004. HIV/AIDS knowledge and the implications for health promotion programs among Chinese college students: Geographic, gender and age differences. *Health Promotion International* 19(3): 345–356.

Li, L., C. Lin, Z. Wu, S. Wu, M. J. Rotherum-Borus, R. Detels, et al. 2007. Stigmatization and shame: Consequences of caring for HIV/AIDS patients in China. *AIDS Care* 19(2): 258–263.

Li, D., G. Xia, R. Qiu, J. Hamblin, and T. Yue. 2003. *Law, policies and regulations concerning HIV/AIDS prevention and containment: An assessment and recommendations.* Beijing: United Nations Development Programme.

Liu, B. 2006. *Needle exchange programs in China: Effectiveness and factors associated with operation in two provinces [MSc].* Beijing: Chinese Center for Disease Control and Prevention.

Liu, H., O. Grusky, Y. Zhu, and X. Li. 2006. Do drug users in China who frequently receive detoxification treatment change their risky drug use practices and sexual behavior? *Drug and Alcohol Dependence* 84(1): 114–121.

Liu, Y., J. Liang, C. Zhao, and W. Zhou. 2010. Looking for a solution for drug addiction in China: Exploring the challenges and opportunities in the way of China's new Drug Control Law. *International Journal of Drug Policy* 21(3): 149–154.

Liu, H., H. Yang, X. Li, N. Wang, H. Liu, B. Wang, et al. 2006. Men who have sex with men and human immunodeficiency virus/sexually transmitted disease control in China. *Sexually Transmitted Diseases* 33(2): 68–76.

Luo, M., H. Liu, K. Zhuang, L. Liu, B. Su, R. Yang, et al. 2009. Prevalence of drug-resistant HIV-1 in rural areas of Hubei province in the People's Republic of China. *Journal of Acquired Immune Deficiency Syndromes* 50(1): 1–8.

Ma, Y., Z. Z. Li, and K. X. Zhang. 1990. Identification of HIV infection among drug users in China. *Zhonghua Liu Xing Bing Xue Za Zhi* 11: 184–185.

Malcolm, A., P. Aggleton, M. Bronfman, J. Galvao, P. Mane, and J. Verrall. 1998. HIV-related stigmatization and discrimination: Its forms and contexts. *Critical Public Health* 8(4): 347–370.

Mao Y, Wu Z, Poundstone K, Wang C, Qin Q, Ma Y, et al. 2010. Development of a unified web-based national HIV/AIDS information system in China. *International Journal of Epidemiology* 39 Suppl 2: ii79–ii89.

Marsch, L. A. 1998. The efficacy of methadone maintenance interventions in reducing illicit opiate use, HIV risk behavior and criminality: A meta-analysis. *Addiction* 93(4): 515–532.

Ministry of Health of China and General Office of Customs of China. 1986. *Notice on banning importing factor III and other blood products.* Beijing: Ministry of Health.

Ministry of Health of China. 1987.. *Notice on strengthening management of imported blood products.* Beijing.

Ministry of Health of China. 1998. *Medium and long-term plan on prevention and control of HIV/AIDS 1998.* Beijing: Ministry of Health.

Ministry of Health of China. 2001. *Action plan on HIV/AIDS prevention and containment (2001–2005).* Beijing: Ministry of Health.

Ministry of Health of China. 2005. *Report on China's healthcare system and reform.* Beijing: Ministry of Health. August 2005.

Ministry of Health of China, UNAIDS, and WHO. 2006. *2005 Update on the HIV/AIDS epidemic and response in China.* Beijing: Ministry of Health. January 24.

Ministry of Health of the People's Republic of China. 2010. *China 2010 UNGASS Country progress report (2008–2009).* Beijing: Ministry of Health. April 2.

Ministry of Health of the People's Republic of China. 2012. *2012 China AIDS Response Progress Report.* Beijing: Ministry of Health. March 31.

Ministry of Health, State Development Planning Commission, Ministry of Science and Technology, and Ministry of Finance. 1998. *Medium and long-term plan on prevention and control of HIV/AIDS Beijing.* Beijing.

National Center for AIDS/STD Control and Prevention. 2010. *Annual report on HIV/AIDS/STD epidemiology, prevention and treatment in China in 2009.* Beijing: China CDC.

National People's Congress Standing Committee. 1985a. *Frontier entry and exit administration law for Chinese citizens.* Beijing.

National People's Congress Standing Committee. 1985b. *Frontier entry and exit administration law for foreign nationals.* Beijing.

NNCC. 2006. *Annual report on drug control in China.* Beijing: National Narcotics Control Commission.

NNCC. 2008. China's drug control efforts. Beijing: National Narcotics Control Commission.

People's Daily. 2005. Chinese government invites private sector to join HIV/AIDS campaign. *People's Daily Online.* March 19.

People's Republic of China. 2008. *Narcotics control law of The People's Republic of China*. Adopted at the Thirty-First Meeting of the Standing Committee of the Tenth National People's Congress.

Qian, H. Z., J. E. Schumacher, H. T. Chen, and Y. H. Ruan. 2006. Injection drug use and HIV/AIDS in China: Review of current situation, prevention and policy implications. *Harm Reduction Journal* 3(1): 4.

Qian, H. Z., S. H. Vermund, and N. Wang. 2005. Risk of HIV/AIDS in China: Subpopulations of special importance. *Sexually Transmitted Infections* 81(6): 442–447.

Rou, K., Z. Wu, S. G. Sullivan, F. Li, J. Guan, C. Xu, et al. 2007. A five-city trial of a behavioral intervention to reduce sexually transmitted disease/HIV risk among sex workers in China. *AIDS* 21 (Suppl 8): S95–S101.

Secretariat of the National Working Group for Community-Based Methadone Maintenance Treatment. 2006. *Implementation protocol of the community-based methadone maintenance treatment program for opiate addicts in China*. Beijing: China CDC.

Settle, E. 2003. *AIDS in China: An annotated chronology: 1985–2003*. Montreal: China AIDS Survey.

Standing Committee of the National People's Congress. 1987. *Frontier health and quarantine law*. Beijing.

Standing Committee of the National People's Congress. 1990. *Decision on the prohibition of narcotic drugs*. Beijing.

Standing Committee of the National People's Congress. 1991. *Decision on the strict prohibition against prostitution and whoring*. Beijing.

Standing Committee of the National People's Congress. 1998. *Blood donation law*. Beijing.

State Council AIDS Working Committee Office, and UN Theme Group on HIV/AIDS in China. 2004. *A joint assessment of HIV/AIDS prevention, treatment and care in China*. Beijing: China Ministry of Health. December 1.

State Council AIDS Working Committee Office, and UN Theme Group on HIV/AIDS in China. 2007. *A joint assessment of HIV/AIDS prevention, treatment and care in China (2007)*. Beijing: China Ministry of Health. December 1.

State Council of P.R. China. 1996. *Regulations for the management of blood products*. Beijing.

State Council of P.R. China. 1998. *Chinese national medium-and long-term strategic plan for HIV/AIDS (1998–2010)*. Beijing.

State Council of P.R. China. 2001. *Action plan on HIV/AIDS prevention and containment (2001–2005)*. Beijing.

State Council of P.R. China. 2006a. *China's action plan for reducing and preventing the spread of HIV/AIDS (2006–2010)*. Beijing.

State Council of P.R. China. 2006b. *Regulations on AIDS prevention and treatment*. Beijing.

Sullivan, L. E., D. S. Metzger, P. J. Fudala, and D. A. Fiellin. 2005. Decreasing international HIV transmission: The role of expanding access to opioid agonist therapies for injection drug users. *Addiction* 100(2): 150–158.

Sullivan, S. G. 2011. Implementation of the Chinese methadone maintenance treatment program: analysis of national data (thesis). Los Angeles: University of California.

Sun, X., N. Wang, D. Li, X. Zheng, S. Qu, L. Wang, et al. 2007. The development of HIV/AIDS surveillance in China. *AIDS 21* (Suppl 8): S33–S38.

Teixeira, P. R., M. A. Vitoria, and J. Barcarolo. 2004. Antiretroviral treatment in resource-poor settings: The Brazilian experience. *AIDS 18* (Suppl 3): S5–S7.

The UN Theme Group on HIV/AIDS in China. 2002. *China's titanic peril: 2001 update of the AIDS situation and needs assessment report*. Beijing: UNAIDS.

UNAIDS. 2003. *Stigma and Discrimination Fact Sheet*. http://siteresources.worldbank.org/INTEAPREGTOPHIVAIDS/Resources/fs_stigma_discrimination_en_pdf.pdf (accessed February 10, 2006).

UNODC, UNAIDS. 2011. China Country Advocacy Brief Injecting Drug Use and HIV. https://www.unodc.org/documents/eastasiaandpacific/topics/hiv-aids/UNRTF/CHI_CAB_27_Sept_10.pdf (accessed November 23, 2012.

UNODC. 2012. *World Drug Report*. Geneva: United Nations Office on Drugs and Crime.

Wang, L. H., and X. Qiu. 2006. Prevention mother to child transmission of HIV. In: L. D. Wang (Ed.), *Epidemics of and responses to HIV/AIDS in China*. Beijing: Beijing Press.

Watts, J. 2003. China faces up to HIV/AIDS epidemic. World AIDS day is marked by launch of huge public-awareness campaign. *The Lancet* 362 (9400): 1983.

Watts, J. 2006. AIDS in China: New legislation, old doubts. *The Lancet* 367 (9513): 803–804.

WHO Technical Consultation UNFPA/UNICEF/WHO/UNAIDS Inter-Agency Task Team on Mother-to-Child Transmission of HIV. 2000. *New data on the prevention of mother-to-child transmission of HIV and their policy implications*. Geneva: World Health Organization.

Wong, F. Y., Z. J. Huang, W. Wang, N. He, J. Marzzurco, S. Frangos, et al. 2009. STIs and HIV among men having sex with men in China: A ticking time bomb? *AIDS Education and Prevention* 21(5): 430–446.

Wong, W. C., J. Zhang, S. C. Wu, T. S. Kong, and D. C. Ling. 2006. The HIV related risks among men having sex with men in rural Yunnan, China: A qualitative study. *Sexually Transmitted Infections* 82(2): 127–130.

Wu, Z. 2002. *Evaluation of a needle social marketing strategy for control of the HIV epidemic among injecting drug users in China (unpublished report)*. Beijing: Chinese Academy of Preventive Medicine.

Wu, Z. 2004. Landmark government methadone maintenance program in mainland China. From 15th international AIDS conference, July 2004. Bangkok.

Wu, Z. 2005. Methadone Maintenance Program in Mainland China: From Pilot to Scale-up. From International conference on the reduction of drug related harm, March 2005. Belfast.

Wu, Z. 2006. Overview of behavioral interventions in China. In: L.D. Wang (Ed.), *Epidemics of and responses to HIV/AIDS in China*. Beijing: Beijing Press.

Wu, Z., P. Lin, W. Liu, Z. Q. Ming, and L. Pang. 2004. Randomized community trial to reduce HIV risk behaviors among injecting drug users using needle social marketing strategies in China. From *15th* international AIDS conference, July 2004. Bangkok.

Wu, Z., Z. Liu, and R. Detels. 1995. HIV-1 infection in commercial plasma donors in China. *The Lancet* 346(8966): 61–62.

Wu, Z., G. Qi, Y. Zeng, and R. Detels. 1999. Knowledge of HIV/AIDS among health care workers in China. *AIDS Education and Prevention* 11(4): 353–363.

Wu, Z., K. Rou, and H. Cui. 2004. The HIV/AIDS epidemic in China: history, current strategies and future challenges. *AIDS Education and Prevention* 16 (3 Suppl A): 7–17.

Wu, Z., K. Rou, and R. Detels. 2001. Prevalence of HIV infection among former commercial plasma donors in rural eastern China. *Health Policy and Planning* 16(1): 41–46.

Wu, Z., K. Rou, M. Jia, S. Duan, and S. G. Sullivan. 2007. The first community-based sexually transmitted disease/HIV intervention trial for female sex workers in China. *AIDS 21* (Suppl 8): S89–S94.

Wu, Z., K. Rou, C. Xu, W. Lou, R. Detels. 2005. Acceptability of HIV/AIDS counseling and testing among premarital couples in China. *AIDS Education and Prevention* 17(1): 12–21.

Wu, Z., and S. G. Sullivan. 2006. China. In: T. Yamamoto, and S. Itoh (Eds.) *Fighting a rising tide: The response to AIDS in East Asia*, 1st ed., 76–95. Tokyo: Japan Center for International Exchange.

Wu, Z., Sullivan, S. G., Wang, Y., Rotheram-Borus, M. J., and Detels, R. 2007. Evolution of China's response to HIV/AIDS. *Lancet* 369(9562): 679–690.

Wu, Z., X. Sun, S. G. Sullivan, and R. Detels. 2006. Public health. HIV testing in China. *Science* 312(5779): 1475–1476.

Xu, H., Y. Zeng, and A.F. Anderson. 2005. Chinese NGOs in action against HIV/AIDS. *Cell Research* 15(11–12): 914–918.

Xu, J., E. Liu, G. Mi, K. Rou, Z. Dou, Z. Wu, et al. 2010. HIV, Syphilis, HCV and HSV-2 prevalence among men who have sex with men in urban China. From XVIII international AIDS conference, July 2010. Vienna.

Xue, B. 2005. HIV/AIDS policy and policy evolution in China. *International Journal of STD & AIDS* 16(7): 459–464.

Yang, H., X. Li, B. Stanton, X. Fang, D. Lin, R. Mao, et al. 2004. Willingness to participate in HIV/STD prevention activities among Chinese rural-to-urban migrants. *AIDS Education and Prevention* 16(6): 557–570.

Yang, H., X. Li, B. Stanton, H. Liu H, H. Liu, N. Wang, et al. 2005. Heterosexual transmission of HIV in China: A systematic review of behavioral studies in the past two decades. *Sexually Transmitted Diseases 32*(5): 270–280.

Yap, L., Z. Wu, W. Liu, Z. Q. Ming, and S. Liang. 2002. A rapid assessment and its implications for a needle social marketing intervention among injecting drug users in China. *International Journal of Drug Policy 13*: 57–68.

Yip, R. 2006. Opportunity for effective prevention of AIDS in China. In: J. Kaufman, A. Kleinman, and T. Saich (Eds.), *AIDS and Social Policy in China*, 177–189. Cambridge, MA: Harvard University Asia Center.

Zhang, B. C., and Q. S. Chu. 2005. MSM and HIV/AIDS in China. *Cell Research 15*(11–12): 858–864.

Zhang, F., M. C. Au, P. D. Bouey, Y. Zhao, Z. J. Huang, Z. Dou, et al. 2007. The diagnosis and treatment of HIV-infected children in China: Challenges and opportunities. *Journal of Acquired Immune Deficiency Syndromes 44*(4): 429–434.

Zhang, F., J. E. Haberer, Y. Wang, Y. Zhao, Y. Ma, D. Zhao, et al. 2007. The Chinese free antiretroviral treatment program: Challenges and responses. *AIDS 21* (Suppl 8): S143–S148.

Zhang, F., J. E. Haberer, Y. Zhao, Z. Dou, H. Zhao, Y. He, et al. 2007. Chinese pediatric highly active antiretroviral therapy observational cohort: A 1-year analysis of clinical, immunologic, and virologic outcomes. *Journal of Acquired Immune Deficiency Syndromes 46*(5): 594–598.

Zhang, F., M. Hsu, L. Yu, Y. Wen, and J. Pan. 2006. Initiation of the national free antiretroviral therapy program in rural China. In: J. Kaufman, A. Kleinman, and T. Saich (Eds.), *AIDS and Social Policy in China*, 96–124. Cambridge, MA: Harvard University Asia Center.

Zhang, K., D. Li, H. Li, E. J. Beck. 1999. Changing sexual attitudes and behavior in China: Implications for the spread of HIV and other sexually transmitted diseases. *AIDS Care 11*(5): 581–589.

Zhang, F J., J. Pan, L. Yu, Y. Wen, and Y. Zhao. 2005. Current progress of China's free ART program. *Cell Research 15*(11–12): 877–882.

Zhang, H., B. Stanton, X. Li, R. Mao, Z. Sun, L. Kaljee, et al. 2004. Perceptions and attitudes regarding sex and condom use among Chinese college students: A qualitative study. *AIDS and Behavior 8*(2): 105–117.

Zhao, C., Z. Liu, D. Zhao, Y. Liu, J. Liang, Y. Tang, et al. 2004. Drug abuse in China. *Annals of the New York Acadedmy of Sciences 1025*: 439–445.

Zhou, Y. Z., M. M. Zhang, S. Wei, H. T. Guan, P. Yin, N. Ren, et al. 2009. Survey on knowledge, attitude, practice related to contraception among college students in Beijing. *Zhonghua Liu Xing Bing Xue Za Zhi 30*(7): 710–712.

Zhuang, K., X. Gui, B. Su, P. Tien, Z. Chen, L. Zhang. 2003. High prevalence of HIV infection among women and their children in Henan Province, China. *Journal of Acquired Immune Deficiency Syndromes 33*(5): 649–650.

Zou, K. 2002. The "re-education through labour" system in China's legal reform. *Criminal Law Forum 12*: 459–485.

# INDEX

aging population, 199. *See also* elderly migration and residential mobility
agriculture, the transition from, 80–81
AIDS. *See* HIV/AIDS
amenity migration, 199
"Asian Social Protection in Comparative Perspective" conference, 3

bilingual education, 180, 182, 186–87. *See also* education policy
bisexual men and HIV/AIDS, 279–80

"capitalism"
   from above, 30
   vs. market economies, 29
   meanings and connotations of the term, 29
centralization. *See* decentralization
central transfers, 40, 40t
child care support for adult children, providing, 212–14
China Health and Nutrition Survey (CHNS), 106, 108, 116, 224, 229–31, 242
"Chinese" path, 29
Chongqing, 91–94, 92t, 93t, 95–96t, 97–98t
college. *See also* higher education
   transition from senior high school to, 263
college attendance, subgroup comparison of, 259–63

college expansion, 249, 263–66
   in the late 1990s, 249, 252–56
college expansion policy, 263–66
   as reducing educational inequality, 256–57
commune health stations (CHSs), 37, 38
Communist Party of Vietnam (CPV), 21, 26, 35, 41
communities, rooted and uprooted
   social policy challenges of, 10–12
"community building" movement, 215–16
Compulsory Education Law, 145, 149, 150
cooperative health insurance rate by province, 110, 111t
cooperative health insurance status. *See also* health insurance; rural cooperative health insurance
   income and, 110, 112t
   and self-reported health status, 110, 112t
cooperative health insurance take-up rate, 109t, 109–10
cooperative medical schemes, history of, 102–6
Cultural Revolution, 3, 71, 102, 163, 250

*danwei*, 12, 98, 214–16
   definitions and meanings of, 12, 197, 202, 209–11
   as welfare institution in the socialist era, a life historical perspective on, 203–9

298　INDEX

*danwei*, (Cont.)
　from welfare institution to urban community, 209–11
　workplaces, welfare institutions, and urban communities, 202–3
*danwei*-bound housing career, 208–9
decentralization, 22, 129, 251
　vs. centralization, 126
　of "public" services, 38
decentralized education financing system, 145–47, 146f, 156
decentralized fiscal expenditure system, 26, 27, 121–24, 123f, 138
demographic transition, 77–80
differential citizenship. *See* local citizenship
drug use, injecting, 277–78
　needle social marketing and needle exchange program, 276–77
　and transmission of HIV, 275–77
"dual-track pricing," 2
"dual-track" system, 2

"East Asian" path, 29
economic institutions and trajectories of economic change, 29–30
economic transitions, 1, 3–4
　multiple, 7
education, 31, 34t. *See also* college; higher education; migrant child education
　equity, family arrangements, and, 12–14
educational spending
　across regions, 147, 147t
　national, 145, 146f
education financing, 36
　in international perspective, 153–55
education financing system, decentralized, 145–47, 146f, 156
education policy, 180–82, 191–92. *See also* college expansion policy; migrant child education
　design, 183–84
　implementation, 184–87
　outcomes, 187–89
　policy recommendations for sustainable curriculum design and implementation, 189–91
education policy recommendations, toward, 189–91
education spending, 36. *See also* education financing

elder care. *See* child care support for adult children, providing; old-age insurance
elderly migration and residential mobility, 198–200, 214–16. *See also danwei*
employer-based social protection, 2
employment, 235–38. *See also* gender gaps in labor market outcomes; labor market outcomes
　guarantees of lifetime, 2
employment-driven evolution of transition policy, 70–74
employment policy, 81–82
ethnic minority groups, 180–81
ethnic minority languages, 180–82, 184t, 186–92. *See also* education policy
　roles of, 183, 184t

family structure and wage income, 234, 235t
family ties, effects of, 212–14
family-work conflicts. *See under* labor market outcomes
financial crisis of 2007–2008, 3
financial responsibility system, 27
fiscal federalism, 121, 124, 126, 136, 138, 139. *See also* welfare spending equalization
fiscal system, China's compound, 122–26
"Five Guarantees" program, 51
Foshan, 91–94, 92t, 93t, 95–96t, 97–98t, 99
"Four Free and One Care" policy, 280–84

gay men and HIV/AIDS, 279–80
gender gaps in labor market outcomes, 228–29, 232–37t, 239–40t
　comparative perspectives, 224–25
　research in China, 226–28
　in urban areas, 226–28
Great Leap Forward, 3, 23, 250

"harmonious society," building a, 11, 64, 122, 124, 216, 252
health care, 2, 31, 33t
　public spending on, 36–38, 37t
health insurance, 52, 88, 95–96t, 97–98t. *See also* cooperative health insurance; rural cooperative health insurance
　exogenous variation in individual probability of taking up, 107
　and perceptions of health and self-reported health, 107

# Index

higher education, 250–52. *See also* college; education
  marketization of, 255
  "mass," 252, 263
HIV/AIDS
  annual government spending on, 281f
  epidemiology, 272f, 288f
HIV/AIDS epidemic, 270, 287–89
  challenges ahead, 285–87
  cumulative reported cases by province, 288f
  "Four Free and One Care" policy for control of, 280–84
  influential forces
    changes in government, 280–81
    media, 281–82
    severe acute respiratory syndrome (SARS), 282
  overview, 272–73
    information and communication networks, 273–74
HIV/AIDS policy development
  program scale-up
    antiretroviral treatment for persons with AIDS, 284–85
    case finding, 282–83
    educating the public, 283–84
    monitoring the scale-up, 285
    prevention of mother-to-child transmission, 285
  scientific evidence for innovative policies, 274–75
    commercial sex work, 278–79
    men who have sex with men (MSM), 279–80
    reduction of transmission via injecting drug use, 275–76
    sexual transmission, 278
  and scientific evidence for innovative policies
    methadone maintenance treatment (MMT) programs, 277–78
    needle social marketing and needle exchange program, 276–77
HIV/AIDS policy development, timeline of events in China's, 271f
homosexuality and HIV/AIDS, 279–80
household income, 230
household registration system, 143–45
  "The Provisional Regulations on the Management of the Population Living Temporarily in the Cities," 143–44

"The State Council Notification on the Household Registration Reform," 143–44
*hukou* (household registration) status, 10, 86, 89, 94, 161–62, 259
human capital, 230–31
human capital theory, 256

Ignatius, David, 1
income, 230. *See also* inequality
  annual wage, 238–41
  family structure and, 234, 235t
India
  labor migration in, 162–69, 173–75
  long-term impact of sending communities, 170–71
inequality, economic, 2, 64
Interim Measure of School Education for Temporary Migrant Children in 1998 (1998 measure), 149, 150
interregional transfers, 9–10

King, Lawrence P., 29
Krishak Sabha, 175

labor market outcomes, 229–30
  family-work conflicts and gender gaps in, 228–29, 232–37t, 239–40t, 241–43
  comparative perspectives, 224–25
  research in China, 226–28
  in rural vs. urban China, 231–35, 232t, 236–37t, 238, 239–40t, 241–42
labor migration in China and India, 162–69, 173–75
language policy. *See also* education policy; ethnic minority languages
  sustainable, 189–91
layoffs, 82, 91, 226. *See also xiagang* (layoff) policy
Leonard, Mark, 1
local citizenship, 162, 166, 174, 175

marital status and wage employment, 232–33, 233f
market-based economy, 2
market-Leninism
  political economy of, 27–30
  political institutions of, 28

# 300 INDEX

market-Leninist welfare regimes, divergence in East Asia's, 30–32
    China, 38–40
    Vietnam, 32, 34–38
market transition, problems for countries undergoing, 25
market transition theory (Nee), 25
maximum maintained inequality (MMI) hypothesis, 257, 264
medical insurance. *See* health insurance
men who have sex with men (MSM), 279–80
methadone maintenance treatment (MMT) programs, 277–78
migrant child education, 142, 155–56
    challenges of, 148–49
    major policies for, 149–50
migrant child education policy implementation, 150–51
    in Beijing, 151–52
    in Zhejiang Province, 152–53, 156
migrant-sending and receiving regions, major, 162, 163t
Minimum Livelihood Guarantee (MLG), 50, 51

Nee, Victor, 25
New Rural Co-operative Medical Care System (NRCMCS), 51, 103–6, 109, 110, 112, 113
985 Project, 251, 254
non-financial defined contribution (NDC), 78
nongovernmental organizations (NGOs), 280, 287
Notice of Improve Education of Children of Rural Migrant Workers in 2003 (2003 Notice), 149–50, 152

old-age insurance, 88, 95–96t, 97–98t

parental status and wage employment, 233–34, 234f
pay-as-you-go (PAYGO) pension system, 78
pensions, 2, 78–80
    evidence on the impact of *xiagang* policy on, 74–77
Plan of Revitalizing Education, 252
policy learning, collaborative, 14–15
population aging, 199. *See also* elderly migration and residential mobility
Project 211, 251

Project 985, 251, 254
prostitution, 278–79

retirement age, 79–80
"revolution from above," 29
"revolution from without," 29
rural and urban gaps in social insurance, 7–9
rural cooperative health insurance, 118n8
    and health outcomes, 101–4, 106, 112–17
    marginal effects of individual cooperative insurance on health, 113, 114t
Rural Cooperative Medical System (RCMS), 51, 101–3
Rural People's Communes, 26
rural-to-urban migrants, social benefits for, 63–64
rural vs. urban China, 26, 232t
    labor market outcomes in, 231–35, 232t, 236–37t, 238, 239–40t, 241–42
    population share and social benefit share in, 57, 57f
    size of social benefits in, 56–58
    social benefit structure in, 58t, 58–59, 65

SARS (severe acute respiratory syndrome), 282
self-employment, 88
sending communities, long-term impact of, 169
    the China case, 171–73
    the India case, 170–71
Senior Rights and Interests Protection Law, 215
severe acute respiratory syndrome (SARS), 282
Shenyang, 91–94, 92t, 93t, 95–96t, 97–98t
social benefit programs, quintile shares of, 60f, 60–61
social benefits
    and income inequality, 61–63, 62t
    progressive vs. regressive distribution of, 59–61
    for rural-to-urban migrants, 63–64
    size of, and urban-rural contrast, 56–58
social benefit structure, urban-rural differences in, 58–59
social benefit system
    Chinese, 50–51
    defined, 49
    Vietnamese, 52–53
social insurance
    urban and rural gaps in, 7–9
    workplace ownership and access to, 93t, 93–94

Index 301

social insurance provision, urban, 86–87, 91–98
  reforms and expansion, 87–89
  segmentation and disparity, 89–90
social insurance reforms in Chinese context, 98–99
socialism. *See also* state-socialism
  the transition from, 70–77
  what comes after, 5–6
socialist "universalism." *See* universalism
socialist workplaces. *See* danwei
socialization, 36, 52
  defined, 36, 52
social policy developments, future, 64–65
social services, 2
social "universalism." *See* universalism
state-owned enterprises (SOEs), 30, 68, 70, 71
state-socialism. *See also* socialism
  paths from, 19–21
state-socialist welfare regimes
  degeneration of regimes in Vietnam and China, 25–27
  demise of, 24–25
Szelényi, Ivan, 29, 30

township and village enterprises (TVEs), 23
trilingual education. *See also* education policy
  justifications for, 188–89
  models of, 184–87, 185t, 189
211 Higher Education Development Project (211 Project), 251

unemployment insurance (UI), 71–73, 88–89, 95–96t, 97–98t
universalism, 34–35, 41, 52
urban-rural differences. *See* rural vs. urban China

Vietnam
  Communist Party, 21, 26, 35, 41
  degeneration of state-socialist welfare, 25–27
  market transition, 21–24
  social benefit system, 52–53
  well-being in, 31
Vietnam and China, 64–65
  commitment to and development of social benefits, 49. *See also* social benefits; social benefit system
  composition of social benefits in, 58t, 58–59
  divergence in East Asia's market-Leninist welfare regimes, 32, 34–40
  education indicators, 31, 34t
  general indicators, 31–32, 32t
  health indicators, 31, 33t
  levels of economic and social development, 48–49

welfare regimes
  and institutional change, 19–20
  in the path from state-socialism, 19–25
  varieties of, 5–6
welfare spending disparities, per capita, 126–27, 128t
welfare spending equalization, 129–39
  determinants of, 126–29
  regional patterns for, 135–36
welfare spending size disparities, 127, 128t, 129
women, rural. *See also* gender gaps in labor market outcomes
  participation in wage employment, 228
work experience, 230
workplace ownership and access to social insurance, 93t, 93–94
workplaces/work units. *See danwei*
Wuxi, 91–94, 92t, 93t, 94, 95–96t, 97–98t, 99

*xiagang* (layoff) policy, 73–77

Zhejiang Province, 152–53, 156